Lovell

IN THE SHADOW OF
ORGANIZATION

IN THE SHADOW OF ORGANIZATION

ROBERT B. DENHARDT

THE REGENTS PRESS OF KANSAS
Lawrence

Library of Congress Cataloging in Publication Data

Denhardt, Robert B
In the shadow of organization.

Bibliography: p.
Includes index.
1. Organization. I. Title.
HM131.D47   305   80-23775
ISBN 0-7006-0210-0

CONTENTS

PREFACE

In the context of organization we find today the same contest between self and society, between autonomy and domination, that has characterized so much of our history. Through organization, we have sought growth and productivity in society, but our success has come at some cost to the individual. While organizations have proven both useful and attractive in many ways, they have done so by limiting personal autonomy and responsibility. More important, as large and complex organizations have come to play such a prominent role in our society, we have been presented with a new and encompassing *ethic of organization,* a new way of seeing the world, a new metaphor for living. It is not the relationship between individuals and particular organizations that now seems most troublesome; it is rather the ethic of organization that casts its shadow over our lives.

Even in the face of these developments, academic studies of organizational life have largely given preference to the concerns of the organization and its management rather than to those of individual members. At best, studies have sought to make more palatable the "integration" of individuals into organizations. In this book, I urge a radical reordering of these priorities by suggesting that we give primacy to the growth of the individual rather than the efficiency of the productive process. More broadly, I argue that we must begin to construct a practical philosophy of modern life, one cognizant of the impact of organizations on our lives, yet one not controlled by that circumstance. Since the ethic of organization prescribes a way of viewing the world, to confront that ethic we must explore new ways of knowing, new modes of knowledge acquisition. Through developments in phenomenology, critical theory, and depth psychology, I suggest that we may find the basis for an alternative personalist approach to life in an organizational society.

Chapter one provides an overview of some of the issues faced by individuals seeking to achieve a sense of meaning, action, and continuity in modern society, while chapter two focuses on the commitments that seem to be part of the new ethic of organization. Chapters three, four, and five return to the themes of meaning, action, and continuity, in each case assessing the impact of organizations on our personal efforts, then suggesting some new ways of viewing life in an organizational society. Chapter six brings these issues together using insights from phenomenology, critical theory, and depth psychology; and finally, chapter seven sketches the beginning steps we might take toward creating an alternative philosophy of life in an organizational society.

A number of people have provided help and encouragement for me to complete this work. My wife Kathryn G. Denhardt and my good friend, Sloane Dugan, made important substantive contributions (especially in chapter three), but more importantly they provided special and much-needed personal support during the completion of this work. Orion White read the entire manuscript and made detailed and extremely helpful comments; his own work was indeed an inspiration. Others who have contributed either through their comments on the manuscript or more generally include Guy Adams, John Forester, Marvin Harder, Philip Jeffress, Larry Kirkhart, Charlene May, Lynn Miller, John Nalbandian, Jan Perkins, and Jay White. Though I must accept responsibility for the final product, I note their complicity—with appreciation. The last part of the manuscript was completed while I was a fellow in the Interdisciplinary Studies Program at the Menninger Foundation, an excellent place to work.

I sometimes think we worry too much about the future, about "discovering ourselves" before it's too late. More often, we don't even know ourselves until we've done something—and even then we may not be very sure what we've done. I've written a book. But I've also discovered a group of people—some scholars, some managers, some athletes, some poets—who reside at least in the penumbra. To them I present this work.

THE INDIVIDUAL
IN AN AGE OF ORGANIZATION

I returned, and saw under the sun, that the race is not to the swift, nor the battle to the strong, neither yet bread to the wise, nor yet riches to men of understanding, nor yet favour to men of skill; but time and chance happeneth to them all. For man also knoweth not his time: as the fishes that are taken in an evil net, and as the birds that are caught in the snare; so are the sons of men snared in an evil time, when it falleth suddenly upon them.

Ecclesiastes 9:11–12

Because "time and chance" present themselves to us daily, we are bound to a process of living in which we are constantly called upon to expand and to fulfill our images of ourselves and our surroundings. Experience presents itself to us as a series of choices—some made by us and some made for us. By these choices we develop a pattern of life which, in our best dreams, expands the possibilities of our existence. We seek always to transcend the realities of the present and move toward the opportunities that the future presents. But, in doing so, we are beset with many difficulties and we must struggle to avoid the "evil time" which may snare us.

The deepest concerns of persons living today are very much like those of previous generations: we are concerned with our identity, with establishing meaning in our lives; we are concerned with developing ways of acting through which we may pursue the meaning which we hold important; and we are concerned with the relationship between our lives and the life of the universe, past,

1

present, and future. By establishing an independent perspective on the world, we are presented with the opportunity for choice; given the opportunity for choice, we may elaborate the meaning of our lives through action; and beyond this we may pursue our own role in infinity. This, then, is the struggle—to establish one's own *meaning*, to develop contexts for *action*, and to establish *continuity* with our surroundings.

But the struggle is not easily won. We must learn to operate within the context of our time and our culture. Each generation must develop an approach to living appropriate to the circumstances of its age, and ours is an age uniquely marked by its preoccupation with bureaucracy. Recent decades have seen an immense proliferation of organizations, whether judged in terms of number, size, or complexity. Today bureaucratic arrangements not only mark large governmental and industrial concerns, they extend as well to much smaller groups. Organization has become a model form of human association and a guide to "appropriate" human behavior.

To the extent that the bureaucratic experience is central to modern living, contemporary approaches to the central tasks of life must take that circumstance into account. In this book, therefore, we will explore the way in which the emerging "ethic" of organization may affect our search for meaning, action, and continuity. We will examine the contest between the individual, on the one hand, and the organizational society, on the other. In doing so we will encounter a number of important, though difficult, questions: How can we sustain our search for autonomy in a positive and effective way, mediating our vision and our experience, our meaning and our action? How can we work with the relationship between the individual and the group in such a way as to facilitate the development of contexts for meaningful human action as well as to develop an authentic connection between our lives and the life of the universe? Finally, how can we create conditions within society so that regulation and control may be displaced by opportunities for creativity and expressiveness?

I

As individuals, our first task, and the task which opens all others to us, is to construct an image of the world which is personally and uniquely our own. This is basic. We must learn to control our own view of the world; we must develop a sense in which we can distinguish truth from falsity, *our* truth. As we come to understand the world, not simply as it presents itself, but rather on our own terms, we can move from passivity to activity, from dependency to autonomy. Only then can we begin to work in the world, to enjoy its pleasures and to learn from its pain, to expand its opportunities, and to rely on it as we seek our salvation.

The search for meaning is deep-seated, underlying many of our more conscious undertakings. Edward Whitmont writes of the essentiality of meaning in our lives: "The one thing we can under no circumstances tolerate is lack of meaning. Everything, even death and destruction, can be faced so long as it has meaning."[1] We seek a context, a way of understanding how events relate to one another and a way of ordering our values. We create our world through our thoughts and our actions, and those formulations which help us make sense of that world are especially meaningful to us.

But our world is not constructed in a vacuum. On all sides we are confronted with cultural forces which attempt to socialize us into existing patterns of belief. To some extent, we find it necessary to accept these patterns simply in order to act effectively in the world as it is given, to understand others and to be understood by them. But typically we accept more of the outer world than is necessary and permit ourselves to become dominated by images which we may not find intrinsically persuasive, but which we accept simply in order to "get along." Our effort to establish autonomous meaning is very difficult; in practice we negotiate and renegotiate our understanding of the world around us day by day.

How, then, is our task of establishing meaning, a task at the outset bounded by many potential difficulties, affected by the fact that we live in an age of organization? To begin with, since complex organizations play such a large part in our lives, the way in which we construct reality is obviously guided by our experiences and our training in organizations. Like other major social institutions, large organizations draw our attention toward certain objects and away from others. Consequently, when we look at problems through the lenses provided by these organizations, we "selectively perceive" some things and we selectively neglect others. Specifically, our attention is directed to those ideas, attitudes, and behaviors that will maintain and enhance the power of organized systems.

Many organizational analysts have noted that persons entering their first organization or transferring from one organization to another must undergo a process of socialization to acquaint them with their new setting. Robert Presthus comments on the parallel to larger socialization processes: "The mechanisms that society employs to inculcate its values may also be seen at work within the organization. The organization, in a word, socializes its members in a way similar to that of a society."[2] But, even prior to the learning which occurs as we enter any specific organization, we develop a generalized understanding of and commitment to the values of the organization. We learn the norms, values, and standards of behavior "appropriate" to organizational life in general. The organization as an agent of socialization operates, then, at two levels, first presenting us with the generalized values of bureaucracy, then indoctrinating us in terms of a particular organization.

This internalization of organization values by members and clients through the process of socialization is quite basic to the survival of organizations. For example, most organizations, built on the concept of hierarchical authority, depend on the acceptance of this idea as a proper form of social interaction prior to its application in specific organizational situations. According to French and Raven, the exercise of legitimate power stems from internalized values in one individual which dictate that a second person has a right to influence him and that he has an obligation to accept this influence.[3] Since the standard bureaucratic model of organization specifies extensive use of such power as a means of control, the internalization of the concept of hierarchical authority must precede any specific exercise of bureaucratic power.

It is important to note that the process of bureaucratic socialization may not require a setting of massive organization in order to provide instruction as to the values associated with organization. Amitai Etzioni, whose comments on socialization are of particular relevance, has noted that, in the case of complex organizations, "The amount of socialization required by organizations depends, of course, on the degree to which organizational behavior differs from behavior the participants have learned elsewhere."[4] As organizations proliferate, extending patterns of organizational life to innumerable new areas of social interaction, bureaucratic socialization may be provided in other social contexts, developing and maintaining an organizational society. So, as Herbert Wilcox has documented, by the time students are in high school they have fully assimilated "the cultural trait of hierarchy," a trait which other research has shown may even displace more traditional cultural values.[5] It is through the process of socialization, therefore, that organization spreads through society and is maintained over time.

The result of this socialization process is the widespread assumption of a particular viewpoint, a sort of organizational ethic, one which supports the extension of an organizational society and offers itself as a way of life for persons in our society. To the extent we accept that ethic, we will come to see the world in terms of order and structure rather than conflict and change; we will come to value discipline, regulation, and obedience in contrast to independence, expressiveness, and creativity. And we will see the world in terms of techniques for resolving inconveniences in the smooth and efficient administration of human affairs. What is especially important is that this new ethic of organization does not just instruct our activities in organizations (as do theories of organization); rather, its power is so great that it recommends those same patterns of thought and behavior for our lives generally.

This condition is illustrated most poignantly in Tom Wicker's account of the Attica prison revolt. Wicker was among a set of observers called to Attica to monitor the negotiations between the rebellious prisoners and the prison bureaucracy. In the course of his attempts to mediate between the opposing groups, Wicker came to realize the vast differences between the prisoners' view of their own humanity and the bureaucracy's concern for restoring normal patterns of authority. In what he describes as one of the most peculiar aspects of the uprising, Wicker writes, "Many of its participants and supporters regarded it less as a power play or an unexpected opportunity (or danger) or even a political act (whether in the cause of prison reform, black power, or social revolution) than as a *proper condition* in itself, of greater validity than the restoration of accustomed authority."[6]

Obviously, from the point of view of the prison officials, the only "proper condition" was a return to the normal operation of the prison, a reassertion of established authority and the smooth

5

administration of the affairs of the institution. In this view there was no room for the prisoners' attempt to recognize the validity of their own individuality. This was simply not an issue. As a consequence, Wicker was brought to wonder whether "those institutions, processes, and arrangements by which humans had sought to order their affairs had become, finally, more important than the people who had erected them and sought to live by them."[7]

We can, of course, think of many other instances in which we are asked to adopt a bureaucratic outlook in preference to other concerns; and we can think of nearly as many cases in which we allow ourselves to adopt such a view. But the more significant point is this: time after time we are asked to focus our attention on the technical problems of maintaining the organization, to concentrate on the bureaucratic "usefulness" of a project rather than on its broader impact, and to suspend our own moral judgment in favor of organizational decree; and each time we submit we aid in establishing an ethic of organization. We reconfirm the power of a reality that is not our own. And as we become more and more dominated by that reality, our lives take on, in their most perverted form, the characteristics which that reality prescribes for us—to be docile; to be technically competent; to be practical, objective, and impersonal; and to be limited in our vision.

The complex psychological impact of these pressures on the individual is well illustrated in Joseph Heller's novel *Something Happened.* While the hero (?) of the novel is terrified by the pressures of organizational life, he is also fascinated with organizational processes. For example, after describing his aversion to hospitals and his anxiety about becoming involved with patients, he describes his extreme interest in a particular organizational technique:

> One time, though (ha, ha), after someone I knew did die, I braced myself, screwed up my valor, and, feigning ignorance, telephoned the hospital that same day to inquire about his condition. I was curious: I wanted to see what it would feel like to hear the hospital tell me that someone I knew was dead. I wondered how it was done; I was preoccupied and even titillated by this problem of technique. Would they decide he had died, passed away, succumbed, was deceased, or perhaps even had expired? (Like a magazine subscription or an old library card?)

The woman on the telephone at the hospital surprised me. She said:

"Mr. ———— is no longer listed as a patient."[8]

This fascination with the "tactful procedure" which the hospital employed was clearly more important than the death of a friend. "Mr. ———— was no longer listed as a patient, and I had to go to his funeral three days later."[9] That an individual could be so "preoccupied" and "titillated" by organizational technique as to be more interested in the announcement of a death than in the death itself suggests the incredible impact of bureaucratic thought on our lives.

We have described the search for meaning as an attempt to assert one's own view of the world in the face of strong pressures to submit to social and bureaucratic standards. As we have seen, there is a special tension which exists between individual meaning and the ethic of organization, so it is very difficult for the individual to succeed in establishing an identity that is personal and unique. Yet, even where this occurs, there is another problem: beyond the search for meaning there lie further questions of social action and individual morality. We still need a context, a practical arena in which the projects of life can be carried out. And, beyond this, we must face the fact that our seeking power extends even past death, as we strive for some sense of immortality.

II

We act. And through our actions we give expression to the personal and social commitments we have made. At best, this expression is incomplete in the sense that neither our actions nor the language we use to embody the idea of action can fully represent the complete psychic circumstance upon which our actions are based; yet we are inevitably forced to act and to be judged by our actions. Here we encounter the problem of choice—the independent comprehension of reality permits authentic and informed choices about the way in which we carry out the tasks of life. Choice, then, provides the connecting link between meaning and action; to seek the clearest expression of our passions, we must constantly seek to expand the possibilities for choice.

It is important that the question of action be approached both in its existential and its institutional senses.[10] Indeed, individual actions are embodied in institutional structures to the point that one must take into account the context of any action in order to understand it most completely. In this sense, the bureaucratization of modern society provides a special backdrop against which we must view particular actions. The question that presents itself is how the individual's opportunities for meaningful action are affected by the bureaucratization of society. Or, more specifically, how may we visualize our efforts to develop appropriate contexts for action in light of society's efforts to channel our activities into organizationally acceptable patterns?

The dilemma faced by the individual seeking a context for meaningful action is that as the continued bureaucratization of society displaces earlier political, vocational, and religious concerns, the individual is left with few opportunities to engage in actions outside organized systems. The problem with this, as we will see later, is that organized systems are inherently based around notions of regulation and control. This means that the organized individual is placed in the contradictory position of attempting to pursue meaningful choice within systems of regulation, a result that is both confounding and alienating in its impact. As one illustration of this process of displacement and the consequences it may have in terms of restricting personal action, we may examine what one prominent political theorist, Sheldon Wolin, has called "the sublimation of the political."[11]

According to Wolin, political theorists traditionally viewed politics as capable of drawing together the various experiences of human existence in some meaningful way and then expanding these experiences so as to achieve the greatest individual and social potential. While some persons still view politics in this way, for many people today political action has been largely dismissed as either trivial or totally useless. Studies of voting behavior, for example, indicate that only about two-thirds of the eligible voters in this country exercise their prerogative to vote in national elections. Speaking more generally, Lester Milbrath, reviewing early studies of political participation, comments, "About one-third of the American adult population can be characterized as politically apathetic or passive. . . . Another 60 percent play largely spectator roles in the political process. . . ."[12] Obviously, figures such as these are not expressive of the inherent values so long associated with political involvement in the traditional sense; yet these findings are only the beginning. Additionally, politically dismal conclusions must also be drawn from the relative lack of political knowledge, the low regard for politics as a vocation, and the general disenchantment with political affairs—all of which were much in evidence even before the Watergate scandals of the Nixon administration.

In contrast to these findings, however, other institutions are competing for our interest and, in many cases, apparently proving more satisfying to the individual than political activities. The development of loyalties directed to the community and the working group rather than to the nation state is of considerable importance. Elaborating on this last point, Peter Drucker has written, "Increasingly it is in his work that the citizen of a modern industrial society looks for the satisfaction of his creative drive and instinct, for those satisfactions which go beyond the economic, for his pride, his self-respect, his self-esteem."[13] Though these new forms of membership may be more limited than the citizenship role, it is clear that they are neither less attractive nor any less demanding of our allegiance.

Waning interest in politics as a framework for human action has not only been manifest in the practical operations of politics and organizations, but has also appeared as a central theme in recent social theory. The first of two such streams of thought is most clearly exemplified by the early European sociologists. According to Wolin, the antipoliticism of these writers was derived from their exaltation of society as the guiding force in human behavior. In this view, it is through our participation in social actions, in groups and institutions, that our existence is given meaning. The various contrivances of the political order, therefore, were seen by these theorists as false and futile attempts to alter the course of social change—false in that they contravened the "nature" of society, futile in that they were powerless against the social structure. Political impulse, at best a reflection of social conditions, could not provide any creative direction for life; political imagination was seen as practically a contradiction in terms.

Another part of the sociologists' rejection of politics was based on the isolation of effective political action from the masses. Government was simply far too remote and far too distant from the individual to offer meaningful participation. On the other hand, social living, through its capacity for intimate association, was capable of providing various types of roles, including membership in social groups. "Reality was socio-economic in nature; political action could not appreciably modify the fundamental character of reality, nor could political theory truly understand it."[14] To achieve understanding, it was necessary to adopt a sociological stance, viewing political processes in terms of social interactions and seeing political units (such as the state) as social organizations. The substitute for the political was, therefore, the organizational.

Similar patterns of thought underlie much recent utopian thinking. Utopias are generally designed to overcome some inherent deficiency in the existing situation. In recent times, the object of scorn has most frequently been the political system. To some utopians, politics has become obsolete and is simply unable to solve the problems of contemporary life; to others, the political system represents a tryannical force foreign to the development of spontaneity and imagination. For example, a passage from *Walden Two*, in which B. F. Skinner wrote about a psychologically based utopia operated on the principle of "cultural engineering," is characteristic:

> Government and Politics! It's not a problem of government and politics at all. That's the first plank in the Walden Two platform. You can't make progress toward the Good Life by political action! Not under *any* current form of government! You must operate upon another level entirely. What you need is a sort of Nonpolitical Action Committee: keep out of politics and away from government except for practical and temporary purposes. It's not the place for men of good will or vision.[15]

In his study of modern utopians, Thomas Molnar writes, "The central concept on which atheistic and religious utopians all agree is the need for the individual to reabsorb the citizen, the need to be redeemed following his fall as a political animal."[16] To replace politics, modern utopians, like some early European sociologists, have generally chosen some type of organizational principle. Precise and impartial, such a technique is felt to provide the structure and social solidarity which the realm of politics lacks. Since the dictates of the new utopian order are shaped by science and by organization (and are therefore presumably objective and rational), their execution supposedly brings people into harmony with their social situation.

Having been deserted by politics, we are seized by organization. And for many reasons this seizure seems only right and proper—in this way (we are told) we may obtain increasing goods, comforts, and leisure; we may develop a more stable economic circumstance, both at the personal and societal level; and we may enjoy the psychological stability so often missing in a turbulent society. Yet the tension between the individual and the organization remains, and it manifests itself by circumscribing the available contexts for action. So our seizure is not without its costs in terms of human meaning and human action. This, then, is the problem with bureaucracy—that in exchange for the benefits it brings, it exacts an enormous price in our lives. We have examined the way in which bureaucracy impinges on the search for identity and meaningful human activity; we may now turn to a final consideration, the impact of bureaucracy on our quest for immortality.

III

Still before us, beyond meaning and beyond action, is the fact that those images which are ultimately most cherished are those which relate to our own immortality. We seek finally to establish a connection between the meaning of our own lives and the meaning of the world around us, between our own potential and the possibilities of the universe. In this, we seek what all other organisms seek —a continuing experience, a way to extend beyond the limitations of life. But unlike other organisms, we do so with a consciousness of our own impending death. Accordingly, we seek to achieve in a spiritual way that which we are unable to achieve in a physical way—an extension of our own potential and a connection between our individual lives and the life of the universe. This we do through culture.

As Otto Rank and others have demonstrated, our search for immortality guides our social and psychological development in curious ways. In seeking a sense of transcendence, we construct entire cultures in such a way that we can use them to demonstrate our own heroic immortality. Indeed, the major cultural institutions of our time may be read as primarily immortality symbols. This point is made with special clarity in Ernest Becker's book *The Denial of Death*, in which Becker marshals impressive sociological and psychological evidence to demonstrate that what people desire most in any age is a way of achieving some sense of duration, and that culture provides them with necessary ideologies or symbols of immortality to accomplish this.[17] We depend on culture to provide what our physical bodies cannot—life after death.

In part, our culture presents us with a set of social activities or projects which presumably will enhance our chances to achieve some sense of transcendence; in part, we are presented with standards by which to judge our behavior, the implication being that performance at a certain level (typically at a level of moral distinction) will qualify us for salvation. In the first instance, for example, we may write books, raise children, or build buildings—each of which may endure beyond the limits of our own lives; in the second instance, we may engage in religious practices, or behave according to a particular "ethic," designated by the group as extending our immortality power.

Our dependence on organizational symbols as aids in our search for immortality can be demonstrated in several ways. One theme, based largely in sociopsychological terms, argues in this way: the contemporary individual, lost in the maze of mass society, is frequently denied fulfillment of certain rather basic psychological needs. Organization, on the other hand, when conceived as a system of social and psychological transactions, has the ability to provide such need-gratifications, even to the point of appearing to meet our spiritual needs. The elaborate symbols of approval offered by large organizations provide ample testimony to the value which individuals place on recognition in organizational contexts; and in such recognition there is an intimation of immortality. By attaining the symbols of organizational success, we seem to feel we can live forever. For this reason, we are not only willing but eager to participate in organized endeavor.

The organization may also provide standards of moral behavior by which we can judge our conduct. Through its presumption of impersonality, the organization can accommodate grievances which are morally untenable for the individual, a characteristic frequently manifest in the transfer of attributed responsibility from the individual to the organization. The organization is called upon to justify the actions of individuals; and, through its amorality (which derives from its impersonality), it can easily do so. The organization is equipped, through its own logic, to accept blame for the failings and incapabilities of the human personality. As we will see, the rhetoric of organization is so structured that individual limitations theoretically make little difference in the outcome of administrative rationality. As a result, the individual has the option of appealing directly to the system as a means of defense.

Unfortunately, as we examine the moral dimensions of our involvement in complex organizations, we are time and time again confronted with instances in which the viewpoint of the organization takes precedence over individual morality. There are obviously many illustrations of this phenomenon; however, the most dramatic remains the German effort to destroy the European Jews during the Second World War. German bureaucrats, at all levels, claimed time after time that their actions were justified because they were simply carrying out orders given from above. As recent trials in this country related to atrocities in Viet Nam indicate, the same bureaucratic form of justification is still very much in vogue. The appeal to hierarchy continues to be an essential part of the defense.

After reviewing the transcripts of various military trials, as well as his own research on obedience to authority, Stanley Milgram writes, "We find a set of people carrying out their jobs and dominated by an administrative, rather than moral, outlook."[18] Milgram comes to the conclusion that "something far more dangerous is revealed: the capacity for man to abandon his humanity, indeed, the inevitability that he does so, as he merges his unique personality into larger institutional structures."[19] In an age of organization, the individual's quest for immortality may appear to be assisted by the power of society and its institutions. And yet, though we deeply invest ourselves in organizational life, seeing this as a way to achieve transcendence, in the end we discover that organizations cannot bear such a spiritual burden.

IV

We seek to achieve meaning, to develop contexts of action, and to establish a sound relationship with that which is universal. But, in an age of organization, this task is enormously complicated, and we find ourselves engaged in a struggle to promote our own individuality against pressures to become merely a function of the group. What seems called for, therefore, is an approach to life in organizations which would enable us to counter the pressures of organizational life. But as Carl Jung reminds us, *"Resistance to the organized mass can be effected only by the man who is as well organized in his individuality as the mass itself."*[20] For this reason, a primary intent of this book is to redirect our attention back from the organization to the individual in order that we might then establish a clearer sense of individual autonomy and responsibility in an age of organization.

In the chapters which follow, we will seek to outline the commitments which we make as members of an organizational society and the way in which these commitments impinge on our efforts to achieve meaning, action, and continuity. First we will review the terms in which modern students of organizational life have given expression to our contemporary ethic of organization. Then we will examine in more detail the themes of meaning, action, and continuity, in particular the impact of modern organization on the individual's work in each of these areas. Having demonstrated the limitations placed on our efforts by the ethic of organization, in the final chapters we will attempt to develop an alternative understanding of organizational life—one which places the individual rather than the productive process at the center of our analysis, and which seeks its justification not in organizational efficiency or hierarchical control but rather in personal growth and development.

14

THE RATIONAL
MODEL OF ORGANIZATION

The power of social systems over individuals becomes understandable, I think, only if we see that social systems provide for their members not only sources of livelihood, protection against outside threat, and the promise of economic security, but a framework of theory, values, and related technology which enables individuals to make sense of their lives.

Donald A. Schon, *Beyond the Stable State*

. . . men will not give in to power unless it is accompanied by mystification, as in the service of something that has a grander aura of legitimacy, of symbolic compellingness.

Ernest Becker, *Escape from Evil*

The true system, the real system, is our present construction of systematic thought itself, rationality itself, and if a factory is torn down but the rationality which produced it is left standing, then that rationality will simply produce another factory.

Robert M. Pirsig, *Zen and the Art of Motorcycle Maintenance*

We have described bureaucratic thought as constituting a sort of contemporary ethic, one with practical implications, but also one with a certain moral and philosophical importance. In accord with this ethic, we have been able to extend our technology and our control to points unparalleled in earlier times. Yet we have done so at some substantial cost to our personal effectiveness in the world. As a result, we may as individuals and as a culture exhibit the same ambivalence toward organization as the central character in *Something Happened*: while we are terribly attracted to organizations and even fascinated by organizational technique, we are somewhat discomforted by the commitments we seem to be making. A first step in finding out exactly where we stand with respect to bureaucracy is to examine the role of complex organizations in our daily lives and the demands such organizations place on us.

Both scholars and popular commentators have pointed out the recent and rapid ascent of the "organizational society." Their evidence rightly shows that, by almost any measure, today's bureaucracies far surpass those of only a few generations ago (to say nothing of earlier times). The growth of giant corporate empires, the vast expansion of the labor movement, the development of massive governmental agencies—all these examples, and many more like them, provide testimony to the rising strength of complex organizations. This is an age of bigness, it is argued, and bigness, in this age, means organization.

But even beyond the vastness of modern organization, there is another important dimension of our organizational society, its depth. Organization today not only dominates, it penetrates. As we have seen, bureaucratic patterns not only mold our work life, but also our political and even religious involvements. In the course of a lifetime, we are likely to join many different organizations, quite dissimilar in many respects, but alike in their admiration for a common form—that of bureaucracy.

This fact does not, however, diminish the power of organization. To the contrary, the seeming dispersion of organization enables us to participate in an array of experiences, each reinforcing certain basic patterns of thought and action. By acquainting us with the central values of bureaucracy in varying contexts, the fragmentation of organization actually serves an important socializing function. The very pervasiveness of organization acts to promote and to extend the idea of organization in many new directions, while at the same time supporting the continued power of existing bureaucracies. It contributes to an organizational way of life.

I

Probably the clearest expression of the bureaucratic experience to-day is that articulated by scholars in the field of organization theory. While these persons—drawn from the disciplines of sociology, psychology, management, economics, and political science—have been intent on providing an objective view of the "facts" of organizational life, their descriptions and explanations also provide a most important commentary on the "values" of people in an organizational society. For this reason, it is through contemporary theories of organization that we will view the commitments we now associate with the ethic of organization.

Like other areas of social science, organizational analysis first looks broadly at human behavior, suggesting that such behavior may be most clearly understood by focusing on the interactions of individuals and that social activity, if it is not indeed the primary form of human action, at least provides the broadest insight into "human nature." At the next level of specificity, however, organizational analysis distinguishes itself from other areas of social science by arguing that social behavior may best be understood by studying people involved in ordered associations, especially complex organizations. An important assumption here is that behavior in organizations is somehow significantly different from that outside organizations. After all, if this were not the case, there would be little justification for a separate and distinct line of inquiry.

How, then, is organizational behavior different? Typically, according to the organizational analyst, this behavior is different because there are certain constraints which one may anticipate in organizational activity. Specifically, the dependence of organizations on strict lines of authority distinguishes the behavior of individuals as participants of organizations from their behavior outside organizations. This is a very important point—for, to the extent that theories of organization are based on the assumption that organizational life is different in certain ways, then those differences will be retained in the resulting theories. Other patterns of action will, by definition, be said to be outside the scope of the study. In this sense, to define organization is to outline a theory of organization, one which will meet certain expectations. For this reason, it is necessary to pay considerable attention to the way in which organizational scientists have defined the object of their study.

If there is one person or one formulation that has pointed the way for organization theory today, the theorist is Max Weber and the theory his analysis of rational bureaucracy. So strong has the influence of the German sociologist remained that even today, over fifty years after his death, students of organization are seemingly required to make at least some passing reference to Weber before going on to their chosen topics. Although we will be concerned with more contemporary formulations of organization, it is important to note that the strong overtones of rationality, impersonality, and hierarchical authority which so dominate contemporary thinking on organizations were predated by Weber's work.

Weber was concerned with the increasing number of social institutions designed solely to achieve given purposes in the most efficient way possible, a development which he described as the "rationalization" of society. This preoccupation with means rather than ends troubled Weber—indeed, he described the resulting institutional framework as constituting an "iron cage" for mankind —yet at the same time he felt such an outcome was a historical inevitability. Bureaucratic organization was, according to Weber, the epitome of rationality (meaning "efficiency"). "For bureaucratic administration is, other things being equal, always, from a formal, technical point of view, the most rational type."[1] Anticipating the continued growth of bureaucracy, Weber sought to delineate the "ideal type" of bureaucracy, bureaucracy in its purest form. In doing so, Weber was not necessarily recommending bureaucracy as a way of organizing, but illustrating what he felt was inevitable. As we will see later, however, his analysis has often given a quite different impression. In any case, the concept of bureaucracy developed by Weber has continued to be prominent in the sociological literature on complex organizations. According to a recent work, the concept includes the following features:

1. A division of labor based on functional specialization
2. A well-defined hierarchy of authority
3. A system of rules covering the rights and duties of positional incumbents
4. A system of procedures for dealing with work situations
5. Impersonality of interpersonal relations

6. Promotion and selection for employment based upon technical competence[2]

Contemporary students of organization closest to the Weberian tradition view organizations as subsystems of the larger social system in which they reside; as one writer puts it, organizations are "miniatures of society."[3] But while organizations are seen as more limited social systems, they are also seen as having important distinguishing characteristics—specifically, a strong emphasis on structure, stable role expectations, and a primary interest in the attainment of goals. Since these features form the bases of modern organization, it is important to examine each carefully.

Although structure is only one element of formal organization, most writers recognize the importance of structure as a defining characteristic of organizations. Organizational behavior occurs within a highly structured environment. Of course, the degree to which various writers emphasize structure varies; however, some seem to regard structure in organization as comparable to physical structures: ". . . imagine one of the models chemists make of molecular structures, with different-colored balls to represent atoms, and connecting rods to represent chemical bonds. This model can be taken to represent an organization as well as a molecule: the atoms are the offices, jobs to be filled, which have titles, authorities, and responsibilities; the bonds are working relationships among offices."[4] In any case, structure provides organization with a degree of formalism and directedness rarely encountered in other social situations. Elements of the organization are clearly defined, relationships are carefully prescribed, and patterns of behavior are stabilized over time.

There is, of course, a particular type of structure preferred by complex organizations today: hierarchy. Specifically, control is vested in a small number of leaders who, acting through an often lengthy chain of command reflective of a structural division of labor, direct the activities of numerous subordinates. Authority— that is, institutionalized control—is expected to extend downward through the various echelons of organization, enabling the leadership to determine the consequences which ultimately flow from their decisions. While current theories of organization rarely assume this strict and rigid pattern to be fully maintained in practice, hierarchical structure is clearly seen as a standard against which deviations may be judged; the burden of proof seems to lie with exceptions to this rule.

Theories of organization are not limited to consideration of organizational structure, but are also attentive to patterns of human behavior within organizations. The interactions of persons within organizations are assumed to be highly directed—that is, regulated from above. While some organizational analysts have described behavior in organizations as "cooperative," both the form and nature of the cooperation among members is determined in advance and enforced by the organization's management group. Through its manipulation of power and authority, the leadership exercises dominance over the activities of persons in the organization.

A final, commonly accepted element of organization, the feature which gives direction to formal organizational structure and to hierarchical patterns of expectations, is some form of goal orientation. Chris Argyris writes that organizations are intricate strategies to achieve certain objectives; Talcott Parsons uses the primacy of an orientation toward a specific goal as the distinguishing characteristic of organization.[5] With the postulation of a goal or purpose, organizational analysts are immediately drawn to the question of how that goal might best be achieved. The organization becomes an instrument, and the chief question facing both students and practitioners becomes how to most effectively employ it. This concern for efficiency clearly underlies what we will term the rational model of administration, a model which well captures the sense of the contemporary ethic of organization.

II

While the rational model stands as the most complete articulation of organizational thought today, its classic exposition is found in Herbert A. Simon's *Administrative Behavior*, written over thirty years ago.[6] For this reason, we will focus on Simon's work in describing the rational model. It is important to note, however, that work in the field of organizational analysis, both before and after the publication of *Administrative Behavior*, bears striking resemblance to the rational model as expressed by Simon. Especially in its adherence to the assumptions of positivistic social science and instrumental rationality, contemporary organization theory stands firmly in the tradition established by Simon some thirty years ago. But even more important for our purposes, the rational model of administration accurately portrays the bureaucratic ethic which seems so much a part of organizational practice. For this reason, an examination of the rational model of administration may help us understand more clearly the range of commitments required by that ethic.

In *Administrative Behavior*, Simon undertakes the formidable project of developing a new set of categories through which to view the operations of complex administrative bodies. Since he is interested in a truly "scientific" study of administrative behavior, Simon begins with a sharp distinction between facts and values in organizations, then recommends that scientists focus on facts rather than values. That which is factual about administrative life is that which is objectively observable: "Factual propositions are statements about the observable world and the way in which it operates."[7] Such propositions, according to Simon, "may be tested to determine whether they are *true* or *false*—whether what they say about the world actually occurs, or whether it does not."[8] It is on the basis of such "verifiable" propositions that Simon urges we build a theory of administration. Those statements which are of interest to the student of rational organization, therefore, are either those which can be validated through the objective observation of manifest behavior or those which can be logically inferred from such empirically justified postulates.

Simon does note, interestingly enough, that the terms "good" and "bad" are often encountered in the literature on administration, but that where they are used in the context of organization they lose their valuational character.[9] Rather, in terms of administration, "good" and "bad" refer only to judgments about the attainment of specific organizational objectives—those actions which contribute to the accomplishment of the organization's purposes are good, those which do not are bad. The use of such terms, according to Simon, does not compromise the scientific character of the rational model. Rather, it comprises the practical side of administrative science, that which shows persons how to behave in order to achieve certain objectives in the most efficient manner.

21

Simon's reliance on a positivistic interpretation of social science in many ways foreshadowed what has now come to be the "mainstream" view of scientific research into human behavior. At the base of this viewpoint, which we will examine in more detail later, are the assumptions that fact and value can be separated and that the role of the scientist is to build theoretical frameworks based on observation of the "factual" behavior of individuals and groups. As we will see, however, this view of social science is not the only one available. Indeed, Simon's choice of this interpretation has had important consequences for the theory of administration which resulted. These consequences will become particularly evident as we develop Simon's interpretation of organizational rationality.

Simon's argument begins with the suggestion that human beings are so limited in their capacity to deal with the complexity of modern times that they must band together in groups and organizations in order to attain mastery over their environment. In *Models of Man*, Simon presents the principle of "bounded rationality," as follows: "The capacity of the human mind for formulating and solving complex problems is very small compared with the size of the problem whose solution is required for objectively rational behavior in the real world—or even for a reasonable approximation to such objective rationality."[10] It is only through their participation in complex organizations that persons are able to make the problems they encounter manageable. James Thompson, a later proponent of the rational model, puts it this way: "By delimiting responsibilities, control over resources, and other matters, organizations provide their participating members with boundaries within which efficiency may be a reasonable expectation."[11] In this view, adherence to the norms of organization is essential for the individual to achieve rationality: "The rational individual is, and must be, an organized and institutionalized individual."[12]

It is critical to note that the concept of rationality used by Simon is "rationality when that behavior is evaluated in terms of the objectives of the larger organization."[13] The rational model does not argue that individuals are at all likely to act in a rational way—though that clearly would be desirable. In fact, being bounded in their rationality, human beings must "satisfice" in their decision-making.[14] It is only with reference to the goals of the organization that an individual's actions are described as rational; it is only as an organizational function that we attain rationality. "The stenographer's rationality is exercised in translating a piece of copy, whatever its content, into a typewritten manuscript. Her employer's rationality is exercised in determining the content of the copy. . . ." That which is efficient is said to be rational.[15]

But this interpretation of "rationality" is not the only one available. Indeed, a view of rationality as concerned merely with the efficient accomplishment of given purposes is quite different from a more comprehensive view of reason. The distinction between these two modes of rationality has been analyzed by Max Horkheimer, who notes that entire philosophical systems have been built on a notion of rationality as existing in the world, not simply as a relationship between means and ends, but as a criterion against which to judge the reasonableness of various ideas and proposals.[16] This mode of reason, in its best expressions, focuses on "the idea of the greatest good, on the problem of human destiny, and on the way of realization of ultimate goals."[17]

The other view of reason (Simon's view) is essentially concerned with means and ends, ". . . the ability to calculate probabilities and thereby coordinate the right means with a given end."[18] To say (in the language of the rational model), therefore, that a particular organization is rational is not to say that it serves politically or morally reasonable purposes, but simply to say that it operates in such a way as to maximize efficiency.

Simon describes the organization as a complex system for decision-making, broadly defined to include "attention-directing or intelligence processes that determine the occasions of decision, processes for discovering and designing possible courses of action, and processes for evaluating alternatives and choosing among them."[19] Whether speaking of the organization or the individual, decisions must be made in the light of the organization's purpose. For the individual, there are two important sets of decisions which must be made—important, that is, to the achievement of organizational purpose. One is concerned with the decisions of people to join, remain in, or leave organizations; the other is concerned with their behavior while they are in organizations.

In Simon's view, a "controlling group" has the power to set the terms of the membership for all participants. Membership is then treated in a rather formal, legalistic manner, being discussed in terms of an employment contract which the member either accepts or rejects. In keeping with the instrumental pursuit of organizational objectives, it is expected that the members of the organization will soon learn to behave in a way consistent with the organization's goals. They may do so for various reasons—because the goals of the organization are compatible with their personal goals, because they are trained to behave in the appropriate manner, or because they respond to the organization's authority or to the inducements it provides.

Typically, the new member is put through a period of training in which the organization presents the entrant with an appropriate set of norms, values, and patterns of behavior which are consistent with the organization's objectives. More bluntly, Philip Selznick speaks of ways in which an organization may indoctrinate its members in terms of the organization's character. Those who can't adapt are dismissed: ". . . one of the signs of 'healthy' organization is the ability to effectively orient new members and readily slough off those who cannot be adapted to the established outlook."[20] In any case, those who enter will be given rigorous instructions with respect to the goals of the organization and the ways in which their behavior will contribute to those goals, a process which ultimately seeks to replace some of the individual's own premises for making choices with those of the organization.

. Simon clearly recognizes that not all persons will find continued involvement in the organization suitable and will leave. "It may be postulated that each participant will remain in the organization if the satisfaction (or utility) he derives . . . is greater than the satisfaction he could obtain if he withdrew. The zero point in such a 'satisfaction function' is defined, therefore, in terms of the opportunity cost of participation."[21] Similarly, the organizational member is expected to contribute to the organization in return for certain inducements provided by the organization. It is this inducements-contributions formula which lies at the heart of the rational model; and it is here that the utility-seeking "economic man" of classical economic theory is joined by the more modern but quite similar "administrative man." And though "administrative man" is limited in his capacity for rational choice, he is no less interested in seeking gains or avoiding losses than his economic counterpart.

What choice does the individual have to withhold "contributions"? Or to leave the organization? Theoretically, the individual member "establishes an area of acceptance in behavior within which the subordinate is willing to accept the decisions made for him by his superior."[22] (Earlier Chester Barnard had discussed a similar "zone of indifference."[23] Simon suggests that this concept does not have the same "positive" tone as the area of acceptance.) But the area of acceptance is not unaffected by the organization. Indeed, it is assumed from the outset that the organization will do everything possible to expand the area so that the member will act in such a way as to pursue the organizational objective.

> Administrative man accepts the organization goals as the value premises of his decisions, is particularly sensitive and reactive to the influences upon him of the other members of his organization, forms stable expectations regarding his own role in relation to others and the roles of others in relation to him, and has high morale in regard to the organization's goals. What is perhaps most remarkable and unique about administrative man is that the organizational influences do not merely cause him to do certain specific things (e.g., putting out a forest fire, if that is his job), but induce in him a habit pattern of doing *whatever* things are appropriate to carry out in cooperation with others the organization goals. *He develops habits of cooperative behavior* [emphasis added].[24]

"The organization, then, takes from the individual some of his decisional autonomy, and substitutes for it an organization decision-making process." To the extent that this occurs, the members' behavior is more likely to be consistent with the instrumental purpose of the organization. Decisions by the individual will be made with organizationally correct premises, and the corresponding behavior will contribute directly to the achievement of the organization's goals. Again, the willingness of the organizational member to be molded to the purposes of the group is justified in terms of the increased rationality to be achieved by organizations. "Since these institutions largely determine the mental sets of the participants, they set the conditions for the exercise of docility, and hence of rationality in human society."[25]

III

While the rational model provides a comprehensive and well-integrated view of organizational life, it is not without its difficulties, many of which become apparent upon closer examination. Clearly, the rational model expects that the individual will be molded by the influence of the organization so as to perform the tasks required for the achievement of the organization's purpose. As Simon points out, the operative employee is the focus of attention, but only because the efficient operation of the organization is dependent on the individual's performance.[26] If the goals of the organization are clear, it is fairly easy to arrange the abstract tasks of the organization in an efficient pattern. The only problem, then, is to fit people to the roles which have been established, a task which is made considerably easier if the organization's "controlling group" understands the factors which determine one's "zone of acceptance" or "satisfaction function."

In providing such information, the rational model is not concerned with the ethical posture of the individual nor even with the correspondence of the theory to actual behavior. It is strictly interested in making accurate predictive statements based on the accumulation of "factual" data; it is interested "in sentences only with regard to their verification."[27] Science, it is argued, is based on facts; values may be introduced only under certain conditions (that is, specified with respect to given ends). The role of the scientist is, therefore, to make more efficient the process of making the organization more efficient.

Under these circumstances, the rational model can only make *instrumental* statements about the organizational member; it can speak only in hypothetical terms about the behavioral outcomes typically associated with various combinations of the events. Simon acknowledges that the only guidance the rational model can give is to say, "In order to produce such and such a state of affairs, such and such must be done."[28] (For example, in order to secure greater obedience, the organization should encourage the development of "habits of cooperative behavior.") The model cannot, however, make *expressive* statements, those which comment on the meaning or value of human action. The rational model places its emphasis on efficiency, but it does so by disregarding the issue of human meaning. As we will see later, many other theorists have urged formulations that would assist in the expression of meaning, but neither the meaning which individual members or clients derive from their experience nor the way in which they use their experience for personal development is a major concern of the rational model.

Given this view, there is little room for the individual to become fully engaged in the process of constructing a reality, or even a personality, apart from that decreed by the organization. The organizational member is merely instructed to become "docile" and "reactive," hardly the characteristics of the model democratic citizen. We may draw an analogy from Herbert Reid: "The image of man in much of American social science—an essentially calculating animal bound to the pursuit of the necessities of life and the satisfaction of organic needs—is in considerable contrast to [a] conception of man as an originating agent in the social construction of a political reality-world."[29] Similarly, the image of "administrative man"—an essentially calculating animal bound to pursue the necessities of organizational life—is quite different from the individual actively engaged in seeking a more fulfilling and responsible associational life.

One might, of course, take the position that this conception of the organizational member is simply an abstraction used at the level of theory, that it does not really provide a model for actual human behavior; however, there is reason to believe otherwise. In a recent exchange with Simon, Chris Argyris argues that "all descriptive concepts, once they are used to organize reality and guide behavior, become normative."[30] Such statements take on a connotation which exceeds their descriptive intent and serves to advise the reader concerning future behaviors. Interestingly enough, Simon himself addresses his work to practitioners as well as to academicians, obviously suggesting that they may learn new ways of acting from reading his material. And what behaviors are endorsed? The reader is told that rationality is to be achieved as one molds oneself to an organizational role and becomes an efficient part of the machine. Even where terms such as "rational" and "good" have been reduced to a limited technical meaning—that is, "rational" or "good" only with respect to the goals of the organization—their use certainly bears the connotation of social approval; and what they approve is an extraordinarily limited conception of the organizational member. Clearly, though "administrative man" is not seen as a fully rational decision-maker, rationality (now technically defined) is seen as desirable. Indeed, a major justification of organization in the beginning is that it can help eliminate those bothersome, inefficient human qualities, such as feelings, that interfere with rational endeavor. For example, one recent text consistent with the rational model laments, "Efficiency also suffers when emotions or personal considerations influence administrative decisions."[31] But such a process obviously involves a serious depersonalization of the member or client. Even Simon acknowledges that under these conditions the member participant "acquires an 'organization personality' rather distinct from his personality as an individual."[32] Because organizational rationality is ultimately concerned with roles rather than those who fill them, the resulting personality bears few human qualities. Robert Dahl and Charles Lindblom write: "A bias in favor of a deliberate adaptation of organizational means to ends requires that human relationships be viewed as instrumental means to the prescribed goals of the organization, not as sources of direct prime goal achievement. Joy, love, friendship, pity, and affection must all be curbed—unless they happen to foster the prescribed goals of the organization."[33] As the model attempts to bring rationality to the decision process, it eliminates other qualities. And, in doing so, it both depersonalizes us and limits our capacity for self-reflection.

Argyris notes, "Simon appears to make rational activity the basis for effective nonprogrammed problem solving. As such he excludes intuition, spontaneity, and faith."[34] But choices *are* made and in many cases must and should be made on the basis of human capacities other than those which accord with technical rationality. Though Simon's position is supported by the cognitive school of psychology, upon which he relies, there are certainly many other psychologists who would argue that the full capacities of human beings are not adequately expressed by attending only to logical, inferential processes. Names such as Jung, Rank, Allport, Maslow, and Rogers easily come to mind in this regard.[35] As we will see in the following chapter, in the works of these writers, there is an insistence that intuition and feelings are important aspects of the human experience and should not be overlooked or de-emphasized.

Interestingly enough, perhaps the clearest statement of this view in the literature on organizations come from Chester Barnard. In a long appendix to *The Functions of the Executive*, a book upon which Simon relies heavily, Barnard suggests that there are two kinds of mental processes that are important in organizational work —the logical and the nonlogical.[36] While recognizing the importance of rationality, Barnard suggests that there are other human processes "not capable of being expressed in words or as reasoning" but which can only be described as "intuition," "good judgment," "inspiration," or "common sense."[37] More important, Barnard, in expressing a strong moral concern for the possible dangers of increasing organization, emphasizes "the insufficiency of logical processes for many purposes and conditions and the desirability of their development in intelligent coordination with the non-logical, the intuitional, even the inspirational processes, which manifest mental energy and enthusiasm."[38]

What is particularly distressing about the rational model's disdain for nonrational processes is that just such processes lie at the base of many contemporary understandings of moral behavior. Rationality, especially the narrowly defined technical rationality of the rational model, cannot inform the process of making moral judgments; the most difficult moral choices of the individual require that we move beyond rationality. Edward Whitmont, a Jungian psychologist, makes this point as follows: ". . . ethos, morality, and the meaningfulness of existence rest basically upon emotional and intuitive foundations. These areas may be secondarily rationalized, but mere reason alone never touches or moves them."[39]

This leads, then, to the ultimate difficulty with the rational model: its preoccupation with technical efficiency omits any concern for the moral consciousness of the individual. As we noted earlier, the stenographer's rationality is achieved by successfully typing a piece of copy. That such a task might have outrageous moral implications—for example, if the copy is an order to execute a group of civilians in wartime—makes little difference to the model. Read as moral theory, the rational model of organization provides the same justification for action as that presented at the Nuremberg trials, that the efficient execution of one's orders is the proper task of the organizational member. Even if one argues, as Simon does, that greater societal benefits will occur if only we submit to occasional authority, the resulting picture of the organizational member is hardly in keeping with even the most fundamental standards of democratic morality.

The rational model, then, excludes certain values from the rationality of the system, but this is not to say that the model is without values. Even though the positive scientist claims objectivity, values do play an important part, interests are expressed. Simon, in keeping with his concern for technical rationality, claims that organizations are neutral instruments to be used in seeking designated purposes: "The efficiency criterion is completely neutral as to what goals are to be attained."[40] But this statement actually veils important valuational concerns. In the first place, the selection of efficiency does not address the question of how social and organizational goals may be rationally chosen. The German bureaucracy, for example, performed quite efficiently the task of murdering millions of people. Moreover, efficiency is itself a value, the selection of which may preclude other values. Having chosen efficiency as a central value, other values such as those of justice, equality, or participation necessarily assume less significance. And, third, the efficient pursuit of any single goal effectively precludes our consideration of others. Carl Rogers sees this as a limitation based in our interpretation of science: "If we choose some particular goal or series of goals for human beings, and then set out on a large scale to control human behavior to the end of achieving these goals, we are locked in the rigidity of our initial choice, because such a scientific endeavor can never transcend itself to select new goals."[41] The neutrality of the rational model is therefore an illusion—by presupposing the existence of social goals and by focusing on their accomplishment, the rational model clearly contributes to the maintenance of existing social and political circumstances.

The central value of the rational model, therefore, becomes the preservation of existing structures of power in society. Those who are in power—the "controlling group"—select the goals of the organization and its members. They then define as rational only those activities which efficiently contribute to the achievement of these goals. William G. Scott and David K. Hart comment on the primacy of this view of rationality in our society by saying, ". . . the predominant value paradigm that instructs the theory and practice of administration assumes the following form: What is desirable or undesirable in our society is measured by the degree to which a cluster of norms, an act, or an event contributes to or obstructs the progress of scientific and technical rationality applied to all planes of human existence."[42] In practically a play on words, if an act is consistent with the rational (meaning "efficient") pursuit of the organization's purpose, it is seen as rational (meaning "reasonable").

Such a view, however, tends to conceal the inevitable tension that underlies organizational action at all levels. In reality the rationality of the larger system and the rationality of the individual often are in direct conflict. From a phenomenological viewpoint, David Silverman writes, "There is thus not one rationality (residing in the work organisation or the official goals of the system), but a *multitude* of rationalities each of which generates the 'in-order-to' motives of the participants and allows them to make their own sense of the actions and intentions of others."[43] For the ordinary member of the organization, money, prestige, interpersonal satisfaction, and so forth may be much more important than efficient behavior and not always obtainable through such behavior. Consequently, the interests of the organization and the individual may be in conflict with one another, conflict which the rational model can only deal with by bringing the individual in line with the rational pattern of organizational behavior or by replacing one member with another more "suited" to the task.

As we have seen, many members, especially those in the lower regions of the organization, will not directly benefit from the operation of a highly efficient organization; *but someone will.* It is therefore for the benefit of that "someone" that the employee must be made to fit in, to become part of the organization's technical structure. Of course, the benefit accrues to those who control the organization's purpose, the "controlling group." The basis of organization is regulation; and regulation, of course, benefits most those who regulate.

Furthermore, there is implicit in the model a particular approach to the way power is to be structured. In the decision-making process, we, being guided by the rational model, choose those alternatives which lead most directly to the desired ends. As Simon puts it, "Ends themselves, however, are often merely instrumental to more final objectives. We are thus led to the conception of a series, or hierarchy, of ends."[44] Since this hierarchy of ends directly implies structural hierarchy, it becomes clear that the rational accomplishment of organizational objectives is dependent on hierarchical authority. In this conception, the rational model regulates facts and value, means and ends, through the establishment of rationalized hierarchical power.

In any case, the rational model extends important human values through our society, yet does so by disguising them as rational science and by forbidding their discussion as *values*. There is, of course, the possibility that these values may be socially acceptable, but they are not acceptable just because they are consistent with a particular interpretation of organizational theory. Indeed, the more likely and more problematic possibility is that these values are not always those we would freely choose to maintain—and that the rational model therefore partakes of a particular version of social reality, bound to existing social arrangements and existing distributions of power, then acts to serve and refine those patterns and those powers.

IV

All of this leads us back once again to the incongruities and contradictions which seem to mark our involvement in complex organizations. We originally designed and employed organizations to help us in attaining our goals. Yet now organization seems to have assumed an institutional character so strong that it comprises a model of thought and action which we are compelled to follow. The ethic of organization suggests itself as a new model for living. We originally sought to construct social institutions that would reflect our beliefs and our values; now there is a danger that our values may reflect our institutions. Here we encounter a most serious problem: as we continue to permit organizations to structure our lives, rather than vice versa, we may become locked in their grasp. We may begin innocently enough, engaging in organizational activities which we hope will promote useful social goals, yet wind up doing certain things not because we choose to do them, but because "that's how things are done" in the world of organization.

As we saw earlier, people today are engaged in a struggle to establish a meaningful identity, to determine a proper context for action, and to relate their individual lives to the life of the universe. In the next three chapters, we will return to these three themes— meaning, action, and continuity—in each case asking first how the ethic of organization restricts our personal development, then how we might begin to construct an alternative view of organizational life which would aid us in this respect. In doing so, we will move well beyond the traditional interests of students of organization, especially those bound to the rational model of administration, and begin to reconstruct the psychology, the sociology, and even the "theology" of organizational life. We will seek to outline what may be taken as a practical philosophy of organizational life.

SCIENCE,
ORGANIZATION, AND PSYCHE

"But how do you know when a path has no heart, don Juan?"

"Before you embark on it you ask the question: Does this path have a heart? If the answer is no, you will know it, and then you must choose another path."

"But how will I know for sure whether a path has a heart or not?"

"Anybody would know that. The trouble is nobody asks the question; and when a man finally realizes that he has taken a path without a heart, the path is ready to kill him. At that point very few men can stop to deliberate, and leave the path."

"How should I proceed to ask the question properly, don Juan?"

"Just ask it."

"I mean, is there a proper method, so I would not lie to myself and believe the answer is yes when it is really no?"

"Why would you lie?"

"Perhaps because at the moment the path is pleasant and enjoyable."

"That is nonsense. A path without a heart is never enjoyable. You have to work hard even to take it. On the other hand, a path with heart is easy; it does not make you work at liking it."

Carlos Castaneda, *The Teachings of Don Juan*

There is a special irony in our modern attempt to choose "a path with a heart"—in an effort to serve our own purposes, we have vastly expanded our capacity to manipulate nature and society; yet

35

in that very process we seem to have lost the capacity to deal with ourselves. In seeking control, we have lost control; in seeking power, we have lost power. As a result, we no longer experience the world in its fullness, but only in the stagnant categories provided by our organizations and other institutions; we have moved away from the realm of action and involvement, toward life-spaces that are dull and routine; and most important, we have forgotten the fascination of the impractical and the transcendent, preferring a rationalized here and now.

In chapter one, we depicted the individual's quest for meaning as a process of negotiation and renegotiation with the world around us. Indeed, it is this dialectical relationship between the individual and the group which underlies any number of philosophical statements. We are individuals living in a social situation, a very basic fact of life, but one which causes us enormous difficulties. On one hand, our solitary self seeks autonomy, growth, and creativity; on the other hand, our social self seeks stability, confirmation, and order. Yet neither can fully exist without the other. The social self needs the solitary self to give it depth; the solitary self needs the social self to sustain it.

In our struggle to develop meaning, therefore, we move back and forth between our individuality and our sociality, our uniqueness and our similarity, our difference and our likeness. That the resulting patterns of meaning may be quite varied for different yet equally strong individuals is nicely illustrated in *Crazy Horse and Custer*, a parallel biography of the two warriors by Stephen Ambrose.[1] Crazy Horse and Custer grew up in vastly different cultures, and the way in which each led his own life naturally reflected his heritage. Custer's culture was disciplined, productive, specialized, and inventive; it was strictly ordered in terms of functions to be fulfilled. Crazy Horse's culture, on the other hand, permitted him and even encouraged him to follow his own wishes, to seek his own vision; no one could tell him what to do. "Custer's fantasy life was terribly constricted, while Crazy Horse's was boundless. Custer could imagine only what he felt, saw, touched, understood. Crazy Horse could imagine almost anything. Custer's culture taught him to be practical; Crazy Horse's culture encouraged him to dream. Custer spent his teenage years trying to do something, to be somebody; Crazy Horse spent his teenage years seeking a vision."[2]

As each of these great American warriors sought to develop his personal power, he developed an orientation toward life and living that at once bore the mark of his individual personality and the stamp of his society. Nowhere was this more evident than in the way the two men approached the possibilities of life. "Living for the future almost had the effect of making Custer's society live *in* the future, while Crazy Horse, caring only for the present, lived in it."[3] While Custer was never satisfied with his present position and sought to move to the next higher level in the social structure, Crazy Horse accepted his role as a respected warrior and sought nothing more. Custer was always in a state of becoming; Crazy Horse was in a state of being. "Custer believed that things could be better than they were. Crazy Horse did not."[4]

To reflect the prevailing images of one's culture, as did these two leaders, is understandable, even necessary; but to become dominated by those images is quite another question. Where the dialectical relationship between the individual and the collective is over-balanced in favor of the group, the tension may be unbearable for the individual psyche. In place of the creative, even heroic, pursuits of individuals who achieve some measure of control over their lives, we witness among those dominated by the images of others exactly the opposite tendency—an amazing capacity for destruction and violence. For many such people, the potential for violence may lie smoldering just beneath the surface of the personality, manifesting itself in projections of fear, hatred, and guilt. For others, violence may erupt in terror and revenge.

Eugene Genovese discusses the often-violent relationship between masters and slaves in the pre–Civil War South in terms of the mutual acceptance of a particular social reality. What is important to note here, however, is that the nature of the relationship between master and slave held inherent contradictions which sometimes led to great violence. "The everyday instances in which 'docile' slaves suddenly rebelled and 'kind' masters suddenly behaved like wild beasts had their origins, apart from frequent instabilities in the participating personalities, in this dialectic."[5] For widely differing reasons, both masters and slaves were forced to agree to a particular conception of reality characterized in part by its paternalistic content. "Master and slave had both 'agreed' on the paternalistic basis of their relationship, the one from reasons of self-aggran-

37

dizement and the other from lack of an alternative. But they understood very different things by their apparently common assent. And every manifestation of that contradiction threatened the utmost violence."[6]

Of course, one might argue, the peculiar nature of the master-slave relationship presents an extreme case, not necessarily characteristic of a broad range of persons in contemporary society. Yet in more subdued (more repressed?) form, many of the same tendencies may be noted among persons today who experience an inability to achieve meaning in their lives. While the psychic damage in these cases may not result in extreme cases of violence directed toward self and others, it may lead to a retreat to depersonalization and an inability to relate to one's fellows in a positive, noninstrumental way. Even here actual physical violence may be just below the surface. Rollo May sees the issue in terms of a failure of society to provide individuals with significant experiences. "We are going to have upheavals of violence for as long as experiences of significance are denied people. Everyone has a need for some sense of significance; and if we can't make that possible, or even probable, in our society, then it will be obtained in destructive ways."[7]

There is much to suggest that the ethic of organization restricts our search for meaning and significance. We will argue in this chapter that the concept of instrumental rationality associated with organizations—and supported by a related concept of rationality in science—has severely limited our efforts to find meaning in our day-to-day lives, and is therefore potentially destructive to ourselves and our society. The power of organization has become so great we are presented with a set of realities structured around technical and managerial categories; and to the extent that we follow, we lose the capacity for unmediated experience, that sense of openness which permits the most complete growth of the individual personality. Our efforts to establish an independent perspective on the world have been severely restricted.

I

In this effort, organization does not stand alone; indeed, the instrumental orientation which we have associated with the ethic of organization is characteristic not only of organization, but also of the mainstream view of social science. This feature of science and organization, which was implicit in our discussion of the rational model of administration, may now be made more explicit, especially as it bears on the question of achieving meaning. Here we will argue that modes of knowledge acquisition and modes of social organization are deeply intertwined and profoundly affect both the way we see the world and the way we construct the world. In fact, science and organization may be viewed as related (perhaps even inseparable) attempts to meet a particular human demand, the demand for control—originally, control over nature, and later, control over other human beings.

Certainly, it is easy to see how science has been justified by its supporters as a way of controlling a potentially hostile environment. The effort to provide protection against the perils of nature has been a continuing concern of mankind. More recently, science has assumed a central role in our attempts to control our social environment, especially problems such as crime, human resources, and the economy. Our standard reaction to problems such as these is to seek a solution through science; in this way, we feel we will reestablish control. Indeed, most scientists describe their work as providing explanation, prediction, and *control* of events and behaviors.

Similarly, organization has been conceived as a method of control, a strategy for the advancement of domination. Through organization, we are said to be able to transcend both the restrictions inherent in our physical make-up and our limited rationality. Thomas Molnar points out in his study of utopianism the high regard for organization as a means of control: " 'Organization' is the key-word of the contemporary utopian. It suffices because his ideal for mankind is control over nature."[8] As we have already seen, organization is viewed as a way of regulating human behavior in order to achieve predictable outcomes; it is deeply based in attempts to control nature and does so by controlling human behavior.

To the extent that both science and organization have developed in response to the demand for control over nature, we should not be surprised that they share many common characteristics. Just as science promises not solutions to problems but rather an approach to seeking solutions, so does organization offer not accomplishments but rather a strategy to be used in their pursuit.

Both rely on rationality, objectivity, and impersonality; both offer themselves as instruments. Just as does scientific methodology, organization suggests a means through which ordinary people may participate in extraordinary achievements. In Simon's words, "It is only because individual human beings are limited in knowledge, foresight, skill, and time that organizations are useful instruments for the achievement of human purpose. . . ."[9] Just as science is concerned with controlling inquiry in order to verify certain assertions, organization is concerned with the control of behavior in order to yield rational action. Following the rational model of administration, the isolated individual has little chance of attaining rationality. It is through our participation in organizations that rationality is supposedly attainable.

In the realm of science, rational outcomes are sought through an adherence to the "rules" of the scientific method by which all inquiry must properly be conducted. It is only through following the particular method of science that we may be successful; and through our respect for that method, we are made equal by science. Yet in that very equality we may have lost our identity. The same is true of modern organization; we all must correspond to "job descriptions" and follow "standard operating procedures," all designed to equalize and therefore impersonalize. As the individual is absorbed into the organization, personal identity must be restrained by the prescriptions of the group.

The equalizing and regularizing effect of science and organization is, in each case, achieved through a particular arrangement which denies personality in favor of technique. Michael Polanyi has pointedly commented that "modern science is the outcome of a rebellion against all authority."[10] Science sought to remove the acquisition of knowledge from the authority of the individual personality and place it in a more public realm. However, while science was able to subvert authority of a personal nature, the authority of the individual, it offered as a replacement its own authority, one shrouded in impersonality. To appeal to science is no longer to appeal to a particular individual or group, but rather to a supposedly impartial and unbiased form, one providing a measure of validity to be challenged only on its own neutral grounds. In the very same way, modern organization detaches its power from the individual who might rule by virtue of personality or competence and attaches it to impersonal positions. The organization urges that personal authority submit to the impersonal standards of the organization; the authority of the individual is only possible in terms of the authority of the organization. The individual's competency is less the issue than the individual's location in the hierarchy.

Richard Braithwaite has offered the following definition: "A scientific theory is a deductive system in which the observable consequences logically follow from the connection of observed facts with the set of the fundamental hypotheses of the system."[11] The model administrative system is much the same. The "observable consequences" which flow from organization are, of course, typically goods and services, but their production is hardly random. Indeed, organization demands that production, in its broadest sense, follow a logical or rational pattern coherent with the design of the organization and, moreover, that the "observed" behavior of the members of the organization concur with the "fundamental hypotheses"—that is, the "standard operating procedures" of the system. In a sense, each organizational act is hypothetical in that it is a prediction of the anticipated reactions of other persons and groups. But as organizational hypotheses are verified through the behavior of the organization's members, the administrative system, like the theoretical system, is firmly established.

As science and organization have taken on a greater institutional significance, they have come to appear much larger than they originally were; they have become important for their own sake, not simply as tools to accomplish certain purposes. Being valued in themselves, not as methods alone, but in a substantive way, science and organization now offer their own values—the values of rationality and control—to the society and its members. What were intended as instruments to control nature have become institutions concerned with maintaining their own existence and controlling their own members and clients. The interest of science and organization in regulation and control has been applied to human relationships as well as to physical objects. Moreover, science and organization have become models for human behavior, making it more structured, more directed, and more impersonal. Over the years, therefore, our efforts to control nature have become intertwined with our efforts to control one another, to the point that

41

Horkheimer has written, "The history of man's efforts to subjugate nature is also the history of man's subjugation by man."[12]

This effect has been further assured as both science and organization have utilized various mechanisms to create and re-create a demand for their services. Advertising and the mass media reinforce our desire for further goods and services as well as our belief that these may best be obtained through science and organization. In the words of one advertisement, "The system is the solution." Moreover, science and organization have attempted to establish themselves as "natural" developments, proper outgrowths of human history or even responses to innate needs of human beings. To say that they are "natural" provides science and organization with an even stronger base than otherwise might be the case. Erich Fromm writes, "For the apologists of a social order based on control by an elite, it is of course very convenient to believe that the social structure is the outcome of an innate need of man, and hence, natural and unavoidable."[13]

In any case, modern organization seems inextricably intertwined with modern science, so that each lends support to and provides justification for the other. The result is a very powerful and persuasive set of institutional commitments, but commitments made at least in part at the expense of the individual. Implicit in a view of science and organization as neutral technical instruments is the assumption that those using these instruments treat their subjects (whether the scientific subjects being analyzed or the organizational subjects being administered) as objects. This process means that those being studied by science or managed by organization are ultimately required to fill roles not of their own design, either the conceptual models of the researcher or the "job descriptions" of the organization.

The instrumental logic of science and organization is predicated on the value of productivity, a value which now underlies claims to legitimacy by those in positions of power. Previously, the major justifications for elite domination were primarily mythical or religious—for example, kings and queens ruled by "divine right." However, according to several theorists, in industrial society we increasingly find the dominant group in society (which roughly corresponds to the scientific and organizational elite) justifying its position of dominance in terms of providing needed goods and services. In doing so, this group moves beyond earlier justifications of its preeminence to defend its role in terms of its technical capabilities. "One of the most important developments of recent years," writes Christopher Lasch, "is that the ruling class in advanced countries has largely outgrown its earlier dependence on general culture and a unified world view and relies instead on an instrumental culture resting its claims to legitimacy, not on the elaboration of a world view that purports to explain the meaning of life, but purely on its capacity to solve technological problems and thereby to enlarge the supply of material goods."[14] In other words, the mystification employed to justify the domination of a particular group is a technical or instrumental one.

What are the consequences of this mystification? In order to deliver supposedly scarce goods and services in what seems to be sufficient quantity, the dominant group finds it necessary to seek "rationality" in the productive process. This, in turn, requires a view of organization as a neutral technical instrument engaged in the larger purpose of maintaining social and economic stability. In turn, the various components of the organization, including raw materials, technology, and human labor, must be made to fit the instrumental orientation of the organization—that is, to follow the prescribed method in the most efficient manner possible. Such a concept, however, makes it necessary for those who employ the organizational instrument to objectify the lower participants. This process of depersonalization means, of course, that those being managed by the organization are required to fill organizationally prescribed roles; they must become part of the machine.

The interest of organization in efficiency leads us to treat one another in impersonal ways, as tools to be used or as data to be manipulated. But neither tools nor data need be concerned about meaning; so as we treat others impersonally we fail to recognize the importance of their search for meaning and do little to encourage them in that effort. Moreover, our treatment of others affects the way we think of ourselves. If we see little need to concern ourselves with the inner life of others, we will likely see little need to concern ourselves with our own inner life. Our lives will be devoid of the sense of self-reflection which adds balance and dignity to our endeavors. Our attention will instead be riveted on the outer world of behavior, performance, and accomplishment.

There are, of course, many illustrations of our contemporary preoccupation with performance, but there are also examples of people trying to break out of the restrictive language of achievement and talk about the meaning of their experiences. A number of these examples can be found in recent writings on sports. Obviously, the world of sports is one in which ordinary language places a great deal of emphasis on technique and accomplishment. Yet when athletes talk about sports, they are equally compelled to talk about the meaning their activity has for them. Bill Bradley, former professional basketball player turned politician, describes "being addicted to the nights when something special happens on the court," an experience he calls "one of beautiful isolation."[15] "It cannot be deducted from the self-evident, like a philosophical proposition. It cannot be generally agreed upon like an empirically verifiable fact, and it is far more than a passing emotion. It is as if a lightning bolt strikes, bringing insight into an unchartered area of human experience."[16]

A similar comment was made several years ago by John Brodie, former quarterback with the San Francisco 49'ers: "Often, in the heat and excitement of the game, a player's perception and coordination will improve dramatically. At times, and with increasing frequency now, I experience a kind of clarity that I've never seen adequately described in a football story. Sometimes, for example, time seems to slow way down, in an uncanny way, as if everyone were moving in slow motion."[17] There seems to be something special happening here, something which goes beyond the standard categories of sports accomplishment. What these athletes seem to be saying is that there are moments of exceptional meaning which occur on the field, and that we have few words to adequately express the inner experience of those moments.

The same is true of the organizational member. The sterile words which comprise the ethic of organization—rationality, efficiency, objectivity—appear foreign to our actual experience. Those surges of emotion and meanings, those "special moments" which occur from time to time in our lives and our work simply cannot be comprehended in instrumental terms. Yet these are important, vital experiences, deserving of our attention, for they represent our efforts to break free from the restrictive categories of a rationalized existence. They should not be defiled by imposing on them standards or concepts which do damage to their essential meaning. To do so not only draws our attention away from such experiences, it deprives us of an essential element of our humanity, which is another way of saying that it is an act of violence.

There are, of course, many examples of organizational members attempting to assert themselves against the pressures of organization to conform and to submit. The "accidental" breakdowns of assembly lines, the disruptions of bureaucratic paperwork, the new demands for worker involvement—all signify the efforts of individuals objecting to the instrumental treatment they are accorded in organizations. More recently, as further attention has been given to the stages of adult development, we have recognized more clearly those transitions in which persons simply choose to leave the organizational life behind. In these cases, we see most explicitly the desire of individuals to find meaning in their lives and their work, and the failure of the organizational society to provide such meaning.

As we have seen, modern science and organization express a common interest in controlling behavior in order to yield socially "useful" products. But this choice sets in motion a particular logic, either that of the scientist or the organizationally powerful—the belief that in order to control behavior it is necessary to treat as objects those things or those persons being controlled. Since to do so implies depersonalization and a limit on reflexivity, the logic is clearly that of those in control, not those who are being controlled. While we may momentarily accept the ideological justifications for our submission, we are ultimately restricted in our efforts to arrive at a clear and meaningful identity.

II

To confront the instrumental logic of organization is a psychological task of considerable difficulty. And unfortunately, most cognitive and behavioristic psychologies provide little help in this effort because they see the individual personality as merely a consequence of social forces impinging on the intellect; they conceive of the person in the same mechanistic way as the rational model of administration. By portraying the individual as passively responding to the manipulation of the environment by those in control, these psychologies contribute to a condition of elite domination. Moreover, by describing the individual as seeking merely to rationally maximize (or even "satisfice"), they characterize the individual as achieving meaning only through the acquisition of certain "utilities."

Many more humanistically oriented psychologists seem to fall into the same trap, failing to recognize the cultural forces which restrain our development, and even, in some cases, coming very close to defining the "healthy" or "self-actualized" person as one who best fits the cultural mold. For example, Maslow's procedure of citing those who had achieved success as defined in Western culture as models of self-actualization obviously biased his later studies of human motivation in favor of culturally approved modes of action.[18] Russell Jacoby has taken this point even further in his book *Social Amnesia*, in which he argues that nearly all post-Freudian psychologists have neglected the central lesson on which psychoanalysis was constructed—that the individual and the group are in a constant state of tension.[19] Under such circumstances, we can hardly expect psychology to assist the individual in that struggle.

In the psychoanalytic tradition, we find a much clearer recognition of the dialectical relationship between self and society, pleasure and reality, life and death. Here we see the interplay of opposites which marks the development of the individual and the group psyche. While there are obviously important differences among theorists such as Sigmund Freud, Alfred Adler, Carl Jung, and Otto Rank, from their collective work we may draw insights that might enable us to formulate more clearly the individual's struggle against organization.[20]

Jung's work is of particular interest as it provides an understanding of the limits of rational action and the possibilities inherent in other modes of psychic functioning. In Jungian psychology, each individual has a personality, or psyche, which embraces "all thought, feeling, and behavior, both conscious and unconscious."[21] The psyche serves as the base from which all social and environmental orientations are formed; therefore, all behavior and attitudes can be explained through an understanding of the psyche. The psyche, or personality, is made up of three parts: the consciousness, the personal unconscious, and the collective unconscious.[22] The consciousness consists of the feelings and attitudes each individual is aware of. The personal unconscious is that part of the personality which stores personal experiences of which the individual is not cognitively aware, but which nevertheless affect conscious activities. The collective unconscious embraces the evolutionary and hereditary characteristics which link people in today's society with the past. It consists of images which are held by all people and which influence their perception of their experiences. It is the interaction among these three parts of the psyche and the various functions of each which makes up the complete personality.

Of primary importance in Jung's discussions of the personality is the idea that there is a "wholeness" of the personality—that the personality is more than just the sum of its parts. Although Jung defines certain dominant functions and orientations in the individual, it is always with the assumption that the opposite of each function also plays an important role. There is a complete duality in the personality—a rational and a nonrational side, an extraverted and an introverted side, as well as many others. However, while one side may be dominant in daily activities, without the recognition and development of both sides—without the recognition and development of the wholeness of the personality—it is impossible to become truly "individuated."

Jung defines individuation as "the process of differentiation, having for its goal the development of the individual personality."[23] This self-knowledge, or the discovery of how every function of the personality is related to experience, is necessary for psychological health. If one or more functions of the personality are repressed, or not allowed expression, then a neurosis will develop. Jung reached the following conclusion: "there are in a neurosis two tendencies standing in strict opposition to one another, one of which is unconscious."[24] Under such a circumstance, the individual will have unexpressed tendencies in the unconscious which will manifest themselves as, for example, phobias or compulsive behavior. This condition will be maintained until self-knowledge allows full expression of all the different parts of the personality.

To clarify the many variations of the human personality, Jung first describes two types of people—the extravert, who is more interested in the object or the outside world, and the introvert, who is more interested in the subject or the self.[25] The extravert looks to the outside world for facts and orientations, then bases decisions and actions on what is discovered there. The subject, or self, is important but plays a subordinate role to the outside world. For instance, the extravert derives a sense of morality more from the norms of society than from personal conscience. The introvert, on the other hand, is principally oriented by his or her own psychic structure, the self rather than the outside world. For example, a sense of right and wrong is determined more through the subject rather than through the norms of society. According to Jung, each person is aware of both subjective and objective factors but generally relies on one set more than the other.

Jung next distinguishes two ways of *perceiving* (sensing and intuition) and two ways of *judging* (thinking and feeling). Sensing refers to the accumulation of data through the senses, through seeing, touching, hearing, and so forth, while intuition refers to that process by which we take in information but are unable to identify the source. Typically, sensing concerns itself with the immediate and concrete, while intuition involves a perception of the deeper meanings or possibilities inherent in any situation. Among the decision-making functions, thinking refers to making judgments based on impersonal and logical considerations, while feeling relies more on emotions and personal values. While each of us uses all of these functions, we do so in varying degrees at different times. In fact, we tend to develop patterns in which we emphasize one function more than the others—that is, one function becomes dominant in our personality. By combining these four functions with our tendencies toward extravertism or introvertism, we arrive at eight psychological types, each of which we will briefly outline.

(1) A person of the Extraverted Thinking type relies on data gathered from the outside world in order to draw logical, impersonal conclusions. Whether the data is in the form of facts or ideas, it is always dealt with in a logical fashion. In a work situation, this means that the person likes to work with a wide variety of analytical problems and to be able to treat these in an impersonal manner. Fairness is of great importance to the person, while feelings are rarely taken into consideration. This indeed comprises their most frequent source of problems, for if feelings are suppressed or neglected too long, they can emerge in damaging ways.

(2) A person of the Introverted Thinking type also has an intense concern with ideas and facts but applies these to the inner

subjective world rather than the outer objective world. This person, too, is logical and impersonal, and can work with either ideas or facts, but studiously avoids applying them to the outer world. This type prefers a work situation in which there is much time for thinking before making each decision, and where work is done in solitude. The person tends to be unaware of other people's feelings about any given situation and, like the Extraverted Thinking type, may have difficulties when feelings are inadequately expressed.

(3) A person of the Extraverted Feeling type is one who depends on feelings as a guide through life. Since the person is extraverted, these feelings are usually in harmony with the external world. The person exhibits warmth and friendliness and judges situations according to the personal values from which feelings are generated. These personal values, however, are largely based on the judgments of others. The best work environment for this person is one in which harmony prevails and in which feelings can enter into the decision-making process. On the other hand, this person may become the captive of incorrect assumptions that were chosen for their immediate attractiveness rather than by careful logic.

(4) A person of the Introverted Feeling type judges the world in terms of independently arrived at personal feelings. Being introverted, the person is unlikely to show great warmth or emotion in new situations or with strangers; but when the people and situations become familiar, this type can be expected to be warm and enthusiastic. This person generally prefers to work alone but will deal with tasks in a way which takes people's feelings into consideration and promotes harmony in the environment. This person, however, may become overly sensitive and consequently vulnerable to pressures both from the outside world and from his or her own excessive expectations.

(5) A person of the Extraverted Sensing type deals almost entirely with objective facts. Personal feelings and other people's values are of little consequence. This type deals primarily with the outside world and accumulates data on which all decisions are based. Little consideration is given to abstract possibilities. This person likes to work with concrete situations where standard problem-solving methods can be used rather than with abstractions. This person may, however, suffer from a lack of clear direction,

preferring to live only for the moment, a characteristic which can lead to some instability.

(6) A person of the Introverted Sensing type gathers objective data in a systematic and continuous fashion and applies these data to the inner world in a way which provides a sound basis for intense ideas. These ideas are then applied in a routine and systematic fashion. This type works best in jobs which require routine analysis of hard data. The work done by this type will be precise, and accurate conclusions based on the given data can be expected. The greatest problem for this individual may be a preoccupation with impressions generated from within and transmitted to the outside as stubbornness and intractability.

(7) A person of the Extraverted Intuitive type is one who approaches the outside world with an eye toward the possibilities a situation offers, rather than dealing only with the actualities of the situation. This person does not draw on logical cause-and-effect relationships, but rather leaps to the potentialities of whatever is at hand. This type is innovative in a work situation but becomes bored with a project once all the possibilities have been discovered. The discovery, not the doing, is what appeals to this person. Of course, this tendency may lead this person to drop projects after they lose their initial appeal, which may be interpreted as indifference.

(8) A person of the Introverted Intuitive type sees the possibilities in situations in terms of personal ideas rather than the outside world. This can result in highly innovative conclusions, but these may not be in harmony with the view of the outside world. A solitary work environment that is out of the ordinary and allows for substantial creativity appeals to this type, but this type cannot be expected to enthusiastically convey new ideas to others. At times this preoccupation with one's own visions may become excessive, leading to isolation and defeat.

As noted above, the goal in Jungian psychoanalysis is self-knowledge leading to individuation. Through self-knowledge each function of the psyche is differentiated and becomes understood in terms of one's life experiences. Individuation, then, is the smooth interaction of all functions resulting in a unified personality. The inherent wholeness of the psyche that Jung refers to requires that *all* functions and orientations be expressed in some way; every function has an opposite (or "inferior") which must also be allowed expression. Nonproductive functioning results from the repression of one or more parts of the personality. Any attempt to repress the opposite functions will result in their expression in some primitive or nonproductive manner. Some neuroses are socially debilitating, while others can be functional in a given setting, but all are a denial of the true individuality of the person. Only through individuation can a person be completely healthy psychologically. Jung says: "If people can be educated to see the shadow-side of their nature clearly, it may be hoped that they will also learn to understand and love their fellow men better. A little less hypocrisy and a little more self-knowledge can only have good results in respect to our neighbour; for we are all too prone to transfer to our fellows the injustice and violence we inflict upon our own natures."[26]

Jung discusses various reasons a person might be unable to achieve individuation, one being that the orientations and ideas which appeal to the individual do not correspond to the dominant ideas of the outside world. According to this theory, which Jung terms the "political theory of neurosis," the outside world imposes constraints on the individual far beyond those necessary to inhibit "animal passions."[27] (This formulation is, of course, similar to Herbert Marcuse's notion of "surplus repression.") These constraints deny many new ideas their proper expression. Since the person holding these ideas continues to live in the society, it is natural that the individual will either adopt the dominant view or suppress his or her own view in an attempt to avoid discord; but the adaptation fails to allow a true expression of self and, consequently, cannot be psychologically healthy.

At another point Jung describes the collective psyche, which lies outside the individual psyche and consists of conscious and unconscious dispositions which influence the individual psyche.[28] While these dispositions have meaning in the collectivity, they do not necessarily reflect the true needs of the individual. The collective psyche involves such conscious but impersonal symbols as offices, titles, and positions, as well as the unconscious rationalizations for the existence of these. Just as a person can become so wrapped up in society that individuality is forgotten, so too can one become so attached to the collective psyche that the individual psyche is neglected. However functional or easy this may be for the outside social world, the person still must deal with his or her individuality.

Failure to do so results in neurotic disturbances and alienation of the self.

According to Jung, even though one function may be consciously more dominant, it is important that all functions of the individual psyche find outlets. Only through free expression can each function develop in a mature and acceptable fashion while at the same time contributing to a balanced whole. Individuation will be facilitated if society allows all functions of the psyche equal opportunity for expression. Unfortunately, the ethic of organization directly contradicts this requirement—the expression of certain functions is rewarded while other functions are repressed.

Specifically, as the ethic of organization gives preference to decisions made (1) on the basis of specific "factual" data, and (2) in line with strict logical procedures, there is an obvious emphasis on two of the four functions: sensing and thinking. Moreover, the functions of intuition and feeling are neglected. This means, first of all, that persons of these latter psychological predispositions who find themselves in highly rationalized bureaucratic systems are located in situations which simply do not match their preferences. These individuals will consequently be subject to special pressures. Whitmont states the problem in this way: "In our present time and culture, environmental influence is primarily exerted in the direction of extroversion and of thinking and sensation. We quite often find that a distorted typological adaptation has been pressed into these molds. The type most likely to be injured in this respect—victims of our current Western cultural bias—are those of introverted feeling and intuition."[29]

But the injury is not exclusive to the less preferred types. The ethic of organization obviously favors a general shift toward the extremes of sensing and thinking—toward the "psychological type" of the machine, a perfect sensing-thinking combination. While those who are initially inclined toward these functions may find the process of adaptation easier, they too will be limited in their growth to the extent that they are prevented from developing a more complete or "whole" personality. The ethic of organization, therefore, provides a significant impediment to the individual's effort to achieve wholeness.

The reaction of the individual to this situation can take various forms, but few contribute to a healthy psychological state. One response might be a repression of those natural tendencies of the individual which do not fit the mold of the organization. For feeling types, this would mean repressing the personal values on which judgments are generally made, in favor of processing objective data through the thinking function. For the intuitive person, this means that the individual, rather than trying to discover the possibilities of a situation (which is the preferred task), would instead deal only with the actualities. For the introverted type, this means adopting an attitude toward the outside world which is alien to natural preferences.

A second reaction might be to shift reliance (and also responsibility) from the individual to the collective. Rather than being concerned with personal feelings or attitudes, the individual would take on all the characteristics of the collective and feel, at least superfluously, well integrated in the society. This is a phenomenon Jung refers to as "inflation," identifying with the collective psyche to such a great extent that the personal psyche atrophies. Indeed, inflation can be carried to such an extreme that the individual psyche no longer exists outside the collective.

The ethic of organization clearly encourages reliance on the collective rather than the individual psyche. The hierarchical structure of organizations, which rewards good performance (as defined by the benefit of the act to the organization) by a promotion in the ranks, is a perfect example of the impersonal structure of Jung's collective psyche. Since few other rewards are available in an organizational society, failure to identify with the collective psyche can leave the individual without psychological support. Harry Levinson has summarized this view by saying, "In brief, the man-organization relationship is important to the person because it meets certain needs; in addition he uses the organization to replace certain psychological losses, to reinforce his psychological defenses, and to serve as a major object of transference."[30] Even though identification with the collective psyche requires some negation of individuality, organizational participants may take this step in order to receive the reinforcement available in the collective. When this identification becomes widespread in organizations, participants express their alienation while maintaining the collective identification; thus we often find individuals complaining about specific procedures or "red tape" as a psychological substitute for their opposition to bureaucratic *policies* they find oppressive.[31] In this way participants can express their alienation while still maintaining their collective identification.

These reactions will allow the individual to function in the society with apparent harmony. However, beneath the surface, they will actually create disharmony by limiting the expression of the individual's preferences. This disharmony may be manifest in phobias, psychosomatic illnesses, or other neurotic responses to the situation (many of which we have already outlined). There is, of course, a third possible reaction, basically a rejection of imposed roles. That is to say, one might simply choose to withdraw from those imposed roles which restrict the individual's growth processes. But this is very difficult. As we have repeatedly indicated, organizationally imposed roles seem increasingly to be the only roles available—whether we speak of work, politics, religion, or any other field. To withdraw from one imposed role may simply be to move to another, with the same limits to personal development as the first.

III

If we momentarily suspend the rationalized "explanations" for our behavior which the ethic of organization proposes, we find that the meanings we hold as important are not as one-sided as they seem. It is clear that *both* subjectivity and objectivity assert themselves in our lives from time to time, even from moment to moment. At some times we are more interested in privacy; at other times we are more interested in publicity. We can in fact conceive of the *process* of moving back and forth from privacy to publicity as a very basic impulse in our lives, one essential to establishing meaning.

At certain times, the flow of our lives is markedly toward privatization. We are concerned with ourselves as individuals, with differentiating ourselves from other people, with establishing our separateness. Here we permit ourselves to operate in terms of the "irrational" images of feeling and intuition; we hope to release our pent-up energies through imagination and creativity. We seek only ourselves. At other times, however, we are much more inclined toward social interaction, emphasizing our relationships with other people, if only to acknowledge that we have something in common with them. Here we are concerned with likeness, with similarity. Here we operate more in terms of the "rational" images of sensing and thinking; we are concerned with the immediate and the given, and we seek to establish logical relationships. We seek others, at least in part because in others we hope to find ourselves.

Of course, what is most common is that our lives play themselves out somewhere between these two extremes. Indeed, we are in fact never at one point or the other, we are always moving in some direction. We can thus express the on-going-ness of our experience as a *process* of movement, sometimes toward privacy and sometimes toward publicity. However, as our lives flow in one direction or another, we may encounter blockages or restrictions.

For example, if we are "in the process" of moving toward a more private, personal moment and something occurs to display us publicly, a certain tension occurs. We might say that we have struck a nerve, in this case, a "process nerve." Or if we are being guided by our logical faculties and something happens around us which we take as an emotional surge, we may react sharply. Again we have struck a "nerve." When this occurs, we may respond in any one of a number of ways. Externally, we may appear angry, resentful, jealous, and so forth. However, that appearance will often seem out of place to others, for it will have been stimulated by processes having nothing to do with the task at hand, with what is happening on the surface, but rather with processes which are much deeper and more personal. Of course, we may attempt to resolve the contradiction which created the tension in the first place, a resolution which, if successful, will be tremendously relieving. But this is usually quite difficult, partially because we may be unwilling to confront the issue being raised (perhaps for "process" reasons!), but more often because we simply do not understand ourselves what happened. (Incidentally, probably the best example of the relief obtained from resolving such a contradiction is laughter. Humor is built around our being led in one direction, then having that direction contradicted. When we resolve the contradiction, our tension is released through laughter.)

The tension resulting from striking a "process nerve" may also be psychologically repressed, stored away in the depths of our psyche (often in a somewhat perverted form). There it resides, waiting for the moment when it can reemerge and "get even." Elias

Canetti provides an excellent and particularly relevant example of this response in his book *Crowds and Power*.[32] Canetti suggests that any command carries with it an implicit threat connected to the symbolism of death. For this reason, the one who receives the command experiences it as an imposition (in our words, an intrusion on his or her privacy) which, if the order is carried out (in our words, "not resolved"), will be repressed only to emerge later as an effort to command others. Canetti calls this a "sting." "Anyone who has carried out an order as an individual keeps his original resistance as a sting, a hard crystal of resentment. This he can only get rid of by himself giving the same order to someone else. The sting is nothing but the hidden replica of the command he once received and could not immediately pass on."[33]

While the correspondence between our repressions and their later consequences is rarely as direct as Canetti suggests, we have here another illustration of the dynamic process by which meaning is established in our lives. Clearly, dependence on one mode of psychic functioning prevents us from achieving the kind of wholeness of the personality which Jung described; indeed, whether exclusively private or exclusively public, intuitive-feeling or sensing-thinking, our lives are incomplete. In order to achieve an integration of our life experience, we must not attend solely to one set of functions or the other. But that is the image of our lives urged by the ethic of organization. It is clear that we must resist that definition of our lives or they will have little meaning.

What emerges from Jung's work is that meaning is concerned with getting in touch with one's own evolving experiences, with opening one's world to its fullness rather than rationalizing its incompleteness, with facing up to the fact that we must live with both light and dark, love and hate, joy and sorrow. In achieving meaning we can never fully depend on instruction from others, and certainly not on instruction from the one-sided organizations of our age. Only through the active cultivation of our inner resources may we begin to see the way forward. In the continuity of our lives there are no dualities, no dilemmas, only temporary struggles which we create (or which are created for us) to keep us busy. In this sense, our conscious life lags far behind our inner life. Where our spirit has moved, so shall we follow. And though we may not even know that the movement has begun (until we look back and see where we have been), we will soon begin to feel a direction—unless we become so bogged down in the present that we fail to attend to the past and the future.

PRAXIS
AS ENLIGHTENED ACTION

Modern man has lost the capacity for subjective experience, and experiences the world only in terms of practical ends.

Erich Fromm, *The Anatomy of Human Destructiveness*

When we realize that life itself is an art, that man can play a decisive role in shaping his own environment and thereby shaping himself, we turn our attention to the best and most enlightened ways in which this can be done.

Richard Bernstein, *Praxis and Action*

But action is human only when it is not merely an occupation but also a preoccupation, that is, when it is not dichotomized from reflection.

Paulo Freire, *The Pedagogy of the Oppressed*

As we open ourselves to the possibilities of our existence and begin to establish a firmer sense of personal identity, we make choices about both the content and the direction of our lives. While these choices may not always be stated, or even conscious for that matter, they establish deeply personal patterns of development to which we are bound. These psychic processes underlie the surface of our existence just as currents lie beneath the ocean's waves. But they nonetheless affect, even direct, the course of our development.

59

Those energies which lie within must ultimately express themselves in the outer world. As Ira Progoff puts it, "The inward process of growth moves in an external direction in order to fulfill itself."[1] We are drawn to those projects and activities which we see as best able to provide a context for the fullest expression of our inner desires and potentialities. We seek action contexts in which we can show the world who we are, but also seek those activities which will provide opportunities for growth, ways of drawing forth literally the best that is in us. Our choices lead inevitably to action, and in our actions we are fulfilled or denied.

As we have indicated, in an age of organization, the available contexts for action are increasingly limited. If we move from business to government to labor, we simply move from organization to organization to organization. The form remains the same; the expectations remain the same; and, in all likelihood, our behavior will remain the same. If this is the case, we must ask in what ways complex organizations, as contexts for human action, assist or restrict the development of our potential.

I

In order to examine this question, we may turn to the work of what has come to be called the Frankfurt School of critical social theory.[2] The Frankfurt School began as the Institute of Social Research at the University of Frankfurt in the early 1920s. The Institute was designed as a center for radical scholarship featuring, though not limited to, Marxist social science. Under the intellectual and administrative leadership of Max Horkheimer, members of the Frankfurt School, while in Germany and later in exile in the United States, engaged in a broad range of research, from the authoritarian personality to aesthetics and mass culture. Such scholars as Theodore Adorno, Herbert Marcuse, Erich Fromm, Leo Lowenthal, Walter Benjamin, and Franz Neuman participated in the work of the Institute and made important contributions to the research program of the Institute as well as to the critical perspective generally. Recently, this perspective has been carried forward most prominently by Jurgen Habermas, a contemporary German philosopher whose work we will examine in some detail.

In an early publication, Habermas developed a distinction between two modes of social action, symbolic or communicative interaction and purposive-rational action.[3] Symbolic or communicative interaction is concerned with the reciprocal expectations of interacting individuals, while purposive-rational action seeks defined goals in an instrumental fashion. This formulation, drawn from Hegel and implicit in Marx, expresses the distinction between interaction and work (or labor), and leads directly to an argument concerning the relationship of one to the other.

These two fields of action may be described in more detail. By "interaction," Habermas suggests "binding *consensual norms*, which define reciprocal expectations about behavior and which must be understood and recognized by at least two acting subjects."[4] These norms of behavior are embedded in ordinary language and in the mutual understanding of participating parties. Communicative interaction is characterized by works consistent with the values and maxims of society and expressed in intersubjectively shared language. The role of communicative interaction is the maintenance of a normative order intended to achieve "emancipation, individuation, [and the] extension of communication free of domination."[5] Through this activity, persons engage in free and meaningful dialogue based on self-reflection and self-understanding.

The realm of "work" or "purposive-rational" action, on the other hand, is concerned with either instrumental action based on technical rules or strategic choices deriving from analytic knowledge; in either case there are implied predictions about observable events which can be proven correct or incorrect. "Purposive-rational action realizes defined goals under given conditions. But while instrumental action organizes means that are appropriate or inappropriate according to criteria of an effective control of reality, strategic action depends only on the correct evaluation of possible alternative choices. . . ."[6] In purposive-rational systems, technical rules define the orientation of those who act; technical efficiency becomes the main criterion for judging various activities.

Each field, of course, establishes rules or maxims for behavior, the violator of which is subject to punishment. However, the conditions of violation are quite different in the two realms. Violating technical rules or strategies is simply deemed "incompetent," while violating consensual norms understood by the society is labeled "deviant." Similarly, "Learned rules of purposive-rational action supply us with *skills*, internalized norms with *personality structures*. Skills put us in a position to solve problems; motivations allow us to follow norms."[7] Most important, extrapolating from Habermas, we may say that the reason which underlies purposive-rational action is *regulation*, the extension of technical control in the pursuit of productive growth; the reason supporting communicative interaction is ultimately that of human *choice*, the autonomous resolution of matters of personal and social concern.

Habermas distinguishes analytically between the broad institutional framework of a society, which consists of the guiding norms of the society, and subsystems based either on purposive-rational action (such as the economic system or the public bureaucracy) or on moral rules of interaction (such as the family or kinship structures). The question which arises is whether one subsystem, that of purposive-rational action, has come to dominate the institutional structure. Following Weber's formulation, precapitalist societies maintained their legitimacy through the preeminence of the institutional or cultural framework. " 'Traditional' societies exist as long as the development of subsystems of purposive-rational action keep[s] within the limits of the legitimating efficacy of cultural traditions."[8] As modern social organization emerged, however, rationality increasingly became the property of purposive-rational systems, thus challenging the older forms of legitimacy.

Habermas's conclusion is that the institutional framework within which systems of purposive-rational action were traditionally embedded may now be shifting, even to the point that the institutional framework may be overwhelmed, and indeed become embedded in the field of purposive-rational action. Where Weber's elaboration of this point leads to the pessimistic conclusion that humanity is condemned to the "iron cage" of social domination, Habermas rejects this dismal conclusion, suggesting that rationalization of the type described here is not a historical inevitability but rather a historical possibility subject to change through human action.

Such change may be brought about by clearly differentiating the spheres of communicative interaction and purposive-rational action, choice and regulation, so as not to permit our vision of the possibilities of life to be limited by the scope of technical interests alone. In his more recent work, Habermas has highlighted the role of language in maintaining patterns of domination. Without going into details of his attempt to develop a "universal pragmatics," we should note an important implication of this work, that truly rational (not technically rational) action at the level of the institutional framework can only occur where distorted patterns of communications are revealed and altered.[9] Moreover, he suggests, *"Rationalization at the level of the institutional framework* can occur only in the medium of symbolic interaction itself, that is, through *removing restrictions on communication."*[10] As long as one party holds greater power in any dialogue, the resulting communications will prevent the parties from arriving at consensus. It is, therefore, in the reassertion of undominated, and consequently undistorted, communication that Habermas sees the possibility of escaping the seemingly inevitable bonds of domination.

Habermas's discussion of labor and interaction is especially instructive in our analysis of life in complex organizations. Clearly, if the realm of purposive-rational action is vastly expanding in modern times, a major agent of that expansion is complex organization. At the same time, an equally important justification for increasing social domination is provided by the ethic of organization. In organization, then, we find a conjunction of a particular pattern of social domination and an elaborate justification of that pattern. What emerges is a picture of the organization as a final (?) battleground on which the struggle between work and interaction, labor and humanity may be fought.

There can be little question that the primary contexts for human action, whether economic, artistic, or even spiritual, are those of organization and are consequently guided by the interests of purposive-rational action. As we seek activities in which we may develop our potential, we are increasingly thrown into complex organizations—that is, into the midst of the battle. The question we then face is whether there are possibilities for growth, creativity, and indeed *choice* which may still be found in systems that are based on a concern for stability, control, and *regulation.*

This question takes us once again to an exploration of the human consequences of our deepening involvement in complex organizations. In the preceding chapter, we examined some of the ways in which the collective consciousness of organization restricts our search for *meaning* and how some of those restrictions might be lessened. Now we must ask how our being limited to action contexts characterized by purposive-rational intent limits our capacity to *act* in pursuit of our personal goals. Here we will argue that the contemporary ethic of organization gives its approval to a narrow range of actions, specifically those (1) guided by a particular mode of rationality, (2) consistent with a special interpretation of power and social change, and (3) carried out on the basis of a certain relationship with our fellow actors.

As we have seen, complex organizations, in keeping with their purposive-rational character, are concerned with the adaptation of the proper means to reach given ends. Their instrumental purpose requires a mode of rationality which can roughly be transposed into the modern concern for productive efficiency; that which is "rational" is that which most efficiently moves us toward established goals. But to define rationality in this way is to severely limit its contribution to building the normative structure of a society. In its larger sense, reason might provide commentary on questions of justice, freedom, and equality, or poverty, hunger, and war. Stripped of its normative interest, however, reason becomes little more than a calculus for reaching certain purposes. Horkheimer makes this point by saying, "Reason has become completely harnessed to the social process. Its operational value, its role in the domination of men and nature, has been made the sole criterion."[11] As a central dynamic in systems concerned primarily with regulation, technical rationality becomes merely a servant of established powers, acting not in the interest of change but in the interest of stability.

Moreover, the success of purposive-rational systems in extending their interest in technical rationality raises the possibility that such systems may so dominate our thinking that the very distinction between work and interaction is lost. This is Habermas's key point, that "the potential of the productive forces has assumed a form owing to which men lose consciousness of the dualism of work and interaction."[12] Through the self-justifying logic of organization, only those problems which are capable of technical solution (that is, solution within the context of existing structures of science or organization) are viewed as appropriate for our consideration. When we come to see all problems as technical, or more precisely when we permit ourselves to focus only on those problems which can be technically defined, we obviously lose our capacity to choose suitable normative directions for ourselves and our society.

That we have already moved substantially in this direction is evidenced by certain trends in contemporary science, organization, and politics. In each case, we find our vision increasingly limited to those concerns which we already know are capable of technical solutions; we entertain only those concerns we see as manageable. P. B. Medawar comments, "Good scientists study the most important problems they think they can solve. It is, after all, their professional business to solve problems, not simply grapple with them."[13] Similarly, Habermas notes the tendency to limit our focus to "administratively soluble technical problems," further noting, "Publicly administered definitions extend to *what* we want for our lives, but not to *how* we would like to live if we could find out, with regard to attainable potentials, how we *could* live."[14] In the realm of government, John Kennedy commented in 1962, "The fact of the matter is that most of the problems . . . that we now face are technical problems, are administrative problems."[15] Finally, one is reminded of Lyndon Johnson's terribly restricted view of politics as merely "the art of the possible."

This leads to a second impact of the extension of purposive-rational systems on human action—the assumption of a special interpretation of power and of social change. We have noted the stabilizing and conservative character of purposive-rational systems, but we should also note that such systems shroud themselves in an ideological justification based on growth and development, either personal or productive. A major symbol of all systems of regulation is an ideology of progress. For example, we noted earlier a shift in the justification presented by elites for their position of domination to one which sees organized systems as essential to productivity. While this position appears to argue for growth and development, it does so only within the context of the existing social structure, including the existing distribution of social power. Similarly, we saw that certain psychologies, particularly cognitive and behavioristic psychologies, stress their capacity to alter the personality, yet the changes which they bring about are basically adjustments which mold the individual to the prevailing cultural norms.

The ideology of purposive-rational action defines change as possible through power, and power in turn as possible through the manipulation of personal, organizational, and societal symbols. That there may be other ways of defining power is illustrated in Robert Pranger's discussion of a "politics of power" and a "politics of participation." In Pranger's view, power politics—"the activities of leaders, activists, and influentials in the public marketplace"—has come to dominate our view of political action.[16] "Power means the relatively greater ability some persons have to control (or dominate) a hierarchically structured group's resources."[17] In contrast, power may be defined in terms of participation and involvement. Through participation, one might suggest opportunities for personal choice and individual expression, particularly as related to issues such as personal freedom and community. But, according to Pranger, for now the politics of power marks the political landscape. Thus, it is not surprising to find Lasswell and Kaplan describing the political man as "one who demands the maximization of his power in relation to all his values, who expects power to determine power, and who identifies with others as a means of enhancing power position and potential."[18] Where power is the only currency, all transactions must be conducted using that currency.

The systems approach to personality and social organization, which is so prominent in the social sciences today, illustrates the narrow boundaries within which change must occur within rationalized systems of power. This approach presents a view of change as movement toward a state of equilibrium. Though turbulence may occur in the environment or disruption may evolve from within, there is an implied tendency toward order and balance. And while turbulence and disruption may temporarily give the appearance of alteration, the central dynamic of the systems approach is that of a return to stable circumstances. Like the thermostat, the mechanical model used to illustrate the operation of systems, personality systems and social systems are described as seeking a return to normality. But, like the thermostat, their ultimate objective is control and regulation. The systems theorist, who may argue that systems may be transformed, is hard pressed to acknowledge the possibility of a completely reconstructed social system. Yet, it is precisely that demand which is made daily by an orientation toward the world which seeks meaningful choices and effective action in pursuit of those choices.

All of this suggests that the issue of change is currently misplaced as it is seen in terms of the manipulation of symbols which are ultimately connected to a dominated view of the world. At the organizational level, the problem of change is said to be one of effectively utilizing the resources of power, money, knowledge, expertise, and so forth, in order to gain a competitive advantage over one's opponent. Systems are created which present only the choice of lesser evils. At the personal level, the process of change (or growth) is seen as the outcome of a struggle between competing images of reality, each powerfully presenting itself to the individual as his or her true identity. As long as the contest continues, the individual is locked into a schizophrenic form of personal alienation from which there is no escape, only submission. Obviously, under such circumstances, individuation or "wholeness" is hardly possible.

This leads directly to the third consequence of our seeking a proper context for action within the confines of organization—the development of a relationship with our fellow actors marked by objectivity and impersonality. As we saw earlier, this tendency is deeply rooted in the history of science and organization. Modern science emerged in an effort to overcome the dogmatism of personal authority as a source of knowledge. The objectivity sought by science was specifically and without question an effort to eliminate the influence of individual judgment, especially with respect to questions having valuational implications. The reliance on science as method was an attempt to depersonalize the research process. In the same way, modern organization arose as a technique for regulating the idiosyncratic behavior of individuals, a way of limiting the excesses of the personality. As we noted in our discussion of the rational model of organization, the chief concern of administration is to fit individual personalities into prescribed nonpersonal roles.

As a result of these efforts, we are left with the image of the "normal scientist" working out the details of research projects, all of which follow the same basic pattern, and of the bureaucrat acting in accord with "standard operating procedures."[19] In either case, the admonition is of two parts: to follow the impersonal method, and to treat others (the subjects of the research or the clients of the organization) in an objective fashion. But what has happened is that the admonition, originally intended to serve a limited purpose and apply only to a limited number of situations, has been generalized into a standard for appropriate human behavior in all circumstances. Thus, we find scientific and organizational activity becoming increasingly objectified, *and* we find the same objectification modeled by science and organization as an appropriate pattern for all relationships among individuals.

Horkheimer makes this connection as follows: "The total transformation of each and every realm of being into a field of means leads to the liquidation of the subject who is supposed to use them."[20] The technical rationality which is at the base of contemporary modes of organization requires the kind of objectivity which is also the boast of positive science; but as that objectivity is displaced from a view of things to a view of other human beings, it seriously limits the way that we relate to others. Moreover, such a displacement also affects the way that we look at ourselves; our objectification of others also affects our self-image.[21] As we come to see ourselves as objects, we begin to rationalize more and more of our own lives. We come to distrust our own capabilities and depend on others for guidance; we tend to lose our emotional vitality and depend on the various "culture industries" to provide our sensuous experience; we even come to see our own bodies as machines which can occasionally be "tuned up" or repaired. Most important, we lose our capacity to experience the world subjectively, as a place in which our own actions count.

It is indeed this side of the psychic damage which results from adherence to the ethic of organization that is most often misunderstood. We can, at least on occasion, recognize the effects of our treating others as objects, for we resent being treated that way ourselves. But what is even more important, though much more concealed, is the deeper sense of estrangement that we experience personally. We not only lose touch with others (and they with us); we lose touch with ourselves. And without a firm base in our self-understanding, our actions will always be limited.

II

Our actions can never be fully explained without due consideration for the social practices and social institutions which surround us. And currently it is against the backdrop of technical rationality, expressed most pointedly in modern organizations, that we seem to play out our lives, that we seek to express in our actions the meaningfulness of our existence. Now that we have indicated some of the limitations which this situation imposes on our actions, we may turn to the question of how those limitations might be displaced. There are at least two preconditions for such an undertaking: first, a thorough understanding of the knowledge base upon which existing social ideologies are constructed; and second, a critical analysis of the contradictions which are inherent in the resulting social institutions. The first point will be examined in this section, the latter in the section which follows.

The role of positive social science in the construction and maintenance of our contemporary organizational society has been alluded to throughout our discussion to this point. Now we can be more specific: the structure of our social institutions is not only similar to but in fact intimately tied to our approach to questions of knowledge acquisition. This suggests that a continued reliance on existing modes of knowledge acquisition would support a continuation of existing organizational arrangements. In contrast, if we were to alter our conception of social understanding, we might in turn open the possibility for restructuring social institutions. Here we will examine the connection between forms of social scientific inquiry and the structure of social relationships from the perspective of critical theory. We will then suggest some ways in which that perspective might be brought to bear on contemporary analyses of complex organizations.

Herbert Marcuse has discussed this issue in detail. In his view, standard approaches to social scientific inquiry conceive of human behavior as the consequence of social forces. The role of science, therefore, is to uncover the antecedent causes of observed manifest behaviors. Such a position, Marcuse argues, neglects the fact that human actions occur within a historical context and that human beings contribute to the formulation of that context as much as they respond to it. If we are able to shape our own actions, then the observation of those actions at any single point and the construction of explanations based on those observations is doomed from the outset. To mechanistically explain a given set of behaviors is not to establish the base for a critical examination of the future of human action. It certainly does little to project the possibilities of human beings developing alternative patterns of action, including those which might be suggestive of greater human freedom. To the contrary, by taking a particular historical moment as representative or "natural," social science builds an implicit argument in behalf of the continuation of the circumstances of that period. More specifically, to see human beings as inevitably bound to rationalized patterns of domination, as Marcuse reads Weber to say, is to promote that historical occurrence.

In a review of Weber's work, Marcuse indicates the sway of such thinking.[22] Through the concept of rationalization, Weber described the course of Western historical development, a pattern of increasing domination culminating in the inevitable power of rational bureaucracy. Marcuse formulates Weber's position in this way: ". . . the specifically Western idea of reason realizes itself in a system of material and intellectual culture (economy, technology, 'conduct of life' science, art) that develops to the full in industrial capitalism, and this system tends towards a specific type of domination which becomes the fate of the contemporary period: total bureaucracy."[23] It is the notion of "fate" to which Marcuse reacts most strongly, suggesting that, if our "fate" has been humanly constructed, it can also be humanly reconstructed. Moreover, he argues, any theory of society which does not allow for the possibility of a rejection of domination encourages it.

Social theory based on an acceptance of the validity of facts as given must remain bound to those facts and to the historical circumstance which produced them. This is characteristic of much contemporary sociology, including organizational sociology, which remains interested in a functional analysis of society, one which takes the existing circumstances, including the existing value-consensus, as given, then focuses on the norms, rules, and beliefs which sustain those conditions. The clear bias in functionalist sociology is toward order and regulation rather than toward change. By taking the existing facts as the final source of validation, functional analysis, like systems analysis, fails to comprehend the possibility for shifts in the normative structure of the society and indeed serves to prevent such shifts.

It is important to note that Marcuse does not simply argue in behalf of a different approach to theory-construction in the social sciences, but in fact ties social science itself to existing patterns of domination. In rejecting the dogmatism of earlier modes of knowledge, science undermined the normative justifications for the institutional structure. But as science itself took on a greater role in the rationalization of society, it also became an ideology favoring the existing structure of society. By first focusing our interest on technical problems of production, then by "solving" those problems through producing greater goods and leisure time, science provides its own justification: one which exactly parallels that of the accompanying social organization. The new forms of social domination implied in the extension of technical rationality to all realms of human existence are given legitimacy by the operations of rational science and instrumental organization.

While he does not fully agree with Marcuse's suggestion that science inherently serves the interest of domination, Habermas does recognize the "scientization" of social and political life in contemporary society and offers an alternative perspective. Again the argument begins with the failure of the older legitimations to sustain the political order. Specifically, where Marx focused on the realm of production as the locus for the institutional framework of society, and consequently the basis for an ideology of exchange, Habermas suggests that increasing state intervention, coupled with the impact of modern science, has displaced this ideology and has led to a search for alternative forms of legitimation. A new situation has emerged, according to Habermas, one which "obliges the political system to maintain stabilizing conditions for an economy that guards against risks to growth and guarantees social security and the chance for individual upward mobility."[24] In this new role, the political system is no longer concerned with the realization of major social goals (the good life?), but rather is concerned with making whatever technical adjustments are necessary in order to assure the smooth functioning of the economic system.

But as government becomes concerned merely with the administration of technical problems, there is decreasing need for the involvement of the masses. Under an older politics, based in a normative commitment to interaction relations, dialogue and communication in the public sphere concerning social goals were the bases for the legitimacy of the political order. But when technical questions are the only questions to be resolved, there is no need for the involvement of the masses; indeed, their participation might interfere with the application of corrective techniques. To justify

71

the required shift in the political structure toward an exclusive politics of power, science and technology take on an ideological aura. Habermas concludes, "It is the singular achievement of this ideology to detach society's self-understanding from the frame of reference of communicative action and from the concepts of symbolic interaction and replace it with a scientific model."[25] Accordingly, the institutional framework of society is absorbed by the subsystems of purposive-rational action, and the consciousness of the people is re-ordered to accommodate this shift.

III

Bound by this new consciousness, we have come to view human action as limited to the solution of technical problems rather than oriented to the pursuit of larger interests. Guided by such a vision, we may in fact believe we are performing acts of great significance when in actuality we are simply making minor adjustments in the existing system. And we may be so deluded by the ideology supporting that system that we fail to see our own domination and think we act freely. In contrast to this condition, what seems required is a new concept of action based on truly rational choice.

To begin, we may return to the distinction made earlier between symbolic or communicative action and purposive-rational action. We will argue that the fundamental evaluative characteristic of the former is *choice*, while that of the latter is *regulation*. Through interaction, we may arrive at fundamental decisions about the directions of our lives and our societies. In this area, where values such as truth, justice, and freedom prevail, it is essential that we be free to choose among real alternatives and to then follow the possibilities which they present to us. Marcuse is succinct in his treatment of this issue: "Reason presupposes freedom, the power to act in accordance with knowledge of the truth, the power to shape reality in line with its potentialities."[26] In the field of work or purposive-rational action, on the other hand, we are faced with the necessity of directing our energies in specific ways in order to accomplish the tasks before us. This is the realm of discipline and order, of rigor and efficiency, of regulation.

When the issue is stated in this way, it is clear that we would prefer that free and meaningful choice guided our actions (including those which are necessarily regulatory), rather than having our choices defined for us by systems of regulation. But in an age of organization, that outcome is made considerably more difficult for the individual. As we have seen, both organization theory and management practice conspire to limit our options to those consistent with the accomplishment of the organization's goals. As elaborated in the rational model of administration, the value of efficiency becomes the instrument of regulation, acting so as to eliminate those human characteristics or actions which would deviate from the prescribed path. The resulting social institutions and an accompanying social science mystification are bound tightly to the notion of regulation.

The construction of an alternative sociology of organizations, which would be suggestive of new patterns of organizational activity, is of course not the intent of this essay. However, it is appropriate to outline some directions in which a reformed sociology of organizations might proceed. First, such a study would necessarily attempt to discern the tensions and contradictions of existing patterns of organization. In this it would be dialectical. Second, the alternative would seek a concept of enlightened organizational action, or praxis, which would enable us to begin to reconcile the realms of choice and regulation. In this it would be critical.

A reconstructed sociology of organizational life would first move dialectically to determine the latent tensions which lie beneath the surface regularities of organizational life. Such an approach would not view organizations as natural phenomena nor individuals as the consequences of mechanistic laws, but rather would assume the historical viability of both. That is, organizations would be seen as historically constituted, humanly derived institutions, always subject to analysis and reformulation; individuals would be seen as active participants in the process of constructing and modifying these institutions.

In looking beneath the "facts" of existing organizational practices, a dialectical analysis might well proceed from a historical analysis of the development of organizational relationships. At several points, we have noted the new legitimation offered by the dominant group in society—one geared toward increasing productivity. Moreover, we have seen the consequent treatment of lower organizational participants in a strictly instrumental fashion. Under these circumstances, members are required to fit themselves into predetermined organizational roles. We may now extend that argument to consider the dialectical relationship which is thus established between those at the top of the organization and those below.

In many cases, the activities "required" by those in control are resisted by organizational members, in part because the social roles imposed on them are contrary to their own beliefs, but also because these roles were not developed by them as a continuation of *their* life experience. It is important to note that the contradiction of interests described here is inevitable (though it may not be recognized as such by all concerned). That is, the imposition of organizational roles reflects the interests of a dominant group seeing the world in terms of an extended, albeit perverted, version of the control of nature; the development of individual needs represents the interests of a subordinate group seeking to establish its own lifespace. In order to act responsibly in terms of its own interest, each group must inevitably oppose the other. The dominant group can only develop its version of "responsible" action as it suppresses the subordinate; the subordinate group can only act responsibly as it resists domination.

What this suggests is an inherent tension between the rule of a controlling group and the subordination of most organizational members. In modern society, the organizationally powerful seek to enhance their position through guiding the productive activities of the society, but in doing so they inevitably view lower organizational participants in an instrumental (and therefore impersonal) fashion. This is obviously alienating to those who are lower in the hierarchy, though this alienation is often not apparent, but rather is experienced as a vague sense of discomfort. Where the instrumental viewpoint of the controlling group does become apparent, the subordinate group will actively resist their domination. Individuals for whom meaningful action is important cannot allow their life-spaces to be designed by others somewhere above in the hierarchy; they must object. In any case, growing from the displaced attempt to control nature, there is created a tension which underlies organizational action at all levels.

In this view, then, it is the tension that inevitably accompanies domination which provides the motive for personal action in organizational settings. Yet acts of resistance only occasionally occur; bound by socialized patterns of belief, organizational actors may fail to comprehend their own condition, accepting their chains, even identifying with their masters. What seems called for, therefore, is a critical analysis of the ethic of organization, one which would reveal the ideological commitments of science and organization, then act to reopen channels of free and unrestricted communication as a basis for personal and societal development. Such an approach would proceed from an interest in enlightenment—that is, an interest in providing insight into the hidden relationships of domination which characterize organizational action today. Based on this insight, organizational members would be called to new modes of action, not action in pursuit of technical possibilities, but action in pursuit of their own freedom and personal development.

While we will return to this question in a later chapter, we should note the importance of this last point: there is implicit in the notion of critique a commitment to action. For this reason, an important component of the critical approach is the recognition of the interrelatedness—indeed, the inseparability—of thought and action. The proper relationship between theory and practice in human action has been a concern of theoreticians since the time of the Greek philosophers. For example, Aristotle made clear the distinction between the meaning of the Greek words *theoria* and *praxis*. *Theoria* refers to the "contemplative life," or to those activities concerned with knowing for its own sake. In pursuit of the "good life," the life of theoretical reflection, persons would engage in the search for truth, understanding, and meaning in human existence. *Praxis*, on the other hand, was used to signify the mundane tasks of daily life, including practice and production. Practice refers to *doing*, or those activities which are an end in themselves, while production describes an act of *making*, with an end outside the act itself.

Over the centuries philosophers became dissatisfied with this separation of theory and practice. Interpreters of Hegel felt that philosophy should deal more directly with political activity, that no longer could theory remain distinct from action. In a well-known passage, Marx wrote, "The philosophers have only *interpreted* the world, in various ways; the point, however, is to *change* it."[27] In order to provide a basis for social change, Marx found it necessary to reconnect theory with practice. In his synthesis of theory (or "consciousness") with practice, he employed the older term "praxis." Marx's "revolutionary praxis" was considered a way of connecting theory to practice in order to overcome alienation and to achieve a humanistic society. In the notion of praxis we find a conjunction between reflection and action directed toward the transformation of social structures.

According to Habermas, when theory and practice are truly related, society is seen "as a system of action by human beings, who communicate through speech and thus must realize social intercourse within the context of conscious communication. Through this communication they must form themselves into a collective subject of the whole, that is capable of action. . . ."[28] It is only in conjunction with the ascendance of technical rationality and the consequent sublimation of the normative order that theory and practice diverge. As technical questions so absorb the human consciousness that they take on the aura of practical questions (those related to social practices informed by reflection), there is no longer any need to attend to that which is theoretical or that which is normative. There is only attention to the technical and behavioral system by which actions are directed toward the efficient accomplishment of pregiven ends. In contrast, the emancipatory interest described by Habermas and others as the basis for a new social understanding implies that theory and practice be recognized as differentiated yet complementary modes of action. In their conjunction, praxis, we find the true bridge between personal reflection and societal action, that which we may describe as enlightened action.

ORGANIZATION
AND IMMORTALITY

The infinity of the universe encompasses man. It excites his wonder, but it eludes his knowledge. Nonetheless, some quality of its infinity seems to be part of the nature of the human being.
Ira Progoff, The Symbolic and the Real

The fact is that this is what society is and always has been: a symbolic action system, a structure of statuses and roles, customs and rules for behavior, designed to serve as a vehicle for earthly heroism. Each script is somewhat unique, each culture has a different hero system.
Ernest Becker, The Denial of Death

The struggle is to maintain the meaningfulness of particular expressions of the sense of immortality, or to find new expressions, as historical conditions change. This makes it possible, in a more complex way, to affirm life in the face of death.
Robert Jay Lifton and Eric Olson, Living and Dying

Beyond the search for meaning, even beyond our attempts to establish satisfactory contexts for action, there lies another challenge. While this challenge may be expressed in many ways—as transcendence, as salvation, as immortality—the final challenge, most simply stated, is death. We live but we know we will die. And knowing that we will die makes all the more urgent our living, especially as we seek in our lives to provide for our deaths, to provide some connection between our own minute and passing existence and the timelessness of the universe. We seek a way in which we can live on—through our dreams, through our experiences, through our works.

It seems so simple. For a moment, it seems almost rational. If we can do this or that, if we can act in this way or that, then we may be spared the indignity of death. Our legacy may somehow endure; the torch may pass. But, alas, death intervenes, making all our plans empty and unfulfilled. We have taken our penchant for instrumentalism to the limit: we have again sought the proper means to an end; but, paradoxically, this time the end is unending —it is immortality. So as rational as we try to be about death, death defies our rationality. Indeed, it comprises our greatest irony, our greatest problem, our greatest irrationality.

This most fundamental human quest, our striving for immortality, was central to the psychoanalytic work of one of the most important post-Freudian thinkers, Otto Rank, and has appeared more recently in the work of Norman O. Brown, Ernest Becker, and Robert Jay Lifton. Through the efforts of these theorists, we may come to understand the urgency of our attempts to move past death, even symbolically, and to establish some sort of relationship with the universe beyond. Moreover, we may recognize more clearly the role which cultural institutions, such as complex organizations, play in our pursuit of a continuing life presence. Finally, we may begin to understand that these systems provide extraordinarily limited avenues for the expression of earthly heroism.

I

Of all the closest disciples of Sigmund Freud, perhaps none had a greater interest in nor understanding of the broad cultural and historical circumstances affecting the development of the human condition than Otto Rank.[1] Like Alfred Adler and Carl Jung before him, Rank began his work as an intimate of the master, but eventually was drawn by the very force of his own work to a painful break with Freud. Throughout his writings, Rank evidenced a strong concern for the artistic and the creative aspects of the human personality, permitting a much more optimistic view of the future of civilization than Freud eventually adopted. But at the base of the creative impulse, indeed at the base of nearly all impulses, Rank saw the fundamental problem of mankind as a religious one—the effort to establish the transcendence of the spirit over the fact of our physical death.

In the Freudian system, the pleasure-principle, variously represented as our desires or our sexuality, contends with the reality-principle, the demands placed on us by society. Though we seek a world of our own making (which presumably would be a world of utmost pleasure), we live in a world in which there are pressures on us to conform, to abide by the "rules of the game." It is almost as if our animal individuality confronts the social collectivity—with the result that our desires are severely restricted by the realities we face. The result is neurosis. As Becker puts it, "The terrible conclusion that we draw from Freud's work is that the *humanization process itself is the neurosis*: the limitation of experience, the fragmentation of perception, the dispossession of *genuine* internal control."[2]

Eventually, of course, Freud began to shift from finding the source of neurosis in our *desires* to locating them as well in our *fears* and specifically in the "death instinct"; it was death that ultimately constituted the reality of our humanness. We die. And in the fear of our death we are burdened with an overwhelming sense of futility and guilt. In contrast, Rank emphasized the importance of the other side of the same coin. To Rank the fact of our impending death is not just a problem to avoid, but a problem to be overcome. The central effort of mankind is the effort to attain immortality. Though immortality cannot be attained in a physical sense, it may be attained symbolically, through culture. Our world is not a world of momentary pleasures (or frustrations), but a world in which we seek some sense of transcendence, some way of defeating death, some way of living on beyond death. As a result, our social world has at its *core* the question of immortality.

We can easily see the ways in which we try to provide for our immortality—through our participation in worthwhile endeavors, through our adherence to moral codes of conduct, through our children and our works, or through spiritual transcendence. What may be less apparent is the depth, the seriousness, the essentiality of these activities. Indeed, as Rank argues, the quest for immortality is so basic that we construct entire cultural systems simply to provide symbolic expression of the particular interpretation of salvation which characterizes our era. Only a culture which seems to provide the necessary symbols of lasting life will be good enough—and will be maintained. Though we know rationally that we cannot exceed death, we cling to the only remaining hope, that we can overcome death ideologically, through our patterns of belief. To discover what pursuits are most valued as a source of "immortality power" is to discover the central commitments of an age.

That our attempts to rationalize death are fictional, indeed irrational to the core, makes them no less important and no less compelling. To some extent, we might even argue that their spiritual nature makes these efforts the *most* important and *most* compelling which we undertake. As Freud points out, it is in our struggle with cultural realities that our personalities are shaped; yet, as Rank adds, our cultures are neither purely accidental on the one hand nor purely rational on the other. Their primary vitality lies in their appeal to or, more precisely, their correspondence with our deeply irrational nature.

But the immortality symbols of one age are not necessarily those of another. For this reason, Rank outlined in sweeping terms the various ways in which mankind has conceived of the quest for immortality, ways which remain even today deeply embedded in our "collective unconscious."[3] In the earliest times, the quest for immortality was closely tied to the maintenance of the group: in the primitive world, the primary reality was that of the tribe or the society into which one was born; there was no individual soul or personal heaven. One's life was bound up in the power of the group, and one's social existence was in turn the key to one's immortality. To participate in the activities of the group, therefore, especially those activities which contributed to the perpetuation of the group and its distinctiveness, was to solve the mystery of death. While individual bodies might pass, the spirit of the group would live on.

The obvious paradox of the "passing" and the "living on" eventually caused problems, as one would certainly expect. As the personal nature of death began to be acknowledged, there was a need for a more personal explanation of immortality. What developed was a belief in the "double," expressed in the famous twins of mythology—a belief that we are of two parts, body and soul, and while our body may die, our soul will live on. This new emphasis, of course, was a much more personal approach to the immortality question, though one still wrapped in the trappings of spirituality. Immortality was no longer to be achieved wholly through a group process; there was now something the individual could do. The quest was still spiritual, but spirituality had been individualized.

Beyond the spiritual era, mankind moved into what Rank termed the "sexual era," one in which the act of procreation became central to the attainment of immortality. To have children was to be, in a sense, born again; children provided one with an enduring identity ("namesakes"). Of course, the new importance of procreation in the quest for immortality made sex a much more serious business, not to be taken lightly or playfully as in earlier (or later) times. Yet the images of freer times lingered on into the sexual era; and, exactly to the extent they did, the new restrictions on sexual activity were viewed as inhibitions, as negative restraints, as well as positive contributors to enduring life. In turn, there emerged a view of the human personality as largely motivated by the darker side of the psyche, our repressed guilt.

At this point, "scientific" psychology and rational organization enter. It is the task of psychology to "explain away" the neuroses of mankind, the negativity, the guilt, and confusion. The ideology characteristic of the psychological era, according to Rank, is basically negative and skeptical in its approach; it is in fact a belief in nonbelief. Psychology enables us to systematically dissect and thereby destroy one by one our previously held justifications for an imagery of continuing life. Through psychology, the realm of the spirit, the realm of the soul, and the realm of sexuality are rationalized away. The only problem is that there is nothing which remains. One by one, the ideologies fall, even until psychology itself, as an ideology, is felled. But at this point we are left with no way of denying our death, and we are consequently left to die.

It is exactly at this point that the ethic of organization asserts itself. Organization urges us to forsake ideology and to assume an instrumental posture, not valuing anything for its own sake but only as it comprises a means to an end. But there is a contradiction here, for the ethic of organization is itself an ideology, something requiring our belief. In the end, organization has to ask that we *believe* in organization, not only instrumentally but spiritually as well. But organization is not equipped to handle the strain of the spirit and its demand for everlasting life. It is not equipped to handle questions which inherently resist formal explanation. In the end, therefore, psychology and organization stand themselves as ideological reconstructions of the historical confusion of conflicting moral beliefs. As such, they offer themselves as modern, rational interpretations of our quest for immortality. Yet they are based in the same forces of irrationality as earlier approaches.

By describing the various stages of history, Rank suggested that our most fundamental views of the world—even our views about that which is universal—are based in the sway of history, in cultural forces which bend with various periods of life. These are not firm and unyielding "principles" upon which we can "analyze" one another; they are rather manifestations of the basic irrationality of humanity, our plodding and uncertain attempts to create a better and more permanent world. Today is no different from before. Norman O. Brown reminds us of our heritage as he writes, "Life remains a war against death—civilized man, no more than archaic man, is not strong enough to die—and death is overcome by accumulating time-defying monuments."[4] If this is the case, then the need today is the same as that of earlier times, to strive individually and collectively to exceed the limitations of our present condition and to achieve a sense of transcendence, a sense of immortality.

We are led back to our own culture and to the institutions which characterize that culture. We can now see, based on our understanding of Rank, that those complex organizations that mark our time hold a far different significance for our lives than their rationalizations would make it appear. Indeed, to say that ours is a society marked by complex organizations is to say that such organizations and the ethic they represent are contemporary expressions of the quest for immortality, means by which we believe that we can find salvation. If they are, it is appropriate that we examine them from a "spiritual" perspective, to ask what they say about our quest for immortality.

II

In doing so, we will first suggest that contemporary organizational thought provides a comprehensive, although often disguised, scheme of moral behavior to which the member's actions can be related; by following this code, we presume our soul will be granted continuity.[5] We may illustrate this use of the ethic of organization by examining the question of obedience to authority. As we have seen, fundamental to bureaucratic organization are hierarchical patterns of authority and adherence to the demands of the leadership. But while orders are generally obeyed, certain orders are difficult, if not impossible, for some members of the organization to carry out. Where the individual would have to violate his or her own values by executing the order, a serious moral dilemma occurs. For example, an advertising executive, convinced of the health hazards of cigarette smoking, yet asked to handle a tobacco company account, faces a serious ethical problem. In a similar way, a mechanic told to install an automobile part known to be unsafe might feel concerned.

While contemporary illustrations of this phenomenon are plentiful, surely the most extreme and thereby most dramatic example of the issue raised here is Hitler's attempt to exterminate the European Jews during the Second World War. While this illustration is admittedly colored by its complex political overtones, it raises in its most grotesque form a fundamental problem facing a member of the bureaucracy—that is, the problem of complete and unquestioning obedience. Though stimulated by political policy, the destruction of the Jews was to be an organized activity, carried out through bureaucratic means. Raul Hilberg writes in his classic *The Destruction of the European Jews*, "A Western bureaucracy had never before faced such a chasm between moral precepts and administrative action; an administrative machine had never been burdened with such a drastic task."[6]

Obviously, the situation created for the individual bureaucrat was most difficult. It was not a problem felt only at the upper echelons of organization; rather, it extended throughout. Under such circumstances, some form of rationalization or justification was imperative. In its ultimate form this apology was not only political; it was administrative as well. As Hilberg explains:

Most bureaucrats composed memoranda, drew up blue-prints, signed correspondence, talked on the telephone, and participated in conferences. . . . However, these men were not stupid; they realized the connection between their paper work and the heaps of corpses in the East. And they realized, also, the shortcomings of those ration-alizations which placed all evil on the Jew and all good on the German. That was why they were compelled to justify their individual activities. The first rationalization was the oldest, the simplest, and therefore the most effective: the doctrine of superior orders. First and foremost there was duty. No matter what objections there might be, orders were given to be obeyed. A clear order was like an abso-lution; armed with such an order, a perpetrator felt that he could pass his responsibility and his conscience upward.[7]

So central was the appeal to organization among the German bureaucrats that this justification assumed a dominant position in the defense of the accused at the Nuremberg trials. Thus, many of the defendants would remark, as did General Alfred Jodl, that it was "not the task of a soldier to act as a judge over his superior commander," and later Adolf Eichmann would speak of blind obedience, "the obedience of corpses," as he called it.[8]

Perhaps the most remarkable feature of this rationalization is that the inherent logic of bureaucracy is extremely well equipped to accept such attributions of responsibility. From the perspective of bureaucratic theory, we are viewed as essentially limited, in terms of both our physical powers and our capacity for understanding. We are, in this sense, incapable of complete rationality. Organi-zation, on the other hand, through its insistence on pure efficiency in the achievement of purpose, is quite different. In place of the "bounded rationality" attributed to the individual, the organization offers a model of rationality. Only through participation in organ-ization, therefore, can we approximate full rationality. But this argument cuts another way: there is also an implication that indi-vidual limitations make little difference in the outcome, in admin-istrative effectiveness. For just as the rational individual must be, to use Simon's words, "the organized and institutionalized individ-ual," so must the individual member be said to participate in the rationality of the group.[9] At times when our human limitations appear, we have the option of appealing directly to the rationality of the system. In other words, any moral "weakness" on the part of the individual can be absorbed by the rationality of the organization. From the standpoint of moral responsibility, bureaucratic theory provides an important justification for individual error. Being impersonal, the organization is amoral, without conscience. To place the blame for improper action on the organization is to relegate this issue to a state oblivious of moral consequences. Personal value is mediated by group standards, and, lost in rational impersonality, the question of responsibility becomes meaningless. The individual, the organizational member, though perhaps feeling slight remorse, is no longer liable.

Because they provide justifications for human action, the valuational concerns examined here are of serious consequence to the organizational member, as a basis for a claim to immortality. As members of organizations, persons can not only perform questionable acts; they can justify them in terms of the greater purpose and superior rationality of bureaucracy. Through organization, we can shed our own morality, even to the point of murder, yet not be at fault. Through organization, we can distort societal standards, acting in a limited frame of interest, yet remain blameless. Simply by invoking the logic of bureaucracy, we are able to make that which is personal impersonal and that which is moral amoral. The organization, intendedly an instrument of achievement, becomes a moral force for absolving personal responsibility.

But to suggest the potential of bureaucratic theory as a form of justification is not enough; we must also ask whether bureaucratic organizations do in fact stimulate such responses as those described here. At first glance, one might question whether the moral consciousness of today's organizational member is so developed as to lead to the type of value conflict for which the logic of bureaucracy provides resolution. Certainly, a conscious, public clash between organizational values and those of the individual or between two sets of values—one bureaucratic, the other political—is a rarity in our present society. But we may ask whether such conflicts of value are not seen because they do not occur or whether they are unseen because bureaucracy effectively prevents their emergence. At least two areas of contemporary organizational research support the latter alternative.

First, bureaucratic organizations as mediators of personal values minimize the possibility of value conflicts by bringing the preferences of the individual in line with those of the organization. To build a basis for such commitment, attempts are made to teach prospective members appropriate patterns of belief and behavior. As we saw earlier, the way in which children develop early images of such generalized bureaucratic norms as the "cultural trait of hierarchy" is now being demonstrated.[10] Indeed, under special circumstances, it has now been shown that the instructive power of organization may even surpass that of the civic culture.[11] Extending this logic to the matter of responsibility, one might anticipate that persons are also socialized to accept the bureaucratic view of responsibility described here.

Secondly, despite the organization's attempts to insure against dissension, an important and growing body of literature indicates that conflicts still do occur. Here several interesting points arise, for most of these situations do not reach the full proportions (nor public view) of the examples just mentioned. However, Kahn and his co-authors note in *Organizational Stress* that 45 percent of the respondents in a national survey reported being bothered by person-role conflicts, while one-third were concerned about inter-role conflicts.[12] For persons involved in such cases, many of which reflect aspects of individual responsibility, various compensatory mechanisms must be employed to cope with the pressures of conflict.

Like so many aspects of human experience, perceptions of individual responsibility are both generated by and sustained for the individual through our affiliations with various groups and institutions. It is not surprising, therefore, that in this age of organization a new form of justification, one distinctly bureaucratic, has arisen. And while one may either agree or disagree with its conception of the individual and of social action, one must surely accept the rhetoric of bureaucracy as an important behavioral referent for members of complex organizations; in the language used above, it becomes a key to immortality.

To act in a way which contributes to the maintenance of the organization—that is, to act "rationally"—is to contribute to purposes far beyond the individual. It is an act which sustains the group, and of course the sustenance of the group spirit is of great importance. Though individuals may come and go, the organization lives on. The logic is simple: if we obey, we may participate in the immortality of the group, thus satisfying our most basic human longing. What is so striking about this formulation, however, is that the question of morality turns completely on the question of power. Since those in power have the capacity to define the "realities" of organizational life, they are able to prescribe what is acceptable moral behavior in the organization. To live according to the morality of organization (and thereby achieve life after death) is not to live by the standards of individual morality or even those of the culture as a whole, but rather by the standards of those who hold positions of power in organizations. This suggests that the relationship between the powerful and the powerless, the *leaders* and the *led*, is itself a spiritual concern, one cut through by the quest for heroic immortality.

III

In the ethic of organization, we see expressed a contemporary version of approved moral behavior, one which would supposedly aid us in attaining immortality; but we also see that this code derives from a purely instrumental interpretation of morality. That which is consistent with the rationality of the organization—that is, that which moves us most efficiently toward the accomplishment of given goals—is that which is valued. But the instrument of organization is used by a "controlling group," making the morality of organization the servant of that group's interest. We see, then, that morality and power are closely related: on the one hand we can never completely solve the riddle of immortality in an age of organization without confronting the question of power, and on the other hand we can never fully understand power without addressing its spiritual as well as secular bases. Rank is correct: "Power is at bottom a magical concept, pertaining ultimately to man's control over life and death."[13]

In the organizational age, power in this sense—power as expressed symbolically in the relationship of the master and the slave, the leader and the led—has been stripped of its fullest meaning. Power is now described in the rationalized language of "attributes" and "contingencies" rather than connected to basic human interests.

Yet social power remains bound in every way to the most basic human interest—the struggle for immortality. The relationship between the leader and the led is based on a reciprocal expectation that each person will, by virtue of his or her involvement in the relationship, attain immortality. Yet, as the parties act out their various understandings of the agreement, different and essentially conflicting interests appear to be represented. As this occurs, and as it is intensified by the increasing rationalization of organizational life, the leader-group relationship in organizations holds forth the promise of affirming *life*, but in the end winds up affirming *death*.

In order to understand the curious ambivalence of this relationship, we must look first at some characteristics of group behavior. Freud, in his own inquiry into the dynamics of group psychology, pointed out that the group mind takes on characteristics quite inconsistent with those exhibited by the normal adult—indeed, characteristics that might better represent the mental life of primitives or children. The group acts strictly according to impulse, without premeditation, without direction, and without tolerance for delay or frustration, but at the same time without the talent to avoid them. "A group is extraordinarily credulous and open to influence, it has no critical faculty, and the improbable does not exist for it," writes Freud. "It thinks in images, which call one another up by association . . . and whose agreement with reality is never checked by any reasonable function. The feelings of a group are always very simple and very exaggerated. So that a group knows neither doubt or uncertainty."[14] At the same time, there is something extremely contradictory in the group experience—something closely related to the matter of leadership. While the group sees itself as very strong, and is intolerant or even aggressive toward others, it also seeks strong, even domineering leadership. In the group, the camaraderie of equals is important, but so is leadership—and it often seems the two together cannot be sustained.

Freud sought to explain the ambivalence of the group in terms of the "scientific myth" of the primal horde.[15] In this myth, the father of many sons holds sway over them, a position which they simultaneously respect, envy, and fear. Finally, as their desire to be free from their father's spell becomes unbearable, they join together to murder him. Their "brotherhood" is fully established in their complicity in the crime, yet through their brotherhood they also seek relief from the guilt of the act. Their guilt is mitigated by their sharing of it. After a period of life in this fatherless world, one brother emerges as the leader, but only after he portrays himself as a hero and assumes by himself the burden of guilt for destroying the father, who is now described only in terms of his tyranny.

Freud, of course, suggests that the image contained in this myth characterizes each individual's renunciation of the controlling father figure and the establishment of a more independent, though guilt-ridden, life. But even more to the point is the possibility that this same process underlies the formation of social groups and social organizations. We come together in groups in order to achieve some object, in order to control some part of our world; but in the act of control (symbolized by the murder of the father), we assume a heavy burden of guilt, which we can only bear by sharing it with others. On this basis, social groups are constructed; therefore, "Social organization (including the division of labor) is a structure of shared guilt."[16]

We may also interpret the psychic structure of modern organizations in these terms. As we have seen, organizations developed out of an interest in controlling nature, in conquering natural forces. But to conquer is to destroy, at least in the sense of denying the independent existence of objects in the environment. For this, we must share a special human guilt. That guilt, however, is even more crucial when we take into account the transition from the domination of nature to the domination of other human beings. To treat other human beings as objects, which is the logic of domination, is to violate their humanity, to dehumanize them, to destroy them. And since destruction, the end of life, is what we fear most ourselves, we must accept a tremendous burden of guilt as we (unwittingly) destroy others.

Again, to some extent, we can assuage our guilt by our involvement in the group, by sharing our guilt with others. It is simply much easier to justify outrageous acts when they are commonplace than when they are the exception. The group is simply overwhelming. "A group impresses the individual with a sense of unlimited power and of insurmountable peril. For the moment it replaces the whole of human society. . . ."[17] For this reason, it is not surprising to see the individual engage in organizationally approved acts which would be out of the question under other circumstances. Moreover, to the extent that these acts seem morally correct, as means to ever-lasting life (as were those we examined in the previous section), they are quite natural. But there comes a time when we can no longer transfer our guilt to others of the "brotherhood"; we must assign responsibility to someone at another level, someone who is not one of us. As we will see in a moment, the leader is an easy target for such a projection.

Becker writes, "From the beginning of time the group has represented big power, big victory, much life."[18] It is this last phrase, signifying the transcendent character of group life, that is of particular interest here. As we saw in Rank's analysis of the various historical interpretations of the quest for immortality, the primitive mind (which is still a part of all of us), holds forth the group as the promise of enduring life. To participate in a group, especially a group connected to vast amounts of power and prestige, is to be a part of something "bigger than life"—indeed, bigger than death. In a sense, the group, the organization, provides a sense of consolation, a consoling belief that through our participation in the group we will live on.

In an age of organization, the group even provides a kind of security against those life-threatening forces which cause our greatest anxiety. In an earlier chapter, we described an individual who, at the time of the death of a friend, became preoccupied with the organizational technique used to tell him of the death. In light of our present discussion, this story would now be interpreted not as a preoccupation with a technique associated with the death of a friend, but rather as a preoccupation with a technique generated *in response to* the death of a friend. Since the irrationality of death was simply too much to bear, the individual redirected his interests to the processes of the group, in this case those of a hospital, again illustrating the connection between the struggle to affirm life and the security of the group.

Rollo May has taken this point a step further by suggesting that it is our fear of the *irrational* in human life which draws us to the order and stability of group life. In this view, mankind is seen as confronted with spiritual challenges which are simply incomprehensible to the modern "rational" mind. Rather than accepting these irrationalities as proper parts of our lives, we are led by our modern psyche to either explain them away or guard ourselves against them. May writes, "What people today do out of fear of irrational elements in themselves as well as in other people is *to put tools and mechanics between themselves and the unconscious world.*"[19] What is especially telling is that we now conceive of the group in technical terms; the group is now important because it provides protection from the irrational. By resorting to technique, we are able to insulate ourselves from the demands of the spirit.

In the group we find a very important expression of our quest for immortality. Just as the primitive believed in the power of the group, we too hold forth the hope that our own participation in the group will enable us to live forever. But this desire for immortality through the maintenance of the group is complicated by the seemingly inherent difficulty of group action. The group mind described by Freud (or anyone else who has carefully observed groups in action) is hardly heroic in its efforts. Instead, one is struck by the chaos, the confusion, the grappling about, all of which seem dreamlike in content and execution.

If this is the case, then we may ask how the unconscious content of the group spirit may be brought to light. One answer may lie in the notion of transference. We are familiar with the process by which the patient attaches special meaning to the therapist. But what is often less clear is that this is a way the patient uses the therapist for the purpose of drawing forth the unconscious content of the mind. Similarly, we might postulate that the group mind, in its unconscious dreamlike style, may require something or someone in the outer world to draw forth its content. This is the role of the leader.

In the leader the group sees an opportunity to actualize its own fantasy, to make real its longing for immortality. The choice of a leader is therefore an attempt to provide the kind of focus which will ensure the continued life of the group (and in turn the immortality of its members). The leader-group relationship is established as a way of protecting and facilitating the members' quest for immortality. The role of the leader, *in the eyes of the group*, is to maintain the integrity of the group and in turn to assure the members' own salvation. In Rank's view, "Social organization originally involved not a restriction of the individual, but a protection and extension of his ego through spiritual belief."[20]

But restrictions soon develop, for the position of the leader—at least as it is currently conceived—is one which seems to demand a certain amount of domination. Though the leader is chosen to assist in the spiritual development of the group, to epitomize the dreams and aspirations of the group, the acts associated with leadership, especially those which are instrumentally based, soon begin to limit rather than to assist the aspirations of the group. To the extent that the leader attempts to impose his or her own will on the group, the leader acts in contradiction to the intent of the group, which is to use the leader to express *its* will. Of course, in a world dominated by hierarchical systems, such attempts are not only possible, they are inevitable.

Meanwhile, the group continues to resist. In the leader the group seeks to find one who can maintain the solidarity of the group; yet, at the same time, the leader is one upon which the members of the group may project their own guilt. By making the leader representative of the group, we also make the leader responsible for the evil of the group. We project our own guilt on the leader, asking only one thing, that the leader, like the hero of the primal myth, accept that guilt (even if it is a lie) and not throw it back on us. Like the emergent brother, the leader assumes leadership only by (implicitly) accepting responsibility for the misdeeds of the group, by living a convenient and self-serving lie. (Note again the parallel to the "doctrine of superior orders," by which guilt is assigned to the leader.)

But the leader-group dynamic has not yet run its course. As soon as the leader seeks to dominate the group, the group recognizes the evil which it has itself imposed on the leader (though it hardly acknowledges that it is the source of that evil); and recognizing this evil, it realizes that no one responsible for such evil should be permitted to lead. The group begins to see the leader as representative of its own unforgivable guilt and therefore someone to be destroyed. The leader becomes the Jungian "shadow," that submerged, often rebellious part of our nature, our Achilles' heel, the focus of our imperfection and our human limitations, our own personal devil. In the leader the group members see expressed the negativity of their own lives, that side which is most clearly connected to the fact of their own impending death—and therefore most to be feared and resisted. Thus, groups create leaders in order to destroy them.

In modern organizations, no less than in primitive tribes, the leader is an available scapegoat, one permitted to rule for a period, but eventually subject to sacrifice by the group. The killing of the leader is a consummate act by the group. In this act the group sees the leader as the symbol of its own guilt, then attempts to expiate that guilt by eliminating the leader. Since this is an act with immense spiritual power, going directly to the heart of our quest for immortality, it is not surprising to find the act accompanied by a high-pitched moral fervor, a deeply self-righteous outcry on the part of the group, such as we witnessed at the resignation of Richard Nixon.

At the point that leadership takes on overtones of personal domination, the group, which originally sought the leader to aid in its quest for immortality, must destroy the leader. But what of the leader? Why would the potential leader—who, one would think, would be aware of the leader's fate—seek leadership? The answer is simple—in the pursuit of the leadership position, the potential leader sees a chance to achieve immortality. The spiritual dependence on the leader as chieftain, as shaman, is not lost on the leader, for the leader understands that his or her own salvation is also tied to the group. To the aspirant, there appears to be an opportunity to move beyond the limitations of the existing reality, one in which all persons are essentially equal, to achieve some distinction; it is immortality, once again, that is on the line.

There is a reason, moreover, that in the modern age the potential leader may fail to recognize the traps hidden in the leader-group relationship. In an age of organization, the rationalization of authority has so confused the leader-group relation that its difficulties are less apparent. No longer does leadership appear as a function of the group; rather, in the world of hierarchical organization, the leadership function is associated with one particular person. There are now leaders rather than acts of leadership. But though the rationalized leadership function appears to have been transferred to the leader as an individual, in fact it remains with the group, latent, beneath the surface, ready to spring forth at any time. But there remains one further step: in an age of organization, leadership is even further rationalized, attached not to particular individuals but to particular roles or positions, to which members are urged to aspire. Presumably, while the group may destroy the leader, it cannot destroy the position—so the rational organization insulates itself from the dynamics of the group. Yet considerable confusion, indeed tension, remains. While the imposition of this rational explanation of leadership on the group may restrict its activities, it does not dissipate the group's displeasure.

Seymour B. Sarason has examined this condition in his book *The Creation of Settings.*[21] There he notes that one important fantasy in our society is that of becoming a leader. From early childhood, the individual is taught the importance of the leadership role and is repeatedly encouraged to seek that role. As the child grows, however, the fantasy becomes more complicated—what was originally a role sought for humanitarian purposes (to do good, to help others, or, in our terms, to seek salvation) takes on tones of self-aggrandizement and the domination of others. "The fantasy has become complex, strongly motivating, and deeply personal; and only a small part of it, that which is perceived as socially acceptable, will receive public expression."[22] Nonetheless, the leadership role is highly valued by society, and the individual strives to attain it; after all, here is a case where society seems to say, "In this way, you can achieve transcendence; you can attain immortality."

The modern organization, of course, is ideally suited to accommodate the ambitions of persons interested in leadership roles; at its most basic level, organization provides a system of rules and behaviors which serve to allocate status and reward contributions to the development (rationalization) of the system. The organization is a modern, ritualized hero system, so it is little wonder that persons pursue their search for immortality by seeking positions of power in the organization. But, as Sarason points out, the pursuit of the leadership fantasy may have severe problems, both for the individual and the group. Though the leader must appear superior (according to the fantasy), the limitations of leadership are soon apparent to the leader, resulting in considerable guilt and agony. But this cannot be revealed without damage to the fantasy itself, so "The leadership fantasy and the social process in our society whereby one becomes a leader insure that the leader will be and will remain a private individual, particularly in regard to thoughts and feelings reflecting anxiety or self-doubt."[23] This complex mix of privacy and superiority, of vision and guilt, places a serious psychological burden on the individual leader, one in which the original quest for immortality gives way to a much more instrumental orientation toward life.

In this sense, modern organization in fact represents both a depersonalization and a despiritualization of the leader and of the group. The modern leader is too often not the classical hero who shows us new directions toward cultural immortality, but rather is the one who most clearly and passionately expresses the existing ideology. Unlike the hero of myth or legend, the modern leader has not developed a critical attitude toward society and its institutions, but rather values that which contributes to the rational and efficient operation of the machine. As a tool of the organization, the leader then becomes much less emotional, much less compassionate, much less humane than we would otherwise expect. Based on a study of 250 corporate executives, Michael Maccoby concludes, "Corporate work in advanced technology stimulates and reinforces attitudes essential for intellectual innovation and teamwork, qualities of the head. And those are the traits required for work. In contrast, compassion, generosity, and idealism, qualities of the heart, remain unneeded and underdeveloped."[24]

IV

To summarize, the relationship between the leader and the led is initiated because the group seeks to sustain itself, to endure, while the leader seeks personal transcendence. The relationship is important to both parties because it holds forth the promise of affirming life. But to the extent that leadership comes to be viewed in terms of domination, especially rationalized hierarchical domination, the quest for immortality is undermined. Both the group and the leader are restricted in their search for continuity. Thus, alienation, the sense of estrangement and despair arising from the tension between the leader and the led, can be seen as a direct manifestation of the death symbolism associated with the eventual collapse of the group. The group and the organization, which at first appear to affirm life, wind up affirming only death.

In the ethic of organization, we find one more effort to control the irrational, another of what Rank called "man's ceaseless attempts to master [life's] irrational forces with his mind."[25] As such, the ethic of organization totally divests itself of spiritual significance and at best provides an *illusion* of affirming life. To be organized is to be certain, certain of one's past, one's present, and one's future. But, though certainty may momentarily appear attractive, it ultimately presents us with the image of death, the final certainty, the only certainty. To the extent that our lives are determined, we have lost our chance to express ourselves, to develop ourselves. We are no longer free. We then recognize that the rationalized certainty of our organizational society can never permit us transcendence; for that we must look to the world of the irrational, the world of the spirit. In the deepest sense, therefore, we must not put our faith in organization.

BEYOND
RATIONAL ORGANIZATION

The only thing that interests me now is the problem of circum-
venting the machine, learning if the inevitable admits a loophole.
                              Albert Camus, *The Stranger*

By imputing significance to human acts, by referring them to
more than they are—to more than the powerful claim them to be
—we connect action with previously unseen and unforeseen purposes.
                              Henry S. Kariel, *Saving Appearances*

The realm of the gods is a forgotten dimension of the world we
know. And the exploration of that dimension, either willingly or
unwillingly, is the whole sense of the deed of the hero.
                      Joseph Campbell, *The Hero with a Thousand Faces*

We are bound by many illusions, and to penetrate these illusions
is the first and most basic step toward autonomy and responsibility.
As we noted earlier, the realities we typically accept, while built by
personal imagination and creativity, are as well the products of particular forms of social interaction. Again, Ernest Becker's language
is compelling: "Man's answers to the problem of his existence are
in large measure *fictional*. His notions of time, space, power, the
character of his dialogue with nature, his venture with his fellow

men, *his primary heroism*—all these are embedded in a network of codified meanings and perceptions that are in large part arbitrary and fictional."[1] The world we come to see as real—including the organizational world we come to see as real—is only real to the extent that we real-ize it—that is, to the extent that we make it real through our acceptance of it.

The way in which reality is socially constructed has been vividly portrayed in a series of encounters between the anthropologist Carlos Castaneda and the Yacqui sorcerer Don Juan. In these works, Castaneda describes his apprenticeship with the Indian medicine man, in which Castaneda was taught the use of various hallucinogenic substances as a technique for developing a mastery of the world of "non-ordinary reality." In order to become a "man of knowledge," Castaneda was led through a series of experiences which introduced him to a completely new world, one incomprehensible to the Western mind. In the introduction to *The Teachings of Don Juan*, Walter Goldschmidt remarks, "The central importance of entering into worlds other than our own . . . lies in the fact that the experience leads us to understand that our own world is also a cultural construct."[2] By understanding the reality of another culture, we come to better understand our own reality as culturally based.

There is a certain magic in the social construction of reality, for the capacity to create, to suspend, and to alter reality is the special talent of the magician. The true magician is the master of illusion, of deceit, of untruth. Yet in this untruth there is embedded a greater truth—that the reality we come to hold as true is an appearance, one which was always available to us, but which has been hidden from us by the very limits of our vision.

But if we recognize the magic by which realities are constructed, we must also recognize that there are several types of magic. On the one hand, magic has to do with the power of the supernatural, the spirit, the transcendent—it allows us to partake of a higher reality than that in which we ordinarily participate. On the other hand, magic may simply have to do with the illusions of the mundane trickster, the one who seeks to manipulate us for personal advantage. We are correct to be skeptical, for there are certainly those who would seek to deceive us; and it seems that our only recourse is to "figure out the trick," to reveal the deception. Moreover, there may be a thin line between illusion and transcendence; that which appears to elevate our spirit may be simply a trick.

Much of what we have said to this point suggests that modern organization and the rationalized science which supports it is the work of a trickster. We have been presented with a certain view of reality by the organizationally powerful and the scientific elite; we have been told that this view is the truth, natural and unchanging. But we have become suspicious that perhaps we have been deceived —especially as we have seen our acceptance of this view aid those who promote it while working to our own disadvantage. The original deception may have been made with malicious intent, in order that we serve the wishes of the powerful; or it may have been made on the basis of a mistake, either the mistake of assuming that the technical objectivity required to deal with a threatening natural environment could be fully translated into a way of ordering and explaining human affairs, or the mistake of assuming that an orientation suitable for one period of time would continue to be suitable for later and far different periods. However the deception originated, it is now a view of reality which is filled with contradictions, especially as it serves the interests of the organizationally powerful to the exclusion of others.

We have seen these conditions illustrated most explicitly in the rational model of administration, and we have seen the difficulties that perspective presents. We have found the rational model of administration inadequate as a guide to organizational life in at least three ways: first, by separating that which is subjective from that which is objective, then concentrating on the latter, the rational model (both in its epistemology and in its psychology) fails to fully comprehend human meaning in organizational settings; second, by directing our attention solely toward the efficiency of technical processes in reaching organizational goals, the model serves to rationalize existing patterns of social domination; and third, by invoking the positivist distinction between fact and value while at the same time endorsing one particular set of values (that is, those related to efficiency) as facts of administrative life, the rational model implies a derogation of personal values.

Obviously, any acceptable alternative viewpoint would have to address each of these issues. But, in order to do so, it would have to base its understanding of organizational life on a quite different conception of the proper basis of social inquiry; it would suggest new ways of knowing as a prelude to new ways of deciding and new ways of acting. It would be concerned with revealing the deceptions inherent in our normally accepted view of the world, with laying bare the contradictions which exist in any given social reality. By exposing the contradictory nature of organized society, such an approach would permit us to "outgrow" that deception and move toward a more mature future.

This implies a quite different approach to the question of knowledge acquisition from that associated with mainstream positivistic social science. As we have seen, modern science shares with modern organization a basically instrumental intent—to control human processes so as to achieve certain ends. In line with this intent, theory is valued only to the extent that it can assist us in explaining, predicting, and *controlling* our world, including our social world. The issue of control is paramount: presumably the individual, armed with the appropriate theoretical understanding of causal relationships within a field, can make the adjustments necessary to produce the desired result. For example, if we fully understand the relationship between inducements and contributions (as portrayed by the rational model of administration), then we can provide exactly the right inducements to secure the contributions we desire. In this instrumental conception of theory, knowledge is indeed power, the power to manipulate others.

Brian Fay has described an alternative model of the relationship between theory and practice, a model which he calls the "educative" model.[3] The educative model views the role of theory as providing people with an understanding of their own lives as a prelude to personal and social development; it seeks to inform people about the needs they have, the social conditions which limit the fulfillment of those needs, and the ways their lives might be changed so that their needs can be met. Such a view implies that social conditions—including the supposed "causal relationships" which seem to exist within organizations—are dependent on our acceptance of those conditions. Moreover, according to Fay, through a critical analysis of existing social circumstances we may educate ourselves in terms of new possibilities for change and development.

Both the instrumentalist and the educative models

promise freedom; but in the former it is the freedom that results from knowing how to achieve what one wants, whereas in the latter it is the freedom to be self-determining in the sense of being able to decide for oneself, on the basis of a lucid, critical self-awareness, the manner in which one wishes to live. In the educative model, the practical result of social theory is not the means for greater manipulative power but rather the self-understanding that allows one's own rational thinking to be the cause of one's actions; i.e., social theory is a means toward increased *autonomy*.[4]

To develop such an educative understanding of organizational life obviously requires several important shifts in the way we view both science and organization, some relating to the way in which we achieve meaning, some relating to the structure of action contexts, and some relating to our quest for immortality. As we have seen, the instrumental conception of science and organization implies a distinction between subject and object. In order to achieve control, persons must be treated as objects; the objectification of goods, services, and personnel is the first step in the rationalization of organized action. The consequences of this outcome in terms of both regulation and dehumanization suggest that the dichotomy of subject and object be taken as an important starting point in developing an alternative understanding of organizational life.

One approach to reconciling the subject-object dichotomy is that suggested by the phenomenological movement in philosophy and the social sciences. Based in the work of Edmund Husserl in the early part of this century, phenomenology rests on a fundamental distinction between the task of the natural sciences and that of the social sciences.[5] While the former seeks to derive causal explanations of the behavior of objects in the physical world, the latter is additionally concerned with deriving an understanding of the meanings human beings attach to their actions. Yet the positivist approach to dealing with the question of meaning is to suggest that meaning can be inferred on the basis of an "objective" observation of manifest behavior. Only in this way, the positivist argues, can we validate our knowledge through independent observations.

We can easily see how this position became popular among social scientists. As social science began to develop, it sought models to follow in developing its approach to its subject matter. The most readily available model, of course, was that of the natural sciences; moreover, the natural science model was one which had produced impressive results and consequently was generally respected. For this reason, it proved attractive to social scientists. It is not surprising, therefore, that most social science has been and continues to be constructed on the basis of a positivistic reinterpretation of the natural sciences translated into the language of the social sciences—one which holds that the facts of social life can be separated from the values people hold, that the relevant facts of social life can be obtained through the objective observation of the manifest behavior of individuals and groups, and that the scientist can rely on social phenomena to be "natural" in the sense that they will follow consistent patterns of behavior over time.

Unfortunately, the easy transfer of techniques from the natural sciences to the social sciences is much more difficult than it might initially seem. While the natural scientist can observe the behavior of physical objects "from the outside" and then make statements concerning the relationships between those objects, the social scientist focusing on the external behavior of human beings must recognize a special problem. Unlike the mechanical response of, say, one billiard ball when it is hit by another, human beings respond to their environment in a creative, even unique, fashion. Not even the accumulation of the varied experiences of different individuals can fully explain the differences in their responses to the same event. Unlike natural objects, human beings carry with them individualized sets of meanings as well as the capacity to create new meanings where it seems appropriate. To the extent that most social scientists continue to follow the model of the natural sciences, we are left with a distorted view of human beings as determined by their environment and as having little impact on the development of their own structures of meaning.

Such a position, according to the phenomenologist, fails to acknowledge the active involvement of the "observed" in shaping and giving meaning to one's actions. In contrast, the phenomenologist would argue, it is the very intentionality of human action that distinguishes it from the behavior of physical objects. Our consciousness does not exist independently, but only in relation to the world around us; it is intentional, it is directed, it is oriented. "All perceptual acts, according to Husserl, have one dominant characteristic; they point toward, or intend, some object. Thus, all thinking is thinking *of* something; all willing is willing *of* something; all imagining is imagining *of* something."[6] To the extent that action is intended, it has meaning for the actor; it is in turn the meaningfulness of human action that is the main concern of phenomenological inquiry.

The meaning which we attach to our actions can be characterized in several ways. Obviously, we establish structures of meaning through our contacts with others. Each individual's act of endowing the world with meaning takes into account the meaning with which the world has previously been endowed by others. In this way, meaning is constituted intersubjectively. Moreover, the pattern by which meaning structures are derived may be viewed historically, as they have been constructed over time. Our social conventions, our value systems, even the structure of our language itself—all serve to shape the meaning that we attribute to the world and to our place in it. In substantial part, the world we come to know is based on conceptual knowledge, but that knowledge is itself founded on preconceptual bases. Hwa Yol Jung comments, "The felt dimension of our experience has an important function in what we think, observe, and perceive, and in how we behave. Meaning involves experiencing that is preconceptual, presymbolic, and preverbal (that is, something felt)."[7] Obviously, this position has important implications for the way we come to understand social (including organizational) action, for it suggests that the task of the observer is to uncover what the action means to the actor, to reconstruct the meaning the action has for the actor.

This orientation differs from the positivist approach in several distinct ways. First, it recognizes that what the actor appears to be doing may not be at all what is intended by the actor. For example, if I sit down in front of my typewriter, an observer might infer that I am getting ready to type; however, I might intend instead to change the ribbon or simply to gaze out the window behind the typewriter. In either case, the inference based on the external observation of my behavior would be misleading. Second, the phenomenological viewpoint recognizes that my actions are oriented not by the observer's characterization of the situation, but by the meaning that I as an individual assign to my circumstance. My actions will be motivated by my own perceptions and the meanings

I assign, not by those of the observer. In turn, my actions will not be satisfactorily understood through categories "imposed" on my behavior "from the outside." Moreover, to the extent that such categories *are* imposed on my behavior, they may act to control that behavior, in the sense of defining a particular construction of reality for the other.

What is observable, then, is always related to the awareness of the actor—a position which immediately begins to undermine the positivist distinction between subjectivity and objectivity. In our everyday relationships with one another, we can never fully separate our perceptions of that which is objective from that which is subjective. While we can see each other as we appear in the external world, we each also must recognize implicitly the inner world of intentions which the other inhabits. In the words of Alfred Schutz, whose phenomenological sociology has been extremely influential, "I can, on the one hand, attend to and interpret in themselves the phenomena of the external world which present themselves to me as indications of the consciousness of other people. When I do this, I say of them that they have objective meaning. But I can, on the other hand, look over and through these external indications into the constituting process within the living consciousness of another rational being. What I am then concerned with is subjective meaning."[8] So each of us appears to the other simultaneously and inseparably as subject and object. To the extent that our meaning structures are affected by our interactions with others, we cannot fully separate our own inner and outer worlds. Because human consciousness is intentional, the internal and the external, the subject and the object, are one.

All of this becomes even more apparent if we return to the relationship of the observer and the observed, for it now becomes clear that the observer is deeply implicated in the world of the actor as well as vice versa. On the one hand, the observer's own subjective evaluations mediate between the actor's behavior and the meaning which the observer assigns to it. On the other hand, the presence of the observer in the world of the observed may even change the behavior itself. In either case, the supposed objectivity of observation sought by the positive science model breaks down.

Parenthetically, we might note that this argument also strikes directly at the positivist's distinction between fact and value. The positivist argues that material which cannot be "objectively" validated—such as human values—must be given over to the world of the subjective and must by definition be unknowable. But, as we have seen, no human interaction—including acts of scientific observation as well as those activities which occur within organizations —takes place without the subjective evaluation that is involved in assigning meaning. In assigning meaning, we are inevitably called upon to make choices based on our values; in the world of action, fact and value are indeed one. According to Michael Polyani, "the act of knowing includes appraisal; and this personal coefficient, which shapes all factual knowledge, bridges in doing so the disjunction between subjectivity and objectivity."[9]

Already there have been several attempts to apply the "action frame of reference" outlined here to the study of organizational life, the most notable being David Silverman's *The Theory of Organisations*. Silverman's work suggests that the bases of everyday life are problematic: "While social action presents a *routine* character, it is in fact socially *accomplished*, i.e., dependent on a series of unstated assumptions, accepted and rejected courses of action."[10] Since we participate in the construction of the institutions which characterize our society, we may legitimately view those institutions as expressions of the meaning of our lives. Organizations may be seen as social products, artifacts which express the various commitments we have made. In contrast to the rational model of administration, which sees the individual as molded into acceptable roles by the organization, the action frame of reference suggests that organizations derive from the way in which we attach meaning to our own acts and to the actions of others. Our own constructions of organizational reality provide the key to understanding meaningful human action and the organizations created by such meaning and such action.

Silverman's effort, of course, is to seek a new basis for the sociological study of complex organizations—a task which he approaches by suggesting that the study of organizations proceed from an examination of the orientations (meaning-structures) of the various participants in the organization, especially as these orientations can be characterized as "ideal-typical." The organization is seen "through the eyes of its members," and the actions taken by the organization are viewed as consequences of the orientations of the individuals who comprise the group. The organization takes shape as a result of the interaction of the individual's store of knowledge (those norms, values, and standards of behavior which individuals bring with them to the organization) and the role-system of the organization (which may modify the individual's definition of the situation). As these forces interact, the individual arrives at a particular structure of meanings with respect to participation in the organization.

Building on this, Silverman suggests six areas which should be investigated by the organizational analyst:

1. The nature of the role-system and pattern of interaction that has been built up in the organisation. . . .
2. The nature of involvement of ideal-typical actors . . . and the characteristic hierarchy of ends which they pursue. . . .
3. The actors' present definitions of their situation within the organisation and their expectations of the likely behaviour of others with particular reference to the strategic resources they perceive to be at their own disposal and at the disposal of others.
4. The typical actions of different actors and the meaning which they attach to their action.
5. The nature and source of the intended and unintended consequences of action. . . .
6. Changes in the involvement and ends of the actors and in the role-system, and their source. . . .[11]

These new possibilities for understanding social relations in organizational settings provide a substantial departure from the more restrictive posture of the rational positivist approach to administration. As we saw earlier, the rational model presumes that human behavior, like the behavior of natural objects, is subject to certain eternal and unchanging "laws of nature," which may be revealed to us by scientists and managers working within the framework of positivism and instrumentalism. The phenomenological perspective, however, permits us to see organizations as constituted through the intended actions of individuals, thus acknowledging the creative role of the individual in producing organizational life. Given this acknowledgment, we begin to see organizations not as central or figural but as settings or backdrops which we construct and against which we play out our lives.

This means that we must ask, with respect to any description or characterization which we might use to assign meaning to our lives in organizations, how that account was generated, how it resulted from the shared experiences of interacting individuals, and how it might be reflected in future constructions. In fact, the process of creating meaning may be seen as more important than the meanings we later articulate. Our first and most decisive choices are those implicit in our own definitions of social situations, those which in turn permit us to articulate more narrow choices. By viewing organizations as created by interacting individuals, we recognize that those same organizations may similarly be re-created or changed, that they are not unalterable. We recognize that the supposedly natural causal relationships which underlie the rational model of administration obtain only to the extent that we believe them to be true, and that even those organizational circumstances which impinge most directly and most harmfully on us merely await our intention to act to change them.

Indeed, the most unchanging aspect of our lives in organizations is change itself: with every act, every exchange, every encounter we alter the meaning of our lives. Since the instrumentalist approach assumes that existing circumstances are subject to alteration only through the application of sheer force, we are led to a preoccupation with a "politics of power" or the "power" of positive thinking. In the action orientation, on the other hand, we recognize that the meaningfulness of our world is constantly changing as we act intentionally. Consequently, the first step in altering social or organizational conditions may be just to suspend our belief in them. But of course that's not really so simple. Indeed, the hardest part of change, really significant change, is not to move the outside world but to move ourselves.

This returns us to the issue of control, where we may now examine both the differences and the similarities of the instrumental model and the phenomenological alternative. In the positivistic approach to social science, we found the abstract categorization of behaviors of persons, irrespective of their lived experience. In organizational systems concerned with technical rationality, we found a clear bias in favor of domination by hierarchical superiors capable

107

of demanding (or "inducing") compliance. In either case, where explanations for actions arise outside the person and then are imposed on the person, they constitute an exercise of control—the definition of "reality" for another.

In contrast, the phenomenological perspective urges a radical openness to experience, a willingness to entertain all phenomena regardless of their scientific or hierarchical justifications. Rather than seeking to find more and more labels to categorize and thereby sterilize the world, we are admonished to hold to a position which accepts the world as it is given, without labels, without prejudices, without "explanations." Of course, as we have seen, there are substantial pressures encouraging us to rationalize, to systematize. There are far fewer which encourage us to see the world in holistic terms, then to act intuitively on the basis of our preconceptual experience. But there is potentially a great advantage in doing so— the advantage of living more creative, more autonomous, and more authentic lives.

Through the action orientation, we see that control is not inevitable, that it is historically based, an ideological reconstruction seeking to explain and thereby direct our lives. But control does occur. In organizations, as elsewhere, people dominate and people submit to domination. At this point the phenomenological perspective can take us no further. For although phenomenology can assist us in exploring the meanings that individuals attach to their actions, the mere accumulation of meanings is not enough; phenomenology cannot take the next decisive step: to seek to determine whether those meanings are freely chosen. In its basic assumption of an ordered and regulated social world, the phenomenological perspective shares with mainstream social science an implicit acceptance of the world as it is given.

There is, however, the possibility that the meanings which individuals hold are the consequence of a systematic distortion of their real intentions, that we are bound by some sort of "false consciousness" which leads us to fail to recognize our true needs. If this is the case, though the world as seen through the eyes of the positivist or those of the phenomenologist may be much the same, imbued with order and regularity, in fact a great deal of conflict may be hidden just beneath the surface. And, if we were able to strip away the distorted view of the world which we have accepted, that conflict would likely erupt in attempts to alter the distribution of social power.

We may be aided in exploring this possibility by returning to the critical perspective, especially its comprehension of social change and the realization of freedom. The Hegelian view of history, which underlies most work in critical theory, sees history as the unfolding of human reason leading to freedom; therefore a central concern is the revelation of the immanent historical consequences of our actions. The world of appearances is historically misleading; indeed, as we noted in our earlier discussion of Marcuse, it cannot be otherwise. Social theory, therefore, has as its central concern the unveiling of the falsity of the superficial, *"the revelation of the lie,"* as Becker puts it.[12] Where the actions of individuals contribute to a pattern of development of which they are unaware—and which indeed may subject them to considerable regulation—it is the task of social theory to reveal that pattern. Only when we come to recognize the larger historical meaning of our actions may we begin to reconstruct our view of the world; and only when we come to recognize existing patterns of domination for what they are may we begin to act in accord with true reason toward the end of human freedom. As Marcuse writes, "Hegel's dialectic is permeated with the profound conviction that all immediate forms of existence—in nature and history—are 'bad,' because they do not permit things to be what they can be. True existence begins only when the immediate state is recognized as negative, when human beings become 'subjects' and strive to adapt their outward state to their potentialities."[13]

The method by which this shall be achieved is the dialectical method. In contrast to the functionalist or systems emphasis on stability and regulation consistent with existing social arrangements, the dialectical method sees society in terms of the dynamics of interacting social forces leading to inevitable change. "Dialectical method understands the existent in terms of the negativity it contains and views realities in light of their change."[14] Following the dialectic, the contradictions and tensions implicit within any existing circumstance provide the driving force which impels us to transcend that condition and to move beyond our present limitations.

Of course, the best-known application of the dialectical method was that of Karl Marx.[15] Marx developed a specific dialectical critique of society based on his exploration of the interaction of the mechanisms of production. In terms applicable to our study of life in complex organizations, Marx found the instruments of capitalism expressive of an inherent contradiction between the interests of the powerful and the powerless. Not only did Marx see the capitalist system of production depriving workers of the value of their labor, he also recognized the sheer alienation which resulted from that exploitation. Importantly, however, Marx also saw in this situation a basic contradiction inevitably leading to an accentuated class struggle in which the oppressed would recognize their oppression and act to overthrow their oppressors. While Marx largely based his understanding of the dialectical movement of history on his analysis of economic forces, his work provides an excellent model of the uses of critique, a model which later theorists, especially critical social theorists, have adapted to many purposes.

In an essay titled "Traditional and Critical Theory," Horkheimer elaborated the differences between earlier theory and the critical approach of the Frankfurt School.[16] In its broadest conception, according to Horkheimer, traditional theory seems to mean much the same thing to natural scientists and social scientists, including phenomenological sociologists; theory means "stored-up knowledge," a systematic and internally consistent set of propositions based on factual observations of a given phenomenon. The keys to traditional theory are a certain harmony which must exist among the various elements of the theory as well as congruence between the theory and the actual facts. Horkheimer sees this mode of knowledge acquisition as inseparably linked to a historical process in which the role of theory development is simply another element in the social division of labor. As scientists see the essence of their work as the accumulation of factual materials and the construction of integrated theories, their efforts are confined to a limited sphere, one defined historically in relation to the productive process. Not surprisingly, this enterprise is similar to other enterprises in advanced society. "The assiduous collecting of facts in all the disciplines dealing with social life, the gathering of great masses of detail in connection with problems, the empirical inquiries, through careful questionnaires and other means . . . all this adds up to a pattern which is, outwardly, much like the rest of life in a society dominated by industrial production techniques."[17] What is perhaps most striking about this view of traditional theory is the limited role that such theory can play in the larger process of human development. Whatever its pretensions, traditional theory, bound by its historically circumscribed role, can do little to address the possibilities of an improved social life guided by true (not technical) reason.

In contrast to traditional theory, Horkheimer points to a different mode of inquiry, that involved in the dialectical critique of society. The critical viewpoint relativizes the relationship between the individual and the society by suggesting that standard norms of conduct be regarded as suspect, as parts of a reality historically derived rather than naturally given. Moreover, these norms incorporate patterns of social control that are inconsistent with truly rational pursuits. While we experience the world as a human creation, we also see that it contains cultural forms such as war and oppression that are clearly not related to the exercise of humanity but are rather the consequences of social and economic relationships beyond the control of the individual. As a result, there arises a tension between our desire to accept the world as it is given and our recognition of the limiting constraints of a socially imposed reality-world. The possibility of moving beyond those limitations, in order to employ true reason in the pursuit of freedom, depends upon our ability to accurately understand and criticize existing social conditions. According to Horkheimer, "Critical thinking . . . is motivated today by the effort really to transcend the tension and to abolish the opposition between the individual's purposefulness, spontaneity, and rationality, and those work-process relationships on which society is built."[18]

In the work of Habermas, we find a more contemporary examination of the role of critical social science. Earlier we noted a distinction made by Habermas between two spheres of social action: the field of symbolic or communicative interaction (which we characterized by its concern for choice), and the field of purpose-rational action (which we characterized by its concern for regulation). In the realm of symbolic interaction we found emphasized the building of the normative structure of a society through the interaction of members of the society; in purposive-rational action, we found the application of technical means to be used in the pursuit of pregiven ends. Moreover, we noted the increasing extension of purposive-rational systems in our society, perhaps to the point that the institutional or normative structure is now becoming embedded within such systems rather than vice versa.

Now it is important for us to elaborate the concepts of inquiry which underlie our approach to understanding in each of these fields.[19] According to Habermas, as we operate within the field of purposive-rational action, we see the world as consisting of a set of objects which we may manipulate, and we are therefore concerned with establishing a body of theoretical statements which will enable us to pursue that effort at control. In this sense, knowledge is sought for the power it brings us, the power to bend the world to our wishes. On the other hand, as we engage in symbolic or communicative interaction, we need to understand the cultural and historical bases of social norms, and we are therefore concerned with cultural interpretation. We wish to understand the normative structures which our experiences have generated. In the first instance, the appropriate mode of inquiry is that provided by the empirical-analytic sciences (including positivist social science); in the second, the appropriate mode is that provided by the cultural sciences (including hermeneutics, the study of methodological principles of interpretation). In other words, differences in our basic cognitive interests lead to parallel differences in the modes of knowledge acquisition we seek to employ.

In this view, the relationships we have repeatedly noted between positive science and rational organization attain an even greater intimacy. The mode of knowledge acquisition which we permit to guide our understanding of organizations is reflective of the cognitive interests we have in an organizational society. The purposive-rational intent of organizational systems demands that we utilize a mode of inquiry appropriate to the exercise of control and manipulation; the empirical approach of the positivist social scientist serves this instrumental purpose well. There is, then, a clear and historically necessary connection between positive science and the purposive-rational intent of organized systems.

But, as we have seen, from the standpoint of the individuals who inhabit them, organizations must be viewed as more than technical systems; they must be viewed as settings or backdrops for human action. In order to achieve an understanding of organizational life as it occurs in the specific lives of organizational members, an alternative interpretive orientation is required. By focusing on questions of human meaning we open new opportunities for organizational and personal development. It is this interpretation which we derive from a view of the organization as established through the actions and expectations of interacting individuals. But there is still one further interest yet to be served—an interest in emancipation, in freeing us from the deception which the ethic of organization promotes.

The critical stance, which Habermas advocates to achieve this intention, recognizes that the "reasons" we give for our personal actions are often justifications rather than actual motives and that, at the level of the society, much the same thing occurs. Here, however, we refer to those justifications as ideologies. It is the task of critical social analysis to cut through these justifications, or ideologies, and to establish the regularities of social action which lie beneath the surface of our relationships. In turn, the critique permits us to see relationships of dependency and submissiveness which have previously been concealed; it sets off a process of self-reflection in which we begin to comprehend our true condition (unfettered by ideological constraints). To engage in serious and unconstrained self-reflection leads to self-knowledge—and guided by self-reflection, we can engage in responsible social action. Unfortunately, we can never fully reach this goal as long as we are engaged in a process of communications with ourselves or with others in which one facet of our being or one partner in the dialogue is "in control." Only through the restoration of undistorted communications, at the level of both the individual and the society, can we achieve a sound basis for personal reflection and autonomous action.

We can perhaps clarify these points by following Habermas in his discussion of psychoanalysis as an example of the use of critique in the pursuit of emancipation. According to Habermas, "Psychoanalytic interpretation is concerned with those connections of symbols in which a subject deceives itself about itself," those in which our communications with ourselves and with the world have been disturbed.[20] What Freud calls repression, Habermas explains as a privatization of certain aspects of our public communications, a privatization which renders the repressed contents of the consciousness inaccessible to others (except where they are exhibited symptomatically) and, under most circumstances, inaccessible to ourselves.

This being the case, the role of the therapist is to assist the patient in restoring those patterns of communications which have previously been distorted. The therapist seeks, on the one hand, to help the patient reconstruct lost patterns of self-understanding through the careful analysis of dream texts and other manifestations, and, on the other hand, seeks to draw from a broadly framed model of psychic development alternative explanations to suggest to the patient. Only the patient can confirm the correctness of the diagnosis, for the only correct diagnosis is that which assists the patient in recovering a portion of his or her life history. A given interpretation may be disregarded by the patient, even though it is accurate, because the resistances are too strong. Success (verification) only occurs when reflection leads to a new self-formative or developmental phase.

Moving from the individual to the society, Habermas argues that a parallel exists between psychoanalysis and critical social theory. "Both the pathology of social institutions and that of individual consciousness reside in the medium of language and of communicative action and assume the form of a structural deformation of communication."[21] The pathological society suffers from a lack of balance or symmetry among the various parties communicating with one another and thereby constructing a social history. Those who dominate the establishment of interpersonal norms impose their view of the world on others, claiming it to be appropriate for all. But such a representation obviously conceals the rational interests of those with less power—perhaps even in their own eyes! It is therefore the role of social criticism to penetrate the resulting dependencies and suffering that we take to be natural and to reconstruct in their place an alternative explanation based on a greater historical understanding. As in the case of psychoanalysis, the critique is oriented toward self-reflection and, consequently, insight so compelling that action in the pursuit of autonomy and responsibility is inevitable.

We might note at this point that Habermas's analysis seems quite consistent with the interpretation of life in complex organizations which we have presented to this point. We have seen the emergence of systems of hierarchical dominance based on an interest in control, we have seen the orientation of the controlling group concerned toward production leading inevitably to the objectification of human beings, and we have seen the emergence of a widely accepted ideological justification for the dominance of organized systems based in a rationalized scientific account of modern life. As a consequence, there has developed a popular consciousness in which the efficient completion of technically determined tasks takes precedence over the development of more effective patterns of personal growth and freedom. What we now see is that this consciousness is a deception—for to the extent that we are constrained by technical considerations we lose the capacity for personal and social transformation. We may be led then to the postulation of a critical lifestyle, an organizational praxis through which we might be able to counterbalance the dehumanization of organizational life with the fully humanizing quests for meaning, action, and continuity.

There is, however, one more issue to be resolved before we can move from self-reflection to action. Freud and Habermas both acknowledge that self-understanding alone will not trigger change in the individual or the society. In a well-known passage, Freud comments, "If knowledge about the unconscious were as important for the patient as people . . . imagine, listening to lectures or reading books would be enough to cure him."[22] Something in addition to cognitive understanding, an affective response, is necessary for change to occur. Freud rather ambiguously connects this affective motive to the transference mechanism, arguing that the patient's attachment to the therapist may trigger the response required to initiate change. However, this formulation merely provides a further cognitive explanation for what must be a purely affective response.

Similarly, Habermas, in developing his critical theory of society, also notes the need to address the affective element: "Critique would not have the power to break up false consciousness if it were not impelled by a *passion for critique*."[23] But the source of this "passion" is unclear. At best, Habermas seems to argue that the act of seeking help in the beginning propels the patient or the society to act once understanding is achieved. But we should then ask what initiates the former action. It appears in the end that Habermas, like Freud, has remained too close to a cognitive explanation and, as some critics have noted, has failed to take the final step toward a more activist stance.

In both the Marxist and Freudian traditions, we see the suffering of the individual and the society as the key to reconstructive (revolutionary?) action. It is through our remembrance of the pleasures which reality denies that we see our true condition, and it is through the recognition of the alienation which marks our existence that we are motivated to move in opposition to the powers which hold us. For this reason, our suffering must not be "rationalized" away, for it remains at the heart of our "spiritual" quest; it is to transcend our suffering that we act.

On the other hand, simply recognizing or recalling our suffering is not enough; we must also recall the forces of development which, when hindered, led to our suffering. These forces, more positive, though more irrational, propel us to act to return our lives to the path which once was blocked. As we activate these forces, we may begin to reconnect that which appears as rational and that which appears as irrational, those forces of negativity with those more positive. In Freud and Marx, we find the propelling force of negative thought; however, we also must recognize our more positive needs for growth and development.

As we have seen, post-Freudian depth psychologists conceived of a more creative role for the individual than did Freud himself, with the motive for personal growth becoming more central. For Rank, the vehicle of our striving is the will, the active and emergent faculty which draws forth greater and greater capacities of consciousness. In contrast to what he saw as the rationalizing tendency of Freudian psychology, Rank sought to discover the source of the individual's potential for growth, a capacity which he described as "an autonomous organizing force in the individual which . . . constitutes the creative expression of the total personality and distinguishes one individual from another."[24] Since the will acts to balance both our impulses and our inhibitions, it may be manifest either destructively or creatively, yet it is in the will that we find the greatest source of potential growth.

Progoff argues that Rank's conception of the will is "comparable in spirit and intention to Jung's theory of the self." As we saw earlier, the self is the unifying principle in the Jungian interpretation of the psyche, the basis for our attempts to achieve integration or wholeness in our personalities. Similarly, Rank's notion of the will supplies a central dynamic to the growth of the personality, one that is manifest in energy and enthusiasm. "The Self as conceived by Jung is the psychological potentiality that emerges in each individual personality; and the life will as conceived by Rank is the vital force with which that potentiality is expressed and fulfilled in the world."[25]

In any case, the individual is ultimately called upon to establish a sense of being connected to life, even in the face of death. According to Rank, it is through the will that we express our lives, but in the course of doing so we confront the confounding anticipation of our impending death. To conceive of the inevitability of our death has the effect of cutting off the expression of our will; thus, we must find some way to come to terms creatively and symbolically with the fact of our death in order to affirm our life (our will). Out of this deep psychological need, as we have seen, we create cultural symbols and historical interpretations which explain our death—that is, which give us some way of transcending death. For us to try to live in any other way is to invite chaos and confusion in our lives, to be "neurotic." Our most basic and most creative impulse, therefore, is that which urges us to exceed our limitations. Such, of course, is the motive of the hero in myth and legend, so in the image of the hero we may find a symbol of our own personal efforts to achieve transcendence, even in the context of a highly organized society.

MEANING,
ACTION, AND CONTINUITY

Because I have called, and ye refused; I have stretched out my hand, and no man regarded; But ye have set at nought all my counsel, and would none of my reproof: I also will laugh at your calamity; I will mock when your fear cometh; When your fear cometh as desolation, and your destruction cometh as a whirlwind; when distress and anguish cometh upon you. . . . For the turning away of the simple shall slay them, and the prosperity of fools shall destroy them.

Proverbs, 1:24–27, 32

If we are to recover our primary sense of heroism, we must first acknowledge the call by which we are summoned to adventure. The call may come in many ways—through our hopes and our ambitions, through our failures and defeats—but it will come. Too often, however, we are so wrapped up in the immediate that we fail to hear or to heed the call. But if we are open to the possibilities that we may encounter and if we respond to the opportunities they present, then we may engage in adventures far beyond what we might have expected in the ordinary world. Indeed, it is exactly because we will find our quest fascinating that we will devote our fullest energies to it. Our world will become our self, and as we transcend that world we will transcend our self. In that effort we will live our lives as heroic. According to Joseph Campbell, the story of the hero has been told in thousands of variations throughout history, but it always seems to follow the same pattern, one which we may take as a model for our own psychological quest. *"A hero ventures forth from the world of common day into a region of supernatural wonder: fabulous forces are there encountered and a decisive victory is won: the hero comes back from this mysterious adventure with the power to bestow boons on his fellow man."*[1] The hero is called away from everyday life to engage in an adventure far beyond; there the hero engages strong and evil forces, with which the hero must successfully contend in order to be allowed to return to the ordinary world; but the hero can never fully return, for the hero has seen a world, indeed has *made* a world which is very extraordinary; the hero then must assume the role of the teacher and attempt to introduce others to the new world. "The hero has died as a modern man; but as eternal man—perfected, unspecific, universal man—he has been reborn. His second solemn task and deed therefore . . . is to return then to us, transfigured, and teach the lesson he has learned of life renewed."[2] The hero must exceed the given culture, the given rationality, and enter into a "spiritual" dimension. At this point, death is no longer a problem; the life of the hero has become a part of the spiritual realm and is therefore immortalized. The hero embodies the ultimate reconciliation of life and death, and in that act represents the greatest achievement of mankind.

The act of the hero is extraordinary, it is transcendent, yet it is open to all. The story of the hero simply represents what is latent in all others: an urge toward expression and creativity. Both Rank and Jung explored the role of the hero, focusing on the artist as prototypical. Rather than accepting a view of the artist as synthesizing the culture of a particular era, both saw the artist as struggling against the culture, as attempting to be free of the culture in order to re-form it. The work of the artist is heroic in the sense that it achieves an individual expression cognizant of but not bound to the dominant culture. Progoff indicates the expansiveness of this task: "The artist's work . . . is authentic to the extent that it is drawn from the objective, more-than-personal contents of the human spirit."[3] The artist expresses an emergent spiritual yearning in the culture and awakens the spirit of the age. But it must be repeated: the artist as a heroic figure expresses what is latent in all others, our inherent urge toward creativity—expressed in its most basic form as our passion for personal growth and development.

To live the life of the hero we must transcend that which is rationally given, but this is something that is very difficult to do. Rank writes, "it is not sufficient to *see* the importance of the irrational element in human life and point it out in *rational* terms! On the contrary, it is necessary actually to live it and of this only a few individuals in every epoch seem to be capable. They represent the heroic type . . . for the original hero was the one who dared live beyond the accepted 'psychology' or ideology of his time."[4] Obviously, today positive science and instrumental organization are extremely persuasive ideologies. In our age, the person who dares live beyond the limits of science and organization may be deemed heroic.

Unfortunately, even our understanding of heroism itself has been altered by the ethic of organization to reflect a "rational" separation of subject and object. On the one hand, we value the contemplative; on the other hand, we value the celebrity—and in between we find only the mundane. The contemplative, cut off from the rest of the world and willing to forgo worldly pleasures, represents most fully the solitary self, the subject. The contemplative wishes only to withdraw from the outer or public world into the inner or private world. The celebrity, on the other hand, lives solely for the audience, solely as an embodiment of the fantasies of others or as an expression of some abstract status system, such as that provided by the "symbols of success" in modern society. In any case, the celebrity becomes an object, defined by others and in no way transcendent. There are, of course, obvious difficulties with each of these images of heroism. The contemplative, having withdrawn from the world, fails to execute personal responsibility for the creation and evolution of that world; the celebrity, living only in response to others, loses any sense of personal autonomy. But even more important is the dichotomy itself: we are urged toward total withdrawal or total commitment.

Of course we must make choices. Day by day, we encounter the world in its completeness, and in this encounter we derive the meaning of our life's experiences. Yet when we attempt to share that experience with others we must necessarily exclude a great deal. There simply isn't time to tell anyone else the complete story of our lives—and even if we could, that would be just another experience to relate (and so on). Our stories are always false in a sense, because they are incomplete. But they are the best we can do. This being the case, we must make choices about which portions of our experience we wish to share with others. As we have seen, the rationalized ethic of organization provides one set of criteria for choosing what we say and to whom, what we tell of our lives and what we exclude. And it is clear that those criteria push us toward a division between our solitary self and our social self.

In contrast, through an integration of our subjective and our objective experience, we can assert a new sense of heroism. Any time we suspend the solitary versus the social self and experience ourselves as fully being in the world, we begin to sense ecstasy, even transcendence. We experience ourselves as relating to the world with a sense of wholeness and engagement. At that point we know we have moved beyond the limitations of either/or—either self or society—and into a realm in which all things are one; we have entered the world of the hero. The hero asserts a position which extends beyond that which exists and begins to change the world, to create a new world, but most important the hero has established a new relationship with the world. In that relationship, we experience both wholeness and engagement, good and evil, limitation and transcendence, not with an eye toward control but toward reconciliation. At this point, we begin to understand that the connection between autonomy and responsibility resides in the integration of subject and object at both the personal and the social level. *In acts of critical self-reflection, we can begin to relate to our whole selves; in acts of sharing ourselves with others, we can begin to achieve a societal praxis.*

I

How, then, might our heroic impulse be directed toward the organizational society in which we now live? In the course of this essay, we have examined the works of a diverse group of theorists, yet there seems to be a common thread running throughout their work, a point of view which may aid us in reconceptualizing life in complex organizations. Whether we are speaking of the individual or the group, there is agreement that we are engaged in a dialectical struggle between ourselves and the society around us; that we are subject to the imposition of rationalized patterns of explanation and behavior; that these patterns limit the fullest expression of our creative potential; that realizing this, we attempt to break free but often find ourselves locked into a self-defeating effort to fight the power of society on its own grounds (those of domination); that in contrast, critical acts of self-reflection, brought about through an exercise of the will and nurtured by dialogue, may reveal to us our true condition; and that at this point, recalling our suffering, we may act to establish conditions of autonomy and responsibility, communication and choice.

Following the ethic of organization, we participate in organized systems in order to accomplish those things which our survival and our security demand. In order to master the physical world—which threatens us and undermines our well-being—we permit ourselves to submit to a certain amount of domination. But the logic of domination soon takes on a life of its own. Our involvement loses both its personal and its social significance; it becomes a matter of obligation. Our labor is no longer an expression of our own needs; it is instead subjected to organizational rationalization.

As we have seen, the rational model of administration may assist in efforts at prediction and control in the interest of efficiency, but it cannot provide an understanding of the meaning of organizational life or a critique of its limitations. Moreover, where the rational model serves as a model of appropriate human action, it provides an extremely limited view of the individual, especially with respect to the question of moral consciousness. Finally, since the rational model inherently serves the interests of social regulation, it cannot aid in the individual's search for autonomy and responsibility. Yet these are just the issues which must be resolved in order for persons to explore new ways of relating to one another as they share in the tasks of life. Recognizing the limitations which the ethic of organization imposes, we must begin to develop an alternative view of the world, one which, like that of the artist, is cognizant of the existing culture but not bound to it.

The first step is to integrate the various aspects of our personality into an unbiased whole, a step which, in an organizational society, must first confront the issue of work. We often define our identity in terms of the work we do or, even more explicitly, the positions we hold in the organizational hierarchy. For example, when we meet someone, we are likely to ask "What do you do?", meaning what type of work are you engaged in, or "Where do you work?", meaning at what location in what organization. Now it is perfectly appropriate for human beings to define themselves in terms of the work they do *if* that work has been freely undertaken. If our work, like the work of the artist, is in fact an extension of our personality (not vice versa), then one way of communicating to others the quest in which we are engaged is to tell them of the work we do. We are in effect describing ourselves through an analogy: our work, of which we *can* speak, provides a clue to ourselves, which we find more difficult to put into words. But if our work is not freely chosen, if in fact we are engaged in involuntary or enforced labor, then it is not appropriate to equate our identities with our work. In this case, our real identities are distorted by such a description, one which is simply reflective of the substitution of an organizationally imposed structure of meanings for that which we might independently hold.

In contrast to our current image of work as involuntary and restrictive, we might begin to develop a more comprehensive alternative view of human action. We can read Habermas's efforts to return interaction to a position at least equivalent to that of purposive-rational action as expressive of this concern. However, this is not enough. A sounder conceptualization—one which would also restore a more creative element to our activities—would be to return interaction (that is, the realm of normative discourse related to personal and social choice) to a position embracing work and its purer antinomy, play. Such a move would permit a balancing of the rigor of work with the imaginativeness of play in seeking individuation at the personal level and praxis at the societal level.

Play, that voluntary and unconstrained activity bound neither by social constraint nor physical need, has a direct connection to the creative effort to achieve autonomy and responsibility. Play involves free and spontaneous activity limited only by the individual imagination. "Play is a context . . . that is voluntary and open-ended (i.e., free from both external and internal compulsions), non-instrumental (in the sense that it is pursued for its sake and has at its center of interest process rather than goal), and transcendent of ordinary states of being and consciousness."[5] As such, play stands in direct contrast to technically efficient work. In the realm of work, especially purposive-rational activity, we simply carry out functions; in the world of play, we are free to act, to enhance, to expand, without regard for consequences or constraints. Where work is instrumental, play is expressive. The world of play is indeed the world of creativity—and the world of freedom. Through play we may catch a glimpse of the future, a way of seeing all the possibilities.

Moreover, the world of play, in all its creativity, seems very much a part of all of us. To restore play to its proper role in our lives requires only that we release an energy that already lies within. "Underneath the habits of work in every man lies the immortal instinct for play," writes Norman O. Brown. "The foundation on which the man of the future will be built is already there, in the repressed unconscious, the foundation does not have to be created out of nothing, but recovered."[6] Similarly, Johan Huizinga argues that the element of play is deeply embedded in all forms of human culture, merely waiting to be released.[7] The recovery of the spirit of play and the full utilization of it in reconstructing individual lives as well as the social world are made difficult by the restricted vision which the ethic of organization imposes on us, but neither is impossible.

Clearly, play reaches its creative peak under circumstances devoid of regulation or restraint, the same circumstances which facilitate the establishment of structures of shared meaning. For these reasons, we may surmise that our seeking personal heroism within organizational settings would require that we act wherever possible to remove such restrictions. There is indeed some hope that advanced industrial society has created the preconditions for a revised understanding of work processes. This new view will be built around an individual creatively involved in the work experience, but no longer involved in work as we know it today. Work will become a reflection of one's commitment to certain actions, and since pleasure comes from meaningful work, work will in fact become pleasurable. Work will become play!

At the same time, as time for leisure becomes greater and greater, the opportunities for play will increase. As this happens, we will work harder at play; what is one's work will be another's play. Artists may play at science, scientists may play at art; and as this occurs, the barriers which now alienate people from their work will begin to fall. Activities which are playful work for some will be workful play for others. And as work and play finally lead toward one another, the distinction between work and play may be blurred.

At this point, we would expect a reconstituted personal and social consciousness to emerge. The imaginativeness of play would permit a far greater sense of reflexivity than now exists; individuals would be able to turn inward for strength and insight. But such a sense of reflection would not be merely self-indulgent; rather, it would provide a new basis for social obligation. The autonomy which permits self-reflection only occurs in a social context; the essence of freedom resides in the process of our interaction with others. For this reason, autonomy implies responsibility; meaningful self-reflection would necessarily lead to responsible social action, action in pursuit of a more active and creative society.

The reemergence of the spirit of play will enable us to see the world with greater vision, yet we still must confront the realities of suffering and regulation, both of which ultimately symbolize our confrontation with death itself. As we have seen, both historically and symbolically the formation of the group is bound to attempts to control the environment, whether the physical environment and the natural threats to survival which it presents or the social environment and the more symbolic threats to security which it presents. (The well-known tendency of groups to become more cohesive in the face of external threats is simply a manifestation of the group's repressed guilt and its fear of being exploited by others with similar intents.) This tendency becomes especially apparent at the level of the organization, for it is clear that the ethic of organization provides a means of establishing and maintaining control over both the natural environment and those portions of the social environment which can be mechanistically defined.

There is, however, some evidence that the types of problems which are likely to prove most troublesome over the coming years are those dealt with not in terms of control but rather in terms of creativity. E. F. Schumacher has argued that mankind faces two kinds of problems in life: those which he calls "convergent" (those on which persons of good will might initially disagree, but could eventually arrive at a common solution through reasoned dialogue), and those which he calls "divergent" (those which lead persons engaged in dialogue to more and more extreme positions).[8] The latter problems, according to Schumacher, can only be effectively resolved by transcending the immediate issue with a creative solution. For example, in the slogan of the French revolution, the inherent opposition of liberty and equality as political principles was resolved by the third element, fraternity.

There is much to suggest that we will be increasingly called upon to solve more and more questions which fall in the latter category. Not only those problems of personal growth which we have addressed here in the context of an organizational society, but also those problems which we associate most closely with the change and turbulence of society generally revolve around conflicting human values. Unfortunately, instrumental organization is ill-equipped to deal with such problems. Like other tools, organizations are so structured as to concentrate energy at one point in order to produce the maximum effect. In line with the ethic of organization, as in levers or pulleys, the "best" design is that which channels energy most effectively. The trick is to focus, to concentrate, to utilize.

While this process may be effective in solving convergent problems, it is clearly less effective in addressing divergent problems. Here, as Schumacher suggests, questions can only be dealt with by moving beyond the immediate statement of the problem in such a way as to transcend and to synthesize. This requires a great deal of creativity, but creativity is not aided by the concentration of human energies, rather by their dispersion, by remaining flexible and by searching, by moving outside normal channels. With creativity it is no longer simply the power of rationality that is at issue; there is also the matter of intuition. "When the situation is right for a given type of discovery," writes Arthur Koestler, "it still needs the intuitive power of an exceptional mind, and sometimes a favourable chance event, to bring it from potential into actual existence."[9]

To the extent that we continue to be guided by the ethic of organization to employ organizational designs which require a focusing rather than a release of human energies, we will be bound to a set of behaviors which severely limit our potential. We will not pursue an interest in simply protecting ourselves from our natural environment, but will continue our active exploitation of that environment. We will not seek merely to provide an adequate level of goods and services, but will increasingly see our interest perverted into mechanical efforts aimed at the accumulation of excess. And we will not seek rest, leisure, and "the good life," but will continue to follow an orientation toward labor which makes work more and more technical as well as more and more unpleasant.

II

What specific steps might we as individuals take to bring a heroic perspective to bear on the problems of modern life? We might begin by shifting our focus to organizational (or interpersonal) *processes* instead of technical tasks. To focus on organizational processes is to seek an understanding of the underlying dynamics of action, to inquire into the hidden but nonetheless compelling patterns of motivation, communication, and interaction which guide our surface responses. Just as we recognize the depth processes which guide our development as individuals, we also must recognize those elements of group and organizational life which represent the repressed contents of our collective histories. A concern for organizational processes enables us to penetrate the appearances of organizational life and to establish interpretations based on a much deeper level of analysis, one especially sensitive to the interplay of human emotions and human values in organizational settings.

This approach would imply a more phenomenological orientation toward our circumstances. We would not be satisfied with observing and reacting to the behavior of others but would seek to make connections to the meaning structures which they bring to public situations and which we take into account in our own actions. Following such an approach would require that we guard against the fallacy of reducing intentional action to determined behavior, or, in other words, that we fully inquire into the processes through which our structures of meaning and those of others are derived. Any consideration of the problem of developing a deeper understanding of individual meaning, however, brings us to the idea of community. As we seek understanding through autonomous, undominated communication, we recognize a neglected characteristic of public situations—that personal action better connects to questions of community than to those of technical control. In an attempt to displace the dominated character of restricted communication, we must develop means to expand the context of public dialogue and to broaden the range of experience that is engaged when we enter into choice situations.

Once again, sharing ourselves with others is an act which transcends the limits of subject and object, fact and value. To communicate fully and completely is to enter into a normatively based community of shared meanings, meanings which partake of all aspects of our personalities—sensing, intuition, thinking, and feeling. Not only does the act of communicating involve transcending the subject-object dichotomy, the sense of evaluation implicit in interaction incorporates inevitable considerations of value. For this reason, acts of pure communication provide a sort of bonding, one clearly at odds with the ethic of organization. Where organization seeks to divide labor (and laborers), pure communication brings people together. Where the ethic of organization intends to objectify and to separate, our search for meaning, action, and continuity requires sharing and integration.

There is in all of this a sense of seeking, a sense of inquiry and critique missing in our current approach to organizational life. At a minimum, we are called upon to search for our own identity, stripped of the "rational" explanations which others may attempt to impose on it. But just as we search for our own identity, we will recognize the uniqueness of others as well—whether those others are "superiors" or "subordinates," "co-workers" or "clients." Indeed, as we begin to establish more firmly our own identities as well as those of other people, we will eliminate the need for those restrictive labels which currently derive from rationalized systems of social domination. And we can turn our critical faculty to the task of reconstituting the basis for human interaction.

This need is nowhere more apparent than in our approach to the relationship between the leader and the group. In many ways, this relationship is a paradigmatic case in point, in part because it is in this relationship that hierarchical domination is epitomized, in part because this relationship so clearly captures the illusory symbolism of the ethic of organization. As we recall from our earlier discussion, the group's very cohesion is tied to the guilt which the group assumes in its attempt to isolate itself and to establish control over its environment, including its social environment. Similarly, the dissolution of the leader-group relationship is brought about by the leader's attempt to rationalize his or her own position and to impose restraints on the group. In other words, the central dynamic of the leader-group relationship currently resides in efforts to achieve domination, either the domination of the group over the environment or the domination of the leader over the group.

To begin to alter our current notion of leadership, it is helpful to think of leadership in its original sense—as a function rather than an attribute of a particular individual or an organizational office. Leadership is better seen as a capacity of the group, a resource which resides in the group and which must be activated in order for the group to fulfill its potential. Moreover, leadership must be seen as intimately connected to the process of change, in the sense that every act of leadership is oriented toward some alteration in the "consciousness" of the group.

The group may operate in several modes: the intransitive mode, which is characterized by our "being" together; the transitive mode, which is characterized by our "doing" things together. In these terms, leadership activities, change activities, represent the transitive reflexive mode, that in which the group acts with respect to itself as an object. But there are several ways in which the group can be led to "change itself." As we noted earlier, one model of group development suggests that change is essentially based around issues of power or control and that the proper manipulation of the symbols of power will lead to change. But beneath this orientation to·change there lies the symbolism of closure, of death. An alternative model of leadership based in communication and mutual learning would see change instead as involving personal and group growth, activities ultimately connected to the affirmation of life.

As we noted earlier, therapists seeking to aid in the development of the individual recognize that it often takes something more than simply revealing the nature of the unconscious to the person in order for growth to occur. Though the potential for growth lies in the deeper reaches of the self, the affective motive which triggers the process of development may require some object in the outside world, something to which one may attach one's destiny. For the group, the leader (the one or ones who represent the leadership function of the group) may serve in this way. The leader expresses not what the group is but what it might be. The leader expresses one version of the group's potential.

There is a certain tension in this relationship; but unlike the tension generated by patterns of domination, this tension between that which is and that which might be is a healthy one. It is not like the tension of domination, but more like the tension associated with spirited play. The tension of domination is a vertical tension, a relationship brought about by conditions of hierarchy. The tension here is more horizontal, emphasizing the relationship between the existing and the potential, the present and the future. Leadership in this educative, expressive mode would restore a lost spiritual dimension to group activities. It would impart real significance to our acts; it would be life-affirming.

As we have seen, the instrumental orientation of both modern organization and modern science views human behavior largely as a mechanical response to external stimuli. In contrast, the world of heroic action is an immensely personal one, one in which the individual strives to exceed these stimuli. In this apparently simple distinction, we have found critically important implications for both the way we view organizational life and the way we act in organizational settings. For the world of heroic action is precisely a world in which the prevailing images of our present organizational society are reversed: *the central question is no longer how the individual may contribute to the efficient operation of the system, but how the individual may transcend that system.* What becomes most clear is that action in organizations is not simply organizational action, but rather is personal action. To see the individual as central rather than a consequence of organized forces in the environment is to permit the possibility of meaningful self-reflection and in turn the kind of action embraced by the term "praxis."

In one sense, the perspective outlined here seems quite idealistic, impossible to attain; but this is not necessarily the case. If we examine our lived experience (rather than some imposed image), we recognize that we are indeed fully capable of self-reflection and critical inquiry, that we often engage in such efforts, that we frequently enter into successful and creative dialogue with others, even within organizations. Here then—in our daily lives—we find the base for developing an alternative view of the world. To begin where we are and to expand these limited spaces for pure communication into more comprehensive structures is a challenging task, but certainly not an impossible one. Henry Kariel puts this nicely, "We are less in need of lofty plans for transforming closed institutions into ongoing processes than of making specific moves where, as it happens, we have the power to act."[10]

Such an approach does not conceive of grand designs which look different from existing structures, then direct our efforts toward achieving those alternatives. Rather we start with ourselves, our own viewpoints, our own actions. As we begin to reformulate our search for meaning in personal terms, as we find appropriate contexts for individual action, and as we keep an eye on the connection between our lives and the life of the universe, we will provide the basis for far more reaching changes in the future. We may not be at all sure where those changes will take us, but we will be secure knowing that the new frame of reference which guides our actions is not that which emphasizes the extrinsic rewards of technical productivity but rather the intrinsic values of autonomy and responsibility, individuation and praxis.

III

We are basically creative beings—we must be—but if we are frustrated in our striving to be creative, we may be tempted to look elsewhere for the same ego support which the act of creativity provides. That support cannot be found in relationships defined within the context of rational organization. We often fail to realize that the satisfaction of our spiritual needs cannot be found within relationships or institutions designed to fulfill our purely human needs. The satisfaction of certain needs may be supported by the ethic of organization, but the needs of the spirit cannot. In our over-estimation of the rationality of our organizational society, we have restricted our fullest personal and social development. Organizations simply cannot bear the moral quest of the individual.

The struggle for personal and societal growth is very demanding. Yet it is work of a new variety, not work as labor, and especially not as enforced labor, but work informed by the imaginative and creative impulse of art and play. It is a work which urges us to answer the call to adventure when it comes, and, as we respond, it is a work which encourages us, which gives us courage, because it is a work that affirms life. Our efforts to achieve heroism lead directly to action, action through which we may expand the present limits of the human condition. And through our actions we will inevitably express the meanings which we attach to our lives. We will see the culture and its institutions as they are, but we will also see beyond them. And, with this vision, we will express our lives not in the limited rationality of organization, but rather in the reasoned irrationality of our basically spiritual condition.

NOTES

CHAPTER 1

1. Edward Whitmont, *The Symbolic Quest* (New York: Harper and Row Publishers, 1969), p. 82.
2. Robert Presthus, *The Organizational Society* (New York: Vintage Books, 1962), p. 12.
3. J. R. P. French and B. Raven, quoted in James G. March, *Handbook of Organizations* (Chicago: Rand-McNally Co., 1965), p. 30.
4. Amitai Etzioni, *A Comparative Analysis of Complex Organizations*, rev. ed. (New York: The Free Press, 1975), p. 146.
5. Herbert Wilcox, "The Cultural Trait of Hierarchy in Middle Class Children," *Public Administration Review* 28 (May/June, 1968): 222–235; Robert B. Denhardt, "Bureaucratic Socialization and Organizational Accommodation," *Administrative Science Quarterly* 13 (December, 1968): 441–450.
6. Tom Wicker, *A Time to Die* (New York: Quadrangle/The New York Times Book Co., 1975), p. 63.
7. Ibid., p. 218.
8. Joseph Heller, *Something Happened* (New York: Ballantine Books, 1974), p. 5.
9. Ibid.
10. This point is made in an excellent book by Richard J. Bernstein, *Praxis and Action* (Philadelphia: University of Pennsylvania Press, 1971), p. 303.
11. Sheldon Wolin, *Politics and Vision: Continuity and Innovation in Western Political Thought* (Boston: Little, Brown and Company, 1960), chap. 10. For a related view of the organization as a political system, see Robert B. Denhardt, "Organizational Citizenship and Personal Freedom," *Public Administration Review* 28 (January/February, 1968): 47–54.
12. Lester Milbrath, *Political Participation* (Chicago: Rand-McNally and Company, 1965), p. 21.
13. Peter Drucker, *The Practice of Management* (New York: Harper and

Brothers, 1954), p. 183. See also the comments by T. H. Marshall, *Citizenship and Social Class* (Cambridge, England: University Press, 1950), p. 81.

14. Wolin, *Politics and Vision*, p. 415.
15. B. F. Skinner, *Walden Two* (New York: The Macmillan Co., 1948), pp. 193–194.
16. Thomas Molnar, *Utopia: The Perennial Heresy* (New York: Sheed and Ward, 1967), p. 160.
17. Ernest Becker, *The Denial of Death* (New York: The Free Press, 1973).
18. Stanley Milgram, *Obedience to Authority* (New York: Harper and Row, 1974), p. 186.
19. Ibid., p. 188.
20. C. G. Jung, *The Undiscovered Self*, trans. by R. F. C. Hull (New York: New American Library, 1957), p. 72.

CHAPTER 2

Epigraphs: Donald A. Schon, *Beyond the Stable State* (New York: W. W. Norton and Company, 1971), p. 51; Ernest Becker, *Escape from Evil* (New York: The Free Press, 1975), p. 58; Robert M. Pirsig, *Zen and the Art of Motorcycle Maintenance* (New York: William Morrow and Co., Inc., 1974), p. 102.

1. Max Weber, *The Theory of Social and Economic Organization*, trans. by A. M. Henderson and Talcott Parsons (New York: The Free Press, 1947), p. 337.
2. Richard Hall, "The Concept of Bureaucracy," *American Journal of Sociology* 69 (July, 1963): 33.
3. Talcott Parsons, *Structure and Process in Modern Society* (Glencoe: The Free Press, 1960), p. 19; Presthus, *Organizational Society*, p. 94.
4. Robert S. Weiss, *Processes of Organization* (Ann Arbor: University of Michigan Press, 1956), p. 2.
5. Chris Argyris, *Understanding Organizational Behavior* (Homewood, Ill.: The Dorsey Press, 1960), pp. 10–11; Talcott Parsons, "Suggestions for a Sociological Approach to the Theory of Organizations—I," *Administrative Science Quarterly* 1 (June, 1956): 64.
6. Herbert A. Simon, *Administrative Behavior: A Study of Decision-Making Processes in Administrative Organization*, 2nd ed. (New York: The Macmillan Co., 1958); Simon's other major works on complex organizations are Herbert A. Simon, *Models of Man* (New York: John Wiley and Sons, 1957), and James G. March and Herbert A. Simon, *Organizations* (New York: John Wiley and Sons, 1958).
7. Simon, *Administrative Behavior*, p. 45.

8. Ibid., pp. 45–46.
9. Ibid., p. 249.
10. Simon, *Models of Man*, p. 198.
11. James D. Thompson, *Organizations in Action* (New York: McGraw-Hill Book Co., 1967), p. 54.
12. Simon, *Administrative Behavior*, p. 102.
13. Ibid., p. 41.
14. March and Simon, *Organizations*, pp. 140–141.
15. Simon, *Administrative Behavior*, p. 246.
16. Max Horkheimer, *Eclipse of Reason* (New York: The Seabury Press, 1974), pp. 4–5.
17. Ibid., p. 5.
18. Ibid.
19. Herbert A. Simon, "Administrative Decision-making," *Public Administration Review* 25 (March, 1965): 35–36.
20. Philip Selznick, *Leadership in Administration: A Sociological Interpretation* (New York: Harper and Row, 1957), p. 38; Philip Selznick, "Foundations of the Theory of Organization," *American Sociological Review* 1 (February, 1948): 30.
21. Simon, *Models of Man*, p. 173.
22. Simon, *Administrative Behavior*, p. 133; see also Simon, *Models of Man*, pp. 74–75.
23. Chester I. Barnard, *The Functions of the Executive* (Cambridge: Harvard University Press, 1938), p. 168.
24. Herbert A. Simon, Donald W. Smithburg, and Victor A. Thompson, *Public Administration* (New York: Alfred A. Knopf, 1950), p. 82.
25. Simon, *Administrative Behavior*, p. 101.
26. Ibid., p. 172.
27. Ibid., p. 249.
28. Ibid., p. 248.
29. Herbert Reid, "The Politics of Time: Conflicting Philosophical Perspectives and Trends," *Human Context* (Autumn, 1972): 458.
30. Chris Argyris, "Some Limits of Rational Man Organizational Theory," *Public Administration Review* 33 (May–June, 1973): 265.
31. Peter M. Blau and Marshall W. Meyer, *Bureaucracy in Modern Society*, 2nd ed. (New York: Random House, 1971), p. 9.
32. Simon, *Administrative Behavior*, p. 198.
33. Robert A. Dahl and Charles Lindblom, *Politics, Economics, and Welfare* (New York: Torchbooks, 1953), p. 252.
34. Argyris, "Some Limits," 257. Argyris continues with a quotation from James G. March, an early collaborator with Simon, as follows: "By placing primary emphasis on rational techniques, we implicitly have rejected—or seriously impaired—two other procedures for choice: (a) the process of intuition, by means of which people may do things without fully understanding why, (b) the processes of tradition and faith, through which people do things because that is the way they

are done." See Michael B. Cohen and James G. March, *Leadership and Ambiguity* (New York: McGraw-Hill Book Co., 1974), pp. 216–229.

35. The work of Carl Jung will be considered more fully in the following chapter. Representative works of the other writers include Gordon Allport, *Personality: A Psychological Interpretation* (New York: Henry Holt and Co., 1937); Abraham Maslow, *The Farther Reaches of Human Nature* (New York: The Viking Press, 1971); Carl Rogers, *On Becoming a Person* (Boston: Houghton Mifflin Co., 1961).

36. Barnard, *Functions of the Executive,* app.

37. Ibid, p. 304.

38. Ibid., p. 322.

39. Whitmont, *Symbolic Quest,* p. 17.

40. Simon, *Administrative Behavior,* p. 14.

41. Rogers, *On Becoming a Person,* p. 394.

42. William G. Scott and David K. Hart, "Administrative Crisis: The Neglect of Metaphysical Speculation," *Public Administration Review* 33 (September–October, 1973): 419.

43. David Silverman, *The Theory of Organisations* (New York: Basic Books, 1971), p. 194.

44. Simon, *Administrative Behavior,* p. 62.

CHAPTER 3

Epigraph: Carlos Castaneda, *The Teachings of Don Juan* (New York: Ballantine Books, 1968), pp. 166–167.

1. Stephen E. Ambrose, *Crazy Horse and Custer* (Garden City, N.Y.: Doubleday and Company, 1975).

2. Ibid., p. 111.

3. Ibid.

4. Ibid., p. 113.

5. Eugene D. Genovese, *Roll, Jordan, Roll* (New York: Vintage Books, 1976), p. 148.

6. Ibid.

7. Rollo May, *Power and Innocence* (New York: W. W. Norton and Company, 1972), p. 179.

8. Molnar, *Utopia,* p. 209.

9. Simon, *Models of Man,* p. 199.

10. Michael Polanyi, *The Logic of Liberty* (London: Routledge and Kegan Paul, 1951), p. 15.

11. Richard Braithwaite, *Scientific Explanation* (Cambridge, England: University Press, 1959), p. 22.

12. Horkheimer, *Eclipse of Reason,* p. 105.

13. Erich Fromm, *The Anatomy of Human Destructiveness* (New York: Holt, Rinehart, and Winston, 1973), p. 142.
14. Epilogue by Christopher Lasch, in Roderick Aya and Norman Miller (eds.), *The New American Revolution* (New York: The Free Press, 1971), p. 325.
15. Bill Bradley, *Life on the Run* (New York: Quadrangle/The New York Times Book Company, 1976), p. 221.
16. Ibid.
17. John Brodie and Michael Murphy, "Interview with John Brodie," *Intellectual Digest* (January, 1973): 19–20.
18. Maslow, *Farther Reaches.*
19. Russell Jacoby, *Social Amnesia* (Boston: Beacon Press, 1975); Jacoby is also critical of "the spiritualities of the conformists, the blind materialism of the behaviorists, the superficial humanism and confused existentialism, the rampant subjectivism" (p. 150).
20. See Ira Progoff, *The Death and Rebirth of Psychology* (New York: McGraw-Hill Book Company, 1956).
21. Calvin S. Hall and Vernon J. Nordby, *A Primer of Jungian Psychology* (New York: New American Library, 1973), p. 32.
22. Ibid., p. 33.
23. C. G. Jung, *Two Essays in Analytical Psychology* (Princeton: Princeton University Press, 1966), p. 155n.
24. Ibid., p. 19.
25. For more complete descriptions of the Jungian psychological types described in the following paragraphs, see C. G. Jung, *Psychological Types* (Princeton: Princeton University Press, 1971). See also Isabel Briggs Myers, *Introduction to Type* (Gainesville, Fla.: Center for Application of Psychological Type, 1976).
26. Jung, *Two Essays*, p. 26.
27. Ibid., p. 20.
28. Ibid., pp. 145–147.
29. Whitmont, *Symbolic Quest*, p. 155.
30. Harry Levinson, "Reciprocation: The Relationship between Man and Organization," *Administrative Science Quarterly* 9 (March, 1965): 382.
31. For an interesting commentary on this point, see Roger Holmes, "Freud, Piaget, and Democratic Leadership," *British Journal of Sociology* 16 (June, 1965): 123–139.
32. Elias Canetti, *Crowds and Power*, trans. by Carol Stewart (New York: The Seabury Press, 1978).
33. Ibid., p. 311.

CHAPTER 4

Epigraphs: Fromm, *Anatomy of Human Destructiveness*, p. 356; Bernstein, *Praxis and Action*, p. 224; Paulo Freire, *Pedagogy of the Oppressed*, trans. by Myra Bergman Ramos (New York: Herder and Herder, 1972), p. 38.

1. Ira Progoff, *At a Journal Workshop* (New York: Dialogue House Library, 1975), p. 180.
2. The major works of members of the Frankfurt School are reviewed in my bibliographic essay. An overview of the development of the Institute of Social Research is contained in Martin Jay, *The Dialectical Imagination* (Boston: Little, Brown and Company, 1973).
3. Jurgen Habermas, *Toward a Rational Society*, trans. by Jeremy J. Shapiro (Boston: Beacon Press, 1970).
4. Ibid., p. 92.
5. Ibid., p. 93.
6. Ibid., p. 92.
7. Ibid.
8. Ibid., p. 95.
9. Jurgen Habermas, *Communication and the Evolution of Society*, trans. by Thomas McCarthy (Boston: Beacon Press, 1979), especially chaps. 1 and 3.
10. Habermas, *Rational Society*, p. 118.
11. Horkheimer, *Eclipse of Reason*, p. 21.
12. Habermas, *Rational Society*, p. 105.
13. Medawar, quoted in E. F. Schumacher, *A Guide for the Perplexed* (New York: Harper and Row, 1977), p. 134.
14. Habermas, *Rational Society*, pp. 103, 120.
15. John F. Kennedy, quoted in Christopher Lasch, *The Culture of Narcissism* (New York: W. W. Norton and Co., 1978), p. 77.
16. Robert J. Pranger, *The Eclipse of Citizenship* (New York: Holt, Rinehart and Winston, 1968), p. 4.
17. Ibid., p. 13.
18. Harold D. Lasswell and Abraham Kaplan, quoted in Pranger, *Eclipse of Citizenship*, p. 7.
19. For the concept of "normal science," see Thomas Kuhn, *The Structure of Scientific Revolutions* (Chicago: University of Chicago Press, 1962), chap. 4.
20. Horkheimer, *Eclipse of Reason*, p. 93.
21. Richard M. Zaner wryly remarks, "We see ourselves as we see others, and to the extent that others are taken as mere things, so are we to ourselves. We then become incapable of even seeing, much less scientifically understanding, what Yeats calls the 'ceremony of innocence,' and thus we do loose anarchy upon the world." See Zaner, "Solitude and Sociality: Critical Foundations," in George Psathas (ed.), *Phenomenological Sociology* (New York: John Wiley and Sons, 1973), p. 41.
22. "Industrialization and Capitalism in the Work of Max Weber," in

Herbert Marcuse, *Negations: Essays in Critical Theory* (Boston: Beacon Press, 1968).
23. Ibid., p. 203.
24. Habermas, *Rational Society*, p. 102.
25. Ibid., p. 105.
26. Herbert Marcuse, *Reason and Revolution* (Boston: Beacon Press, 1941), p. 9.
27. Karl Marx, "Theses on Feuerbach," in Robert C. Tucker (ed.), *The Marx-Engles Reader*, 2nd ed. (New York: W. W. Norton and Company, 1978), p. 145.
28. Jurgen Habermas, *Theory and Practice*, trans. by John Viertel (Boston: Beacon Press, 1973), p. 255.

CHAPTER 5

Epigraphs: Ira Progoff, *The Symbolic and the Real* (New York: McGraw-Hill Book Company, 1963), p. 95; Becker, *Denial of Death*, p. 4; Robert Jay Lifton and Eric Olson, *Living and Dying* (New York: Bantam Books, 1975), p. 79.

1. Rank's major works are reviewed in my bibliographic essay.
2. Ernest Becker, *The Birth and Death of Meaning*, 2nd ed. (New York: The Free Press, 1971), p. 56.
3. This effort is contained in Otto Rank, *Psychology and the Soul* (Philadelphia: University of Pennsylvania Press, 1950).
4. Norman O. Brown, *Life against Death* (Middletown, Conn.: Wesleyan University Press, 1959), p. 286.
5. Much of the material in this section is taken from Robert B. Denhardt, "Individual Responsibility in an Age of Organization," *Midwest Review of Public Administration* 11 (December, 1977): 259–269. Used by permission.
6. Raul Hilberg, *The Destruction of the European Jews* (Chicago: Quadrangle Books, 1961), p. 649. See also Richard L. Rubenstein, *The Cunning of History* (New York: Harper Colophon Books, 1975), for an interpretation of the captivity of the Jews in a "society of total domination" based on bureaucratic indifference.
7. Hilberg, *European Jews*.
8. Hannah Arendt, *Eichmann in Jerusalem* (New York: The Viking Press, 1963), pp. 133, 120.
9. Simon, *Administrative Behavior*, p. 102.
10. Wilcox, "Cultural Trait."
11. Denhardt, "Bureaucratic Socialization."
12. Robert Kahn et al., *Organizational Stress* (New York: John Wiley and Sons, 1964), pp. 20–21, 59.

13. Otto Rank, *Psychology and the Soul*, p. 74.
14. Sigmund Freud, *Group Psychology and the Ego* in *The Complete Works of Sigmund Freud*, vol. 18 (London: Hogarth Press and the Institute of Psycho-analysis, 1950), p. 78.
15. Ibid., chap. 10; see also Sigmund Freud, *Totem and Taboo* (New York: W. W. Norton and Co., 1952).
16. Brown, *Life against Death*, p. 269.
17. Freud, *Group Psychology*, p. 91. Wilfred R. Bion, whose own work on group relations is of importance, comments, "The first assumption is that the group has met in order to be sustained by a leader on whom it depends for nourishment, material and spiritual, and protection." See Bion, "Selections from 'Experiences in Groups,'" in Arthur D. Colman and W. Harold Bexton (eds.), *Group Relations Reader* (Sausalito, Calif.: GREX, 1975), p. 14.
18. Becker, *Escape from Evil*, p. 36.
19. Rollo May, *The Courage to Create* (New York: W. W. Norton and Co., 1975), pp. 69–70.
20. Rank, *Psychology and the Soul*, p. 74.
21. Seymour B. Sarason, *The Creation of Settings and the Future Societies* (San Francisco: Jossey-Bass Publishers, 1972).
22. Ibid., p. 189.
23. Ibid., p. 218.
24. Michael Maccoby, *The Gamesman* (New York: Simon and Schuster, 1976), p. 175.
25. Rank, *Beyond Psychology* (New York: Dover Publications, 1941), p. 18.

CHAPTER 6

Epigraphs: Albert Camus, *The Stranger*, trans. by Stuart Gilbert (New York: Vintage Books, 1946), p. 136; Henry S. Kariel, *Saving Appearances* (North Scituate, Mass.: Duxbury Press, 1972), p. 72; Joseph Campbell, *The Hero with a Thousand Faces*, 2nd ed. (Princeton: Princeton University Press, 1968), p. 217.

1. Becker, *Birth and Death*, pp. 126–127.
2. Walter Goldschmidt, introduction to Castaneda, *Teachings of Don Juan*, p. viii.
3. Brian Fay, "How People Change Themselves," in Terence Ball (ed.), *Political Theory and Praxis* (Minneapolis: University of Minnesota Press, 1977), pp. 200–238. See also Brian Fay, *Social Theory and Political Practice* (London: George Allen and Unwin, 1975).
4. Ibid., p. 207.
5. A review of works in phenomenology is contained in my bibliographical essay.

6. Maurice Natanson, *Edmund Husserl: Philosopher of Infinite Tasks* (Evanston: Northwestern University Press, 1973), p. 85.
7. Hwa Yol Jung (ed.), *Existential Phenomenology and Political Theory* (Chicago: Henry Regnery Company, 1972), p. xxv.
8. Alfred Schutz, *The Phenomenology of the Social World*, trans. by George Walsh and Frederick Lehnert (Evanston: Northwestern University Press, 1967), p. 37.
9. Michael Polyani, *Personal Knowledge* (New York: Harper Torchbooks, 1964), p. 17.
10. Silverman, *Theory of Organisations*, p. 6.
11. Ibid., p. 154.
12. Becker, *Escape from Evil*, p. 125.
13. Marcuse, *Reason and Revolution*, p. 66.
14. Ibid., p. 214.
15. See the various selections from Marx in Tucker, *Marx-Engels Reader*.
16. Max Horkheimer, *Critical Theory*, trans. by Matthew J. O'Connell and others (New York: The Seabury Press, 1972).
17. Ibid., p. 190–191.
18. Ibid., p. 210.
19. Jurgen Habermas, *Knowledge and Human Interests*, trans. by Jeremy J. Shapiro (Boston: Beacon Press, 1971), app.
20. Ibid., p. 218.
21. Ibid., p. 288.
22. Sigmund Freud quoted in Habermas, ibid., p. 229.
23. Ibid., p. 234.
24. Rank, *Beyond Psychology*, p. 50.
25. Progoff, *Death and Rebirth*, p. 206.

CHAPTER 7

1. Campbell, *Hero with a Thousand Faces*, p .30.
2. Ibid., p. 20.
3. Progoff, *Death and Rebirth*, p. 236
4. Rank, *Beyond Psychology*, p. 14.
5. Francis Hearn, "Toward a Critical Theory of Play," *Telos* 30 (Winter, 1976–77): 145.
6. Brown, *Life against Death*, p. 36.
7. Johan Huizinga, *Homo Ludens* (London: Maurice Temple Smith, 1970).
8. Schumacher, *Guide for the Perplexed*, chap. 10.
9. Arthur Koestler, *The Act of Creation* (London: Hutchinson and Company, 1964), p. 120.
10. Henry Kariel, *Beyond Liberalism* (New York: Harper Colophon Books, 1977), p. 101.

BIBLIOGRAPHICAL ESSAY

The literature on complex organizations has grown enormously in the last thirty years, to the point that many claim that organizational analysis is a separate and distinct field of study, an academic discipline. If so, it is a discipline which has drawn from many different sources and from many different perspectives. Among those contributing to this growing body of literature have been management theorists, sociologists, social psychologists, political scientists, and others. As noted in the text, organizational analysis has for the most part worked within the context of technical rationality and has shared the "mainstream" positivistic perspective of the other social sciences. This position is most clearly stated in Herbert A. Simon, *Administrative Behavior: A Study of Decision-making Processes in Administrative Organization*, 2nd ed. (New York: The Macmillan Company, 1958). Simon's rational model of administration is elaborated in Herbert A. Simon, *Models of Man* (New York: John Wiley and Sons, 1957); James G. March and Herbert A. Simon, *Organizations* (New York: John Wiley and Sons, 1958); and Richard M. Cyert and James G. March, *A Behavioral Theory of the Firm* (Englewood Cliffs, N.J.: Prentice-Hall, 1963). The same concern for issues of rationality evidenced in Simon's work is also important in more recent efforts, most notably the highly influential book by James D. Thompson, *Organizations in Action* (New York: McGraw-Hill Book Company, 1967). Thompson, whose work has often been taken as a departure from Simon's, explicitly states that his work "seeks to extend" the "Simon-March-Cyert stream of study" (p. 9). While Simon has not been as deeply involved in organizational studies more recently as he was earlier in his career, he presented an excellent defense of the rational model in "Organization Man: Rational or Self-Actualizing?", *Public Administration Review* 33 (July/August, 1973): 346–353.

The primary contributors to the study of modern organizations have been persons interested in management theory, sociology, and social psychology (though interestingly enough Simon was trained as a political scientist). Management theorists have largely concentrated on issues of planning and control, with special attention to the interface between social and technical concerns. They have specifically sought more effective approaches to managing behavior in organizations. Among these, Chester I. Barnard, *The Functions of the Executive* (Cambridge: Harvard University Press, 1938), redirected studies of management away from a search for structural "principles" of organization to a focus on human behavior in organizations. In doing so, Barnard's work provided an important grounding for Simon's efforts, but also firmly established an interest in the task of management. Later studies have largely accepted this management focus. See, for example, the work on management styles by Rensis Likert, *New Patterns of Management* (New York: McGraw-Hill Book Company, 1961); Robert R. Blake and Jane S. Mouton, *The Managerial Grid* (Houston: Gulf Publishing Company, 1964); and Douglas McGregor, *The Human Side of Enterprise* (New York: McGraw-Hill Book Company, 1967). Works investigating the relationship between social and technical factors include Joan Woodward, *Industrial Organization* (London: Oxford University Press, 1965); Tom Burns and G. M. Stalker, *The Management of Innovation* (London: Tavistock Publications, 1961); and F. E. Emery and E. L. Trist, *Towards a Social Ecology* (London: Plenum Press, 1972). Closely related to this work is an increasing interest in the relationship between organizations and their environments. See, for example, Paul Lawrence and Jay Lorsch, *Organization and Environment* (Cambridge: Harvard University Press, 1967); and the work of the Aston group: D. S. Pugh and D. J. Hickson, *Organizational Structure in Its Context* (Lexington, Mass.: Lexington Books, 1976).

As Gibson Burrell and Gareth Morgan point out in their excellent review of work in organizational analysis, sociological contributions to the study of organizations have remained largely bound to a functionalist perspective, combining an interest in regulation rather than change with an objectivist or positivist interpretation of social science. See their *Sociological Paradigms and Organisational Analysis* (London: Heinemann, 1979). Among the major contributions by sociologists to the study of complex organizations are Philip Selznick, *Leadership in Administration* (New York: Harper and Row, Inc., 1957); Peter Blau, *The Dynamics of Bureaucracy*, 2nd rev. ed. (Chicago: University of Chicago Press, 1973); Amitai Etzioni, *A Comparative Analysis of Complex Organizations*, rev. ed. (New York: The Free Press, 1975); Charles Perrow, *Complex Organizations: A Critical Essay*, 2nd ed. (Glenview, Ill.: Scott, Foresman and Company, 1979). For an interesting critical perspective on sociological contributions to organizational analysis, see Chris Argyris, *The Applicability of Organizational Sociology* (New York: Cambridge University Press, 1972).

Argyris has been perhaps the leading organizational analyst combining a concern for management with an interest and background in social psychology. His early work largely centered on the integration of the individual and the organization and has been viewed as an important extension of earlier work in human relations. See, for example, *Person-*

ality and Organization (New York: Harper Bros., 1957); *Interpersonal Competence and Organizational Effectiveness* (Homewood, Ill.: The Dorsey Press, Inc., 1962); *Integrating the Individual and the Organization* (New York: John Wiley and Sons, 1964). More recently, Argyris and several others interested in social psychology have turned their attention primarily to organization development. See, for example, Warren G. Bennis, K. D. Benne, and R. Chin (eds.), *The Planning of Change* (New York: Holt, Rinehart and Winston, 1961); Chris Argyris and Donald A. Schon, *Theory in Practice* (San Francisco: Jossey-Bass Publishers, 1974). Among other works based in social psychology, Robert Presthus (a political scientist) developed an assessment of the impact of organizations on the personality structure of organizational members in *The Organizational Society* (New York: Vintage Books, 1962). See also Daniel Katz and Robert Kahn, *Social Psychology of Organizations* (New York: John Wiley and Sons, Inc., 1966); Karl Weick, *The Social Psychology of Organizing* (Reading, Mass.: Addison-Wesley Co., 1969). Again it must be pointed out that nearly all these writers—management theorists, sociologists, social psychologists, and political scientists—adopt a management perspective on organizational problems and a mainstream view of social science. Though there are clear differences among the theorists noted here, there are important similarities as well, similarities which coincide with the central concerns of the rational model of administration.

In contrast, a number of works have appeared over the years which view the bureaucratization of society from a more critical perspective, especially with respect to the impact of bureaucracy on the social structure. Among the earlier books examining the impact of organizations on society were Adolf A. Berle, Jr., and Gardner C. Means, *The Modern Corporation and Private Property* (New York: The Macmillan Co., 1934), James Burnham, *The Managerial Revolution* (New York: The John Day Co., 1941), and Kenneth Boulding, *The Organizational Revolution* (New York: Harper Brothers, 1953). Three more contemporary critiques of the impact of the growth of organizations on modern society are William G. Scott and David K. Hart, *Organizational America* (Boston: Houghton Mifflin Company, 1979); Ralph P. Hummell, *The Bureaucratic Experience* (New York: St. Martin's Press, 1977); and Frederick C. Thayer, *An End to Hierarchy! An End to Competition!* (New York: New Viewpoints, 1973). Two shorter works are also of interest: Orion White, *Psychic Energy and Organizational Change* (Beverly Hills: Sage Publications, 1973); William N. Dunn and Bahman Fozouni, *Toward a Critical Administrative Theory* (Beverly Hills: Sage Publications, 1976). In addition to these academic treatments of the organizational society, there have been a number of popular commentaries, ranging from William H. Whyte's *The Organization Man* (New York: Simon and Schuster, 1956), to novels such as Sloan Wilson's *The Man in the Grey Flannel Suit* (New York: Dell Publishing Co., 1955) and Joseph Heller's *Something Happened* (New York: Ballantine Books, 1974).

Our text draws significantly on literature in depth psychology, phenomenology, and critical theory. For this reason, an overview of works providing a grounding in these fields is appropriate. The term "depth psychology" has been increasingly used to refer to works in the psychoanalytic tradition that seek a relationship between the unconscious "depths" of the human psyche and the sources of meaning in modern life. This work has been well described in several quite readable books by Ira Progoff, most notably *The Death and Rebirth of Psychology* (New York: McGraw-Hill Book Company, 1956). In this survey, Progoff considers the work of Sigmund Freud, Alfred Adler, Carl Jung, and Otto Rank, concluding that a new kind of depth psychology is emerging, bringing together an understanding of the individual psyche and our search for spiritual meaning.

The original works by Freud that relate most clearly to an understanding of the relationship between the individual and society are *Civilization and Its Discontents* and *Group Psychology and the Ego*. Both are contained in *The Complete Works of Sigmund Freud* (London: Hogarth Press and the Institute of Psycho-analysis, 1950). Of course, the standard biographical reference concerning Freud's life and work is Ernest Jones, *The Life and Work of Sigmund Freud*, 3 vols. (New York: Basic Books, Inc., 1953). The "object relations" theorists have developed a further understanding of group processes, though their orientation would seem to implicitly support highly authoritarian group relationships. For selections of this work, see Arthur D. Colman and W. Harold Bexton (eds.), *Group Relations Reader* (Sausalito, Calif.: GREX, 1975).

In this work, we have given far greater attention to the work of Carl Jung and Otto Rank. Both were originally disciples of Freud, but both broke with Freud over theoretical differences. Jung felt that Freud placed too much emphasis on infantile sexuality, while failing to adequately account for the striving of the individual personality for future development. In contrast, Jung sought to develop an understanding of the process by which individuals seek "individuation" or wholeness. There are a number of excellent secondary texts which examine major aspects of Jung's work. Among those which are most direct and accessible are Edward C. Whitmont, *The Symbolic Quest* (New York: Harper and Row Publishers, 1969); June K. Singer, *Boundaries of the Soul* (Garden City, N.Y.: Doubleday and Company, Inc., 1972); Frances Wickes, *The Inner World of Choice* (Englewood Cliffs, N.J.: Prentice-Hall, Inc., 1976).

Several of Jung's own works provide a less technical introduction to his theories. Among these, an autobiography of Jung completed just a few years before his death is particularly interesting: *Memories, Dreams, and Reflections*, rev. ed., ed. by Aniela Jaffe, trans. by Richard and Clara Winston (New York: Vintage Books, 1965). Other works in a more popular vein include *The Undiscovered Self*, trans. by R. F. C. Hull (New York: New American Library, 1957), and *Man and His Symbols* (New York: Dell Publishing Co., Inc., 1964). The more technical works on which the interpretations contained here are based include *Two Essays in Analytical Psychology* (Princeton: Princeton University Press, 1966) and *Psychological Types* (Princeton: Princeton University Press, 1971).

As noted in the text, Rank broke with Freud over matters of "life and death," specifically holding that our attempts to achieve symbolic immortality underlie entire cultural systems. On this premise, Rank developed a remarkably complete and detailed social psychology, giving particular emphasis to the development of mythology and other symbolic systems. Rank felt that psychology itself had assumed a certain symbolic significance for modern individuals and that an effort to move past the limits which this modern system imposed was required. This theme is developed most fully in Rank's last work, *Beyond Psychology* (New York: Dover Publications, 1941). Other works of relevance to any consideration of creativity and heroism in the modern age include *Truth and Reality* (New York: Alfred A. Knopf, Inc., 1936) and *Psychology and the Soul* (Philadelphia: University of Pennsylvania Press, 1950). A set of selections from Rank's writings is contained in Otto Rank, *The Myth of the Birth of the Hero and Other Writings*, edited by Philip Freund (New York: Vintage Books, 1959). Recently, in the work of Ernest Becker, many of the themes prominent in Rank's work emerge in an extraordinary account of modern life—and death. Among Becker's books are *The Birth and Death of Meaning*, 2nd ed. (New York: The Free Press, 1971); *The Denial of Death* (New York: The Free Press, 1973); and *Escape from Evil* (New York: The Free Press, 1975).

In contrast to the mainstream view of social science as basically the same as natural science in its assumptions of objectivity and order, phenomenology suggests a more interpretive account of life, one centering on the intersubjective constitution of meaning structures. A good introduction to the works of Edmund Husserl, considered the "father" of phenomenology, is contained in Maurice Natanson, *Edmund Husserl: Philosopher of Infinite Tasks* (Evanston: Northwestern University Press, 1973). Social scientists interested in exploring phenomenology should be directed to the sociological work of Alfred Schutz, including *The Phenomenology of the Social World* (New York: Northwestern University Press, 1967). Useful introductions to phenomenology include Quentin Lauer, *Phenomenology: Its Genesis and Prospect* (New York: Harper and Row, 1965); William A. Luijpen and Henry J. Koren, *A First Introduction to Existential Phenomenology* (Pittsburgh: Duquesne University Press, 1969); George Psathas (ed.), *Phenomenological Sociology* (New York: John Wiley and Sons, 1973); and Richard M. Zaner, *The Way of Phenomenology* (New York: Pegasus, 1970).

What has come to be called the Frankfurt School of critical social theory began with the development of the Institute of Social Research at the University of Frankfurt in the 1920s. The development of the Frankfurt School has been chronicled by Martin Jay, *The Dialectical Imagination* (Boston: Little, Brown and Company, 1973). Over the years, the various members of the Frankfurt School, both in Germany and later in exile in the United States, treated subjects ranging from Marxism and psychoanalysis to aesthetics and mass culture. For statements of the basic positions around which members of the Frankfurt School came together, see Max Horkheimer, *Critical Theory: Selected Essays*, trans. by Matthew J. O'Connell and others (New York: The Seabury Press, 1971); Max Horkheimer, *Eclipse of Reason*, rev. ed. (New York: The Seabury Press, 1974). Among the members of the Frankfurt School of critical theory, Herbert Marcuse became best known in the United States. Marcuse's works of particular relevance to the present study include *Reason and Revolution* (New York: Oxford University Press, 1941); *One-Dimensional Man* (Boston: Beacon Press, 1964); *Eros and Civilization*, rev. ed. (Boston: Beacon Press, 1966); and *Negations* (Boston: Beacon Press, 1968). The last book contains an interesting exchange with Norman O. Brown, whose work is also relevant. See Norman O. Brown, *Life against Death* (Middletown, Conn.: Wesleyan University Press, 1959).

The most comprehensive contemporary statement of the critical position is found in the work of Jurgen Habermas. Habermas has undertaken the formidable project of reconstructing social history from a critical perspective in order to reveal those conflicts and contradictions which reside within existing patterns of social domination. In *Toward a Rational Society*, trans. by Jeremy J. Shapiro (Boston: Beacon Press, 1970), Habermas examines the "scientization" of politics in the modern age, specifically noting the tension between purposive-rational action and symbolic or communicative interaction. *Knowledge and Human Interests*, trans. by Jeremy J. Shapiro (Boston: Beacon Press, 1971), contains a radical critique of the bases for knowledge acquisition which have been developed in the context of Western philosophy. *Theory and Practice*, trans. by John Viertel (Boston: Beacon Press, 1973), contains a diverse set of essays tied together in an effort to achieve a better integration of theory and practice, a new sense of praxis in modern life; *Legitimation Crisis*, trans. by Thomas McCarthy (Boston: Beacon Press, 1975), examines certain crisis tendencies in advanced capitalistic societies; and *Communication and the Evolution of Society*, trans. by Thomas McCarthy (Boston: Beacon Press, 1979), contains a series of essays, including the latest statement of Habermas's effort to achieve a comprehensive theory of communicative competence or a "universal pragmatics."

The importance of Habermas's work should not be allowed to overshadow that of other theorists who share a critical perspective, including several who have raised concerns with Habermas's efforts. Among the more recent of these works, those which have been especially helpful here include Trent Schroyer, *The Critique of Domination* (Boston: Beacon Press, 1973); John O'Neill, *On Critical Theory* (New York: The Seabury Press, 1976); J. W. Freiberg (ed.), *Critical Sociology* (New York: Irvington Publishers, 1979); and William Leiss, *The Domination of Nature* (Boston: Beacon Press, 1974).

Finally, several recent works provide a comparative analysis of various approaches to knowledge acquisition. One especially lucid account of mainstream social science, phenomenology, language analysis, and critical theory is Richard J. Bernstein, *The Restructuring of Social and Political Theory* (New York: Harcourt, Brace, Jovanovich, 1976). See also Bernstein's *Praxis and Action* (Philadelphia: University of Pennsylvania Press, 1971). A similarly readable discussion of a number of these issues is contained in Brian Fay, *Social Theory and Political Practice* (London: George Allen and Unwin, 1975). See also Brian Fay, "How People Change Themselves," in Terence Ball (ed.), *Political Theory and Praxis* (Minneapolis: University of Minnesota Press, 1977), pp. 200–238. An interesting critique of contemporary psychology from the standpoint of critical theory is contained in Russell Jacoby, *Social Amnesia* (Boston: Beacon Press, 1975). Despite these excellent efforts, there remains a need to more fully integrate the findings of depth psychology and critical social theory so as to connect the individual's search for wholeness and the society's search for emancipation—that is, to relate individuation and praxis.

INDEX

Rave Reviews for John Green!

"What sets this novel apart is the brilliant, insightful, suffering but enduring voice of Miles Halter." *—Chicago Tribune* on *Looking for Alaska*

"Funny, sad, inspiring, and always compelling."

—Bookpage on *Looking for Alaska*

★ "Alive with sweet, self-deprecating humor . . . Like Phineas in John Knowles's *A Separate Peace*, Green draws Alaska . . . lovingly, in self-loathing darkness as well as energetic light." *—SLJ,* starred review of *Looking for Alaska*

"Stunning conclusion . . . one worthy of a book this good."

—Philadelphia Enquirer on *Looking for Alaska*

★ "Miles is an articulate spokesperson for the legions of teens searching for life meaning." *—BCCB,* starred review of *Looking for Alaska*

"The spirit of Holden Caulfield lives on." *—KLIATT* on *Looking for Alaska*

★ "What sings and soars in this gorgeously told tale is Green's mastery of language . . . Girls will cry and boys will find love, lust, loss and longing in Alaska's vanilla-and-cigarettes scent."

—Kirkus Reviews, starred review of *Looking for Alaska*

"Readers will only hope that this is not the last word from this promising new author." *—Publishers Weekly* on *Looking for Alaska*

"Damn near genius." *—TIME Magazine* on *The Fault in Our Stars*

"Funny . . . Poignant . . . Luminous."

—Entertainment Weekly on *The Fault in Our Stars*

"Green writes with empathy about some of the biggest questions there are— Why me? Why now? Why bother with love?—producing a story about two incandescent kids who will live a long time in the minds of the readers who come to know them."

—People, four out of four stars on *The Fault in Our Stars*

"Remarkable . . . A pitch perfect, elegiac comedy."

—USA Today, four out of four stars on *The Fault in Our Stars*

"A smarter, edgier *Love Story* for the Net Generation."

—Family Circle on *The Fault in Our Stars*

★ "In its every aspect, this novel is a triumph."

—*Booklist*, starred review of *The Fault in Our Stars*

★ ". . . an achingly beautiful story about life and loss."

—*SLJ*, starred review of *The Fault in Our Stars*

★ ". . . razor-sharp characters brim with genuine intellect, humor and desire."

—*Kirkus Reviews*, starred review of *The Fault in Our Stars*

★ ". . . [an] acerbic comedy, sexy romance, and a lightly played, extended meditation on the big questions about life and death."

—*The Horn Book*, starred review of *The Fault in Our Stars*

★ ". . . this is [Green's] best work yet."

—*Publishers Weekly*, starred review of *The Fault in Our Stars*

★ "Green's much-anticipated novel is breathtaking in its ability to alternate between iridescent humor and raw tragedy."

—*VOYA*, starred review of *The Fault in Our Stars*

"Funny, sweet, and unpredictable."

—*The Minneapolis Star Tribune* on *An Abundance of Katherines*

★ "Funny, fun, challengingly complex and entirely entertaining."

—*Kirkus Reviews*, starred review of *An Abundance of Katherines*

★ "Green follows his Printz-winning *Looking for Alaska* with another sharp, intelligent story. The laugh-out-loud humor ranges from delightfully sophomoric to subtly intellectual."

—*Booklist*, starred review of *An Abundance of Katherines*

★ "Laugh-out-loud funny . . . A coming-of-age American road trip that is at once a satire of and tribute to its many celebrated predecessors."

—*The Horn Book*, starred review of *An Abundance of Katherines*

"Enjoyable, witty, and even charming."   —*SLJ* on *An Abundance of Katherines*

★ "Green's prose is astounding—from hilarious, hyperintellectual trash talk and shtick, to complex philosophizing, to devastating observation and truths. He nails it—exactly how a thing feels, looks, affects—page after page."

—*SLJ*, starred review of *Paper Towns*

★ "Green ponders the interconnectedness of imagination and perception . . . he is not only clever and wonderfully witty but also deeply thoughtful and insightful."   —*Booklist*, starred review of *Paper Towns*

"Green knows what he does best and delivers once again with this satisfying, crowd-pleasing [book]." —*Kirkus Reviews* on *Paper Towns*

★ "[A] terrific high-energy tale of teen love, lust, intrigue, anger, pain, and friendship." —*Booklist*, starred review of *Will Grayson, Will Grayson*

★ "Complete with honest language, interesting characters, and a heartfelt, gritty edge, this quirky yet down-to-earth collaboration by two master YA storytellers will keep readers turning pages."
—*SLJ*, starred review of *Will Grayson, Will Grayson*

★ "An intellectually existential, electrically ebullient love story that brilliantly melds the ridiculous with the realistic."
—*Kirkus Reviews*, starred review of *Will Grayson, Will Grayson*

"Funny, rude and original."
—*The New York Times Book Review* on *Will Grayson, Will Grayson*

"A comedy as delicious as any whipped up by the Bard."
—*Washington Post Book World* on *Let It Snow*

"There is plenty of physical humor for laugh-out-loud fun and enough dreamy romance to warm up those cold winter nights." —*VOYA* on *Let It Snow*

"This is a great story illuminating the magic of the holidays and the strengths and weaknesses of friendships." —*KLIATT* on *Let It Snow*

"The authors share an ironic, idiosyncratic sense of humor that helps bind their stories, each with a slightly different tone and take on love, into one interconnected volume brimming with romance and holiday spirit."
—*The Horn Book* on *Let It Snow*

Books by John Green

Looking for Alaska
An Abundance of Katherines
Paper Towns
The Fault in Our Stars

Let it Snow
(with Maureen Johnson and Lauren Myracle)
Will Grayson, Will Grayson
(with David Levithan)

looking for alaska

JOHN GREEN

speak
An Imprint of Penguin Group (USA) Inc.

Pages 18–19 and 155: Excerpt from *The General in His Labyrinth*,
by Gabriel García Márquez
Page 85: Poetry quote from "As I Walked Out One Evening," by W. H. Auden
Page 89: Poetry quote from "Not So Far as the Forest," by Edna St. Vincent Millay

SPEAK

Penguin Group (USA) Inc., 345 Hudson Street, New York, New York 10014, U.S.A.
Penguin Group (Canada), 90 Eglinton Avenue East, Suite 700,
Toronto, Ontario M4P 2Y3, Canada (a division of Pearson Penguin Canada Inc.)
Penguin Books Ltd, 80 Strand, London WC2R 0RL, England
Penguin Ireland, 25 St Stephen's Green, Dublin 2, Ireland (a division of Penguin Books Ltd)
Penguin Group (Australia), 707 Collins Street, Melbourne, Victoria 3008, Australia
(a division of Pearson Australia Group Pty Ltd)
Penguin Books India Pvt Ltd, 11 Community Centre,
Panchsheel Park, New Delhi–110 017, India
Penguin Group (NZ), 67 Apollo Drive, Rosedale, Auckland 0632, New Zealand
(a division of Pearson New Zealand Ltd)
Penguin Books, Rosebank Office Park, 181 Jan Smuts Avenue,
Parktown North 2193, South Africa
Penguin China, B7 Jiaming Center, 27 East Third Ring Road North,
Chaoyang District, Beijing 100020, China

Registered Offices: Penguin Books Ltd, 80 Strand, London WC2R 0RL, England

First published in the United States of America by Dutton Books,
a member of Penguin Group (USA) Inc., 2005
Published by Speak, an imprint of Penguin Group (USA) Inc., 2007, 2012

50 49 48 47 46 45 44 43 42 41

THE LIBRARY OF CONGRESS HAS CATALOGED THE DUTTON EDITION AS FOLLOWS:

Green, John.
Looking for Alaska / John Green.—1st ed.
p. cm.
Summary: Sixteen-year-old Miles' first year at Culver Creek Preparatory School in Alabama
includes good friends and great pranks, but is defined by the search for answers about life and
death after a fatal car crash.
ISBN 0-525-47506-0
[1. Interpersonal relations—Fiction. 2. Boarding schools—Fiction.
3. Schools—Fiction. 4. Death—Fiction.] I. Title.
PZ7.G8233Lo 2005
[Fic]—dc22 2004010827

Speak ISBN 978-0-14-240251-1

Designed by Irene Vandervoort

Printed in the United States of America

To my family: Sydney Green, Mike Green, and Hank Green
"I have tried so hard to do right."
(last words of President Grover Cleveland)

acknowledgments

USING SMALL TYPE that does not reflect the size of my debt, I need to acknowledge some things:

First, that this book would have been utterly impossible if not for the extraordinary kindness of my friend, editor, quasi-agent, and mentor, Ilene Cooper. Ilene is like a fairy godmother, only real, and also better dressed.

Second, that I am amazingly fortunate to have Julie Strauss-Gabel as my editor at Dutton, and even luckier to have become her friend. Julie is every writer's dream editor: caring, passionate, and inarguably brilliant. This right here, her acknowledgment, is the one thing in the whole book she couldn't edit, and I think we can agree it suffered as a result.

Third, that Donna Brooks believed in this story from the beginning and did much to shape it. I'm also indebted to Margaret Woollatt of Dutton, whose name contains too many consonants but who is a really top-notch person. And thanks as well to the talented Sarah Shumway, whose careful reading and astute comments were a blessing to me.

Fourth, that I am very grateful to my agent, Rosemary Sandberg, who is a tireless advocate for her authors. Also, she is British. She says "Cheers" when she means to say "Later." How great is that?

Fifth, that the comments of my two best friends in the entire world, Dean Simakis and Will Hickman, were essential to the writing and revision of this story, and that I, uh, you know, love them.

Sixth, that I am indebted to, among many others, Shannon James (roommate), Katie Else (I promised), Hassan Arawas (friend), Braxton Goodrich (cousin), Mike Goodrich (lawyer, and also cousin), Daniel Biss (professional mathematician), Giordana Segneri (friend), Jenny Lawton (long story), David Rojas and Molly Hammond (friends), Bill Ott (role model), Amy Krouse Rosenthal (got me on the radio), Stephanie Zvirin (gave me my first real job), P. F. Kluge (teacher), Diane Martin (teacher), Perry Lentz (teacher), Don Rogan (teacher), Paul MacAdam (teacher—I am a big fan of teachers), Ben Segedin (boss and friend), and the lovely Sarah Urist.

Seventh, that I attended high school with a wonderful bunch of people. I would like to particularly thank the indomitable Todd Cartee and also Olga Charny, Sean Titone, Emmett Cloud, Daniel Alarcon, Jennifer Jenkins, Chip Dunkin, and MLS.

before

THE WEEK BEFORE I left my family and Florida and the rest of my minor life to go to boarding school in Alabama, my mother insisted on throwing me a going-away party. To say that I had low expectations would be to underestimate the matter dramatically. Although I was more or less forced to invite all my "school friends," i.e., the ragtag bunch of drama people and English geeks I sat with by social necessity in the cavernous cafeteria of my public school, I knew they wouldn't come. Still, my mother persevered, awash in the delusion that I had kept my popularity secret from her all these years. She cooked a small mountain of artichoke dip. She festooned our living room in green and yellow streamers, the colors of my new school. She bought two dozen champagne poppers and placed them around the edge of our coffee table.

And when that final Friday came, when my packing was mostly done, she sat with my dad and me on the living-room couch at 4:56 P.M. and patiently awaited the arrival of the Good-bye to Miles

Cavalry. Said cavalry consisted of exactly two people: Marie Lawson, a tiny blonde with rectangular glasses, and her chunky (to put it charitably) boyfriend, Will.

"Hey, Miles," Marie said as she sat down.

"Hey," I said.

"How was your summer?" Will asked.

"Okay. Yours?"

"Good. We did *Jesus Christ Superstar*. I helped with the sets. Marie did lights," said Will.

"That's cool." I nodded knowingly, and that about exhausted our conversational topics. I might have asked a question about *Jesus Christ Superstar*, except that 1. I didn't know what it was, and 2. I didn't care to learn, and 3. I never really excelled at small talk. My mom, however, can talk small for hours, and so she extended the awkwardness by asking them about their rehearsal schedule, and how the show had gone, and whether it was a success.

"I guess it was," Marie said. "A lot of people came, I guess." Marie was the sort of person to guess a lot.

Finally, Will said, "Well, we just dropped by to say good-bye. I've got to get Marie home by six. Have fun at boarding school, Miles."

"Thanks," I answered, relieved. The only thing worse than having a party that no one attends is having a party attended only by two vastly, deeply uninteresting people.

They left, and so I sat with my parents and stared at the blank TV and wanted to turn it on but knew I shouldn't. I could feel them both looking at me, waiting for me to burst into tears or something, as if I hadn't known all along that it would go precisely like this. But I *had* known. I could feel their pity as they scooped artichoke dip with chips intended for my imaginary friends, but they needed pity more than I did: I wasn't disappointed. My expectations had been met.

"Is this why you want to leave, Miles?" Mom asked.

I mulled it over for a moment, careful not to look at her. "Uh, no," I said.

"Well, why then?" she asked. This was not the first time she had posed the question. Mom was not particularly keen on letting me go to boarding school and had made no secret of it.

"Because of me?" my dad asked. He had attended Culver Creek, the same boarding school to which I was headed, as had both of his brothers and all of their kids. I think he liked the idea of me following in his footsteps. My uncles had told me stories about how famous my dad had been on campus for having simultaneously raised hell and aced all his classes. That sounded like a better life than the one I had in Florida. But no, it wasn't because of Dad. Not exactly.

"Hold on," I said. I went into Dad's study and found his biography of François Rabelais. I liked reading biographies of writers, even if (as was the case with Monsieur Rabelais) I'd never read any of their actual writing. I flipped to the back and found the highlighted quote ("NEVER USE A HIGHLIGHTER IN MY BOOKS," my dad had told me a thousand times. But how else are you supposed to find what you're looking for?).

"So this guy," I said, standing in the doorway of the living room. "François Rabelais. He was this poet. And his last words were 'I go to seek a Great Perhaps.' That's why I'm going. So I don't have to wait until I die to start seeking a Great Perhaps."

And that quieted them. I was after a Great Perhaps, and they knew as well as I did that I wasn't going to find it with the likes of Will and Marie. I sat back down on the couch, between my mom and my dad, and my dad put his arm around me, and we stayed there like that, quiet on the couch together, for a long time, until it seemed okay to turn on the TV, and then we ate artichoke dip for dinner and watched the History Channel, and as going-away parties go, it certainly could have been worse.

FLORIDA WAS PLENTY HOT, certainly, and humid, too. Hot enough that your clothes stuck to you like Scotch tape, and sweat dripped like tears from your forehead into your eyes. But it was only hot outside, and generally I only went outside to walk from one air-conditioned location to another.

This did not prepare me for the unique sort of heat that one encounters fifteen miles south of Birmingham, Alabama, at Culver Creek Preparatory School. My parents' SUV was parked in the grass just a few feet outside my dorm room, Room 43. But each time I took those few steps to and from the car to unload what now seemed like far too much stuff, the sun burned through my clothes and into my skin with a vicious ferocity that made me genuinely fear hellfire.

Between Mom and Dad and me, it only took a few minutes to unload the car, but my unair-conditioned dorm room, although blessedly out of the sunshine, was only modestly cooler. The room surprised me: I'd pictured plush carpet, wood-paneled walls, Victorian furniture. Aside from one luxury—a private bathroom—I got a box. With cinder-block walls coated thick with layers of white paint and a green-and-white-checkered linoleum floor, the place looked more like a hospital than the dorm room of my fantasies. A bunk bed of unfinished wood with vinyl mattresses was pushed against the room's back window. The desks and dressers and bookshelves were all attached to the walls in order to prevent creative floor planning. *And no air-conditioning*.

I sat on the lower bunk while Mom opened the trunk, grabbed a stack of the biographies my dad had agreed to part with, and placed them on the bookshelves.

"I can unpack, Mom," I said. My dad stood. He was ready to go.

"Let me at least make your bed," Mom said.

"No, really. I can do it. It's okay." Because you simply cannot draw these things out forever. At some point, you just pull off the Band-Aid and it hurts, but then it's over and you're relieved.

"God, we'll miss you," Mom said suddenly, stepping through the minefield of suitcases to get to the bed. I stood and hugged her. My dad walked over, too, and we formed a sort of huddle. It was too hot, and we were too sweaty, for the hug to last terribly long. I knew I ought to cry, but I'd lived with my parents for sixteen years, and a trial separation seemed overdue.

"Don't worry." I smiled. "I's a-gonna learn how t'talk right Southern." Mom laughed.

"Don't do anything stupid," my dad said.

"Okay."

"No drugs. No drinking. No cigarettes." As an alumnus of Culver Creek, he had done the things I had only heard about: the secret parties, streaking through hay fields (he always whined about how it was all boys back then), drugs, drinking, and cigarettes. It had taken him a while to kick smoking, but his badass days were now well behind him.

"I love you," they both blurted out simultaneously. It needed to be said, but the words made the whole thing horribly uncomfortable, like watching your grandparents kiss.

"I love you, too. I'll call every Sunday." Our rooms had no phone lines, but my parents had requested I be placed in a room near one of Culver Creek's five pay phones.

They hugged me again—Mom, then Dad—and it was over. Out the back window, I watched them drive the winding road off campus. I should have felt a gooey, sentimental sadness, perhaps. But mostly I just wanted to cool off, so I grabbed one of the desk chairs and sat down outside my door in the shade of the overhanging eaves, waiting for a breeze that never arrived. The air outside sat as still and oppressive as the air inside. I stared out over my new digs: Six one-story buildings, each with sixteen dorm rooms, were arranged in a hexagram around a large circle of grass. It looked like an oversize old motel. Everywhere, boys and girls hugged and smiled and walked together. I vaguely hoped that someone would come up and talk to me. I imagined the conversation:

"Hey. Is this your first year?"

"Yeah. Yeah. I'm from Florida."

"That's cool. So you're used to the heat."

"I wouldn't be used to this heat if I were from Hades," I'd joke. I'd make a good first impression. *Oh, he's funny. That guy Miles is a riot.*

That didn't happen, of course. Things never happened like I imagined them.

Bored, I went back inside, took off my shirt, lay down on the heat-soaked vinyl of the lower bunk mattress, and closed my eyes. I'd never been born again with the baptism and weeping and all that, but it couldn't feel much better than being born again as a guy with no known past. I thought of the people I'd read about—John F. Kennedy, James Joyce, Humphrey Bogart—who went to boarding school, and their adventures—Kennedy, for example, loved pranks. I thought of the Great Perhaps and the things that might happen and the people I might meet and who my roommate might be (I'd gotten a letter a few weeks before that gave me his name, Chip Martin, but no other information). Whoever Chip Martin was, I hoped to God he would bring an arsenal of high-powered fans, because I hadn't packed even one, and I could already feel my sweat pooling on the vinyl mattress, which disgusted me so much that I stopped thinking and got off my ass to find a towel to wipe up the sweat with. And then I thought, *Well, before the adventure comes the unpacking.*

I managed to tape a map of the world to the wall and get most of my clothes into drawers before I noticed that the hot, moist air made even the walls sweat, and I decided that now was not the time for manual labor. Now was the time for a magnificently cold shower.

The small bathroom contained a huge, full-length mirror behind the door, and so I could not escape the reflection of my naked self as I leaned in to turn on the shower faucet. My skinniness always surprised me: My thin arms didn't seem to get much bigger as they moved from wrist to shoulder, my chest lacked any hint of either fat or muscle, and I felt embarrassed and wondered if something could be done about the mirror. I pulled open the plain white shower curtain and ducked into the stall.

Unfortunately, the shower seemed to have been designed for someone approximately three feet, seven inches tall, so the cold water hit my lower rib cage—with all the force of a dripping faucet. To wet my sweat-soaked face, I had to spread my legs and squat significantly. Surely, John F. Kennedy (who was six feet tall according to his biography, my height exactly) did not have to *squat* at *his* boarding school. No, this was a different beast entirely, and as the dribbling shower slowly soaked my body, I wondered whether I could find a Great Perhaps here at all or whether I had made a grand miscalculation.

When I opened the bathroom door after my shower, a towel wrapped around my waist, I saw a short, muscular guy with a shock of brown hair. He was hauling a gigantic army-green duffel bag through the door of my room. He stood five feet and nothing, but was well-built, like a scale model of Adonis, and with him arrived the stink of stale cigarette smoke. *Great*, I thought. *I'm meeting my roommate naked*. He heaved the duffel into the room, closed the door, and walked over to me.

"I'm Chip Martin," he announced in a deep voice, the voice of a radio deejay. Before I could respond, he added, "I'd shake your hand, but I think you should hold on damn tight to that towel till you can get some clothes on."

I laughed and nodded my head at him (that's cool, right? the nod?) and said, "I'm Miles Halter. Nice to meet you."

"Miles, as in 'to go before I sleep'?" he asked me.

"Huh?"

"It's a Robert Frost poem. You've never read him?"

I shook my head no.

"Consider yourself lucky." He smiled.

I grabbed some clean underwear, a pair of blue Adidas soccer shorts, and a white T-shirt, mumbled that I'd be back in a second, and ducked back into the bathroom. So much for a good first impression.

"So where are your parents?" I asked from the bathroom.

"My parents? The father's in California right now. Maybe sitting in his La-Z-Boy. Maybe driving his truck. Either way, he's drinking. My mother is probably just now turning off campus."

"Oh," I said, dressed now, not sure how to respond to such personal information. I shouldn't have asked, I guess, if I didn't want to know.

Chip grabbed some sheets and tossed them onto the top bunk. "I'm a top bunk man. Hope that doesn't bother you."

"Uh, no. Whatever is fine."

"I see you've decorated the place," he said, gesturing toward the world map. "I like it."

And then he started naming countries. He spoke in a monotone, as if he'd done it a thousand times before.

Afghanistan.

Albania.

Algeria.

American Samoa.

Andorra.

And so on. He got through the A's before looking up and noticing my incredulous stare.

"I could do the rest, but it'd probably bore you. Something I learned over the summer. God, you can't imagine how boring New Hope, Alabama, is in the summertime. Like watching soybeans grow. Where are you from, by the way?"

"Florida," I said.

"Never been."

"That's pretty amazing, the countries thing," I said.

"Yeah, everybody's got a talent. I can memorize things. And you can . . . ?"

"Um, I know a lot of people's last words." It was an indulgence, learning last words. Other people had chocolate; I had dying declarations.

"Example?"

"I like Henrik Ibsen's. He was a playwright." I knew a lot about Ibsen, but I'd never read any of his plays. I didn't like reading plays. I liked reading biographies.

"Yeah, I know who he was," said Chip.

"Right, well, he'd been sick for a while and his nurse said to him, 'You seem to be feeling better this morning,' and Ibsen looked at her and said, 'On the contrary,' and then he died."

Chip laughed. "That's morbid. But I like it."

He told me he was in his third year at Culver Creek. He had started in ninth grade, the first year at the school, and was now a junior like me. A scholarship kid, he said. Got a full ride. He'd heard it was the best school in Alabama, so he wrote his application essay about how he wanted to go to a school where he could read long books. The problem, he said in the essay, was that his dad would always hit him with the books in his house, so Chip kept his books short and paperback for his own safety. His parents got divorced his sophomore year. He liked "the Creek," as he called it, but "You have to be careful here, with students and with teachers. And I do hate being careful." He smirked. I hated being careful, too—or wanted to, at least.

He told me this while ripping through his duffel bag, throwing clothes into drawers with reckless abandon. Chip did not believe in having a sock drawer or a T-shirt drawer. He believed that all drawers were created equal and filled each with whatever fit. My mother would have died.

As soon as he finished "unpacking," Chip hit me roughly on the shoulder, said, "I hope you're stronger than you look," and walked out the door, leaving it open behind him. He peeked his head back in a few seconds later and saw me standing still. "Well, come on, Miles To Go Halter. We got shit to do."

We made our way to the TV room, which according to Chip contained the only cable TV on campus. Over the summer, it served as a storage unit. Packed nearly to the ceiling with couches, fridges, and rolled-up carpets, the TV room undulated with kids trying to find and haul away their stuff. Chip said hello to a few people but didn't introduce me. As he wandered through the couch-stocked maze, I stood near the room's entrance, trying my best not to block pairs of roommates as they maneuvered furniture through the narrow front door.

It took ten minutes for Chip to find his stuff, and an hour more for us to make four trips back and forth across the dorm circle between the TV room and Room 43. By the end, I wanted to crawl into Chip's minifridge and sleep for a thousand years, but Chip seemed immune to both fatigue and heatstroke. I sat down on his couch.

"I found it lying on a curb in my neighborhood a couple years ago," he said of the couch as he worked on setting up my Play-Station 2 on top of his footlocker. "I know the leather's got some cracks, but come on. That's a damn nice couch." The leather had more than a few cracks—it was about 30 percent baby blue faux leather and 70 percent foam—but it felt damn good to me anyway.

"All right," he said. "We're about done." He walked over to his desk and pulled a roll of duct tape from a drawer. "We just need your trunk."

I got up, pulled the trunk out from under the bed, and Chip situated it between the couch and the PlayStation 2 and started tearing off thin strips of duct tape. He applied them to the trunk so that they spelled out COFFEE TABLE.

"There," he said. He sat down and put his feet up on the, uh, coffee table. "Done."

I sat down next to him, and he looked over at me and suddenly said, "Listen. I'm not going to be your entrée to Culver Creek social life."

"Uh, okay," I said, but I could hear the words catch in my throat. I'd just carried this guy's couch beneath a white-hot sun and now he didn't like me?

"Basically you've got two groups here," he explained, speaking with increasing urgency. "You've got the regular boarders, like me, and then you've got the Weekday Warriors; they board here, but they're all rich kids who live in Birmingham and go home to their parents' air-conditioned mansions every weekend. Those are the cool kids. I don't like them, and they don't like me, and so if you came here thinking that you were hot shit at public school so you'll be hot shit here, you'd best not be seen with me. You did go to public school, didn't you?"

"Uh . . ." I said. Absentmindedly, I began picking at the cracks in the couch's leather, digging my fingers into the foamy whiteness.

"Right, you did, probably, because if you had gone to a private school your freakin' shorts would fit." He laughed.

I wore my shorts just below my hips, which I thought was cool. Finally I said, "Yeah, I went to public school. But I wasn't hot shit there, Chip. I was regular shit."

"Ha! That's good. And don't call me Chip. Call me the Colonel."

I stifled a laugh. "The *Colonel?*"

"Yeah. The Colonel. And we'll call you . . . hmm. Pudge."

"Huh?"

"Pudge," the Colonel said. "Because you're skinny. It's called irony, Pudge. Heard of it? Now, let's go get some cigarettes and start this year off right."

He walked out of the room, again just assuming I'd follow, and this time I did. Mercifully, the sun was descending toward the horizon. We walked five doors down to Room 48. A dry-erase board was taped to the door using duct tape. In blue marker, it read: *Alaska has a single!*

The Colonel explained to me that *1.* this was Alaska's room, and that *2.* she had a single room because the girl who was supposed to be her roommate got kicked out at the end of last year, and that *3.* Alaska had cigarettes, although the Colonel neglected to ask whether *4.* I smoked, which *5.* I didn't.

He knocked once, loudly. Through the door, a voice screamed, "Oh my God come in you short little man because I have the best story."

We walked in. I turned to close the door behind me, and the Colonel shook his head and said, "After seven, you have to leave the door open if you're in a girl's room," but I barely heard him because the hottest girl in all of human history was standing before me in cutoff jeans and a peach tank top. And she was talking over the Colonel, talking loud and fast.

"So first day of summer, I'm in grand old Vine Station with this boy named Justin and we're at his house watching TV on the couch—and mind you, I'm already dating Jake—actually I'm still dating him, miraculously enough, but Justin is a friend of mine from when I was a kid and so we're watching TV and literally chatting about the SATs or something, and Justin puts his arm around me and I think, *Oh that's nice, we've been friends for so long and this is totally comfortable*, and we're just chatting and then I'm in the middle of a sentence about analogies or something and like a hawk he reaches down and he honks my boob. *HONK*. A much-too-firm, two- to three-second *HONK*. And the first thing I thought was *Okay, how do I extricate this claw from my boob before it leaves permanent marks?* and the second thing I thought was *God, I can't wait to tell Takumi and the Colonel*."

The Colonel laughed. I stared, stunned partly by the force of the voice emanating from the petite (but God, curvy) girl and partly by the gigantic stacks of books that lined her walls. Her library filled her bookshelves and then overflowed into waist-high stacks of books everywhere, piled haphazardly against the walls. If just one of them moved, I thought, the domino effect could engulf the three of us in an asphyxiating mass of literature.

"Who's the guy that's not laughing at my very funny story?" she asked.

"Oh, right. Alaska, this is Pudge. Pudge memorizes people's last words. Pudge, this is Alaska. She got her boob honked over the summer." She walked over to me with her hand extended, then made a quick move downward at the last moment and pulled down my shorts.

"Those are the biggest shorts in the state of Alabama!"

"I like them baggy," I said, embarrassed, and pulled them up. They had been cool back home in Florida.

"So far in our relationship, Pudge, I've seen your chicken legs entirely too often," the Colonel deadpanned. "So, Alaska. Sell us some cigarettes." And then somehow, the Colonel talked me into paying five dollars for a pack of Marlboro Lights I had no intention of ever smoking. He asked Alaska to join us, but she said, "I have to find Takumi and tell him about The Honk." She turned to me and asked, "Have you seen him?" I had no idea whether I'd seen Takumi, since I had no idea who he was. I just shook my head.

"All right. Meet ya at the lake in a few minutes, then." The Colonel nodded.

At the edge of the lake, just before the sandy (and, the Colonel told me, fake) beach, we sat down in an Adirondack swing. I made the obligatory joke: "Don't grab my boob." The Colonel gave an obligatory laugh, then asked, "Want a smoke?" I had never smoked a cigarette, but when in Rome . . .

"Is it safe here?"

"Not really," he said, then lit a cigarette and handed it to me. I inhaled. Coughed. Wheezed. Gasped for breath. Coughed again. Considered vomiting. Grabbed the swinging bench, head spinning, and threw the cigarette to the ground and stomped on it, convinced my Great Perhaps did not involve cigarettes.

"Smoke much?" He laughed, then pointed to a white speck across the lake and said, "See that?"

"Yeah," I said. "What is that? A bird?"

"It's the swan," he said.

"Wow. A school with a swan. Wow."

"That swan is the spawn of Satan. Never get closer to it than we are now."

"Why?"

"It has some issues with people. It was abused or something. It'll rip you to pieces. The Eagle put it there to keep us from walking around the lake to smoke."

"The Eagle?"

"Mr. Starnes. Code name: the Eagle. The dean of students. Most of the teachers live on campus, and they'll all bust you. But only the Eagle lives in the dorm circle, and he sees all. He can smell a cigarette from like five miles."

"Isn't his house back there?" I asked, pointing to it. I could see the house quite clearly despite the darkness, so it followed he could probably see us.

"Yeah, but he doesn't really go into blitzkrieg mode until classes start," Chip said nonchalantly.

"God, if I get in trouble my parents will kill me," I said.

"I suspect you're exaggerating. But look, you're going to get in trouble. Ninety-nine percent of the time, your parents never have to know, though. The school doesn't want your parents to think you became a fuckup here any more than *you* want your parents to think you're a fuckup." He blew a thin stream of smoke forcefully toward the lake. I had to admit: He looked cool doing it. Taller, somehow. "Anyway, when you get in trouble, just don't tell on anyone. I mean, I hate the rich snots here with a fervent passion I usually reserve only for dental work and my father. But that doesn't mean I would rat them out. Pretty much the only important thing is never never never never rat."

"Okay," I said, although I wondered: *If someone punches me in the face, I'm supposed to insist that I ran into a door?* It seemed a little stupid. How do you deal with bullies and assholes if you can't get them into trouble? I didn't ask Chip, though.

"All right, Pudge. We have reached the point in the evening when I'm obliged to go and find my girlfriend. So give me a few of those cigarettes you'll never smoke anyway, and I'll see you later."

I decided to hang out on the swing for a while, half because the heat had finally dissipated into a pleasant, if muggy, eighty-something, and half because I thought Alaska might show up. But almost as soon as the Colonel left, the bugs encroached: no-see-ums (which, for the record, you can see) and mosquitoes hovered around me in such numbers that the tiny noise of their rubbing wings sounded cacophonous. And then I decided to smoke.

Now, I did think, *The smoke will drive the bugs away.* And, to some degree, it did. I'd be lying, though, if I claimed I became a smoker to ward off insects. I became a smoker because *1.* I was on an Adirondack swing by myself, and *2.* I had cigarettes, and *3.* I figured that if everyone else could smoke a cigarette without coughing, I could damn well, too. In short, I didn't have a very good reason. So yeah, let's just say that *4.* it was the bugs.

I made it through three entire drags before I felt nauseous and dizzy and only semipleasantly buzzed. I got up to leave. As I stood, a voice behind me said:

"So do you really memorize last words?"

She ran up beside me and grabbed my shoulder and pushed me back onto the porch swing.

"Yeah," I said. And then hesitantly, I added, "You want to quiz me?"

"JFK," she said.

"That's obvious," I answered.

"Oh, is it now?" she asked.

"No. Those were his last words. Someone said, 'Mr. President, you can't say Dallas doesn't love you,' and then he said, 'That's obvious,' and then he got shot."

She laughed. "God, that's awful. I shouldn't laugh. But I will," and then she laughed again. "Okay, Mr. Famous Last Words Boy. I have one for you." She reached into her overstuffed backpack and pulled out a book. "Gabriel García Márquez. *The General in His Labyrinth*. Absolutely one of my favorites. It's about Simón Bolívar." I didn't know who Simón Bolívar was, but she didn't give me time to ask. "It's a historical novel, so I don't know if this is true, but in the book, do you know what his last words are? No, you don't. But I am about to tell you, Señor Parting Remarks."

And then she lit a cigarette and sucked on it so hard for so long that I thought the entire thing might burn off in one drag. She exhaled and read to me:

"'He'—that's Simón Bolívar—'was shaken by the overwhelming

revelation that the headlong race between his misfortunes and his dreams was at that moment reaching the finish line. The rest was darkness. "Damn it," he sighed. "How will I ever get out of this labyrinth!"''"

I knew great last words when I heard them, and I made a mental note to get ahold of a biography of this Simón Bolívar fellow. Beautiful last words, but I didn't quite understand. "So what's the labyrinth?" I asked her.

And now is as good a time as any to say that she was beautiful. In the dark beside me, she smelled of sweat and sunshine and vanilla, and on that thin-mooned night I could see little more than her silhouette except for when she smoked, when the burning cherry of the cigarette washed her face in pale red light. But even in the dark, I could see her eyes—fierce emeralds. She had the kind of eyes that predisposed you to supporting her every endeavor. And not just beautiful, but hot, too, with her breasts straining against her tight tank top, her curved legs swinging back and forth beneath the swing, flip-flops dangling from her electric-blue-painted toes. It was right then, between when I asked about the labyrinth and when she answered me, that I realized the *importance* of curves, of the thousand places where girls' bodies ease from one place to another, from arc of the foot to ankle to calf, from calf to hip to waist to breast to neck to ski-slope nose to forehead to shoulder to the concave arch of the back to the butt to the etc. I'd *noticed* curves before, of course, but I had never quite apprehended their significance.

Her mouth close enough to me that I could feel her breath warmer than the air, she said, "That's the mystery, isn't it? Is the labyrinth living or dying? Which is he trying to escape—the world or the end of it?" I waited for her to keep talking, but after a while it became obvious she wanted an answer.

"Uh, I don't know," I said finally. "Have you really read all those books in your room?"

She laughed. "Oh God no. I've maybe read a third of 'em. But I'm *going to* read them all. I call it my Life's Library. Every summer since I was little, I've gone to garage sales and bought all the books that looked interesting. So I always have something to read. But there is so much to do: cigarettes to smoke, sex to have, swings to swing on. I'll have more time for reading when I'm old and boring."

She told me that I reminded her of the Colonel when he came to Culver Creek. They were freshmen together, she said, both scholarship kids with, as she put it, "a shared interest in booze and mischief." The phrase *booze and mischief* left me worrying I'd stumbled into what my mother referred to as "the wrong crowd," but for the wrong crowd, they both seemed awfully smart. As she lit a new cigarette off the butt of her previous one, she told me that the Colonel was smart but hadn't done much living when he got to the Creek.

"I got rid of that problem quickly." She smiled. "By November, I'd gotten him his first girlfriend, a perfectly nice non–Weekday Warrior named Janice. He dumped her after a month because she was too rich for his poverty-soaked blood, but whatever. We pulled our first prank that year—we filled Classroom 4 with a thin layer of marbles. We've progressed some since then, of course." She laughed. So Chip became the Colonel—the military-style planner of their pranks, and Alaska was ever Alaska, the larger-than-life creative force behind them.

"You're smart like him," she said. "Quieter, though. And cuter, but I didn't even just say that, because I love my boyfriend."

"Yeah, you're not bad either," I said, overwhelmed by her compliment. "But I didn't just say that, because I love my girlfriend. Oh, wait. Right. I don't have one."

She laughed. "Yeah, don't worry, Pudge. If there's one thing I can get you, it's a girlfriend. Let's make a deal: You figure out what the labyrinth is and how to get out of it, and I'll get you laid."

"Deal." We shook on it.

Later, I walked toward the dorm circle beside Alaska. The cicadas hummed their one-note song, just as they had at home in Florida. She turned to me as we made our way through the darkness and said, "When you're walking at night, do you ever get creeped out and even though it's silly and embarrassing you just want to run home?"

It seemed too secret and personal to admit to a virtual stranger, but I told her, "Yeah, totally."

For a moment, she was quiet. Then she grabbed my hand, whispered, "Run run run run run," and took off, pulling me behind her.

one hundred twenty-seven days before

EARLY THE NEXT AFTERNOON, I blinked sweat from my eyes as I taped a van Gogh poster to the back of the door. The Colonel sat on the couch judging whether the poster was level and fielding my endless questions about Alaska. *What's her story?* "She's from Vine Station. You could drive past it without noticing—and from what I understand, you ought to. Her boyfriend's at Vanderbilt on scholarship. Plays bass in some band. Don't know much about her family." *So she really likes him?* "I guess. She hasn't cheated on him, which is a first." And so on. All morning, I'd been unable to care about anything else, not the van Gogh poster and not video games and not even my class schedule, which the Eagle had brought by that morning. He introduced himself, too:

"Welcome to Culver Creek, Mr. Halter. You're given a large measure of freedom here. If you abuse it, you'll regret it. You seem like a nice young man. I'd hate to have to bid you farewell."

And then he stared at me in a manner that was either serious or seriously malicious. "Alaska calls that the Look of Doom," the Colonel told me after the Eagle left. "The next time you see that, you're busted."

"Okay, Pudge," the Colonel said as I stepped away from the poster. Not entirely level, but close enough. "Enough with the Alaska already. By my count, there are ninety-two girls at this school, and every last one of them is less crazy than Alaska, who, I might add, *already has a boyfriend*. I'm going to lunch. It's bufriedo day." He walked out, leaving the door open. Feeling like an overinfatuated idiot, I got up to close the door. The Colonel, already halfway across the dorm circle, turned around. "Christ. Are you coming or what?"

You can say a lot of bad things about Alabama, but you can't say that Alabamans as a people are unduly afraid of deep fryers. In that first week at the Creek, the cafeteria served fried chicken, chicken-fried steak, and fried okra, which marked my first foray into the delicacy that is the fried vegetable. I half expected them to fry the iceberg lettuce. But nothing matched the bufriedo, a dish created by Maureen, the amazingly (and understandably) obese Culver Creek cook. A deep-fried bean burrito, the bufriedo proved beyond the shadow of a doubt that frying *always* improves a food. Sitting with the Colonel and five guys I didn't know at a circular table in the cafeteria that afternoon, I sank my teeth into the crunchy shell of my first bufriedo and experienced a culinary orgasm. My mom cooked okay, but I immediately wanted to bring Maureen home with me over Thanksgiving.

The Colonel introduced me (as "Pudge") to the guys at the wobbly wooden table, but I only registered the name Takumi, whom Alaska had mentioned yesterday. A thin Japanese guy only a few inches taller than the Colonel, Takumi talked with his mouth full as I chewed slowly, savoring the bean-y crunch.

"God," Takumi said to me, "there's nothing like watching a man eat his first bufriedo."

I didn't say much—partly because no one asked me any questions and partly because I just wanted to eat as much as I could.

But Takumi felt no such modesty—he could, and did, eat and chew and swallow while talking.

The lunch discussion centered on the girl who was supposed to have been Alaska's roommate, Marya, and her boyfriend, Paul, who had been a Weekday Warrior. They'd gotten kicked out in the last week of the previous school year, I learned, for what the Colonel called "the Trifecta"—they were caught committing three of Culver Creek's expellable offenses at once. Lying naked in bed together ("genital contact" being offense #1), already drunk (#2), they were smoking a joint (#3) when the Eagle burst in on them. Rumors had it that someone had ratted them out, and Takumi seemed intent on finding out who—intent enough, anyway, to shout about it with his mouth jam-packed with bufriedo.

"Paul was an asshole," the Colonel said. "I wouldn't have ratted on them, but anyone who shacks up with a Jaguar-driving Weekday Warrior like Paul deserves what she gets."

"Dude," Takumi responded, "yaw guhfwend," and then he swallowed a bite of food, "is a Weekday Warrior."

"True." The Colonel laughed. "Much to my chagrin, that is an incontestable fact. But she is not as big an asshole as Paul."

"Not quite." Takumi smirked. The Colonel laughed again, and I wondered why he wouldn't stand up for his girlfriend. I wouldn't have cared if my girlfriend was a Jaguar-driving Cyclops with a beard—I'd have been grateful just to have someone to make out with.

That evening, when the Colonel dropped by Room 43 to pick up the cigarettes (he seemed to have forgotten that they were, technically, *mine*), I didn't really care when he didn't invite me out with him. In public school, I'd known plenty of people who made it a habit to hate this kind of person or that kind—the geeks hated the preps, etc.—and it always seemed like a big waste of time to me.

The Colonel didn't tell me where he'd spent the afternoon, or where he was going to spend the evening, but he closed the door behind him when he left, so I guessed I wasn't welcome.

Just as well: I spent the night surfing the Web (no porn, I swear) and reading *The Final Days,* a book about Richard Nixon and Watergate. For dinner, I microwaved a refrigerated bufriedo the Colonel had snuck out of the cafeteria. It reminded me of nights in Florida—except with better food and no air-conditioning. Lying in bed and reading felt pleasantly familiar.

I decided to heed what I'm sure would have been my mother's advice and get a good night's sleep before my first day of classes. French II started at 8:10, and figuring it couldn't take more than eight minutes to put on some clothes and walk to the classrooms, I set my alarm for 8:02. I took a shower, and then lay in bed waiting for sleep to save me from the heat. Around 11:00, I realized that the tiny fan clipped to my bunk might make more of a difference if I took off my shirt, and I finally fell asleep on top of the sheets wearing just boxers.

A decision I found myself regretting some hours later when I awoke to two sweaty, meaty hands shaking the holy hell out of me. I woke up completely and instantly, sitting up straight in bed, terrified, and I couldn't understand the voices for some reason, couldn't understand why there were any voices at all, and what the hell time was it anyway? And finally my head cleared enough to hear, "C'mon, kid. Don't make us kick your ass. Just get up," and then from the top bunk, I heard, "Christ, Pudge. Just *get up.*" So I got up, and saw for the first time three shadowy figures. Two of them grabbed me, one with a hand on each of my upper arms, and walked me out of the room. On the way out, the Colonel mumbled, "Have a good time. Go easy on him, Kevin."

They led me, almost at a jog, behind my dorm building, and then across the soccer field. The ground was grassy but gravelly, too, and

I wondered why no one had shown the common courtesy to tell me to put on shoes, and why was I out there in my underwear, chicken legs exposed to the world? A thousand humiliations crossed my mind: *There's the new junior, Miles Halter, handcuffed to the soccer goal wearing only his boxers.* I imagined them taking me into the woods, where we now seemed headed, and beating the shit out of me so that I looked great for my first day of school. And the whole time, I just stared at my feet, because I didn't want to look at them and I didn't want to fall, so I watched my steps, trying to avoid the bigger rocks. I felt the fight-or-flight reflex swell up in me over and over again, but I knew that neither fight nor flight had ever worked for me before. They took me a roundabout way to the fake beach, and then I knew what would happen—a good, old-fashioned dunking in the lake—and I calmed down. I could handle that.

When we reached the beach, they told me to put my arms at my sides, and the beefiest guy grabbed two rolls of duct tape from the sand. With my arms flat against my sides like a soldier at attention, they mummified me from my shoulder to my wrists. Then they threw me down on the ground; the sand from the fake beach cushioned the landing, but I still hit my head. Two of them pulled my legs together while the other one—Kevin, I'd figured out—put his angular, strong-jawed face up so close to mine that the gel-soaked spikes of hair pointing out from his forehead poked at my face, and told me, "This is for the Colonel. You shouldn't hang out with that asshole." They taped my legs together, from ankles to thighs. I looked like a silver mummy. I said, "Please guys, don't," just before they taped my mouth shut. Then they picked me up and hurled me into the water.

Sinking. Sinking, but instead of feeling panic or anything else, I realized that "Please guys, don't" were terrible last words. But then the great miracle of the human species—our buoyancy— came through, and as I felt myself floating toward the surface,

I twisted and turned as best I could so that the warm night air hit my nose first, and I breathed. I wasn't dead and wasn't going to die.

Well, I thought, *that wasn't so bad.*

But there was still the small matter of getting to shore before the sun rose. First, to determine my position vis-à-vis the shoreline. If I tilted my head too much, I felt my whole body start to roll, and on the long list of unpleasant ways to die, "facedown in soaking-wet white boxers" is pretty high up there. So instead I rolled my eyes and craned my neck back, my eyes almost underwater, until I saw that the shore—not ten feet away—was directly behind my head. I began to swim, an armless silver mermaid, using only my hips to generate motion, until finally my ass scraped against the lake's mucky bottom. I turned then and used my hips and waist to roll three times, until I came ashore near a ratty green towel. They'd left me a towel. How thoughtful.

The water had seeped under the duct tape and loosened the adhesive's grip on my skin, but the tape was wrapped around me three layers deep in places, which necessitated wiggling like a fish out of water. Finally it loosened enough for me to slip my left hand up and out against my chest and rip the tape off.

I wrapped myself in the sandy towel. I didn't want to go back to my room and see Chip, because I had no idea what Kevin had meant—maybe if I went back to the room, they'd be waiting for me and they'd get me for real; maybe I needed to show them, "Okay. Got your message. He's just my roommate, not my friend." And anyway, I didn't feel terribly friendly toward the Colonel. *Have a good time,* he'd said. *Yeah*, I thought. *I had a ball.*

So I went to Alaska's room. I didn't know what time it was, but I could see a faint light underneath her door. I knocked softly.

"Yeah," she said, and I came in, wet and sandy and wearing only a towel and soaking boxers. This was not, obviously, how you want the world's hottest girl to see you, but I figured she could explain to me what had just happened.

She put down a book and got out of bed with a sheet wrapped around her shoulders. For a moment, she looked concerned. She looked like the girl I met yesterday, the girl who said I was cute and bubbled over with energy and silliness and intelligence. And then she laughed.

"Guess you went for a swim, huh?" And she said it with such casual malice that I felt that everyone had known, and I wondered why the whole damn school agreed in advance to possibly drown Miles Halter. But Alaska *liked* the Colonel, and in the confusion of the moment, I just looked at her blankly, unsure even of what to ask.

"Give me a break," she said. "Come on. You know what? There are people with real problems. I've got real problems. Mommy ain't here, so buck up, big guy."

I left without saying a word to her and went to my room, slamming the door behind me, waking the Colonel, and stomping into the bathroom. I got in the shower to wash the algae and the lake off me, but the ridiculous faucet of a showerhead failed spectacularly, and how could Alaska and Kevin and those other guys already dislike me? After I finished the shower, I dried off and went into the room to find some clothes.

"So," he said. "What took you so long? Get lost on your way home?"

"They said it was because of you," I said, and my voice betrayed a hint of annoyance. "They said I shouldn't hang out with you."

"What? No, it happens to everybody," the Colonel said. "It happened to me. They throw you in the lake. You swim out. You walk home."

"I couldn't just swim out," I said softly, pulling on a pair of jean shorts beneath my towel. "They duct-taped me. I couldn't even move, really."

"Wait. Wait," he said, and hopped out of his bunk, staring at me through the darkness. "They *taped* you? How?" And I showed him: I stood like a mummy, with my feet together and my hands at my sides, and showed him how they'd wrapped me up. And then I plopped down onto the couch.

"Christ! You could have drowned! They're just supposed to throw you in the water in your underwear and run!" he shouted. "What the hell were they thinking? Who was it? Kevin Richman and who else? Do you remember their faces?"

"Yeah, I think."

"Why the hell would they do that?" he wondered.

"Did you do something to them?" I asked.

"No, but I'm sure as shit gonna do something to 'em now. We'll get them."

"It wasn't a big deal. I got out fine."

"You could have *died*." And I could have, I suppose. But I didn't.

"Well, maybe I should just go to the Eagle tomorrow and tell him," I said.

"Absolutely not," he answered. He walked over to his crumpled shorts lying on the floor and pulled out a pack of cigarettes. He lit two and handed one to me. I smoked the whole goddamned thing. "You're not," he continued, "because that's not how shit gets dealt with here. And besides, you really don't want to get a reputation for ratting. But we will deal with those bastards, Pudge. I promise you. They will regret messing with one of my friends."

And if the Colonel thought that calling me his friend would make me stand by him, well, he was right. "Alaska was kind of mean to me tonight," I said. I leaned over, opened an empty desk drawer, and used it as a makeshift ashtray.

"Like I said, she's moody."

I went to bed wearing a T-shirt, shorts, and socks. No matter how miserably hot it got, I resolved, I would sleep in my clothes every night at the Creek, feeling—probably for the first time in my life—the fear and excitement of living in a place where you never know what's going to happen or when.

one hundred twenty-six days before

"WELL, NOW IT'S WAR," the Colonel shouted the next morning. I rolled over and looked at the clock: 7:52. My first Culver Creek class, French, started in eighteen minutes. I blinked a couple times and looked up at the Colonel, who was standing between the couch and the COFFEE TABLE, holding his well-worn, once-white tennis shoes by the laces. For a long time, he stared at me, and I stared at him. And then, almost in slow motion, a grin crept across the Colonel's face.

"I've got to hand it to them," he said finally. "That was pretty clever."

"What?" I asked.

"Last night—before they woke you up, I guess—they pissed in my shoes."

"Are you sure?" I said, trying not to laugh.

"Do you care to smell?" he asked, holding the shoes toward me. "Because I went ahead and smelled them, and yes, I am sure. If there's one thing I know, it's when I've just stepped in another man's piss. It's like my mom always says: 'Ya think you's a-walkin' on water, but turns out you just got piss in your shoes.' Point those guys out to me if you see them today," he added, "because we need to figure out why they're so, uh, pissed at me. And then we need to go ahead and start thinking about how we're going to ruin their miserable little lives."

When I received the Culver Creek Handbook over the summer and noticed happily that the "Dress Code" section contained only two words, *casual modesty,* it never occurred to me that girls would show up for class half asleep in cotton pajama shorts, T-shirts, and flip-flops. Modest, I guess, and casual.

And there *was* something about girls wearing pajamas (even if modest), which might have made French at 8:10 in the morning bearable, if I'd had any idea what Madame O'Malley was talking about. *Comment dis-tu* "Oh my God, I don't know nearly enough French to pass French II" *en français?* My French I class back in Florida did not prepare me for Madame O'Malley, who skipped the "how was your summer" pleasantries and dove directly into something called the *passé composé,* which is apparently a verb tense. Alaska sat directly across from me in the circle of desks, but she didn't look at me once the entire class, even though I could notice little but her. Maybe she could be mean . . . but the way she talked that first night about getting out of the labyrinth—so smart. And the way her mouth curled up on the right side all the time, like she was preparing to smirk, like she'd mastered the right half of the *Mona Lisa's* inimitable smile . . .

From my room, the student population seemed manageable, but it overwhelmed me in the classroom area, which was a single, long building just beyond the dorm circle. The building was split into fourteen rooms facing out toward the lake. Kids crammed the narrow sidewalks in front of the classrooms, and even though finding my classes wasn't hard (even with my poor sense of direction, I could get from French in Room 3 to precalc in Room 12), I felt unsettled all day. I didn't know anyone and couldn't even figure out whom I should be trying to know, and the classes were *hard,* even on the first day. My dad had told me I'd have to study, and now I believed him. The teachers were serious and smart and a lot of them went by "Dr.," and so when the time came for my last class before lunch, World Religions, I felt tremendous relief. A vestige from when Culver Creek was a Christian boys' school, I figured the World Religions class, required of every junior and senior, might be an easy A.

It was my only class all day where the desks weren't arranged either in a square or a circle, so, not wanting to seem eager, I sat down in the third row at 11:03. I was seven minutes early, partly because I liked to be punctual, and partly because I didn't have anyone to chat with out in the halls. Shortly thereafter, the Colonel came in with Takumi, and they sat down on opposite sides of me.

"I heard about last night," Takumi said. "Alaska's pissed."

"That's weird, since she was such a bitch last night," I blurted out.

Takumi just shook his head. "Yeah, well, she didn't know the whole story. And people are moody, dude. You gotta get used to living with people. You could have worse friends than—"

The Colonel cut him off. "Enough with the psychobabble, MC Dr. Phil. Let's talk counterinsurgency." People were starting to file into class, so the Colonel leaned in toward me and whispered, "If any of 'em are in this class, let me know, okay? Just, here, just put X's where they're sitting," and he ripped a sheet of paper out of his notebook and drew a square for each desk. As people filed in, I saw one of them—the tall one with immaculately spiky hair—Kevin. Kevin stared down the Colonel as he walked past, but in trying to stare, he forgot to watch his step and bumped his thigh against a desk. The Colonel laughed. One of the other guys, the one who was either a little fat or worked out too much, came in behind Kevin, sporting pleated khaki pants and a short-sleeve black polo shirt. As they sat down, I crossed through the appropriate squares on the Colonel's diagram and handed it to him. Just then, the Old Man shuffled in.

He breathed slowly and with great labor through his wide-open mouth. He took tiny steps toward the lectern, his heels not moving much past his toes. The Colonel nudged me and pointed casually to his notebook, which read, *The Old Man only has one lung,* and I did not doubt it. His audible, almost desperate breaths reminded me of my grandfather when he was dying of lung cancer. Barrel-chested and ancient, the Old Man, it seemed to me, might die before he ever reached the podium.

"My name," he said, "is Dr. Hyde. I have a first name, of course. So far as you are concerned, it is Doctor. Your parents pay a great deal of money so that you can attend school here, and I expect that you will offer them some return on their investment by reading what I tell you to read when I tell you to read it and consistently attending this class. And when you are here, you will listen to what I say." Clearly not an easy A.

"This year, we'll be studying three religious traditions: Islam, Christianity, and Buddhism. We'll tackle three more traditions next year. And in my classes, I will talk most of the time, and you will listen most of the time. Because you may be smart, but I've been smart longer. I'm sure some of you do not like lecture classes, but as you have probably noted, I'm not as young as I used to be. I would love to spend my remaining breath chatting with you about the finer points of Islamic history, but our time together is short. I must talk, and you must listen, for we are engaged here in the most important pursuit in history: the search for meaning. What is the nature of being a person? What is the best way to go about being a person? How did we come to be, and what will become of us when we are no longer? In short: What are the rules of this game, and how might we best play it?"

The nature of the labyrinth, I scribbled into my spiral notebook, *and the way out of it.* This teacher rocked. I hated discussion classes. I hated talking, and I hated listening to everyone else stumble on their words and try to phrase things in the vaguest possible way so they wouldn't sound dumb, and I hated how it was all just a game of trying to figure out what the teacher wanted to hear and then saying it. I'm in *class*, so *teach me*. And teach me he did: In those fifty minutes, the Old Man made me take religion seriously. I'd never been religious, but he told us that religion is important whether or not *we* believed in one, in the same way that historical events are important whether or not you personally lived through them. And then he assigned us fifty pages of reading for the next day—from a book called *Religious Studies*.

That afternoon, I had two classes and two free periods. We had nine fifty-minute class periods each day, which means that most everyone had three "study periods" (except for the Colonel, who had an extra independent-study math class on account of being an Extra Special Genius). The Colonel and I had biology together, where I pointed out the other guy who'd duct-taped me the night before. In the top corner of his notebook, the Colonel wrote, *Longwell Chase. Senior W-day Warrior. Friends w/Sara. Weird.* It took me a minute to remember who Sara was: the Colonel's girlfriend.

I spent my free periods in my room trying to read about religion. I learned that *myth* doesn't mean a lie; it means a traditional story that tells you something about people and their worldview and what they hold sacred. Interesting. I also learned that after the events of the previous night, I was far too tired to care about myths or anything else, so I slept on top of the covers for most of the afternoon, until I awoke to Alaska singing, "WAKE UP, LITTLE PUHHHHHDGIE!" directly into my left ear canal. I held the religion book close up against my chest like a small paperback security blanket.

"That was terrible," I said. "What do I need to do to ensure that never happens to me again?"

"Nothing you can do!" she said excitedly. "I'm unpredictable. God, don't you hate Dr. Hyde? Don't you? He's so condescending."

I sat up and said, "I think he's a genius," partly because I thought it was true and partly because I just felt like disagreeing with her.

She sat down on the bed. "Do you always sleep in your clothes?"

"Yup."

"Funny," she said. "You weren't wearing much last night." I just glared at her.

"C'mon, Pudge. I'm teasing. You have to be tough here. I didn't know how bad it was—and I'm sorry, and they'll regret it—but you have to be tough." And then she left. That was all she had to say on the subject. *She's cute*, I thought, *but you don't need to like a girl who treats you like you're ten: You've already got a mom.*

one hundred twenty-two days before

AFTER MY LAST CLASS of my first week at Culver Creek, I entered Room 43 to an unlikely sight: the diminutive and shirtless Colonel, hunched over an ironing board, attacking a pink button-down shirt. Sweat trickled down his forehead and chest as he ironed with great enthusiasm, his right arm pushing the iron across the length of the shirt with such vigor that his breathing nearly duplicated Dr. Hyde's.

"I have a date," he explained. "This is an emergency." He paused to catch his breath. "Do you know"—breath--"how to iron?"

I walked over to the pink shirt. It was wrinkled like an old woman who'd spent her youth sunbathing. If only the Colonel didn't ball up his every belonging and stuff it into random dresser drawers. "I think you just turn it on and press it against the shirt, right?" I said. "I don't know. I didn't even know we *had* an iron."

"We don't. It's Takumi's. But Takumi doesn't know how to iron, either. And when I asked Alaska, she started yelling, 'You're not going to impose the patriarchal paradigm on *me*.' Oh, God, I need to smoke. I need to smoke, but I can't reek when I see Sara's parents. Okay, screw it. We're going to smoke in the bathroom with the shower on. The shower has steam. Steam gets rid of wrinkles, right?

"By the way," he said as I followed him into the bathroom, "if you want to smoke inside during the day, just turn on the shower. The smoke follows the steam up the vents."

Though this made no scientific sense, it seemed to work. The shower's shortage of water pressure and low showerhead made it all but useless for showering, but it worked great as a smoke screen.

Sadly, it made a poor iron. The Colonel tried ironing the shirt once more ("I'm just gonna push really hard and see if that helps") and finally put it on wrinkled. He matched the shirt with a blue tie decorated with horizontal lines of little pink flamingos.

"The one thing my lousy father taught me," the Colonel said as his hands nimbly threaded the tie into a perfect knot, "was how to tie a tie. Which is odd, since I can't imagine when he ever had to wear one."

Just then, Sara knocked on the door. I'd seen her once or twice before, but the Colonel never introduced me to her and didn't have a chance to that night.

"Oh. My God. Can't you at least press your shirt?" she asked, even though the Colonel was standing in front of the ironing board. "We're going out with my *parents*." Sara looked awfully nice in her blue summer dress. Her long, pale blond hair was pulled up into a twist, with a strand of hair falling down each side of her face. She looked like a movie star—a bitchy one.

"Look, I did my best. We don't all have maids to do our ironing."

"Chip, that chip on your shoulder makes you look even shorter."

"Christ, can't we get out the door without fighting?"

"I'm just saying. It's *the opera*. It's a big deal to my parents. What-ever. Let's go." I felt like leaving, but it seemed stupid to hide in the bathroom, and Sara was standing in the doorway, one hand cocked on her hip and the other fiddling with her car keys as if to say, *Let's go*.

"I could wear a tuxedo and your parents would still hate me!" he shouted.

"That's not my fault! You antagonize them!" She held up the car keys in front of him. "Look, we're going now or we're not going."

"Fuck it. I'm not going anywhere with you," the Colonel said.

"Fine. Have a great night." Sara slammed the door so hard that a sizable biography of Leo Tolstoy (last words: "The truth is . . . I care a great deal . . . what they . . . ") fell off my bookshelf and landed with a thud on our checkered floor like an echo of the slamming door.

"AHHHHH!!!!!!!!!!!!" he screamed.

"So that's Sara," I said.

"Yes."

"She seems nice."

The Colonel laughed, knelt down next to the minifridge, and pulled out a gallon of milk. He opened it, took a swig, winced, half coughed, and sat down on the couch with the milk between his legs.

"Is it sour or something?"

"Oh, I should have mentioned that earlier. This isn't milk. It's five parts milk and one part vodka. I call it ambrosia. Drink of the gods. You can barely smell the vodka in the milk, so the Eagle can't catch me unless he actually takes a sip. The downside is that it tastes like sour milk and rubbing alcohol, but it's Friday night, Pudge, and my girlfriend is a bitch. Want some?"

"I think I'll pass." Aside from a few sips of champagne on New Year's under the watchful eye of my parents, I'd never really drunk any alcohol, and "ambrosia" didn't seem like the drink with which to start. Outside, I heard the pay phone ring. Given the fact that 190 boarders shared five pay phones, I was amazed at how infrequently it rang. We weren't supposed to have cell phones, but I'd noticed that some of the Weekday Warriors carried them surreptitiously. And most non-Warriors called their parents, as I did, on a regular basis, so parents only called when their kids forgot.

"Are you going to get that?" the Colonel asked me. I didn't feel like being bossed around by him, but I also didn't feel like fighting.

Through a buggy twilight, I walked to the pay phone, which was drilled into the wall between Rooms 44 and 45. On both sides of the phone, dozens of phone numbers and esoteric notes were written in pen and marker (205.555.1584; *Tommy to airport 4:20;* 773.573.6521; *JG—Kuffs?*). Calling the pay phone required a great deal of patience. I picked up on about the ninth ring.

"Can you get Chip for me?" Sara asked. It sounded like she was on a cell phone.

"Yeah, hold on."

I turned, and he was already behind me, as if he knew it would be her. I handed him the receiver and walked back to the room.

A minute later, three words made their way to our room through the thick, still air of Alabama at almost-night. "Screw you too!" the Colonel shouted.

Back in the room, he sat down with his ambrosia and told me, "She says I ratted out Paul and Marya. That's what the Warriors are saying. That I ratted them out. *Me*. That's why the piss in the shoes. That's why the nearly killing you. 'Cause you live with me, and they say I'm a rat."

I tried to remember who Paul and Marya were. The names were familiar, but I had heard so many names in the last week, and I couldn't match "Paul" and "Marya" with faces. And then I remembered why: I'd never seen them. They got kicked out the year before, having committed the Trifecta.

"How long have you been dating her?" I asked.

"Nine months. We never got along. I mean, I didn't even briefly like her. Like, my mom and my dad—my dad would get pissed, and then he would beat the shit out of my mom. And then my dad would be all nice, and they'd have like a honeymoon period. But with Sara, there's never a honeymoon period. God, how could she think I was a rat? I know, I know: Why don't we break up?" He ran a hand through his hair, clutching a fistful of it atop his head, and said, "I guess I stay with her because she stays with me. And that's not an easy thing to do. I'm a bad boyfriend. She's a bad girlfriend. We deserve each other."

"But—"

"I can't believe they think that," he said as he walked to the bookshelf and pulled down the almanac. He took a long pull off his ambrosia. "Goddamn Weekday Warriors. It was probably one of them that ratted out Paul and Marya and then blamed me to cover their tracks. Anyway, it's a good night for staying in. Staying in with Pudge and ambrosia."

"I still—" I said, wanting to say that I didn't understand how you could kiss someone who believed you were a rat if being a rat was the worst thing in the world, but the Colonel cut me off.

"Not another word about it. You know what the capital of Sierra Leone is?"

"No."

"Me neither," he said, "but I intend to find out." And with that, he stuck his nose in the almanac, and the conversation was over.

one hundred ten days before

KEEPING UP WITH MY CLASSES proved easier than I'd expected. My general predisposition to spending a lot of time inside reading gave me a distinct advantage over the average Culver Creek student. By the third week of classes, plenty of kids had been sunburned to a bufriedo-like golden brown from days spent chatting outside in the shadeless dorm circle during free periods. But I was barely pink: I studied.

And I listened in class, too, but on that Wednesday morning, when Dr. Hyde started talking about how Buddhists believe that all things are interconnected, I found myself staring out the window. I was looking at the wooded, slow-sloping hill beyond the lake. And from Hyde's classroom, things did seem connected: The trees seemed to clothe the hill, and just as I would never think to notice a particular cotton thread in the magnificently tight orange tank top Alaska wore that day, I couldn't see the trees for the forest—everything so intricately woven together that it made no sense to think of one tree as independent from that hill. And then I heard my name, and I knew I was in trouble.

"Mr. Halter," the Old Man said. "Here I am, straining my lungs for your edification. And yet *something* out there seems to have caught your fancy in a way that I've been unable to do. Pray tell: What have you discovered out there?"

Now I felt my own breath shorten, the whole class watching me, thanking God they *weren't* me. Dr. Hyde had already done this three times, kicking kids out of class for not paying attention or writing notes to one another.

"Um, I was just looking outside at the, uh, at the hill and thinking about, um, the trees and the forest, like you were saying earlier, about the way—"

The Old Man, who obviously did not tolerate vocalized rambling, cut me off. "I'm going to ask you to leave class, Mr. Halter, so that you can go out there and discover the relationship between the um-trees and the uh-forest. And tomorrow, when you're ready to take this class seriously, I will welcome you back."

I sat still, my pen resting in my hand, my notebook open, my face flushed and my jaw jutting out into an underbite, an old trick I had to keep from looking sad or scared. Two rows behind me, I heard a chair move and turned around to see Alaska standing up, slinging her backpack over one arm.

"I'm sorry, but that's bullshit. You can't just throw him out of class. You drone on and on for an hour every day, and we're not allowed to glance out the *window?*"

The Old Man stared back at Alaska like a bull at a matador, then raised a hand to his sagging face and slowly rubbed the white stubble on his cheek. "For fifty minutes a day, five days a week, you abide by my rules. Or you fail. The choice is yours. Both of you leave."

I stuffed my notebook into my backpack and walked out, humiliated. As the door shut behind me, I felt a tap on my left shoulder. I turned, but there was no one there. Then I turned the other way, and Alaska was smiling at me, the skin between her eyes and temple crinkled into a starburst. "The oldest trick in the book," she said, "but everybody falls for it."

I tried a smile, but I couldn't stop thinking about Dr. Hyde. It was worse than the Duct Tape Incident, because I always knew that the Kevin Richmans of the world didn't like me. But my teachers had always been card-carrying members of the Miles Halter Fan Club.

"I told you he was an asshole," she said.

"I still think he's a genius. He's right. I wasn't listening."

"Right, but he didn't need to be a jerk about it. Like he needs to prove his power by humiliating you?! Anyway," she said, "the only real geniuses are artists: Yeats, Picasso, García Márquez: *geniuses.* Dr. Hyde: bitter old man."

And then she announced we were going to look for four-leaf clovers until class ended and we could go smoke with the Colonel and Takumi, "both of whom," she added, "are big-time assholes for not marching out of class right behind us."

When Alaska Young is sitting with her legs crossed in a brittle, periodically green clover patch leaning forward in search of four-leaf clovers, the pale skin of her sizable cleavage clearly visible, it is a plain fact of human physiology that it becomes impossible to join in her clover search. I'd gotten in enough trouble already for looking where I wasn't supposed to, but still . . .

After perhaps two minutes of combing through a clover patch with her long, dirty fingernails, Alaska grabbed a clover with three full-size petals and an undersize, runt of a fourth, then looked up at me, barely giving me time to avert my eyes.

"Even though you were *clearly* not doing your part in the clover search, perv," she said wryly, "I really would give you this clover. Except luck is for suckers." She pinched the runt petal between the nails of her thumb and finger and plucked it. "There," she said to the clover as she dropped it onto the ground. "Now you're not a genetic freak anymore."

"Uh, thanks," I said. The bell rang, and Takumi and the Colonel were first out the door. Alaska stared at them.

"What?" asked the Colonel. But she just rolled her eyes and started walking. We followed in silence through the dorm circle and then across the soccer field. We ducked into the woods, following the faint path around the lake until we came to a dirt road. The Colonel ran up to Alaska, and they started fighting about something quietly enough that I couldn't hear the words so much as the mutual annoyance, and I finally asked Takumi where we were headed.

"This road dead-ends into the barn," he said. "So maybe there. But probably the smoking hole. You'll see."

From here, the woods were a totally different creature than from Dr. Hyde's classroom. The ground was thick with fallen branches, decaying pine needles, and brambly green bushes; the path wound past pine trees sprouting tall and thin, their stubbly needles providing a lace of shade from another sunburned day. And the smaller oak and maple trees, which from Dr. Hyde's classroom had been invisible beneath the more majestic pines, showed hints of an as-yet-thermally-unforeseeable fall: Their still-green leaves were beginning to droop.

We came to a rickety wooden bridge—just thick plywood laid

over a concrete foundation—over Culver Creek, the winding rivulet that doubled back over and over again through the outskirts of campus. On the far side of the bridge, there was a tiny path leading down a steep slope. Not even a path so much as a series of hints—a broken branch here, a patch of stomped-down grass there—that people had come this way before. As we walked down single file, Alaska, the Colonel, and Takumi each held back a thick maple branch for one another, passing it along until I, last in line, let it snap back into place behind me. And there, beneath the bridge, an oasis. A slab of concrete, three feet wide and ten feet long, with blue plastic chairs stolen long ago from some classroom. Cooled by the creek and the shade of the bridge, I felt unhot for the first time in weeks.

The Colonel dispensed the cigarettes. Takumi passed; the rest of us lit up.

"He has no right to condescend to us is all I'm saying," Alaska said, continuing her conversation with the Colonel. "Pudge is done with staring out the window, and I'm done with going on tirades about it, but he's a terrible teacher, and you won't convince me otherwise."

"Fine," the Colonel said. "Just don't make another scene. Christ, you nearly killed the poor old bastard."

"Seriously, you'll never win by crossing Hyde," Takumi said. "He'll eat you alive, shit you out, and then piss on his dump. Which by the way is what we should be doing to whoever ratted on Marya. Has anyone heard anything?"

"It must have been some Weekday Warrior," Alaska said. "But apparently they think it was the Colonel. So who knows. Maybe the Eagle just got lucky. She was stupid; she got caught; she got expelled; it's over. That's what happens when you're stupid and you get caught." Alaska made an O with her lips, moving her mouth like a goldfish eating, trying unsuccessfully to blow smoke rings.

"Wow," Takumi said, "if I ever get kicked out, remind me to even the score myself, since I sure can't count on you."

"Don't be ridiculous," she responded, not angry so much as dismissive. "I don't understand why you're so obsessed with figuring out everything that happens here, like we have to unravel every mystery. God, it's over. Takumi, you gotta stop stealing other people's problems and get some of your own." Takumi started up again, but Alaska raised her hand as if to swat the conversation away.

I said nothing—I hadn't known Marya, and anyway, "listening quietly" was my general social strategy.

"Anyway," Alaska said to me. "I thought the way he treated you was just awful. I wanted to cry. I just wanted to kiss you and make it better."

"Shame you didn't," I deadpanned, and they laughed.

"You're adorable," she said, and I felt the intensity of her eyes on me and looked away nervously. "Too bad I love my boyfriend." I stared at the knotted roots of the trees on the creek bank, trying hard not to look like I'd just been called adorable.

Takumi couldn't believe it either, and he walked over to me, tussling my hair with his hand, and started rapping to Alaska. "Yeah, Pudge is adorable / but you want incorrigible / so Jake is more endurable / 'cause he's so—damn. Damn. I almost had four rhymes on *adorable*. But all I could think of was *unfloorable,* which isn't even a word."

Alaska laughed. "That made me not be mad at you anymore. God, rapping is sexy. Pudge, did you even know that you're in the presence of the sickest emcee in Alabama?"

"Um, no."

"Drop a beat, Colonel Catastrophe," Takumi said, and I laughed at the idea that a guy as short and dorky as the Colonel could have a rap name. The Colonel cupped his hands around his mouth and started making some absurd noises that I suppose were intended to be beats. *Puh-chi. Puh-puhpuh-chi.* Takumi laughed.

"Right here, by the river, you want me to kick it? / If your smoke was a Popsicle, I'd surely lick it / My rhymin' is old school, sort of like the ancient Romans / The Colonel's beats is sad like Arthur Miller's Willy Loman / Sometimes I'm accused of being a showman / ICanRhymeFast and I can rhyme slow, man."

He paused, took a breath, and then finished.

"Like Emily Dickinson, I ain't afraid of slant rhyme / And that's the end of this verse; emcee's out on a high."

I didn't know slant rhyme from regular rhyme, but I was suitably impressed. We gave Takumi a soft round of applause. Alaska finished her cigarette and flicked it into the river.

"Why do you smoke so damn fast?" I asked.

She looked at me and smiled widely, and such a wide smile on her narrow face might have looked goofy were it not for the unimpeachably elegant green in her eyes. She smiled with all the delight of a kid on Christmas morning and said, "Y'all smoke to enjoy it. I smoke to die."

one hundred nine days before

DINNER IN THE CAFETERIA the next night was meat loaf, one of the rare dishes that didn't arrive deep-fried, and, perhaps as a result, meat loaf was Maureen's greatest failure—a stringy, gravy-soaked concoction that did not much resemble a loaf and did not much taste like meat. Although I'd never ridden in it, Alaska apparently had a car, and she offered to drive the Colonel and me to McDonald's, but the Colonel didn't have any money, and I didn't have much either, what with constantly paying for his extravagant cigarette habit.

So instead the Colonel and I reheated two-day-old bufriedos—unlike, say, french fries, a microwaved bufriedo lost nothing of its taste or its satisfying crunch—after which the Colonel insisted on attending the Creek's first basketball game of the season.

"Basketball in the fall?" I asked the Colonel. "I don't know much about sports, but isn't that when you play football?"

"The schools in our league are too small to have football teams, so we play basketball in the fall. Although, man, the Culver Creek football team would be a thing of beauty. Your scrawny ass could probably start at lineman. Anyway, the basketball games are great."

I hated sports. I hated sports, and I hated people who played them, and I hated people who watched them, and I hated people who didn't hate people who watched or played them. In third grade—the very last year that one could play T-ball—my mother wanted me to make friends, so she forced me onto the Orlando Pirates. I made friends all right—with a bunch of kindergartners, which didn't really bolster my social standing with my peers. Primarily because I towered over the rest of the players, I nearly made it onto the T-ball all-star team that year. The kid who beat me, Clay Wurtzel, had one arm. I was an unusually tall third grader with two arms, and I got beat out by kindergartner Clay Wurtzel. And it wasn't some pity-the-one-armed-kid thing, either. Clay Wurtzel could flat-out *hit*, whereas I sometimes struck out even with the ball sitting on the tee. One of the things that appealed to me most about Culver Creek was that my dad assured me there was no PE requirement.

"There is only one time when I put aside my passionate hatred for the Weekday Warriors and their country-club bullshit," the Colonel told me. "And that's when they pump up the air-conditioning in the gym for a little old-fashioned Culver Creek basketball. You can't miss the first game of the year."

As we walked toward the airplane hangar of a gym, which I had seen but never even thought to approach, the Colonel explained to me the most important thing about our basketball team: They were not very good. The "star" of the team, the Colonel said, was a senior named Hank Walsten, who played power forward despite being five-foot-eight. Hank's primary claim to campus fame, I already knew, was that he always had weed, and the Colonel told me that for four years, Hank started every game without ever once playing sober.

"He loves weed like Alaska loves sex," the Colonel said. "This is a man who once constructed a bong using only the barrel of an air rifle, a ripe pear, and an eight-by-ten glossy photograph of Anna Kournikova. Not the brightest gem in the jewelry shop, but you've got to admire his single-minded dedication to drug abuse."

From Hank, the Colonel told me, it went downhill until you reached Wilson Carbod, the starting center, who was almost six feet tall. "We're so bad," the Colonel said, "we don't even have a mascot. I call us the Culver Creek Nothings."

"So they just suck?" I asked. I didn't quite understand the point of watching your terrible team get walloped, though the air-conditioning was reason enough for me.

"Oh, they suck," the Colonel replied. "But we always beat the shit out of the deaf-and-blind school." Apparently, basketball wasn't a big priority at the Alabama School for the Deaf and Blind, and so we usually came out of the season with a single victory.

When we arrived, the gym was packed with most every Culver Creek student—I noticed, for instance, the Creek's three goth girls reapplying their eyeliner as they sat on the top row of the gym's bleachers. I'd never attended a school basketball game back home, but I doubted the crowds there were quite so inclusive. Even so, I was surprised when none other than Kevin Richman sat down on the bleacher directly in front of me while the opposing school's cheerleading team (their unfortunate school colors were mud-brown and dehydrated-piss-yellow) tried to fire up the small visitors' section in the crowd. Kevin turned around and stared at the Colonel.

Like most of the other guy Warriors, Kevin dressed preppy, looking like a lawyer-who-enjoys-golfing waiting to happen. And his hair, a blond mop, short on the sides and spiky on top, was always soaked through with so much gel that it looked perennially wet. I didn't hate him like the Colonel did, of course, because the Colonel hated him on principle, and principled hate is a hell of a lot stronger than "Boy, I wish you hadn't mummified me and thrown me into the lake" hate. Still, I tried to stare at him intimidatingly as he looked at the Colonel, but it was hard to forget that this guy had seen my skinny ass in nothing but boxers a couple weeks ago.

"You ratted out Paul and Marya. We got you back. Truce?" Kevin asked.

"I didn't rat them out. Pudge here *certainly* didn't rat them out, but you brought him in on your fun. Truce? Hmm, let me take a poll real quick." The cheerleaders sat down, holding their pom-poms close to their chest as if praying. "Hey, Pudge," the Colonel said. "What do you think of a truce?"

"It reminds me of when the Germans demanded that the U.S. surrender at the Battle of the Bulge," I said. "I guess I'd say to this truce offer what General McAuliffe said to that one: Nuts."

"Why would you try to kill this guy, Kevin? He's a genius. Nuts to your truce."

"Come on, dude. I know you ratted them out, and we had to defend our friend, and now it's over. Let's end it." He seemed very sincere, perhaps due to the Colonel's reputation for pranking.

"I'll make you a deal. You pick one dead American president. If Pudge doesn't know that guy's last words, truce. If he does, you spend the rest of your life lamenting the day you pissed in my shoes."

"That's retarded."

"All right, no truce," the Colonel shot back.

"Fine. Millard Fillmore," Kevin said. The Colonel looked at me hurriedly, his eyes saying, *Was that guy a president?* I just smiled.

"When Fillmore was dying, he was super hungry. But his doctor was trying to starve his fever or whatever. Fillmore wouldn't shut up about wanting to eat, though, so finally the doctor gave him a tiny teaspoon of soup. And all sarcastic, Fillmore said, 'The nourishment is palatable,' and then died. No truce."

Kevin rolled his eyes and walked away, and it occurred to me that I could have made up any last words for Millard Fillmore and Kevin probably would have believed me if I'd used that same tone of voice, the Colonel's confidence rubbing off on me.

"That was your first badass moment!" The Colonel laughed. "Now, it's true that I gave you an easy target. But still. Well done."

Unfortunately for the Culver Creek Nothings, we weren't playing the deaf-and-blind school. We were playing some Christian school from downtown Birmingham, a team stocked with huge, gargantuan apemen with thick beards and a strong distaste for turning the other cheek.

At the end of the first quarter: 20–4.

And that's when the fun started. The Colonel led all of the cheers.

"Cornbread!" he screamed.

"CHICKEN!" the crowd responded.

"Rice!"

"PEAS!"

And then, all together: "WE GOT HIGHER SATs."

"Hip Hip Hip Hooray!" the Colonel cried.

"YOU'LL BE WORKIN' FOR US SOMEDAY!"

The opposing team's cheerleaders tried to answer our cheers with "The roof, the roof, the roof is on fire! Hell is in your future if you give in to desire," but we could always do them one better.

"Buy!"

"SELL!"

"Trade!"

"BARTER!"

"YOU'RE MUCH BIGGER, BUT WE ARE SMARTER!"

When the visitors shoot a free throw on most every court in the country, the fans make a lot of noise, screaming and stomping their feet. It doesn't work, because players learn to tune out white noise. At Culver Creek, we had a much better strategy. At first, everyone yelled and screamed like in a normal game. But then everyone said, *"Shh!"* and there was absolute silence. Just as our hated opponent stopped dribbling and prepared for his shot, the Colonel stood up and screamed something. Like:

"For the love of God, please shave your back hair!" Or:

"I need to be saved. Can you minister to me after your shot?!"

Toward the end of the third quarter, the Christian-school coach called a time-out and complained to the ref about the Colonel, pointing at him angrily. We were down 56–13. The Colonel stood up. "What?! You have a problem with me!?"

The coach screamed, "You're bothering my players!"

"THAT'S THE POINT, SHERLOCK!" the Colonel screamed back. The ref came over and kicked him out of the gym. I followed him.

"I've gotten thrown out of thirty-seven straight games," he said.

"Damn."

"Yeah. Once or twice, I've had to go really crazy. I ran onto the court with eleven seconds left once and stole the ball from the other team. It wasn't pretty. But, you know. I have a streak to maintain."

The Colonel ran ahead of me, gleeful at his ejection, and I jogged after him, trailing in his wake. I wanted to be one of those people who have streaks to maintain, who scorch the ground with their intensity. But for now, at least I knew such people, and they needed me, just like comets need tails.

one hundred eight days before

THE NEXT DAY, Dr. Hyde asked me to stay after class. Standing before him, I realized for the first time how hunched his shoulders were, and he seemed suddenly sad and kind of old. "You like this class, don't you?" he asked.

"Yessir."

"You've got a lifetime to mull over the Buddhist understanding of interconnectedness." He spoke every sentence as if he'd written it down, memorized it, and was now reciting it. "But while you were looking out the window, you missed the chance to explore the equally interesting Buddhist belief in being present for every facet of your daily life, of being truly present. Be present in this class. And then, when it's over, be present out there," he said, nodding toward the lake and beyond.

"Yessir."

one hundred one days before

ON THE FIRST MORNING of October, I knew something was wrong as soon as I woke up enough to turn off the alarm clock. The bed didn't smell right. And I didn't feel right. It took me a groggy minute before I realized: I felt *cold*. Well, at the very least, the small fan clipped to my bunk seemed suddenly unnecessary. "It's cold!" I shouted.

"Oh God, what time is it?" I heard above me.

"Eight-oh-four," I said.

The Colonel, who didn't have an alarm clock but almost always woke up to take a shower before mine went off, swung his short legs over the side of the bed, jumped down, and dashed to his dresser. "I suppose I missed my window of opportunity to shower," he said as he put on a green CULVER CREEK BASKETBALL T-shirt and a pair of shorts. "Oh well. There's always tomorrow. And it's not cold. It's probably eighty."

Grateful to have slept fully dressed, I just put on shoes, and the Colonel and I jogged to the classrooms. I slid into my seat with twenty seconds to spare. Halfway through class, Madame O'Malley turned around to write something in French on the blackboard, and Alaska passed me a note.

Nice bedhead. Study at McDonald's for lunch?

Our first significant precalc test was only two days away, so Alaska grabbed the six precalc kids she did not consider Weekday Warriors and piled us into her tiny blue two-door. By happy coincidence, a cute sophomore named Lara ended up sitting on my lap. Lara'd been born in Russia or someplace, and she spoke with a slight accent. Since we were only four layers of clothes from doing it, I took the opportunity to introduce myself.

"I know who you are." She smiled. "You're Alaska's freend from FlowReeda."

"Yup. Get ready for a lot of dumb questions, 'cause I suck at precalc," I said.

She started to answer, but then she was thrown back against me as Alaska shot out of the parking lot.

"Kids, meet Blue Citrus. So named because she is a lemon," Alaska said. "Blue Citrus, meet the kids. If you can find them, you might want to fasten your seat belts. Pudge, you might want to serve as a seat belt for Lara." What the car lacked in speed, Alaska made up for by refusing to move her foot from the accelerator, damn the consequences. Before we even got off campus, Lara was lurching helplessly whenever Alaska took hard turns, so I took Alaska's advice and wrapped my arms around Lara's waist.

"Thanks," she said, almost inaudibly.

After a fast if reckless three miles to McDonald's, we ordered seven large french fries to share and then went outside and sat on the lawn. We sat in a circle around the trays of fries, and Alaska taught class, smoking while she ate.

Like any good teacher, she tolerated little dissension. She smoked and talked and ate for an hour without stopping, and I scribbled in my notebook as the muddy waters of tangents and cosines began to clarify. But not everyone was so fortunate.

As Alaska zipped through something obvious about linear equations, stoner/baller Hank Walsten said, "Wait, wait. I don't get it."

"That's because you have eight functioning brain cells."

"Studies show that marijuana is better for your health than those cigarettes," Hank said.

Alaska swallowed a mouthful of french fries, took a drag on her cigarette, and blew smoke across the table at Hank. "I may die young," she said. "But at least I'll die smart. Now, back to tangents."

one hundred days before

"NOT TO ASK the obvious question, but why *Alaska?*" I asked. I'd just gotten my precalc test back, and I was awash with admiration for Alaska, since her tutoring had paved my way to a B-plus. She and I sat alone in the TV lounge watching MTV on a drearily cloudy Saturday. Furnished with couches left behind by previous generations of Culver Creek students, the TV room had the musty air of dust and mildew—and, perhaps for that reason, was almost perennially unoccupied. Alaska took a sip of Mountain Dew and grabbed my hand in hers.

"Always comes up eventually. All right, so my mom was something of a hippie when I was a kid. You know, wore oversize sweaters she knitted herself, smoked a lot of pot, et cetera. And my dad was a real Republican type, and so when I was born, my mom wanted to name me Harmony Springs Young, and my dad wanted to name me Mary Frances Young." As she talked, she bobbed her head back and forth to the MTV music, even though the song was the kind of manufactured pop ballad she professed to hate.

"So instead of naming me Harmony *or* Mary, they agreed to let me decide. So when I was little, they called me Mary. I mean, they called me sweetie or whatever, but like on school forms and stuff, they wrote *Mary Young*. And then on my seventh birthday, my present was that I got to pick my name. Cool, huh? So I spent the whole day looking at my dad's globe for a really cool name. And so my first choice was Chad, like the country in Africa. But then my dad said that was a boy's name, so I picked Alaska."

I wish my parents had let me pick *my* name. But they went ahead and picked the only name firstborn male Halters have had for a century. "But why Alaska?" I asked her.

She smiled with the right side of her mouth. "Well, later, I found out what it means. It's from an Aleut word, *Alyeska*. It means 'that which the sea breaks against,' and I love that. But at the time, I just saw Alaska up there. And it was big, just like I wanted to be. And it was damn far away from Vine Station, Alabama, just like I wanted to be."

I laughed. "And now you're all grown up and fairly far away from home," I said, smiling. "So congratulations." She stopped the head bobbing and let go of my (unfortunately sweaty) hand.

"Getting out isn't that easy," she said seriously, her eyes on mine like I knew the way out and wouldn't tell her. And then she seemed to switch conversational horses in midstream. "Like after college, know what I want to do? Teach disabled kids. I'm a good teacher, right? Shit, if I can teach you precalc, I can teach anybody. Like maybe kids with autism."

She talked softly and thoughtfully, like she was telling me a secret, and I leaned in toward her, suddenly overwhelmed with the feeling that we must kiss, that we ought to kiss right now on the dusty orange couch with its cigarette burns and its decades of collected dust. And I would have: I would have kept leaning toward her until it became necessary to tilt my face so as to miss her ski-slope nose, and I would have felt the shock of her so-soft lips. I would have. But then she snapped out of it.

"No," she said, and I couldn't tell at first whether she was reading my kiss-obsessed mind or responding to herself out loud. She turned away from me, and softly, maybe to herself, said, "Jesus, I'm not going to be one of those people who sits around talking about what they're gonna do. I'm just going to do it. Imagining the future is a kind of nostalgia."

"Huh?" I asked.

"You spend your whole life stuck in the labyrinth, thinking about how you'll escape it one day, and how awesome it will be, and imagining that future keeps you going, but you never do it. You just use the future to escape the present."

I guess that made sense. I had imagined that life at the Creek would be a bit more exciting than it was—in reality, there'd been more homework than adventure—but if I hadn't imagined it, I would never have gotten to the Creek at all.

She turned back to the TV, a commercial for a car now, and made a joke about Blue Citrus needing its own car commercial. Mimicking the deep-voiced passion of commercial voice-overs, she said, "It's small, it's slow, and it's shitty, but it runs. Sometimes. Blue Citrus: See Your Local Used-Car Dealer." But I wanted to talk more about her and Vine Station and the future.

"Sometimes I don't get you," I said.

She didn't even glance at me. She just smiled toward the television and said, "You never get me. That's the whole point."

ninety-nine days before

I SPENT MOST of the next day lying in bed, immersed in the miserably uninteresting fictional world of *Ethan Frome*, while the Colonel sat at his desk, unraveling the secrets of differential equations or something. Although we tried to ration our smoke breaks amid the shower's steam, we ran out of cigarettes before dark, necessitating a trip to Alaska's room. She lay on the floor, holding a book over her head.

"Let's go smoke," he said.

"You're out of cigarettes, aren't you?" she asked without looking up.

"Well. Yes."

"Got five bucks?" she asked.

"Nope."

"Pudge?" she asked.

"Yeah, all right." I fished a five out of my pocket, and Alaska handed me a pack of twenty Marlboro Lights. I knew I'd smoke maybe five of them, but so long as I subsidized the Colonel's smoking, he couldn't really attack me for being another rich kid, a Weekday Warrior who just didn't happen to live in Birmingham.

We grabbed Takumi and walked down to the lake, hiding behind a few trees, laughing. The Colonel blew smoke rings, and Takumi called them "pretentious," while Alaska followed the smoke rings with her fingers, stabbing at them like a kid trying to pop bubbles.

And then we heard a branch break. It might have been a deer, but the Colonel busted out anyway. A voice directly behind us said, "Don't run, Chipper," and the Colonel stopped, turned around, and returned to us sheepishly.

The Eagle walked toward us slowly, his lips pursed in disgust. He wore a white shirt and a black tie, like always. He gave each of us in turn the Look of Doom.

"Y'all smell like a North Carolina tobacco field in a wildfire," he said.

We stood silent. I felt disproportionately terrible, like I had just been caught fleeing the scene of a murder. Would he call my parents?

"I'll see you in Jury tomorrow at five," he announced, and then walked away. Alaska crouched down, picked up the cigarette she had thrown away, and started smoking again. The Eagle wheeled around, his sixth sense detecting Insubordination To Authority Figures. Alaska dropped the cigarette and stepped on it. The Eagle shook his head, and even though he must have been crazy mad, I swear to God he smiled.

"He loves me," Alaska told me as we walked back to the dorm circle. "He loves all y'all, too. He just loves the school more. That's the thing. He thinks busting us is good for the school and good for us. It's the eternal struggle, Pudge. The Good versus the Naughty."

"You're awfully philosophical for a girl that just got busted," I told her.

"Sometimes you lose a battle. But mischief always wins the war."

ninety-eight days before

ONE OF THE UNIQUE THINGS about Culver Creek was the Jury. Every semester, the faculty elected twelve students, three from each class, to serve on the Jury. The Jury meted out punishment for nonexpellable offenses, for everything from staying out past curfew to smoking. Usually, it was smoking or being in a girl's room after seven. So you went to the Jury, you made your case, and they punished you. The Eagle served as the judge, and he had the right to overturn the Jury's verdict (just like in the real American court system), but he almost never did.

I made my way to Classroom 4 right after my last class—forty minutes early, just to be safe. I sat in the hall with my back against the wall and read my American history textbook (kind of remedial reading for me, to be honest) until Alaska showed up and sat down next to me. She was chewing on her bottom lip, and I asked whether she was nervous.

"Well, yeah. Listen, just sit tight and don't talk," she told me. "*You* don't need to be nervous. But this is the seventh time I've been caught smoking. I just don't want — whatever. I don't want to upset my dad."

"Does your mom smoke or something?" I asked.

"Not anymore," Alaska said. "It's fine. You'll be fine."

I didn't start to worry until it got to be 4:50 and the Colonel and Takumi were still unaccounted for. The members of the Jury filed in one by one, walking past us without any eye contact, which made me feel worse. I counted all twelve by 4:56, plus the Eagle.

At 4:58, the Colonel and Takumi rounded the corner toward the classrooms.

I never saw anything like it. Takumi wore a starched white shirt with a red tie with a black paisley print; the Colonel wore his wrinkled pink button-down and flamingo tie. They walked in step, heads up and shoulders back, like some kind of action-movie heroes.

I heard Alaska sigh. "The Colonel's doing his Napoleon walk."

"It's all good," the Colonel told me. "Just don't say anything."

We walked in—two of us wearing ties, and two of us wearing ratty T-shirts—and the Eagle banged an honest-to-God gavel against the podium in front of him. The Jury sat in a line behind a rectangular table. At the front of the room, by the blackboard, were four chairs. We sat down, and the Colonel explained exactly what happened.

"Alaska and I were smoking down by the lake. We usually go off campus, but we forgot. We're sorry. It won't happen again."

I didn't know what was going on. But I knew my job: sit tight and shut up. One of the kids looked at Takumi and asked, "What about you and Halter?"

"We were keeping them company," Takumi said calmly.

The kid turned to the Eagle then and asked, "Did you see anyone smoking?"

"I only saw Alaska, but Chip ran away, which struck me as cowardly, as does Miles and Takumi's aw-shucks routine," the Eagle said, giving me the Look of Doom. I didn't want to look guilty, but I couldn't hold his stare, so I just looked down at my hands.

The Colonel gritted his teeth, like it pained him to lie. "It is the truth, sir."

The Eagle asked if any of us wanted to say anything, and then asked if there were any more questions, and then sent us outside.

"What the hell was that?" I asked Takumi when we got outside.

"Just sit tight, Pudge."

Why have Alaska confess when she'd already been in trouble so many times? Why the Colonel, who literally couldn't afford to get in serious trouble? Why not me? I'd never been busted for anything. I had the least to lose. After a couple minutes, the Eagle came out and motioned for us to come back inside.

"Alaska and Chip," a member of the Jury said, "you get ten work hours—doing dishes in the cafeteria—and you're both officially one problem away from a phone call home. Takumi and Miles, there's nothing in the rules about watching someone smoke, but the Jury will remember your story if you break the rules again. Fair?"

"Fair," Alaska said quickly, obviously relieved. On my way out, the Eagle spun me around. "Don't abuse your privileges at this school, young man, or you will regret it." I nodded.

"WE FOUND YOU A GIRLFRIEND," Alaska said to me. Still, no one had explained to me what happened the week before with the Jury. It didn't seem to have affected Alaska, though, who was *1.* in our room after dark with the door closed, and *2.* smoking a cigarette as she sat on the mostly foam couch. She had stuffed a towel into the bottom of our door and insisted it was safe, but I worried— about the cigarette and the "girlfriend."

"All I have to do now," she said, "is convince you to like her and convince her to like you."

"Monumental tasks," the Colonel pointed out. He lay on the top bunk, reading for his English class. *Moby-Dick.*

"How can you read and talk at the same time?" I asked.

"Well, I usually can't, but neither the book nor the conversation is particularly intellectually challenging."

"I like that book," Alaska said.

"Yes." The Colonel smiled and leaned over to look at her from his top bunk. "You would. Big white whale is a metaphor for everything. You live for pretentious metaphors."

Alaska was unfazed. "So, Pudge, what's your feeling on the former Soviet bloc?"

"Um. I'm in favor of it?"

She flicked the ashes of her cigarette into my pencil holder. I almost protested, but why bother. "You know that girl in our precalc class," Alaska said, "soft voice, says *thees,* not *this.* Know that girl?"

"Yeah. Lara. She sat on my lap on the way to McDonald's."

"Right. I know. And she liked you. You thought she was quietly discussing precalc, when she was clearly talking about having hot sex with you. Which is why you need me."

"She has great breasts," the Colonel said without looking up from the whale.

"DO NOT OBJECTIFY WOMEN'S BODIES!" Alaska shouted. Now he looked up. "Sorry. Perky breasts."

"That's not any better!"

"Sure it is," he said. "*Great* is a judgment on a woman's body. *Perky* is merely an observation. They *are* perky. I mean, Christ."

"You're hopeless," she said. "So she thinks you're cute, Pudge."

"Nice."

"Doesn't mean anything. Problem with you is that if you talk to her you'll 'uh um uh' your way to disaster."

"Don't be so hard on him," the Colonel interrupted, as if he was my mom. "God, I understand whale anatomy. Can we move on now, Herman?"

"So Jake is going to be in Birmingham this weekend, and we're going on a triple date. Well, triple and a half, since Takumi will be there, too. Very low pressure. You won't be able to screw up, because I'll be there the whole time."

"Okay."

"Who's my date?" the Colonel asked.

"Your girlfriend is your date."

"All right," he said, and then deadpanned, "but we don't get along very well."

"So Friday? Do you have plans for Friday?" And then I laughed, because the Colonel and I didn't have plans for this Friday, or for any other Friday for the rest of our lives.

"I didn't think so." She smiled. "Now, we gotta go do dishes in the cafeteria, Chipper. God, the sacrifices I make."

eighty-seven days before

OUR TRIPLE-AND-A-HALF DATE started off well enough. I was in Alaska's room—for the sake of getting me a girlfriend, she'd agreed to iron a green button-down shirt for me—when Jake showed up. With blond hair to his shoulders, dark stubble on his cheeks, and the kind of faux-ruggedness that gets you a career as a catalog model, Jake was every bit as good-looking as you'd expect Alaska's boyfriend to be. She jumped onto him and wrapped her legs around him (*God forbid anyone ever does that to me,* I thought. *I'll fall over*). I'd heard Alaska *talk* about kissing, but I'd never seen her kiss until then: As he held her by her waist, she leaned forward, her pouty lips parted, her head just slightly tilted, and enveloped his mouth with such passion that I felt I should look away but couldn't. A good while later, she untangled herself from Jake and introduced me.

"This is Pudge," she said. Jake and I shook hands.

"I've heard a lot about ya." He spoke with a slight Southern accent, one of the few I'd heard outside of McDonald's. "I hope your date works out tonight, 'cause I wouldn't want you stealin' Alaska out from under me."

"God, you're so adorable," Alaska said before I could answer, kissing him again. "I'm sorry." She laughed. "I just can't seem to stop kissing my boyfriend."

I put on my freshly starched green shirt, and the three of us gathered up the Colonel, Sara, Lara, and Takumi and then walked to the gym to watch the Culver Creek Nothings take on Harsden Academy, a private day school in Mountain Brook, Birmingham's richest suburb. The Colonel's hatred for Harsden burned with the fire of a thousand suns. "The only thing I hate more than rich people," he told me as we walked to the gym, "is stupid people. And all the kids at Harsden are rich, and they're all too stupid to get into the Creek."

Since we were supposed to be on a date and all, I thought I'd sit next to Lara at the game, but as I tried to walk past a seated Alaska on my way to Lara, Alaska shot me a look and patted the empty spot next to her on the bleachers.

"I'm not allowed to sit next to my date?" I asked.

"Pudge, one of us has been a girl her whole life. The other of us has never gotten to second base. If I were you, I'd sit down, look cute, and be your pleasantly aloof self."

"Okay. Whatever you say."

Jake said, "That's pretty much my strategy for pleasing Alaska."

"Aww," she said, "so sweet! Pudge, did I tell you that Jake is recording an album with his band? They're fantastic. They're like Radiohead meets the Flaming Lips. Did I tell you that I came up with their name, Hickman Territory?" And then, realizing she was being silly: "Did I tell you that Jake is hung like a horse and a beautiful, sensual lover?"

"Baby, Jesus." Jake smiled. "Not in front of the kids."

I wanted to hate Jake, of course, but as I watched them together, smiling and fumbling all over each other, I didn't hate him. I wanted to *be* him, sure, but I tried to remember I was ostensibly on a date with someone else.

Harsden Academy's star player was a six-foot-seven Goliath named Travis Eastman that everyone—even his mother, I suspect—called the Beast. The first time the Beast got to the free-throw line, the Colonel could not keep himself from swearing while he taunted:

"You owe everything to your daddy, you stupid redneck bastard."

The Beast turned around and glared, and the Colonel almost got kicked out after the first free throw, but he smiled at the ref and said, "Sorry!"

"I want to stay around for a good part of this one," he said to me.

At the start of the second half, with the Creek down by a surprisingly slim margin of twenty-four points and the Beast at the foul line, the Colonel looked at Takumi and said, "It's time." Takumi and the Colonel stood up as the crowd went, "*Shhh . . .*"

"I don't know if this is the best time to tell you this," the Colonel shouted at the Beast, "but Takumi here hooked up with your girl-friend just before the game."

That made everyone laugh—except the Beast, who turned from the free throw line and walked calmly, with the ball, toward us.

"I think we run now," Takumi said.

"I haven't gotten kicked out," the Colonel answered.

"Later," Takumi said.

I don't know whether it was the general anxiety of being on a date (albeit one with my would-be date sitting five people away from me) or the specific anxiety of having the Beast stare in my direction, but for some reason, I took off running after Takumi. I thought we were in the clear as we began to round the corner of the bleachers, but then I saw, out of the corner of my eye, a cylindrical orange object getting bigger and bigger, like a fast-approaching sun.

I thought: *I think that is going to hit me.*

I thought: *I should duck.*

But in the time between when something gets thought and when it gets done, the ball hit me square across the side of the face. I fell, the back of my head slamming against the gym floor. I then stood up immediately, as if unhurt, and left the gym.

Pride had gotten me off the floor of the gym, but as soon as I was outside, I sat down.

"I am concussed," I announced, entirely sure of my self-diagnosis.

"You're fine," Takumi said as he jogged back toward me. "Let's get out of here before we're killed."

"I'm sorry," I said. "But I can't get up. I have suffered a mild con-cussion."

Lara ran out and sat down next to me.

"Are you okay?"

"I am concussed," I said.

Takumi sat down with me and looked me in the eye. "Do you know what happened to you?"

"The Beast got me."

"Do you know where you are?"

"I'm on a triple-and-a-half date."

"You're fine," Takumi said. "Let's go."

And then I leaned forward and threw up onto Lara's pants. I can't say why I didn't lean backward or to the side. I leaned forward and aimed my mouth toward her jeans—a nice, butt-flattering pair of jeans, the kind of pants a girl wears when she wants to look nice but not look like she is trying to look nice—and I threw up all over them.

Mostly peanut butter, but also clearly some corn.

"Oh!" she said, surprised and slightly horrified.

"Oh God," I said. "I'm so sorry."

"I think you might have a concussion," Takumi said, as if the idea had never been suggested.

"I am suffering from the nausea and dizziness typically associated with a mild concussion," I recited. While Takumi went to get the Eagle and Lara changed pants, I lay on the concrete sidewalk. The Eagle came back with the school nurse, who diagnosed me with—get this—a concussion, and then Takumi drove me to the hospital with Lara riding shotgun. Apparently I lay in the back and slowly repeated the words "The. Symptoms. Generally. Associated. With. Concussion."

So I spent my date at the hospital with Lara and Takumi. The doctor told me to go home and sleep a lot, but to make sure and have someone wake me up every four hours or so.

I vaguely remember Lara standing in the doorway, the room dark and the outside dark and everything mild and comfortable but sort of spinny, the world pulsing as if from a heavy bass beat. And I vaguely remember Lara smiling at me from the doorway, the glittering ambiguity of a girl's smile, which seems to promise an answer to the question but never gives it. *The* question, the one we've all been asking since girls stopped being gross, the question that is too simple to be uncomplicated: Does she like me or *like* me? And then I fell deeply, endlessly asleep and slept until three in the morning, when the Colonel woke me up.

"She dumped me," he said.

"I am concussed," I responded.

"So I heard. Hence my waking you up. Video game?"

"Okay. But keep it on mute. My head hurts."

"Yeah. Heard you puked on Lara. Very suave."

"Dumped?" I asked, getting up.

"Yeah. Sara told Jake that I had a hard-on for Alaska. Those words. In that order. And I was like, 'Well, I don't have a hard-on for *anything* at this moment. You can check if you'd like,' and Sara thought I was being too glib, I suppose, because then she said she knew for a fact I'd hooked up with Alaska. Which, incidentally, is ridiculous. I. Don't. Cheat," he said, and finally the game finished loading and I half listened as I drove a stock car in circles around a silent track in Talladega. The circles nauseated me, but I kept at it.

"So Alaska went ballistic, basically." He affected Alaska's voice then, making it more shrill and headache-inducing than it actually was. "'No woman should ever lie about another woman! You've violated the sacred covenant between women! How will stabbing one another in the back help women to rise above patriarchal oppression?!' And so on. And then Jake came to Alaska's defense, saying that she would never cheat because she loved him, and then I was like, 'Don't worry about Sara. She just likes bullying people.' And then Sara asked me why I never stood up for her, and somewhere in there I called her a crazy bitch, which didn't go over particularly well. And then the waitress asked us to leave, and so we were standing in the parking lot and she said, 'I've had enough,' and I just stared at her and she said, 'Our relationship is over.'"

He stopped talking then. "'Our relationship is over?'" I repeated.

I felt very spacey and thought it was just best to repeat the last phrase of whatever the Colonel said so he could keep talking.

"Yeah. So that's it. You know what's lame, Pudge? I really care about her. I mean, we were hopeless. Badly matched. But still. I mean, I said I loved her. I lost my virginity to her."

"You lost your virginity to her?"

"Yeah. Yeah. I never told you that? She's the only girl I've slept with. I don't know. Even though we fought, like, ninety-four percent of the time, I'm really sad."

"You're really sad?"

"Sadder than I thought I'd be, anyway. I mean, I knew it was inevitable. We haven't had a pleasant moment this whole year. Ever since I got here, I mean, we were just on each other relentlessly. I should have been nicer to her. I don't know. It's sad."

"It is sad," I repeated.

"I mean, it's stupid to miss someone you didn't even get along with. But, I don't know, it was nice, you know, having someone you could always fight with."

"Fighting," I said, and then, confused, barely able to drive, I added, "is nice."

"Right. I don't know what I'll do now. I mean, it was nice to have her. I'm a mad guy, Pudge. What do I do with that?"

"You can fight with me," I said. I put my controller down and leaned back on our foam couch and was asleep. As I drifted off, I heard the Colonel say, "I can't be mad at you, you harmless skinny bastard."

eighty-four days before

THREE DAYS LATER, the rain began. My head still hurt, and the sizable knot above my left temple looked, the Colonel thought, like a miniaturized topographical map of Macedonia, which I had not previously known was a place, let alone a country. And as the Colonel and I walked over the parched, half-dead grass that Monday, I said, "I suppose we could use some rain," and the Colonel looked up at the low clouds coming in fast and threatening, and then he said, "Well, use it or not, we're sure as shit going to get some."

And we sure as shit did. Twenty minutes into French class, Madame O'Malley was conjugating the verb *to believe* in the subjunctive. *Que je croie. Que tu croies. Qu'il ou qu'elle croie.* She said it over and over, like it wasn't a verb so much as a Buddhist mantra. *Que je croie; que tu croies; qu'il ou qu'elle croie.* What a funny thing to say over and over again: I would believe; you would believe; he or she would believe. *Believe what?* I thought, and right then, the rain came.

It came all at once and in a furious torrent, like God was mad and wanted to flood us out. Day after day, night after night, it rained. It rained so that I couldn't see across the dorm circle, so that the lake swelled up and lapped against the Adirondack swing, swallowing half of the fake beach. By the third day, I abandoned my umbrella entirely and walked around in a perpetual state of wetness. Everything at the cafeteria tasted like the minor acid of rainwater and everything stank of mildew and showers became ludicrously inappropriate because the whole goddamned world had better water pressure than the showers.

And the rain made hermits of us all. The Colonel spent every not-in-class moment sitting on the couch, reading the almanac and playing video games, and I wasn't sure whether he wanted to talk or whether he just wanted to sit on the white foam and drink his ambrosia in peace.

After the disaster that was our "date," I felt it best not to speak to Lara under any circumstances, lest I suffer a concussion and/or an attack of puking, even though she'd told me in precalc the next day that it was "no beeg deal."

And I saw Alaska only in class and could never talk to her, because she came to every class late and left the moment the bell rang, before I could even cap my pen and close my notebook. On the fifth evening of the rain, I walked into the cafeteria fully prepared to go back to my room and eat a reheated bufriedo for dinner if Alaska and/or Takumi weren't eating (I knew full well the Colonel was in Room 43, dining on milk 'n' vodka). But I stayed, because I saw Alaska sitting alone, her back to a rain-streaked window. I grabbed a heaping plate of fried okra and sat down next to her.

"God, it's like it'll never end," I said, referring to the rain.

"Indeed," she said. Her wet hair hung from her head and mostly covered her face. I ate some. She ate some.

"How've you been?" I finally asked.

"I'm really not up for answering any questions that start with *how, when, where, why,* or *what.*"

"What's wrong?" I asked.

"That's a *what.* I'm not doing *what*'s right now. All right, I should go." She pursed her lips and exhaled slowly, like the way the Colonel blew out smoke.

"What—" Then I stopped myself and reworded. "Did I do something?" I asked.

She gathered her tray and stood up before answering. "Of course not, sweetie."

Her "sweetie" felt condescending, not romantic, like a boy enduring his first biblical rainstorm couldn't possibly understand her problems—whatever they were. It took a sincere effort not to roll my eyes at her, though she wouldn't have even noticed as she walked out of the cafeteria with her hair dripping over her face.

"I FEEL BETTER," the Colonel told me on the ninth day of the rainstorm as he sat down next to me in religion class. "I had an epiphany. Do you remember that night when she came to the room and was a complete and total bitch?"

"Yeah. The opera. The flamingo tie."

"Right."

"What about it?" I asked.

The Colonel pulled out a spiral notebook, the top half of which was soaking wet, and slowly pulled the pages apart until he found his place. "That was the epiphany. She's a complete and total bitch."

Hyde hobbled in, leaning heavily on a black cane. As he made his way toward his chair, he drily noted, "My trick knee is warning me that we might have some rain. So prepare yourselves." He stood in front of his chair, leaned back cautiously, grabbed it with both hands, and collapsed into the chair with a series of quick, shallow breaths—like a woman in labor.

"Although it isn't due for more than two months, you'll be receiving your paper topic for this semester today. Now, I'm quite sure that you've all read the syllabus for this class with such frequency and seriousness that by now you've committed it to memory." He smirked. "But a reminder: This paper is fifty percent of your grade. I encourage you to take it seriously. Now, about this Jesus fellow."

Hyde talked about the Gospel of Mark, which I hadn't read until the day before, although I was a Christian. I guess. I'd been to church, uh, like four times. Which is more frequently than I'd been to a mosque or a synagogue.

He told us that in the first century, around the time of Jesus, some of the Roman coins had a picture of the Emperor Augustus on them, and that beneath his picture were inscribed the words *Filius Dei*. The Son of God.

"We are speaking," he said, "of a time in which gods had sons. It was not so unusual to be a son of God. The miracle, at least in that time and in that place, was that *Jesus*—a peasant, a Jew, a nobody in an empire ruled exclusively by somebodies—was the son of *that* God, the all-powerful God of Abraham and Moses. That God's son was not an emperor. Not even a trained rabbi. A peasant and a Jew. A nobody like you. While the Buddha was special because he abandoned his wealth and noble birth to seek enlightenment, Jesus was special because he lacked wealth and noble birth, but inherited the ultimate nobility: King of Kings. Class over. You can pick up a copy of your final exam on the way out. Stay dry." It wasn't until I stood up to leave that I noticed Alaska had skipped class—how could she skip the only class worth attending? I grabbed a copy of the final for her.

The final exam: *What is the most important question human beings must answer? Choose your question wisely, and then examine how Islam, Buddhism, and Christianity attempt to answer it.*

"I hope that poor bastard lives the rest of the school year," the Colonel said as we jogged home through the rain, "because I'm sure starting to enjoy that class. What's your most important question?"

After thirty seconds of running, I was already winded. "What happens . . . to us . . . when we die?"

"Christ, Pudge, if you don't stop running, you're going to find out." He slowed to a walk. "My question is: Why do good people get rotten lots in life? Holy shit, is that Alaska?"

She was running at us at full speed, and she was screaming, but I couldn't hear her over the pounding rain until she was so close to us that I could see her spit flying.

"The fuckers flooded my room. They ruined like a hundred of my books! Goddamned pissant Weekday Warrior shit. Colonel, they poked a hole in the gutter and connected a plastic tube from the gutter down through my back window into my room! The whole place is soaking wet. My copy of *The General in His Labyrinth* is absolutely *ruined*."

"That's pretty good," the Colonel said, like an artist admiring another's work.

"Hey!" she shouted.

"Sorry. Don't worry, dude," he said. "God will punish the wicked. And before He does, we will."

sixty-seven days before

SO THIS IS HOW NOAH FELT. You wake up one morning and God has forgiven you and you walk around squinting all day because you've forgotten how sunlight feels warm and rough against your skin like a kiss on the cheek from your dad, and the whole world is brighter and cleaner than ever before, like central Alabama has been put in the washing machine for two weeks and cleaned with extra-superstrength detergent with color brightener, and now the grass is greener and the bufriedos are crunchier.

I stayed by the classrooms that afternoon, lying on my stomach in the newly dry grass and reading for American history—the Civil War, or as it was known around these parts, the War Between the States. To me, it was the war that spawned a thousand good last words. Like General Albert Sidney Johnston, who, when asked if he was injured, answered, "Yes, and I fear seriously." Or Robert E. Lee, who, many years after the war, in a dying delirium, announced, "Strike the tent!"

I was mulling over why the Confederate generals had better last words than the Union ones (Ulysses S. Grant's last word, "Water," was pretty lame) when I noticed a shadow blocking me from the sun. It had been some time since I'd seen a shadow, and it startled me a bit. I looked up.

"I brought you a snack," Takumi said, dropping an oatmeal cream pie onto my book.

"Very nutritious." I smiled.

"You've got your oats. You've got your meal. You've got your cream. It's a fuckin' food pyramid."

"Hell yeah it is."

And then I didn't know what to say. Takumi knew a lot about hip-hop; I knew a lot about last words and video games. Finally, I said, "I can't believe those guys flooded Alaska's room."

"Yeah," Takumi said, not looking at me. "Well, they had their reasons. You have to understand that with like everybody, even the Weekday Warriors, Alaska is famous for pranking. I mean, last year, we put a Volkswagen Beetle in the library. So if they have a reason to try and one-up her, they'll try. And that's pretty ingenious, to divert water from the gutter to her room. I mean, I don't *want* to admire it . . ."

I laughed. "Yeah. That will be tough to top." I unwrapped the cream pie and bit into it. Mmm . . . hundreds of delicious calories per bite.

"She'll think of something," he said. "Pudge," he said. "Hmm. Pudge, you need a cigarette. Let's go for a walk."

I felt nervous, as I invariably do when someone says my name twice with a *hmm* in between. But I got up, leaving my books behind, and walked toward the Smoking Hole. But as soon as we got to the edge of the woods, Takumi turned away from the dirt road. "Not sure the Hole is safe," he said. *Not safe?* I thought. *It's the safest place to smoke a cigarette in the known universe.* But I just followed him through the thick brush, weaving through pine trees and threatening, chest-high brambly bushes. After a while, he just sat down. I cupped my hand around my lighter to protect the flame from the slight breeze and lit up.

"Alaska ratted out Marya," he said. "So the Eagle might know about the Smoking Hole, too. I don't know. I've never seen him down that way, but who knows what she told him."

"Wait, how do you know?" I asked, dubious.

"Well, for one thing, I figured it out. And for another, Alaska admitted it. She told me at least part of the truth, that right at the end of school last year, she tried to sneak off campus one night after lights-out to go visit Jake and then got busted. She said she was careful—no headlights or anything—but the Eagle caught her, and she had a bottle of wine in her car, so she was fucked. And the Eagle took her into his house and gave her the same offer he gives to everyone when they get fatally busted. 'Either tell me everything you know or go to your room and pack up your stuff.' So Alaska broke and told him that Marya and Paul were drunk and in her room right then. And then she told him God knows what else. And so the Eagle let her go, because he needs rats to do his job. She was smart, really, to rat on one of her friends, because no one ever thinks to blame the friends. That's why the Colonel is so sure it was Kevin and his boys. I didn't believe it could be Alaska, either, until I figured out that she was the only person on campus who could've known what Marya was doing. I suspected Paul's roommate, Long-well—one of the guys who pulled the armless-mermaid bit on you. Turns out he was at home that night. His aunt had died. I checked the obit in the paper. Hollis Burnis Chase—hell of a name for a woman."

"So the Colonel doesn't know?" I asked, stunned. I put out my cigarette, even though I wasn't quite finished, because I felt spooked. I'd never suspected Alaska could be disloyal. Moody, yes. But not a rat.

"No, and he can't know, because he'll go crazy and get her expelled. The Colonel takes all this honor and loyalty shit pretty seriously, if you haven't noticed."

"I've noticed."

Takumi shook his head, his hands pushing aside leaves to dig into the still-wet dirt beneath. "I just don't get why she'd be so afraid of getting expelled. I'd hate to get expelled, but you have to take your lumps. I don't get it."

"Well, she obviously doesn't like home."

"True. She only goes home over Christmas and the summer, when Jake is there. But whatever. I don't like home, either. But I'd never give the Eagle the satisfaction." Takumi picked up a twig and dug it into the soft red dirt. "Listen, Pudge. I don't know what kind of prank Alaska and the Colonel are going to come up with to end this, but I'm sure we'll both be involved. I'm telling you all this so you can know what you're getting into, because if you get caught, you had better take it."

I thought of Florida, of my "school friends," and realized for the first time how much I would miss the Creek if I ever had to leave it. I stared down at Takumi's twig sticking erect out of the mud and said, "I swear to God I won't rat."

I finally understood that day at the Jury: Alaska wanted to show us that we could trust her. Survival at Culver Creek meant loyalty, and she had ignored that. But then she'd shown me the way. She and the Colonel had taken the fall for me to show me how it was done, so I would know what to do when the time came.

fifty-eight days before

ABOUT A WEEK LATER I woke up at 6:30—6:30 on a Saturday!— to the sweet melody of Decapitation: automatic gunfire blasted out above the menacing, bass-heavy background music of the video game. I rolled over and saw Alaska pulling the controller up and to the right, as if that would help her escape certain death. I had the same bad habit.

"Can you at least mute it?"

"*Pudge,*" she said, faux-condescending, "the sound is an integral part of the artistic experience of this video game. Muting Decapitation would be like reading only every other word of *Jane Eyre*. The Colonel woke up about half an hour ago. He seemed a little annoyed, so I told him to go sleep in my room."

"Maybe I'll join him," I said groggily.

Rather than answering my question, she remarked, "So I heard Takumi told you. Yeah, I ratted out Marya, and I'm sorry, and I'll never do it again. In other news, are you staying here for Thanksgiving? Because I am."

I rolled back toward the wall and pulled the comforter over my head. I didn't know whether to trust Alaska, and I'd certainly had enough of her unpredictability—cold one day, sweet the next; irresistibly flirty one moment, resistibly obnoxious the next. I preferred the Colonel: At least when he was cranky, he had a *reason*.

In a testament to the power of fatigue, I managed to fall asleep quickly, convinced that the shrieking of dying monsters and Alaska's delighted squeals upon killing them were nothing more than a pleasant sound track by which to dream. I woke up half an hour later, when she sat down on my bed, her butt against my hip. *Her underwear, her jeans, the comforter, my corduroys, and my boxers between us*, I thought. Five layers, and yet I felt it, the nervous warmth of touching—a pale reflection of the fireworks of one mouth on another, but a reflection nonetheless. And in the almostness of the moment, I cared at least enough. I wasn't sure whether I liked her, and I doubted whether I could trust her, but I cared at least enough to try to find out. Her on my bed, wide green eyes staring down at me. The enduring mystery of her sly, almost smirking, smile. Five layers between us.

She continued as if I hadn't been asleep. "Jake has to study. So he doesn't want me in Nashville. Says he can't pay attention to musicology while staring at me. I said I would wear a burka, but he wasn't convinced, so I'm staying here."

"I'm sorry," I said.

"Oh, don't be. I'll have loads to do. There's a prank to plan. But I was thinking you should stay here, too. In fact, I have composed a list."

"A list?"

She reached into her pocket and pulled out a heavily folded piece of notebook paper and began to read.

"Why Pudge Should Stay at the Creek for Thanksgiving: A List, by Alaska Young.

"One. Because he is a very conscientious student, Pudge has been deprived of many wonderful Culver Creek experiences, including but not limited to *A.* drinking wine with me in the woods, and *B.* getting up early on a Saturday to eat breakfast at McInedible and then driving through the greater Birmingham area smoking cigarettes and talking about how pathetically boring the greater Birmingham area is, and also *C.* going out late at night and lying in the dewy soccer field and reading a Kurt Vonnegut book by moonlight.

"Two. Although she certainly does not excel at endeavors such as teaching the French language, Madame O'Malley makes a mean stuffing, and she invites all the students who stay on campus to Thanksgiving dinner. Which is usually just me and the South Korean exchange student, but whatever. Pudge would be welcome.

"Three. I don't really have a *Three,* but *One* and *Two* were awfully good."

One and *Two* appealed to me, certainly, but mostly I liked the idea of just her and just me on campus. "I'll talk to my parents. Once they wake up," I said. She coaxed me onto the couch, and we played Decapitation together until she abruptly dropped the controller.

"I'm not flirting. I'm just tired," she said, kicking off her flip-flops. She pulled her feet onto the foam couch, tucking them behind a cushion, and scooted up to put her head in my lap. My corduroys. My boxers. Two layers. I could feel the warmth of her cheek on my thigh.

There are times when it is appropriate, even preferable, to get an erection when someone's face is in close proximity to your penis.

This was not one of those times.

So I stopped thinking about the layers and the warmth, muted the TV, and focused on Decapitation.

At 8:30, I turned off the game and scooted out from underneath Alaska. She turned onto her back, still asleep, the lines of my corduroy pants imprinted on her cheek.

I usually only called my parents on Sunday afternoons, so when my mom heard my voice, she instantly overreacted. "What's wrong, Miles? Are you okay?"

"I'm fine, Mom. I think—if it's okay with you, I think I might stay here for Thanksgiving. A lot of my friends are staying"—lie—"and I have a lot of work to do"—double lie. "I had no idea how hard the classes would be, Mom"—truth.

"Oh, sweetie. We miss you so much. And there's a big Thanksgiving turkey waiting for you. And all the cranberry sauce you can eat."

I hated cranberry sauce, but for some reason my mom persisted in her lifelong belief that it was my very favorite food, even though every single Thanksgiving I politely declined to include it on my plate.

"I know, Mom. I miss you guys, too. But I really want to do well here"—truth—"and plus it's really nice to have, like, *friends*"—truth.

I knew that playing the friend card would sell her on the idea, and it did. So I got her blessing to stay on campus after promising to hang out with them for every minute of Christmas break (as if I had other plans).

I spent the morning at the computer, flipping back and forth between my religion and English papers. There were only two weeks of classes before exams—the coming one and the one after Thanksgiving—and so far, the best personal answer I had to "What happens to people after they die?" was "Well, something. Maybe."

The Colonel came in at noon, his thick übermath book cradled in his arms.

"I just saw Sara," he said.

"How'd that work out for ya?"

"Bad. She said she still loved me. God, 'I love you' really is the gateway drug of breaking up. Saying 'I love you' while walking across the dorm circle inevitably leads to saying 'I love you' while you're doing it. So I just bolted." I laughed. He pulled out a notebook and sat down at his desk.

"Yeah. Ha-ha. So Alaska said you're staying here."

"Yeah. I feel a little guilty about ditching my parents, though."

"Yeah, well. If you're staying here in hopes of making out with Alaska, I sure wish you wouldn't. If you unmoor her from the rock that is Jake, God have mercy on us all. That would be some drama, indeed. And as a rule, I like to avoid drama."

"It's not because I want to make out with her."

"Hold on." He grabbed a pencil and scrawled excitedly at the paper as if he'd just made a mathematical breakthrough and then looked back up at me. "I just did some calculations, and I've been able to determine that you're full of shit."

And he was right. How could I abandon my parents, who were nice enough to pay for my education at Culver Creek, my parents who had always loved me, just because I maybe liked some girl with a boyfriend? How could I leave them alone with a giant turkey and mounds of inedible cranberry sauce? So during third period, I called my mom at work. I wanted her to say it was okay, I guess, for me to stay at the Creek for Thanksgiving, but I didn't quite expect her to excitedly tell me that she and Dad had bought plane tickets to England immediately after I called and were planning to spend Thanksgiving in a castle on their second honeymoon.

"Oh, that—that's awesome," I said, and then quickly got off the phone because I did not want her to hear me cry. I guess Alaska heard me slam down the phone from her room, because she opened the door as I turned away, but said nothing. I walked across the dorm circle, and then straight through the soccer field, bush-whacking through the woods, until I ended up on the banks of Culver Creek just down from the bridge. I sat with my butt on a rock and my feet in the dark dirt of the creek bed and tossed pebbles into the clear, shallow water, and they landed with an empty *plop*, barely audible over the rumbling of the creek as it danced its way south. The light filtered through the leaves and pine needles above as if through lace, the ground spotted in shadow.

I thought of the one thing about home that I missed, my dad's study with its built-in, floor-to-ceiling shelves sagging with thick biographies, and the black leather chair that kept me just uncomfortable enough to keep from feeling sleepy as I read. It was stupid, to feel as upset as I did. *I* ditched *them*, but it felt the other way around. Still, I felt unmistakably homesick.

I looked up toward the bridge and saw Alaska sitting on one of the blue chairs at the Smoking Hole, and though I'd thought I wanted to be alone, I found myself saying, "Hey." Then, when she did not turn to me, I screamed, "Alaska!" She walked over.

"I was looking for you," she said, joining me on the rock.

"Hey."

"I'm really sorry, Pudge," she said, and put her arms around me, resting her head against my shoulder. It occurred to me that she didn't even know what had happened, but she still sounded sincere.

"What am I going to do?"

"You'll spend Thanksgiving with me, silly. Here."

"So why don't you go home for vacations?" I asked her.

"I'm just scared of ghosts, Pudge. And home is full of them."

fifty-two days before

AFTER EVERYONE LEFT; after the Colonel's mom showed up in a beat-up hatchback and he threw his giant duffel bag into the backseat; and after he said, "I'm not much for saying good-bye. I'll see you in a week. Don't do anything I wouldn't do"; and after a green limousine arrived for Lara, whose father was the only doctor in some small town in southern Alabama; and after I joined Alaska on a harrowing, we-don't-need-no-stinking-brakes drive to the airport to drop off Takumi; and after the campus settled into an eerie quiet, with no doors slamming and no music playing and no one laughing and no one screaming; after all that:

We made our way down to the soccer field, and she took me to edge of the field where the woods start, the same steps I'd walked on my way to being thrown into the lake. Beneath the full moon she cast a shadow, and you could see the curve from her waist to her hips in the shadow, and after a while she stopped and said, "Dig."

And I said, "Dig?" and she said, "Dig," and we went on like that for a bit, and then I got on my knees and dug through the soft black dirt at the edge of the woods, and before I could get very far, my fingers scratched glass, and I dug around the glass until I pulled out a bottle of pink wine—Strawberry Hill, it was called, I suppose because if it had not tasted like vinegar with a dash of maple syrup, it might have tasted like strawberries.

"I have a fake ID," she said, "but it sucks. So every time I go to the liquor store, I try to buy ten bottles of this, and some vodka for the Colonel. And so when it finally works, I'm covered for a semester. And then I give the Colonel his vodka, and he puts it wherever he puts it, and I take mine and bury it."

"Because you're a pirate," I said.

"Aye, matey. Precisely. Although wine consumption has risen a bit this semester, so we'll need to take a trip tomorrow. This is the last bottle." She unscrewed the cap—no corks here—sipped, and handed it to me. "Don't worry about the Eagle tonight," she said. "He's just happy most everyone's gone. He's probably masturbating for the first time in a month."

I worried about it for a moment as I held the bottle by the neck, but I wanted to trust her, and so I did. I took a minor sip, and as soon as I swallowed, I felt my body rejecting the stinging syrup of it. It washed back up my esophagus, but I swallowed hard, and there, yes, I did it. I was drinking on campus.

So we lay in the tall grass between the soccer field and the woods, passing the bottle back and forth and tilting our heads up to sip the wince-inducing wine. As promised in the list, she brought a Kurt Vonnegut book, *Cat's Cradle*, and she read aloud to me, her soft voice mingling with the the frogs' croaking and the grasshoppers landing softly around us. I did not hear her words so much as the cadence of her voice. She'd obviously read the book many times before, and so she read flawlessly and confidently, and I could hear her smile in the reading of it, and the sound of that smile made me think that maybe I would like novels better if Alaska Young read them to me. After a while, she put down the book, and I felt warm but not drunk with the bottle resting between us—my chest touching the bottle and her chest touching the bottle but us not touching each other, and then she placed her hand on my leg.

Her hand just above my knee, the palm flat and soft against my jeans and her index finger making slow, lazy circles that crept toward the inside of my thigh, and with one layer between us, God I wanted her. And lying there, amid the tall, still grass and beneath the star-drunk sky, listening to the just-this-side-of-inaudible sound of her rhythmic breathing and the noisy silence of the bullfrogs, the grasshoppers, the distant cars rushing endlessly on I-65, I thought it might be a fine time to say the Three Little Words. And I steeled myself to say them as I stared up at that starriest night, convinced myself that she felt it, too, that her hand so alive and vivid against my leg was more than playful, and fuck Lara and fuck Jake because I do, Alaska Young, I do love you and what else matters but that and my lips parted to speak and before I could even begin to breathe out the words, she said, "It's not life or death, the labyrinth."

"Um, okay. So what is it?"

"Suffering," she said. "Doing wrong and having wrong things happen to you. That's the problem. Bolívar was talking about the pain, not about the living or dying. How do you get out of the labyrinth of suffering?"

"What's wrong?" I asked. And I felt the absence of her hand on me.

"Nothing's wrong. But there's always suffering, Pudge. Homework or malaria or having a boyfriend who lives far away when there's a good-looking boy lying next to you. Suffering is universal. It's the one thing Buddhists, Christians, and Muslims are all worried about."

I turned to her. "Oh, so maybe Dr. Hyde's class isn't total bullshit." And both of us lying on our sides, she smiled, our noses almost touching, my unblinking eyes on hers, her face blushing from the wine, and I opened my mouth again but this time not to speak, and she reached up and put a finger to my lips and said, "Shh. Shh. Don't ruin it."

fifty-one days before

THE NEXT MORNING, I didn't hear the knocking, if there was any.

I just heard, "UP! Do you know what time it is?!"

I looked at the clock and groggily muttered, "It's seven thirty-six."

"No, Pudge. It's party time! We've only got seven days left before everyone comes back. Oh God, I can't even tell you how nice it is to have you here. Last Thanksgiving, I spent the whole time constructing one massive candle using the wax from all my little candles. God, it was boring. I counted the ceiling tiles. Sixty-seven down, eighty-four across. Talk about suffering! Absolute torture."

"I'm really tired. I—" I said, and then she cut me off.

"Poor Pudge. Oh, poor poor Pudge. Do you want me to climb into bed with you and cuddle?"

"Well, if you're offering—"

"NO! UP! NOW!"

She took me behind a wing of Weekday Warrior rooms—50 to 59—and stopped in front of a window, placed her palms flat against it, and pushed up until the window was half open, then crawled inside. I followed.

"What do you see, Pudge?"

I saw a dorm room—the same cinder-block walls, the same dimensions, even the same layout as my own. Their couch was nicer, and they had an actual coffee table instead of COFFEE TABLE. They had two posters on the wall. One featured a huge stack of hundred-dollar bills with the caption THE FIRST MILLION IS THE HARDEST. On the opposite wall, a poster of a red Ferrari. "Uh, I see a dorm room."

"You're not looking, Pudge. When I go into your room, I see a couple of guys who love video games. When I look at my room, I see a girl who loves books." She walked over to the couch and picked up a plastic soda bottle. "Look at this," she said, and I saw that it was half filled with a brackish, brown liquid. Dip spit. "So they dip. And they obviously aren't hygienic about it. So are they going to care if we pee on their toothbrushes? They won't care enough, that's for sure. Look. Tell me what these guys love."

"They love money," I said, pointing to the poster. She threw up her hands, exasperated.

"They *all* love money, Pudge. Okay, go into the bathroom. Tell me what you see there."

The game was annoying me a little, but I went into the bathroom as she sat down on that inviting couch. Inside the shower, I found a dozen bottles of shampoo and conditioner. In the medicine cabinet, I found a cylindrical bottle of something called Rewind. I opened it—the bluish gel smelled like flowers and rubbing alcohol, like a fancy hair salon. (Under the sink, I also found a tub of Vaseline so big that it could have only had one possible use, which I didn't care to dwell on.) I came back into the room and excitedly said, "They love their hair."

"*Precisely!*" she shouted. "Look on the top bunk." Perilously positioned on the thin wooden headboard of the bed, a bottle of STA-WET gel. "Kevin doesn't just *wake up* with that spiky bedhead look, Pudge. He *works* for it. He loves that hair. They leave their hair products here, Pudge, because they have *duplicates* at home. All those boys do. And you know why?"

"Because they're compensating for their tiny little penises?" I asked.

"Ha ha. No. That's why they're macho assholes. They love their hair because they aren't smart enough to love something more interesting. So we hit them where it hurts: the scalp."

"Ohh-kaay," I said, unsure of how, exactly, to prank someone's scalp.

She stood up and walked to the window and bent over to shimmy out. "Don't look at my ass," she said, and so I looked at her ass, spreading out wide from her thin waist. She effortlessly somersaulted out the half-opened window. I took the feetfirst approach, and once I got my feet on the ground, I limboed my upper body out the window.

"Well," she said. "That looked awkward. Let's go to the Smoking Hole."

She shuffled her feet to kick up dry orange dirt on the road to the bridge, seeming not to walk so much as cross-country ski. As we followed the almost-trail down from the bridge to the Hole, she turned around and looked back at me, stopping. "I wonder how one would go about acquiring industrial-strength blue dye," she said, and then held a tree branch back for me.

forty-nine days before

TWO DAYS LATER—Monday, the first real day of vacation—I spent the morning working on my religion final and went to Alaska's room in the afternoon. She was reading in bed.

"Auden," she announced. "What were his last words?"

"Don't know. Never heard of him."

"Never *heard* of him? You poor, illiterate boy. Here, read this line." I walked over and looked down at her index finger. "You shall love your crooked neighbour / With your crooked heart," I read aloud. "Yeah. That's pretty good," I said.

"Pretty good? Sure, and bufriedos are pretty good. Sex is pretty fun. The sun is pretty hot. Jesus, it says so much about love and brokenness—it's perfect."

"Mm-hmm." I nodded unenthusiastically.

"You're hopeless. Wanna go porn hunting?"

"Huh?"

"We can't love our neighbors till we know how crooked their hearts are. Don't you like porn?" she asked, smiling.

"Um," I answered. The truth was that I hadn't seen much porn, but the idea of looking at porn with Alaska had a certain appeal.

We started with the 50s wing of dorms and made our way backward around the hexagon—she pushed open the back windows while I looked out and made sure no one was walking by.

I'd never been in most people's rooms. After three months, I knew most people, but I regularly talked to very few—just the Colonel and Alaska and Takumi, really. But in a few hours, I got to know my classmates quite well.

Wilson Carbod, the center for the Culver Creek Nothings, had hemorrhoids, or at least he kept hemorrhoidal cream secreted away in the bottom drawer of his desk. Chandra Kilers, a cute girl who loved math a little too much, and who Alaska believed was the Colonel's future girlfriend, collected Cabbage Patch Kids. I don't mean that she collected Cabbage Patch Kids when she was, like, five. She collected them now—dozens of them—black, white, Latino, and Asian, boys and girls, babies dressed like farmhands and budding businessmen. A senior Weekday Warrior named Holly Moser sketched nude self-portraits in charcoal pencil, portraying her rotund form in all its girth.

I was stunned by how many people had booze. Even the Weekday Warriors, who got to go home every weekend, had beer and liquor stashed everywhere from toilet tanks to the bottoms of dirty-clothes hampers.

"God, I could have ratted out anyone," Alaska said softly as she unearthed a forty-ounce bottle of Magnum malt liquor from Longwell Chase's closet. I wondered, then, why she had chosen Paul and Marya.

Alaska found everyone's secrets so fast that I suspected she'd done this before, but she couldn't possibly have had advance knowledge of the secrets of Ruth and Margot Blowker, ninth-grade twin sisters who were new and seemed to socialize even less than I did. After crawling into their room, Alaska looked around for a moment, then walked to the bookshelf. She stared at it, then pulled out the King James Bible, and there—a purple bottle of Maui Wowie wine cooler.

"How clever," she said as she twisted off the cap. She drank it down in two long sips, and then proclaimed, "Maui WOWIE!"

"They'll know you were here!" I shouted.

Her eyes widened. "Oh no, you're right, Pudge!" she said. "Maybe they'll go to the Eagle and tell him that someone stole their wine cooler!" She laughed and leaned out the window, throwing the empty bottle into the grass.

And we found plenty of porn magazines haphazardly stuffed in between mattresses and box springs. It turns out that Hank Walsten did like something other than basketball and pot: he liked *Juggs*. But we didn't find a *movie* until Room 32, occupied by a couple of guys from Mississippi named Joe and Marcus. They were in our religion class and sometimes sat with the Colonel and me at lunch, but I didn't know them well.

Alaska read the sticker on the top of the video. "*The Bitches of Madison County*. Well. Ain't that just delightful."

We ran with it to the TV room, closed the blinds, locked the door, and watched the movie. It opened with a woman standing on a bridge with her legs spread while a guy knelt in front of her, giving her oral sex. No time for dialogue, I suppose. By the time they started doing it, Alaska commenced with her righteous indignation. "They just don't make sex look fun for women. The girl is just an object. Look! Look at that!"

I was already looking, needless to say. A woman crouched on her hands and knees while a guy knelt behind her. She kept saying "Give it to me" and moaning, and though her eyes, brown and blank, betrayed her lack of interest, I couldn't help but take mental notes. *Hands on her shoulders*, I noted. *Fast, but not too fast or it's going to be over, fast. Keep your grunting to a minimum.*

As if reading my mind, she said, "God, Pudge. Never do it that hard. That would *hurt*. That looks like torture. And all she can do is just sit there and take it? This is not a *man* and a *woman*. It's a penis and a vagina. What's erotic about that? Where's the kissing?"

"Given their position, I don't think they can kiss right now," I noted.

"That's my point. Just by virtue of how they're doing it, it's objectification. He can't even see her face! This is what can happen to women, Pudge. That woman is someone's daughter. This is what you make us do for money."

"Well, not *me*," I said defensively. "I mean, not technically. I don't, like, produce porn movies."

"Look me in the eye and tell me this doesn't turn you on, Pudge."

I couldn't. She laughed. It was fine, she said. Healthy. And then she got up, stopped the tape, lay down on her stomach across the couch, and mumbled something.

"What did you say?" I asked, walking to her, putting my hand on the small of her back.

"Shhhh," she said. "I'm sleeping."

Just like that. From a hundred miles an hour to asleep in a nanosecond. I wanted so badly to lie down next to her on the couch, to wrap my arms around her and sleep. Not fuck, like in those movies. Not even have sex. Just sleep together, in the most innocent sense of the phrase. But I lacked the courage and she had a boyfriend and I was gawky and she was gorgeous and I was hopelessly boring and she was endlessly fascinating. So I walked back to my room and collapsed on the bottom bunk, thinking that if people were rain, I was drizzle and she was a hurricane.

forty-seven days before

ON WEDNESDAY MORNING, I woke up with a stuffy nose to an entirely new Alabama, a crisp and cold one. As I walked to Alaska's room that morning, the frosty grass of the dorm circle crunched beneath my shoes. You don't run into frost much in Florida—and I jumped up and down like I was stomping on bubble wrap. *Crunch. Crunch. Crunch.*

Alaska was holding a burning green candle in her hand upside down, dripping the wax onto a larger, homemade volcano that looked a bit like a Technicolor middle-school-science-project volcano.

"Don't burn yourself," I said as the flame crept up toward her hand.

"Night falls fast. Today is in the past," she said without looking up.

"Wait, I've read that before. What is that?" I asked.

With her free hand, she grabbed a book and tossed it toward me. It landed at my feet. "Poem," she said. "Edna St. Vincent Millay. You've read that? I'm stunned."

"Oh, I read her biography! Didn't have her last words in it, though. I was a little bitter. All I remember is that she had a lot of sex."

"I know. She's my hero," Alaska said without a trace of irony. I laughed, but she didn't notice. "Does it seem at all odd to you that you enjoy biographies of great writers a lot more than you enjoy their actual writing?"

"Nope!" I announced. "Just because they were interesting people doesn't mean I care to hear their musings on nighttime."

"It's about depression, dumb-ass."

"Oooooh, really? Well, jeez, then it's *brilliant*," I answered.

She sighed. "All right. The snow may be falling in the winter of my discontent, but at least I've got sarcastic company. Sit down, will ya?"

I sat down next to her with my legs crossed and our knees touching. She pulled a clear plastic crate filled with dozens of candles out from underneath her bed. She looked at it for a moment, then handed me a white one and a lighter.

We spent all morning burning candles—well, and occasionally lighting cigarettes off the burning candles after we stuffed a towel into the crack at the bottom of her door. Over the course of two hours, we added a full foot to the summit of her polychrome candle volcano.

"Mount St. Helens on acid," she said

At 12:30, after two hours of me begging for a ride to McDonald's, Alaska decided it was time for lunch. As we began to walk to the student parking lot, I saw a strange car. A small green car. A hatchback. *I've seen that car,* I thought. *Where have I seen the car?* And then the Colonel jumped out and ran to meet us.

Rather than, like, I don't know, "hello" or something, the Colonel began, "I have been instructed to invite you to Thanksgiving dinner at Chez Martín."

Alaska whispered into my ear, and then I laughed and said, "I have been instructed to accept your invitation." So we walked over to the Eagle's house, told him we were going to eat turkey trailer-park style, and sped away in the hatchback.

The Colonel explained it to us on the two-hour car ride south. I was crammed into the backseat because Alaska had called shotgun. She usually drove, but when she didn't, she was shotgun-calling queen of the world. The Colonel's mother heard that we were on campus and couldn't bear the thought of leaving us familyless for Thanksgiving. The Colonel didn't seem too keen on the whole idea—"I'm going to have to sleep in a tent," he said, and I laughed.

Except it turns out he did have to sleep in a tent, a nice four-person green outfit shaped like half an egg, but still a tent. The Colonel's mom lived in a trailer, as in the kind of thing you might see attached to a large pickup truck, except this particular one was old and falling apart on its cinder blocks, and probably couldn't have been hooked up to a truck without disintegrating. It wasn't even a particularly big trailer. I could just barely stand up to my full height without scraping the ceiling. Now I understood why the Colonel was short—he couldn't afford to be any taller. The place was really one long room, with a full-size bed in the front, a kitchenette, and a living area in the back with a TV and a small bathroom—so small that in order to take a shower, you pretty much had to sit on the toilet.

"It ain't much," the Colonel's mom ("That's Dolores, not Miss Martin") told us. "But y'alls a-gonna have a turkey the size o' the kitchen." She laughed. The Colonel ushered us out of the trailer immediately after our brief tour, and we walked through the neighborhood, a series of trailers and mobile homes on dirt roads.

"Well, now you get why I hate rich people." And I did. I couldn't fathom how the Colonel grew up in such a small place. The entire trailer was smaller than our dorm room. I didn't know what to say to him, how to make him feel less embarrassed.

"I'm sorry if it makes you uncomfortable," he said. "I know it's probably foreign."

"Not to me," Alaska piped up.

"Well, you don't live in a trailer," he told her.

"Poor is poor."

"I suppose," the Colonel said.

Alaska decided to go help Dolores with dinner. She said that it was sexist to leave the cooking to the women, but better to have good sexist food than crappy boy-prepared food. So the Colonel and I sat on the pull-out couch in the living room, playing video games and talking about school.

"I finished my religion paper. But I have to type it up on your computer when we get back. I think I'm ready for finals, which is good, since we have an ank-pray to an-play."

"Your mom doesn't know pig Latin?" I smirked.

"Not if I talk fast. Christ, be quiet."

The food—fried okra, steamed corn on the cob, and pot roast that was so tender it fell right off the plastic fork—convinced me that Dolores was an even better cook than Maureen. Culver Creek's okra had less grease, more crunch. Dolores was also the funniest mom I'd ever met. When Alaska asked her what she did for work, she smiled and said, "I'm a culinary engineeyer. That's a short-order cook at the Waffle House to y'all."

"Best Waffle House in Alabama." The Colonel smiled, and then I realized, he wasn't embarrassed of his mom at all. He was just scared that we would act like condescending boarding-school snobs. I'd always found the Colonel's I-hate-the-rich routine a little overwrought until I saw him with his mom. He was the same Colonel, but in a totally different context. It made me hope that one day, I could meet Alaska's family, too.

Dolores insisted that Alaska and I share the bed, and she slept on the pull-out while the Colonel was out in his tent. I worried he would get cold, but frankly I wasn't about to give up my bed with Alaska. We had separate blankets, and there were never fewer than three layers between us, but the possibilities kept me up half the night.

forty-six days before

BEST THANKSGIVING FOOD I'd ever had. No crappy cranberry sauce. Just huge slabs of moist white meat, corn, green beans cooked in enough bacon fat to make them taste like they weren't good for you, biscuits with gravy, pumpkin pie for dessert, and a glass of red wine for each of us. "I believe," Dolores said, "that yer s'posed to drink white with turkey, but—now I don't know 'bout y'all—but I don't s'pose I give a shit."

We laughed and drank our wine, and then after the meal, we each listed our gratitudes. My family always did that before the meal, and we all just rushed through it to get to the food. So the four of us sat around the table and shared our blessings. I was thankful for the fine food and the fine company, for having a home on Thanksgiving. "A trailer, at least," Dolores joked.

"Okay, my turn," Alaska said. "I'm grateful for having just had my best Thanksgiving in a decade."

Then the Colonel said, "I'm just grateful for you, Mom," and Dolores laughed and said, "That dog won't hunt, boy."

I didn't exactly know what that phrase meant, but apparently it meant, "That was inadequate," because then the Colonel expanded his list to acknowledge that he was grateful to be "the smartest human being in this trailer park," and Dolores laughed and said, "Good enough."

And Dolores? She was grateful that her phone was back on, that her boy was home, that Alaska helped her cook and that I had kept the Colonel out of her hair, that her job was steady and her coworkers were nice, that she had a place to sleep and a boy who loved her.

I sat in the back of the hatchback on the drive home—and that is how I thought of it: home—and fell asleep to the highway's monotonous lullaby.

forty-four days before

"COOSA LIQUORS' entire business model is built around selling cigarettes to minors and alcohol to adults." Alaska looked at me with disconcerting frequency when she drove, particularly since we were winding through a narrow, hilly highway south of school, headed to the aforementioned Coosa Liquors. It was Saturday, our last day of real vacation. "Which is great, if all you need is cigarettes. But we need booze. And they card for booze. And my ID blows. But I'll flirt my way through." She made a sudden and unsignaled left turn, pulling onto a road that dropped precipitously down a hill with fields on either side, and she gripped the steering wheel tight as we accelerated, and she waited until the last possible moment to brake, just before we reached the bottom of the hill. There stood a plywood gas station that no longer sold gas with a faded sign bolted to the roof: COOSA LIQUORS: WE CATER TO YOUR SPIRITUAL NEEDS.

Alaska went in alone and walked out the door five minutes later weighed down by two paper bags filled with contraband: three cartons of cigarettes, five bottles of wine, and a fifth of vodka for the Colonel. On the way home, Alaska said, "You like knock-knock jokes?"

"Knock-knock jokes?" I asked. "You mean like, 'Knock knock . . .'"

"Who's there?" replied Alaska.

"Who."

"Who Who?"

"What are you, an owl?" I finished. Lame.

"That was brilliant," said Alaska. "I have one. You start."

"Okay. Knock knock."

"Who's there?" said Alaska.

I looked at her blankly. About a minute later, I got it, and laughed.

"My mom told me that joke when I was six. It's still funny."

So I could not have been more surprised when she showed up sobbing at Room 43 just as I was putting the finishing touches on my final paper for English. She sat down on the couch, her every exhalation a mix of whimper and scream.

"I'm sorry," she said, heaving. Snot was dribbling down her chin.

"What's wrong?" I asked. She picked up a Kleenex from the COFFEE TABLE and wiped at her face.

"I don't . . ." she started, and then a sob came like a tsunami, her cry so loud and childlike that it scared me, and I got up, sat down next her, and put my arm around her. She turned away, pushing her head into the foam of the couch. "I don't understand why I screw everything up," she said.

"What, like with Marya? Maybe you were just scared."

"Scared isn't a good excuse!" she shouted into the couch. "Scared is the excuse everyone has always used!" I didn't know who "everyone" was, or when "always" was, and as much as I wanted to understand her ambiguities, the slyness was growing annoying.

"Why are you upset about this *now?*"

"It's not just that. It's everything. But I told the Colonel in the car." She sniffled but seemed done with the sobs. "While you were sleeping in the back. And he said he'd never let me out of his sight during pranks. That he couldn't trust me on my own. And I don't blame him. I don't even trust me."

"It took guts to tell him," I said.

"I have guts, just not when it counts. Will you—um," and she sat up straight and then moved toward me, and I raised my arm as she collapsed into my skinny chest and cried. I felt bad for her, but she'd done it to herself. She didn't *have* to rat.

"I don't want to upset you, but maybe you just need to tell us all why you told on Marya. Were you scared of going home or something?"

She pulled away from me and gave me a Look of Doom that would have made the Eagle proud, and I felt like she hated me or hated my question or both, and then she looked away, out the window, toward the soccer field, and said, "There's no home."

"Well, you *have* a family," I backpedaled. She'd talked to me about her mom just that morning. How could the girl who told that joke three hours before become a sobbing mess?

Still staring at me, she said, "I try not to be scared, you know. But I still ruin everything. I still fuck up."

"Okay," I told her. "It's okay." I didn't even know what she was talking about anymore. One vague notion after another.

"Don't you know who you love, Pudge? You love the girl who makes you laugh and shows you porn and drinks wine with you. You don't love the crazy, sullen bitch."

And there was something to that, truth be told.

christmas

WE ALL WENT HOME for Christmas break—even purportedly homeless Alaska.

I got a nice watch and a new wallet—"grown-up gifts," my dad called them. But mostly I just studied for those two weeks. Christmas vacation wasn't really a vacation, on account of how it was our last chance to study for exams, which started the day after we got back. I focused on precalc and biology, the two classes that most deeply threatened my goal of a 3.4 GPA. I wish I could say I was in it for the thrill of learning, but mostly I was in it for the thrill of getting into a worthwhile college.

So, yeah, I spent a lot of my time at home studying math and memorizing French vocab, just like I had before Culver Creek. Really, being at home for two weeks was just like my entire life before Culver Creek, except my parents were more emotional. They talked very little about their trip to London. I think they felt guilty. That's a funny thing about parents. Even though I pretty much stayed at the Creek over Thanksgiving because I wanted to, my parents still felt guilty. It's nice to have people who will feel guilty for you, although I could have lived without my mom crying during every single family dinner. She would say, "I'm a bad mother," and my dad and I would immediately reply, "No, you're not."

Even my dad, who is affectionate but not, like, *sentimental*, randomly, while we were watching *The Simpsons*, said he missed me. I said I missed him, too, and I did. Sort of. They're such nice people. We went to movies and played card games, and I told them the stories I could tell without horrifying them, and they listened. My dad, who sold real estate for a living but read more books than anyone I knew, talked with me about the books I was reading for English class, and my mom insisted that I sit with her in the kitchen and learn how to make simple dishes—macaroni, scrambled eggs—now that I was "living on my own." Never mind that I didn't have, or want, a kitchen. Never mind that I didn't like eggs *or* macaroni and cheese. By New Year's Day, I could make them anyway.

When I left, they both cried, my mom explaining that it was just empty-nest syndrome, that they were just so proud of me, that they loved me so much. That put a lump in my throat, and I didn't care about Thanksgiving anymore. I had a family.

eight days before

ALASKA WALKED IN on the first day back from Christmas break and sat beside the Colonel on the couch. The Colonel was hard at work, breaking a land-speed record on the PlayStation.

She didn't say she missed us, or that she was glad to see us. She just looked at the couch and said, "You really need a new couch."

"Please don't address me when I'm racing," the Colonel said. "God. Does Jeff Gordon have to put up with this shit?"

"I've got an idea," she said. "It's great. What we need is a pre-prank that coincides with an attack on Kevin and his minions," she said.

I was sitting on the bed, reading the textbook in preparation for my American history exam the next day.

"A pre-prank?" I asked.

"A prank designed to lull the administration into a false sense of security," the Colonel answered, annoyed by the distraction. "After the pre-prank, the Eagle will think the junior class has done its prank and won't be waiting for it when it actually comes." Every year, the junior and senior classes pulled off a prank at some point in the year—usually something lame, like Roman candles in the dorm circle at five in the morning on a Sunday.

"Is there always a pre-prank?" I asked.

"No, you idiot," the Colonel said. "If there was always a pre-prank, then the Eagle would *expect* two pranks. The last time a pre-prank was used—hmm. Oh, right: 1987. When the pre-prank was cutting off electricity to campus, and then the actual prank was putting five hundred live crickets in the heating ducts of the class-rooms. Sometimes you can still hear the chirping."

"Your rote memorization is, like, *so* impressive," I said.

"You guys are like an old married couple." Alaska smiled. "In a creepy way."

"You don't know the half of it," the Colonel said. "You should see this kid try to crawl into bed with me at night."

"Hey!"

"Let's get on subject!" Alaska said. "Pre-prank. This weekend, since there's a new moon. We're staying at the barn. You, me, the Colonel, Takumi, and, as a special gift to you, Pudge, Lara Buterskaya."

"The Lara Buterskaya I puked on?"

"She's just shy. She still likes you." Alaska laughed. "Puking made you look—vulnerable."

"Very perky boobs," the Colonel said. "Are you bringing Takumi for me?"

"You need to be single for a while."

"True enough," the Colonel said.

"Just spend a few more months playing video games," she said.

"That hand-eye coordination will come in handy when you get to third base."

"Gosh, I haven't heard the base system in so long, I think I've forgotten third base," the Colonel responded. "I would roll my eyes at you, but I can't afford to look away from the screen."

"French, Feel, Finger, Fuck. It's like you skipped third grade," Alaska said.

"I *did* skip third grade," the Colonel answered.

"So," I said, "what's our pre-prank?"

"The Colonel and I will work that out. No need to get you into trouble—yet."

"Oh. Okay. Um, I'm gonna go for a cigarette, then."

I left. It wasn't the first time Alaska had left me out of the loop, certainly, but after we'd been together so much over Thanksgiving, it seemed ridiculous to plan the prank with the Colonel but without me. Whose T-shirts were wet with her tears? Mine. Who'd listened to her read Vonnegut? Me. Who'd been the butt of the world's worst knock-knock joke? Me. I walked to the Sunny Konvenience Kiosk across from school and smoked. This never happened to me in Florida, this oh-so-high-school angst about who likes whom more, and I hated myself for letting it happen now. *You don't* have *to care about her*, I told myself. *Screw her.*

four days before

THE COLONEL WOULDN'T TELL ME a word about the preprank, except that it was to be called Barn Night, and that when I packed, I should pack for two days.

Monday, Tuesday, and Wednesday were torture. The Colonel was always with Alaska, and I was never invited. So I spent an inordinate amount of time studying for finals, which helped my GPA considerably. And I finally finished my religion paper.

My answer to the question was straightforward enough, really. Most Christians and Muslims believe in a heaven and a hell, though there's a lot of disagreement within both religions over what, exactly, will get you into one afterlife or the other. Buddhists are more complicated—because of the Buddha's doctrine of *anatta*, which basically says that people don't have eternal souls. Instead, they have a bundle of energy, and that bundle of energy is transitory, migrating from one body to another, reincarnating endlessly until it eventually reaches enlightenment.

I never liked writing concluding paragraphs to papers—where you just repeat what you've already said with phrases like *In summation,* and *To conclude.* I didn't do that—instead I talked about why I thought it was an important question. People, I thought, wanted security. They couldn't bear the idea of death being a big black nothing, couldn't bear the thought of their loved ones not existing, and couldn't even *imagine* themselves not existing. I finally decided that people believed in an afterlife because they couldn't bear not to.

three days before

ON FRIDAY, after a surprisingly successful precalc exam that brought my first set of Culver Creek finals to a close, I packed clothes ("Think New York trendy," the Colonel advised. "Think black. Think sensible. Comfortable, but warm.") and my sleeping bag into a backpack, and we picked up Takumi in his room and walked to the Eagle's house. The Eagle was wearing his only outfit, and I wondered whether he just had thirty identical white button-down shirts and thirty identical black ties in his closet. I pictured him waking up in the morning, staring at his closet, and thinking, *Hmm . . . hmm . . . how about a white shirt and a black tie?* Talk about a guy who could use a wife.

———————

"I'm taking Miles and Takumi home for the weekend to New Hope," the Colonel told him.

"Miles liked his taste of New Hope that much?" the Eagle asked me.

"Yee haw! There's a gonna be a hoedown at the trailer park!" the Colonel said. He could actually have a Southern accent when he wanted to, although like most everyone at Culver Creek, he didn't usually speak with one.

"Hold on one moment while I call your mom," the Eagle said to the Colonel.

Takumi looked at me with poorly disguised panic, and I felt lunch—fried chicken—rising in my stomach. But the Colonel just smiled. "Sure thing."

"Chip and Miles and Takumi will be at your house this weekend? . . . Yes, ma'am. . . . Ha! . . . Okay. Bye now." The Eagle looked up at the Colonel. "Your mom is a wonderful woman." The Eagle smiled.

"You're tellin' me." The Colonel grinned. "See you on Sunday."

As we walked toward the gym parking lot, the Colonel said, "I called her yesterday and asked her to cover for me, and she didn't even ask why. She just said, 'I sure trust you, son,' and hot damn she does." Once out of sight of the Eagle's house, we took a sharp right into the woods.

We walked on the dirt road over the bridge and back to the school's barn, a dilapidated leak-prone structure that looked more like a long-abandoned log cabin than a barn. They still stored hay there, although I don't know what for. It wasn't like we had an equestrian program or anything. The Colonel, Takumi, and I got there first, setting up our sleeping bags on the softest bales of hay. It was 6:30.

Alaska came shortly after, having told the Eagle she was spending the weekend with Jake. The Eagle didn't check that story, because Alaska spent at least one weekend there every month, and he knew that her parents never cared. Lara showed up half an hour later. She'd told the Eagle that she was driving to Atlanta to see an old friend from Romania. The Eagle called Lara's parents to make sure that they knew she was spending a weekend off campus, and they didn't mind.

"They trust me." She smiled.

"You don't sound like you have an accent sometimes," I said, which was pretty stupid, but a darn sight better than throwing up on her.

"Eet's only soft *i*'s."

"No soft *i*'s in Russian?" I asked.

"Romanian," she corrected me. Turns out Romanian is a language. Who knew? My cultural sensitivity quotient was going to have to drastically increase if I was going to share a sleeping bag with Lara anytime soon.

Everybody was sitting on sleeping bags, Alaska smoking with flagrant disregard for the overwhelming flammability of the structure, when the Colonel pulled out a single piece of computer paper and read from it.

"The point of this evening's festivities is to prove once and for all that we are to pranking what the Weekday Warriors are to sucking. But we'll also have the opportunity to make life unpleasant for the Eagle, which is always a welcome pleasure. And so," he said, pausing as if for a drumroll, "we fight tonight a battle on three fronts:

"Front One: The pre-prank: We will, as it were, light a fire under the Eagle's ass.

"Front Two: Operation Baldy: Wherein Lara flies solo in a retaliatory mission so elegant and cruel that it could only have been the brainchild of, well, me."

"Hey!" Alaska interrupted. "It was *my* idea."

"Okay, fine. It was Alaska's idea." He laughed. "And finally, Front Three: The Progress Reports: We're going to hack into the faculty computer network and use their grading database to send out letters to Kevin et al.'s families saying that they are failing some of their classes."

"We are definitely going to get expelled," I said.

"I hope you didn't bring the Asian kid along thinking he's a computer genius. Because I am not," Takumi said.

"We're not going to get expelled and *I'm* the computer genius. The rest of you are muscle and distraction. We won't get expelled even if we get caught because there are no expellable offenses here—well, except for the five bottles of Strawberry Hill in Alaska's backpack, and that will be well hidden. We're just, you know, wreaking a little havoc."

The plan was laid out, and it left no room for error. The Colonel relied so heavily on perfect synchronicity that if one of us messed up even slightly, the endeavor would collapse entirely.

He had printed up individual itineraries for each of us, including times exact to the second. Our watches synchronized, our clothes black, our backpacks on, our breath visible in the cold, our minds filled with the minute details of the plan, our hearts racing, we walked out of the barn together once it was completely dark, around seven. The five of us walking confidently in a row, I'd never felt cooler. The Great Perhaps was upon us, and we were invincible. The plan may have had faults, but we did not.

After five minutes, we split up to go to our destinations. I stuck with Takumi. We were the distraction.

"We're the fucking Marines," he said.

"First to fight. First to die," I agreed nervously.

"Hell yes."

He stopped and opened his bag.

"Not here, dude," I said. "We have to go to the Eagle's."

"I know. I know. Just—hold on." He pulled out a thick headband. It was brown, with a plush fox head on the front. He put it on his head.

I laughed. "What the hell is that?"

"It's my fox hat."

"Your fox hat?"

"Yeah, Pudge. My *fox hat*."

"Why are you wearing your *fox hat*?" I asked.

"Because no one can catch the motherfucking fox."

Two minutes later, we were crouched behind the trees fifty feet from the Eagle's back door. My heart thumped like a techno drumbeat.

"Thirty seconds," Takumi whispered, and I felt the same spooked nervousness that I had felt that first night with Alaska when she grabbed my hand and whispered *run run run run run*. But I stayed put.

I thought: *We are not close enough.*

I thought: *He will not hear it.*

I thought: *He will hear it and be out so fast that we will have no chance.*

I thought: *Twenty seconds.* I was breathing hard and fast.

"Hey, Pudge," Takumi whispered, "you can do this, dude. It's just running."

"Right." *Just running. My knees are good. My lungs are fair. It's just running.*

"Five," he said. "Four. Three. Two. One. Light it. Light it. Light it."

It lit with a sizzle that reminded me of every July Fourth with my family. We stood still for a nanosecond, staring at the fuse, making sure it was lit. *And now,* I thought. *Now. Run run run run run.* But my body didn't move until I heard Takumi shout-whisper, "Go go go fucking go."

And we went.

Three seconds later, a huge burst of pops. It sounded, to me, like the automatic gunfire in Decapitation, except louder. We were twenty steps away already, and I thought my eardrums would burst.

I thought: *Well, he will certainly hear it.*

We ran past the soccer field and into the woods, running uphill and with only the vaguest sense of direction. In the dark, fallen branches and moss-covered rocks appeared at the last possible second, and I slipped and fell repeatedly and worried that the Eagle would catch up, but I just kept getting up and running beside Takumi, away from the classrooms and the dorm circle. We ran like we had golden shoes. I ran like a cheetah—well, like a cheetah that smoked too much. And then, after precisely one minute of running, Takumi stopped and ripped open his backpack.

My turn to count down. Staring at my watch. Terrified. By now, he was surely out. He was surely running. I wondered if he was fast. He was old, but he'd be mad.

"Five four three two one," and the sizzle. We didn't pause that time, just ran, still west. Breath heaving. I wondered if I could do this for thirty minutes. The firecrackers exploded.

The pops ended, and a voice cried out, "STOP RIGHT NOW!" But we did not stop. Stopping was not in the plan.

"I'm the motherfucking fox," Takumi whispered, both to himself and to me. "No one can catch the fox."

A minute later, I was on the ground. Takumi counted down. The fuse lit. We ran.

But it was a dud. We had prepared for one dud, bringing an extra string of firecrackers. Another, though, would cost the Colonel and Alaska a minute. Takumi crouched down on the ground, lit the fuse, and ran. The popping started. The fireworks *bangbangbanged* in sync with my heartbeat.

When the firecrackers finished, I heard, "STOP OR I'LL CALL THE POLICE!" And though the voice was distant, I could feel his Look of Doom bearing down on me.

"The pigs can't stop the fox; I'm too quick," Takumi said to himself. "I can rhyme while I run; I'm that slick."

The Colonel warned us about the police threat, told us not to worry. The Eagle didn't like to bring the police to campus. Bad publicity. So we ran. Over and under and through all manner of trees and bushes and branches. We fell. We got up. We ran. If he couldn't follow us with the firecrackers, he could sure as hell follow the sound of our whispered *shits* as we tripped over dead logs and fell into briar bushes.

One minute. I knelt down, lit the fuse, ran. *Bang.*

Then we turned north, thinking we'd gotten past the lake. This was key to the plan. The farther we got while still staying on campus, the farther the Eagle would follow us. The farther he followed us, the farther he would be from the classrooms, where the Colonel and Alaska were working their magic. And then we planned to loop back near the classrooms and swing east along the creek until we came to the bridge over our Smoking Hole, where we would rejoin the road and walk back to the barn, triumphant.

But here's the thing: We made a slight error in navigation. We weren't past the lake; instead we were staring at a field and then the lake. Too close to the classrooms to run anywhere but along the lakefront, I looked over at Takumi, who was running with me stride for stride, and he just said, "Drop one now."

So I dropped down, lit the fuse, and we ran. We were running through a clearing now, and if the Eagle was behind us, he could see us. We got to the south corner of the lake and started running along the shore. The lake wasn't all that big—maybe a quarter mile long, so we didn't have far to go when I saw it.

The swan.

Swimming toward us like a swan possessed. Wings flapping furiously as it came, and then it was on the shore in front of us, making a noise that sounded like nothing else in this world, like all the worst parts of a dying rabbit plus all the worst parts of a crying baby, and there was no other way, so we just ran. I hit the swan at a full run and felt it bite into my ass. And then I was running with a noticeable limp, because my ass was on fire, and I thought to myself, *What the hell is in swan saliva that burns so badly?*

The twenty-third string was a dud, costing us one minute. At that point, I wanted a minute. I was dying. The burning sensation in my left buttock had dulled to an intense aching, magnified each time I landed on my left leg, so I was running like an injured gazelle trying to evade a pride of lions. Our speed, needless to say, had slowed considerably. We hadn't heard the Eagle since we got across the lake, but I didn't think he had turned around. He was trying to lull us into complacency, but it would not work. Tonight, we were invincible.

Exhausted, we stopped with three strings left and hoped we'd given the Colonel enough time. We ran for a few more minutes, until we found the bank of the creek. It was so dark and so still that the tiny stream of water seemed to roar, but I could still hear our hard, fast breaths as we collapsed on wet clay and pebbles beside the creek. Only when we stopped did I look at Takumi. His face and arms were scratched, the fox head now directly over his left ear. Looking at my own arms, I noticed blood dripping from the deeper cuts. There were, I remembered now, some wicked briar patches, but I was feeling no pain.

Takumi picked thorns out of his leg. "The fox is fucking tired," he said, and laughed.

"The swan bit my ass," I told him.

"I saw." He smiled. "Is it bleeding?" I reached my hand into my pants to check. No blood, so I smoked to celebrate.

"Mission accomplished," I said.

"Pudge, my friend, we are indefuckingstructible."

We couldn't figure out where we were, because the creek doubles back so many times through the campus, so we followed the creek for about ten minutes, figuring we walked half as fast as we ran, and then turned left.

"Left, you think?" Takumi asked.

"I'm pretty lost," I said.

"The fox is pointing left. So left." And, sure enough, the fox took us right back to the barn.

"You're okay!" Lara said as we walked up. "I was worried. I saw the Eagle run out of hees house. He was wearing pajamas. He sure looked mad."

I said, "Well, if he was mad then, I wouldn't want to see him now."

"What took you so long?" she asked me.

"We took the long way home," Takumi said. "Plus Pudge is walking like an old lady with hemorrhoids 'cause the swan bit him on the ass. Where's Alaska and the Colonel?"

"I don't know," Lara said, and then we heard footsteps in the distance, mutters and cracking branches. In a flash, Takumi grabbed our sleeping bags and backpacks and hid them behind bales of hay. The three of us ran through the back of the barn and into the waist-high grass, and lay down. *He tracked us back to the barn*, I thought. *We fucked everything up.*

But then I heard the Colonel's voice, distinct and very annoyed, saying, "Because it narrows the list of possible suspects by twenty-three! Why couldn't you just follow the plan? Christ, where is everybody?"

We walked back to the barn, a bit sheepish from having overreacted. The Colonel sat down on a bale of hay, his elbows on his knees, his head bowed, his palms against his forehead. Thinking.

"Well, we haven't been caught yet, anyway. Okay, first," he said without looking up, "tell me everything else went all right. Lara?"

She started talking. "Yes. Good."

"Can I have some more detail, please?"

"I deed like your paper said. I stayed behind the Eagle's house until I saw heem run after Miles and Takumi, and then I ran behind the dorms. And then I went through the weendow eento Keveen's room. Then I put the stuff een the gel and the conditioner, and then I deed the same thing een Jeff and Longwell's room."

"The stuff?" I asked.

"Undiluted industrial-strength blue number-five hair dye," Alaska said. "Which I bought with your cigarette money. Apply it to wet hair, and it won't wash out for months."

"We dyed their hair blue?"

"Well, technically," the Colonel said, still speaking into his lap, "they're going to dye their own hair blue. But we have certainly made it easier for them. I know you and Takumi did all right, because we're here and you're here, so you did your job. And the good news is that the three assholes who had the gall to prank us have progress reports coming saying that they are failing three classes."

"Uh-oh. What's the bad news?" Lara asked.

"Oh, c'mon," Alaska said. "The *other* good news is that while the Colonel was worried he'd heard something and ran into the woods, I saw to it that twenty other Weekday Warriors *also* have progress reports coming. I printed out reports for all of them, stuffed them into metered school envelopes, and then put then in the mailbox." She turned to the Colonel. "You were sure gone a long time," she said. "The wittle Colonel: so scared of getting expelled."

The Colonel stood up, towering over the rest of us as we sat. "That is not good news! That was not in the plan! That means there are twenty-three people who the Eagle can eliminate as suspects. Twenty-three people who might figure out it was us and rat!"

"If that happens," Alaska said very seriously, "I'll take the fall."

"Right." The Colonel sighed. "Like you took the fall for Paul and Marya. You'll say that while you were traipsing through the woods lighting firecrackers you were simultaneously hacking into the faculty network and printing out false progress reports on school stationery? Because I'm sure that will fly with the Eagle!"

"Relax, dude," Takumi said. "First off, we're not gonna get caught. Second off, if we do, I'll take the fall with Alaska. You've got more to lose than any of us." The Colonel just nodded. It was an undeniable fact: The Colonel would have no chance at a scholarship to a good school if he got expelled from the Creek.

Knowing that nothing cheered up the Colonel like acknowledging his brilliance, I asked, "So how'd you hack the network?"

"I climbed in the window of Dr. Hyde's office, booted up his computer, and I typed in his password," he said, smiling.

"You guessed it?"

"No. On Tuesday I went into his office and asked him to print me a copy of the recommended reading list. And then I watched him type the password: *J3ckylnhyd3.*"

"Well, shit," Takumi said. "I could have done that."

"Sure, but then you wouldn't have gotten to wear that sexy hat," the Colonel said, laughing. Takumi took the headband off and put it in his bag.

"Kevin is going to be pissed about his hair," I said.

"Yeah, well, I'm really pissed about my waterlogged library. Kevin is a blowup doll," Alaska said. "Prick us, we bleed. Prick him, he pops."

"It's true," said Takumi. "The guy is a dick. He kind of tried to kill you, after all."

"Yeah, I guess," I acknowledged.

"There are a lot of people here like that," Alaska went on, still fuming. "You know? Fucking blowup-doll rich kids."

But even though Kevin had sort of tried to kill me and all, he really didn't seem worth hating. Hating the cool kids takes an awful lot of energy, and I'd given up on it a long time ago. For me, the prank was just a response to a previous prank, just a golden opportunity to, as the Colonel said, wreak a little havoc. But to Alaska, it seemed to be something else, something more.

I wanted to ask her about it, but she lay back down behind the piles of hay, invisible again. Alaska was done talking, and when she was done talking, that was it. We didn't coax her out for two hours, until the Colonel unscrewed a bottle of wine. We passed around the bottle till I could feel it in my stomach, sour and warm.

I wanted to like booze more than I actually did (which is more or less the precise opposite of how I felt about Alaska). But that night, the booze felt great, as the warmth of the wine in my stomach spread through my body. I didn't like feeling stupid or out of control, but I liked the way it made everything (laughing, crying, peeing in front of your friends) easier. Why did we drink? For me, it was just fun, particularly since we were risking expulsion. The nice thing about the constant threat of expulsion at Culver Creek is that it lends excitement to every moment of illicit pleasure. The bad thing, of course, is that there is always the possibility of actual expulsion.

two days before

I WOKE UP EARLY the next morning, my lips dry and my breath visible in the crisp air. Takumi had brought a camp stove in his backpack, and the Colonel was huddled over it, heating instant coffee. The sun shone bright but could not combat the cold, and I sat with the Colonel and sipped the coffee ("The thing about instant coffee is that it smells pretty good but tastes like stomach bile," the Colonel said), and then one by one, Takumi and Lara and Alaska woke up, and we spent the day hiding out, but loudly. Hiding out loud.

At the barn that afternoon, Takumi decided we needed to have a freestyle contest.

"You start, Pudge," Takumi said. "Colonel Catastrophe, you're our beat box."

"Dude, I can't rap," I pled.

"That's okay. The Colonel can't drop beats, either. Just try and rhyme a little and then send it over to me."

With his hand cupped over his mouth, the Colonel started to make absurd noises that sounded more like farting than bass beats, and I, uh, rapped.

"Um, we're sittin' in the barn and the sun's goin' down / when I was a kid at Burger King I wore a crown / dude, I can't rhyme for shit / so I'll let my boy Takumi rip it."

Takumi took over without pausing. "Damn, Pudge, I'm not sure I'm quite ready / but like *Nightmare on Elm Street*'s Freddy / I've always got the goods to rip shit up / last night I drank wine it was like hiccup hiccup / the Colonel's beats are sick like malaria / when I rock the mike the ladies suffer hysteria / I represent Japan as well as Birmingham / when I was a kid they called me yellow man / but I ain't ashamed a' my skin color / and neither are the countless bitches that call me lover."

Alaska jumped in.

"Oh shit did you just diss the feminine gender / I'll pummel your ass then stick you in a blender / you think I like Tori and Ani so I can't rhyme / but I got flow like Ghostbusters got slime / objectify women and it's fuckin' on / you'll be dead and gone like ancient Babylon."

Takumi picked it up again.

"If my eye offends me I will pluck it out / I got props for girls like old men got gout / oh shit now my rhyming got all whack / Lara help me out and pick up the slack."

Lara rhymed quietly and nervously—and with even more fla- grant disregard for the beat than me. "My name's Lara and I'm from Romania / thees is pretty hard, um, I once visited Albania / I love riding in Alaska's Geo / My two best vowels in English are *EO* / I'm not so good weeth the leetle *i*'s / but they make me sound cosmo- poleeteen, right? / Oh, Takumi, I think I'm done / end thees game weeth some fun."

"I drop bombs like Hiroshima, or better yet Nagasaki / when girls hear me flow they think that I'm Rocky / to represent my homeland I still drink sake / the kids don't get my rhymin' so sometimes they mock me / my build ain't small but I wouldn't call it stocky / then again, unlike Pudge, I'm not super gawky / I'm the fuckin' fox and this is my crew / our freestyle's infused with funk like my gym shoes. And we're out."

The Colonel rapped it up with freestyle beat-boxing, and we gave ourselves a round of applause.

"You ripped it up, Alaska," Takumi says, laughing.

"I do what I can to represent the ladies. Lara had my back."

"Yeah, I deed."

And then Alaska decided that although it wasn't nearly dark yet, it was time for us to get shitfaced.

"Two nights in a row is maybe pushing our luck," Takumi said as Alaska opened the wine.

"Luck is for suckers." She smiled and put the bottle to her lips. We had saltines and a hunk of Cheddar cheese provided by the Colonel for dinner, and sipping the warm pink wine out of the bot- tle with our cheese and saltines made for a fine dinner. And when we ran out of cheese, well, all the more room for Strawberry Hill.

"We have to slow down or I'll puke," I remarked after we finished the first bottle.

"I'm sorry, Pudge. I wasn't aware that someone was holding open your throat and pouring wine down it," the Colonel responded, tossing me a bottle of Mountain Dew.

"It's a little charitable to call this shit wine," Takumi cracked.

And then, as if out of nowhere, Alaska announced, "Best Day/Worst Day!"

"Huh?" I asked.

"We are all going to puke if we just drink. So we'll slow it down with a drinking game. Best Day/Worst Day."

"Never heard of it," the Colonel said.

"'Cause I just made it up." She smiled. She lay on her side across two bales of hay, the afternoon light brightening the green in her eyes, her tan skin the last memory of fall. With her mouth half open, it occurred to me that she must already be drunk as I noticed the far-off look in her eyes. *The thousand-yard stare of intoxication,* I thought, and as I watched her with an idle fascination, it occurred to me that, yeah, I was a little drunk, too.

"Fun! What are the rules?" Lara asked.

"Everybody tells the story of their best day. The best story-teller doesn't have to drink. Then everybody tells the story of their worst day, and the best storyteller doesn't have to drink. Then we keep going, second best day, second worst day, until one of y'all quits."

"How do you know it'll be one of us?" Takumi asked.

"'Cause I'm the best drinker *and* the best storyteller," she answered. Hard to disagree with that logic. "You start, Pudge. Best day of your life."

"Um. Can I take a minute to think of one?"

"Couldn'ta been that good if you have to think about it," the Colonel said.

"Fuck you, dude."

"Touchy."

"Best day of my life was today," I said. "And the story is that I woke up next to a very pretty Hungarian girl and it was cold but not too cold and I had a cup of lukewarm instant coffee and ate Cheerios without milk and then walked through the woods with Alaska and Takumi. We skipped stones across the creek, which sounds dumb but it wasn't. I don't know. Like the way the sun is right now, with the long shadows and that kind of bright, soft light you get when the sun isn't quite setting? That's the light that makes everything better, everything prettier, and today, everything just seemed to be in that light. I mean, I didn't do anything. But just sitting here, even if I'm watching the Colonel whittle, or whatever. Whatever. Great day. Today. Best day of my life."

"You think I'm pretty?" Lara said, and laughed, bashful. I thought, *It'd be good to make eye contact with her now*, but I couldn't. "And I'm *Romaneean!*"

"That story ended up being a hell of a lot better than I thought it would be," Alaska said, "but I've still got you beat."

"Bring it on, baby," I said. A breeze picked up, the tall grass outside the barn tilting away from it, and I pulled my sleeping bag over my shoulders to stay warm.

"Best day of my life was January 9, 1997. I was eight years old, and my mom and I went to the zoo on a class trip. I liked the bears. She liked the monkeys. Best day ever. End of story."

"That's it?!" the Colonel said. "That's the best day of your whole life?!"

"Yup."

"I liked eet," Lara said. "I like the monkeys, too."

"Lame," said the Colonel. I didn't think it was lame so much as more of Alaska's intentional vagueness, another example of her furthering her own mysteriousness. But still, even though I knew it was intentional, I couldn't help but wonder: *What's so fucking great about the zoo?* But before I could ask, Lara spoke.

"'Kay, my turn," said Lara. "Eet's easy. The day I came here. I knew Engleesh and my parents deedn't, and we came off the airplane and my relatives were here, aunts and uncles I had not ever seen, in the airport, and my parents were so happy. I was twelve, and I had always been the leetle baby, but that was the first day that my parents needed me and treated me like a grown-up. Because they did not know the language, right? They need me to order food and to translate tax and immigration forms and everytheeng else, and that was the day they stopped treating me like a keed. Also, in Romania, we were poor. And here, we're kinda reech." She laughed.

"All right." Takumi smiled, grabbing the bottle of wine. "I lose. Because the best day of my life was the day I lost my virginity. And if you think I'm going to tell you that story, you're gonna have to get me drunker than this."

"Not bad," the Colonel said. "That's not bad. Want to know my best day?"

"That's the game, Chip," Alaska said, clearly annoyed.

"Best day of my life hasn't happened yet. But I know it. I see it every day. The best day of my life is the day I buy my mom a huge fucking house. And not just like out in the woods, but in the middle of Mountain Brook, with all the Weekday Warriors' parents. With all y'all's parents. And I'm not buying it with a mortgage either. I'm buying it with cash money, and I am driving my mom there, and I'm going to open her side of the car door and she'll get out and look at this house—this house is like picket fence and two stories and everything, you know—and I'm going to hand her the keys to her house and I'll say, 'Thanks.' Man, she helped fill out my application to this place. And she let me come here, and that's no easy thing when you come from where we do, to let your son go away to school. So that's the best day of my life."

Takumi tilted the bottle up and swallowed a few times, then handed it to me. I drank, and so did Lara, and then Alaska put her head back and turned the bottle upside down, quickly downing the last quarter of the bottle.

As she unscrewed the next bottle, Alaska smiled at the Colonel. "You won that round. Now what's your worst day?"

"Worst day was when my dad left. He's old—he's like seventy now—and he was old when he married my mom, and he *still* cheated on her. And she caught him, and she got pissed, so he hit her. And then she kicked him out, and he left. I was here, and my mom called, and she didn't tell me the whole story with the cheating and everything and the hitting until later. She just said that he was gone and not coming back. And I haven't seen him since. All that day, I kept waiting for him to call me and explain it, but he never did. He never called at all. I at least thought he would say good-bye or something. That was the worst day."

"Shit, you got me beat again," I said. "My worst day was in seventh grade, when Tommy Hewitt pissed on my gym clothes and then the gym teacher said I had to wear my uniform or I'd fail the class. Seventh-grade gym, right? There are worse things to fail. But it was a big deal then, and I was crying, and trying to explain to the teacher what happened, but it was so embarrassing, and he just yelled and yelled and yelled until I put on these piss-soaked shorts and T-shirt. That was the day I stopped caring what people did. I just never cared anymore, about being a loser or not having friends or any of that. So I guess it was good for me in a way, but that moment was awful. I mean, imagine me playing volleyball or whatever in pee-soaked gym clothes while Tommy Hewitt tells everyone what he did. That was the worst day."

Lara was laughing. "I'm sorry, Miles."

"All good," I said. "Just tell me yours so I can laugh at *your* pain," and I smiled, and we laughed together.

"My worst day was probably the same day as my best. Because I left everytheeng. I mean, eet sounds dumb, but my childhood, too, because most twelve-year-olds do not, you know, have to feegure out W-2 forms."

"What's a W-2 form?" I asked.

"That's my point. Eet's for taxes. So. Same day."

Lara had always needed to talk for her parents, I thought, and so maybe she never learned how to talk for herself. And I wasn't great at talking for myself either. We had something important in common, then, a personality quirk I didn't share with Alaska or anybody else, although almost by definition Lara and I couldn't express it to each other. So maybe it was just the way the not-yet-setting sun shone against her lazy dark curls, but at that moment, I wanted to kiss her, and we did not need to talk in order to kiss, and the puking on her jeans and the months of mutual avoidance melted away.

"Eet's your turn, Takumi."

"Worst day of my life," Takumi said. "June 9, 2000. My grandmother died in Japan. She died in a car accident, and I was supposed to leave to go see her two days later. I was going to spend the whole summer with her and my grandfather, but instead I flew over for her funeral, and the only time I really saw what she looked like, I mean other than in pictures, was at her funeral. She had a Buddhist funeral, and they cremated her, but before they did she was on this, like—well, it's not really Buddhist. I mean, religion is complicated there, so it's a little Buddhist and a little Shinto, but y'all don't care—point being that she was on this, like, funeral pyre or whatever. And that's the only time I ever saw her, was just before they burned her up. That was the worst day."

The Colonel lit a cigarette, threw it to me, and lit one of his own. It was eerie, that he could tell when I wanted a cigarette. We *were* like an old married couple. For a moment, I thought, *It's massively unwise to throw lit cigarettes around a barn full of hay*, but then the moment of caution passed, and I just made a sincere effort not to flick ash onto any hay.

"No clear winner yet," the Colonel said. "The field is wide open. Your turn, buddy."

Alaska lay on her back, her hands locked behind her head. She spoke softly and quickly, but the quiet day was becoming a quieter night—the bugs gone now with the arrival of winter—and we could hear her clearly.

"The day after my mom took me to the zoo where she liked the monkeys and I liked the bears, it was a Friday. I came home from school. She gave me a hug and told me to go do my homework in my room so I could watch TV later. I went into my room, and she sat down at the kitchen table, I guess, and then she screamed, and I ran out, and she had fallen over. She was lying on the floor, holding her head and jerking. And I freaked out. I should have called 911, but I just started screaming and crying until finally she stopped jerking, and I thought she had fallen asleep and that whatever had hurt didn't hurt anymore. So I just sat there on the floor with her until my dad got home an hour later, and he's screaming, 'Why didn't you call 911?' and trying to give her CPR, but by then she was plenty dead. Aneurysm. Worst day. I win. You drink."

And so we did.

No one talked for a minute, and then Takumi asked, "Your dad blamed you?"

"Well, not after that first moment. But yeah. How could he not?"

"Well, you were a little kid," Takumi argued. I was too surprised and uncomfortable to talk, trying to fit this into what I knew about Alaska's family. Her mom told her the knock-knock joke—when Alaska was six. Her mom used to smoke—but didn't anymore, obviously.

"Yeah. I was a little kid. Little kids can dial 911. They do it all the time. Give me the wine," she said, deadpan and emotionless. She drank without lifting her head from the hay.

"I'm sorry," Takumi said.

"Why didn't you ever tell me?" the Colonel asked, his voice soft.

"It never came up." And then we stopped asking questions. *What the hell do you say?*

In the long quiet that followed, as we passed around the wine and slowly became drunker, I found myself thinking about President William McKinley, the third American president to be assassinated. He lived for several days after he was shot, and toward the end, his wife started crying and screaming, "I want to go, too! I want to go, too!" And with his last measure of strength, McKinley turned to her and spoke his last words: "We are all going."

It was the central moment of Alaska's life. When she cried and told me that she fucked everything up, I knew what she meant now. And when she said she failed everyone, I knew whom she meant. It was the everything and the everyone of her life, and so I could not help but imagine it: I imagined a scrawny eight-year-old with dirty fingers, looking down at her mother convulsing. So she sat down with her dead-or-maybe-not mother, who I imagine was not breathing by then but wasn't yet cold either. And in the time between dying and death, a little Alaska sat with her mother in silence. And then through the silence and my drunkenness, I caught a glimpse of her as she might have been. She must have come to feel so powerless, I thought, that the one thing she might have done—pick up the phone and call an ambulance—never even occurred to her. There comes a time when we realize that our parents cannot save themselves or save us, that everyone who wades through time eventually gets dragged out to sea by the undertow—that, in short, we are all going.

So she became impulsive, scared by her inaction into perpetual action. When the Eagle confronted her with expulsion, maybe she blurted out Marya's name because it was the first that came to mind, because in that moment she didn't want to get expelled and couldn't think past that moment. She was scared, sure. But more importantly, maybe she'd been scared of being paralyzed by fear again.

"We are all going," McKinley said to his wife, and we sure are. There's your labyrinth of suffering. We are all going. Find your way out of that maze.

None of which I said out loud to her. Not then and not ever. We never said another word about it. Instead, it became just another worst day, albeit the worst of the bunch, and as night fell fast, we continued on, drinking and joking.

Later that night, after Alaska stuck her finger down her throat and made herself puke in front of all of us because she was too drunk to walk into the woods, I lay down in my sleeping bag. Lara was lying beside me, in her bag, which was almost touching mine. I moved my arm to the edge of my bag and pushed it so it slightly overlapped with hers. I pressed my hand against hers. I could feel it, although there were two sleeping bags between us. My plan, which struck me as very slick, was to pull my arm out of my sleeping bag and put it into hers, and then hold her hand. It was a good plan, but when I tried to actually get my arm out of the mummy bag, I flailed around like a fish out of water, and nearly dislocated my shoulder. She was laughing—and not with me, at me—but we still didn't speak. Having passed the point of no return, I slid my hand into her sleeping bag anyway, and she stifled a giggle as my fingers traced a line from her elbow to her wrist.

"That teekles," she whispered. So much for me being sexy.

"Sorry," I whispered.

"No, it's a nice teekle," she said, and held my hand. She laced her fingers in mine and squeezed. And then she rolled over and keessed me. I am sure that she tasted like stale booze, but I did not notice, and I'm sure I tasted like stale booze and cigarettes, but she didn't notice. We were kissing.

I thought: *This is good.*

I thought: *I am not bad at this kissing. Not bad at all.*

I thought: *I am clearly the greatest kisser in the history of the universe.*

Suddenly she laughed and pulled away from me. She wiggled a hand out of her sleeping bag and wiped her face. "You slobbered on my nose," she said, and laughed.

I laughed, too, trying to give her the impression that my nose-slobbering kissing style was intended to be funny. "I'm sorry." To borrow the base system from Alaska, I hadn't hit more than five singles in my entire life, so I tried to chalk it up to inexperience. "I'm a bit new at this," I said.

"Eet was a nice slobbering," she said, laughed, and kissed me again. Soon we were entirely out of our sleeping bags, making out quietly. She lay on top of me, and I held her small waist in my hands. I could feel her breasts against my chest, and she moved slowly on top of me, her legs straddling me. "You feel nice," she said.

"You're beautiful," I said, and smiled at her. In the dark, I could make out the outline of her face and her large, round eyes blinking down at me, her eyelashes almost fluttering against my forehead.

"Could the two people who are making out please be quiet?" the Colonel asked loudly from his sleeping bag. "Those of us who are not making out are drunk and tired."

"Mostly. Drunk," Alaska said slowly, as if enunciation required great effort.

We had almost never talked, Lara and I, and we didn't get a chance to talk anymore because of the Colonel. So we kissed quietly and laughed softly with our mouths and our eyes. After so much kissing that it almost started to get boring, I whispered, "Do you want to be my girlfriend?" And she said, "Yes please," and smiled. We slept together in her sleeping bag, which felt a little crowded, to be honest, but was still nice. I had never felt another person against me as I slept. It was a fine end to the best day of my life.

one day before

THE NEXT MORNING, a term I use loosely since it was not yet dawn, the Colonel shook me awake. Lara was wrapped in my arms, folded into my body.

"We gotta go, Pudge. Time to roll up."

"Dude. Sleeping."

"You can sleep after we check in. IT'S TIME TO GO!" he shouted.

"All right. All right. No screaming. Head hurts." And it did. I could feel last night's wine in my throat and my head throbbed like it had the morning after my concussion. My mouth tasted like a skunk had crawled into my throat and died. I made an effort not to exhale near Lara as she groggily extricated herself from the sleeping bag.

We packed everything quickly, threw our empty bottles into the tall grass of the field—littering was an unfortunate necessity at the Creek, since no one wanted to throw an empty bottle of booze in a campus trash can—and walked away from the barn. Lara grabbed my hand and then shyly let go. Alaska looked like a train wreck, but insisted on pouring the last few sips of Strawberry Hill into her cold instant coffee before chucking the bottle behind her.

"Hair of the dog," she said.

"How ya doin'?" the Colonel asked her.

"I've had better mornings."

"Hungover?"

"Like an alcoholic preacher on Sunday morning."

"Maybe you shouldn't drink so much," I suggested.

"Pudge." She shook her head and sipped the cold coffee and wine. "Pudge, what you must understand about me is that I am a deeply unhappy person."

We walked side by side down the washed-out dirt road on our way back to campus. Just after we reached the bridge, Takumi stopped, said "uh-oh," got on his hands and knees, and puked a volcano of yellow and pink.

"Let it out," Alaska said. "You'll be fine."

He finished, stood up, and said, "I finally found something that can stop the fox. The fox cannot summit Strawberry Hill."

Alaska and Lara walked to their rooms, planning to check in with the Eagle later in the day, while Takumi and I stood behind the Colonel as he knocked on the Eagle's door at 9:00 A.M.

"Y'all are home early. Have fun?"

"Yes sir," the Colonel said.

"How's your mom, Chip?"

"She's doing well, sir. She's in good shape."

"She feed y'all well?"

"Oh yes sir," I said. "She tried to fatten me up."

"You need it. Y'all have a good day."

"Well, I don't think he suspected anything," the Colonel said on our way back to Room 43. "So maybe we actually pulled it off." I thought about going over to see Lara, but I was pretty tired, so I just went to bed and slept through my hangover.

It was not an eventful day. I should have done extraordinary things. I should have sucked the marrow out of life. But on that day, I slept eighteen hours out of a possible twenty-four.

the last day

THE NEXT MORNING, the first Monday of the new semester, the Colonel came out of the shower just as my alarm went off.

As I pulled on my shoes, Kevin knocked once and then opened the door, stepping inside.

"You're looking good," the Colonel said casually. Kevin's now sported a crew cut, a small patch of short blue hair on each side of his head, just above the ear. His lower lip jutted out—the morning's first dip. He walked over to our COFFEE TABLE, picked up a can of Coke, and spit into it.

"You almost didn't get me. I noticed it in my conditioner and got right back in the shower. But I didn't notice it in my gel. It didn't show up in Jeff's hair at all. But Longwell and me, we had to go with the Marine look. Thank God I have clippers."

"It suits you," I said, although it didn't. The short hair accentuated his features, specifically his too-close-together beady eyes, which did not stand up well to accentuation. The Colonel was trying hard to look tough—ready for whatever Kevin might do—but it's hard to look tough when you're only wearing an orange towel.

"Truce?"

"Well, your troubles aren't over, I'm afraid," the Colonel said, referring to the mailed-but-not-yet-received progress reports.

"A'ight. If you say so. We'll talk when it's over, I guess."

"I guess so," the Colonel said. As Kevin walked out, the Colonel said, "Take the can you spit in, you unhygienic shit." Kevin just closed the door behind him. The Colonel grabbed the can, opened the door, and threw it at Kevin—missing him by a good margin.

"Jeez, go easy on the guy."

"No truce yet, Pudge."

I spent that afternoon with Lara. We were very cutesy, even though we didn't know the first thing about each other and barely talked.

But we made out. She grabbed my butt at one point, and I sort of jumped. I was lying down, but I did the best version of jumping that one can do lying down, and she said, "Sorry," and I said, "No, it's okay. It's just a little sore from the swan."

We walked to the TV room together, and I locked the door. We were watching *The Brady Bunch*, which she had never seen. The episode, where the Bradys visit the gold-mining ghost town and they all get locked up in the one-room jail by some crazy old gold panner with a scraggly white beard, was especially horrible, and gave us a lot to laugh about. Which is good, since we didn't have much to *talk* about.

Just as the Bradys were getting locked in jail, Lara randomly asked me, "Have you ever gotten a blow job?"

"Um, that's out of the blue," I said.

"The blue?"

"Like, you know, out of left field."

"Left field?"

"Like, in baseball. Like, out of nowhere. I mean, what made you think of that?"

"I've just never geeven one," she answered, her little voice dripping with seductiveness. It was so brazen. I thought I would explode. I never thought. I mean, from Alaska, hearing that stuff was one thing. But to hear her sweet little Romanian voice go so sexy all of the sudden . . .

"No," I said. "I never have."

"Think it would be fun?"

DO I!?!?!?!?!?!?! "Um. yeah. I mean, you don't have to."

"I think I want to," she said, and we kissed a little, and then. And then with me sitting watching *The Brady Bunch*, watching Marcia Marcia Marcia up to her Brady antics, Lara unbuttoned my pants and pulled my boxers down a little and pulled out my penis.

"Wow," she said.

"What?"

She looked up at me, but didn't move, her face nanometers away from my penis. "It's weird."

"What do you mean *weird?*"

"Just beeg, I guess."

I could live with that kind of weird. And then she wrapped her hand around it and put it into her mouth.

And waited.

We were both very still. She did not move a muscle in her body, and I did not move a muscle in mine. I knew that at this point something else was supposed to happen, but I wasn't quite sure what.

She stayed still. I could feel her nervous breath. For minutes, for as long as it took the Bradys to steal the key and unlock themselves from the ghost-town jail, she lay there, stock-still with my penis in her mouth, and I sat there, waiting.

And then she took it out of her mouth and looked up at me quizzically.

"Should I do sometheeng?"

"Um. I don't know," I said. Everything I'd learned from watching porn with Alaska suddenly exited my brain. I thought maybe she should move her head up and down, but wouldn't that choke her? So I just stayed quiet.

"Should I, like, bite?"

"Don't bite! I mean, I don't think. I think—I mean, that felt good. That was nice. I don't know if there's something else."

"I mean, you deedn't—"

"Um. Maybe we should ask Alaska."

So we went to her room and asked Alaska. She laughed and laughed. Sitting on her bed, she laughed until she cried. She walked into the bathroom, returned with a tube of toothpaste, and showed us. In detail. Never have I so wanted to be Crest Complete.

Lara and I went back to her room, where she did exactly what Alaska told her to do, and I did exactly what Alaska said I would do, which was die a hundred little ecstatic deaths, my fists clenched, my body shaking. It was my first orgasm with a girl, and afterward, I was embarrassed and nervous, and so, clearly, was Lara, who finally broke the silence by asking, "So, want to do some homework?"

There was little to do on the first day of the semester, but she read for her English class. I picked up a biography of Argentinian revolutionary Che Guevara—whose face adorned a poster on the wall—that Lara's roommate had on her bookshelf, then I lay down next to Lara on the bottom bunk. I began at the end, as I sometimes did with biographies I had no intention of reading all the way through, and found his last words without too much searching. Captured by the Bolivian army, Guevara said, "Shoot, coward. You are only going to kill a man." I thought back to Simón Bolívar's last words in García Márquez's novel—"How will I ever get out of this labyrinth!" South American revolutionaries, it would seem, died with flair. I read the last words out loud to Lara. She turned on her side, placing her head on my chest.

"Why do you like last words so much?"

Strange as it might seem, I'd never really thought about why. "I don't know," I said, placing my hand against the small of her back. "Sometimes, just because they're funny. Like in the Civil War, a general named Sedgwick said, 'They couldn't hit an elephant from this dis—' and then he got shot." She laughed. "But a lot of times, people die how they live. And so last words tell me a lot about who people were, and why they became the sort of people biographies get written about. Does that make sense?"

"Yeah," she said.

"Yeah?" Just yeah?

"Yeah," she said, and then went back to reading.

I didn't know how to talk to her. And I was frustrated with trying, so after a little while, I got up to go.

I kissed her good-bye. I could do that, at least.

I picked up Alaska and the Colonel at our room and we walked down to the bridge, where I repeated in embarrassing detail the fellatio fiasco.

"I can't believe she went down on you twice in one day," the Colonel said.

"Only technically. Really just once," Alaska corrected.

"Still. I mean. Still. Pudge got his hog smoked."

"The poor Colonel," Alaska said with a rueful smile. "I'd give you a pity blow, but I really am attached to Jake."

"That's just creepy," the Colonel said. "You're only supposed to flirt with Pudge."

"But Pudge has a *giiirrrrlll*friend." She laughed.

That night, the Colonel and I walked down to Alaska's room to celebrate our Barn Night success. She and the Colonel had been celebrating a lot the past couple days, and I didn't feel up to climbing Strawberry Hill, so I sat and munched on pretzels while Alaska and the Colonel drank wine from paper cups with flowers on them.

"We ain't drinkin' out the bottle tonight, hun," the Colonel said. "We classin' it up!"

"It's an old-time Southern drinking contest," Alaska responded. "We's a-gonna treat Pudge to an evening of real Southern livin': We go'n match each other Dixie cup for Dixie cup till the lesser drinker falls."

And that is pretty much what they did, pausing only to turn out the lights at 11:00 so the Eagle wouldn't drop by. They chatted some, but mostly they drank, and I drifted out of the conversation and ended up squinting through the dark, looking at the book spines in Alaska's Life Library. Even minus the books she'd lost in the mini-flood, I could have stayed up until morning reading through the haphazard stacks of titles. A dozen white tulips in a plastic vase were precariously perched atop one of the book stacks, and when I asked her about them, she just said, "Jake and my's anniversary," and I didn't care to continue that line of dialogue, so I went back to scanning titles, and I was just wondering how I could go about learning Edgar Allan Poe's last words (for the record: "Lord help my poor soul") when I heard Alaska say, "Pudge isn't even listening to us."

And I said, "I'm listening."

"We were just talking about Truth or Dare. Played out in seventh grade or still cool?"

"Never played it," I said. "No friends in seventh grade."

"Well, that does it!" she shouted, a bit too loud given the late hour and also given the fact that she was openly drinking wine in the room. "Truth or Dare!"

"All right," I agreed, "but I'm not making out with the Colonel."

The Colonel sat slumped in the corner. "Can't make out. Too drunk."

Alaska started. "Truth or Dare, Pudge."

"Dare."

"Hook up with me."

So I did.

It was that quick. I laughed, looked nervous, and she leaned in and tilted her head to the side, and we were kissing. Zero layers between us. Our tongues dancing back and forth in each other's mouth until there was no her mouth and my mouth but only our mouths intertwined. She tasted like cigarettes and Mountain Dew and wine and Chap Stick. Her hand came to my face and I felt her soft fingers tracing the line of my jaw. We lay down as we kissed, she on top of me, and I began to move beneath her. I pulled away

for a moment, to say, "What is going on here?" and she put one finger to her lips and we kissed again. A hand grabbed one of mine and
she placed it on her stomach. I moved slowly on top of her and felt
her arching her back fluidly beneath me.

I pulled away again. "What about Lara? Jake?" Again, she *sshed*
me. "Less tongue, more lips," she said, and I tried my best. I
thought the tongue was the whole point, but she was the expert.

"Christ," the Colonel said quite loudly. "That wretched beast,
drama, draws nigh."

But we paid no attention. She moved my hand from her waist to
her breast, and I felt cautiously, my fingers moving slowly under her
shirt but over her bra, tracing the outline of her breasts and then
cupping one in my hand, squeezing softly. "You're good at that," she
whispered. Her lips never left mine as she spoke. We moved
together, my body between her legs.

"This is so fun," she whispered, "but I'm so sleepy. To be continued?" She kissed me for another moment, my mouth straining to
stay near hers, and then she moved from beneath me, placed her
head on my chest, and fell asleep instantly.

We didn't have sex. We never got naked. I never touched her
bare breast, and her hands never got lower than my hips. It didn't
matter. As she slept, I whispered, "I love you, Alaska Young."

Just as I was falling asleep, the Colonel spoke. "Dude, did you
just make out with Alaska?"

"Yeah."

"This is going to end poorly," he said to himself.

And then I was asleep. That deep, can-still-taste-her-in-my-mouth
sleep, that sleep that is not particularly restful but is difficult to wake
from all the same. And then I heard the phone ring. I think. And I
think, although I can't know, that I felt Alaska get up. I think I heard
her leave. I think. How long she was gone is impossible to know.

But the Colonel and I both woke up when she returned, whenever that was, because she slammed the door. She was sobbing, like that post-Thanksgiving morning but worse.

"I have to get out of here!" she cried.

"What's wrong?" I asked.

"I forgot! God, how many times can I fuck up?" she said. I didn't even have time to wonder what she forgot before she screamed, "I JUST HAVE TO GO. HELP ME GET OUT OF HERE!"

"Where do you need to go?"

She sat down and put her head between her legs, sobbing. "Just please distract the Eagle right now so I can go. Please."

The Colonel and I, at the same moment, equal in our guilt, said, "Okay."

"Just don't turn on your lights," the Colonel said. "Just drive slow and don't turn on your lights. Are you sure you're okay?"

"Fuck," she said. "Just get rid of the Eagle for me," she said, her sobs childlike half screams. "God oh God, I'm so sorry."

"Okay," the Colonel said. "Start the car when you hear the second string."

We left.

We did not say: *Don't drive. You're drunk.*

We did not say: *We aren't letting you in that car when you are upset.*

We did not say: *We insist on going with you.*

We did not say: *This can wait until tomorrow. Anything—everything—can wait.*

We walked to our bathroom, grabbed the three strings of leftover firecrackers from beneath the sink, and ran to the Eagle's. We weren't sure that it would work again.

But it worked well enough. The Eagle tore out of his house as soon as the first string of firecrackers started popping—he was waiting for us, I suppose—and we headed for the woods and got him in deeply enough that he never heard her drive away. The Colonel and I doubled back, wading through the creek to save time, slipped in through the back window of Room 43, and slept like babies.

after

the day after

THE COLONEL SLEPT the not-restful sleep of the drunk, and I lay on my back on the bottom bunk, my mouth tingling and alive as if still kissing, and we would have likely slept through our morning classes had the Eagle not awoken us at 8:00 with three quick knocks. I rolled over as he opened the door, and the morning light rushed into the room.

"I need y'all to go to the gym," he said. I squinted toward him, the Eagle himself backlit into invisibility by the too bright sun. "Now," he added, and I knew it. We were done for. Caught. Too many progress reports. Too much drinking in too short a time. Why did they have to drink last night? And then I could taste her again, the wine and the cigarette smoke and the Chap Stick and Alaska, and I wondered if she had kissed me because she was drunk. *Don't expel me*, I thought. *Don't. I have just begun to kiss her.*

And as if answering my prayers, the Eagle said, "You're not in any trouble. But you need to go to the gym now."

I heard the Colonel rolling over above me. "What's wrong?"

"Something terrible has happened," the Eagle said, and then closed the door.

As he grabbed a pair of jeans lying on the floor, the Colonel said, "This happened a couple years ago. When Hyde's wife died. I guess it's the Old Man himself now. Poor bastard really *didn't* have many breaths left." He looked up at me, his half-open eyes bloodshot, and yawned.

"You look a little hungover," I observed.

He closed his eyes. "Well, then I'm putting up a good front, Pudge, 'cause I'm actually a lot hungover."

"I kissed Alaska."

"Yeah. I wasn't *that* drunk. Let's go."

We walked across the dorm circle to the gym. I sported baggy jeans, a sweatshirt with no shirt underneath, and a bad case of bedhead. All the teachers were in the dorm circle knocking on doors, but I didn't see Dr. Hyde. I imagined him lying dead in his house, wondered who had found him, how they even knew he was missing before he failed to show up for class.

"I don't see Dr. Hyde," I told the Colonel.

"Poor bastard."

The gym was half full by the time we arrived. A podium had been set up in the middle of the basketball court, close to the bleachers. I sat in the second row, with the Colonel directly in front of me. My thoughts were split between sadness for Dr. Hyde and excitement about Alaska, remembering the up-close sight of her mouth whispering, "To be continued?"

And it did not occur to me—not even when Dr. Hyde shuffled into the gym, taking tiny, slow steps toward the Colonel and me.

I tapped the Colonel on the shoulder and said, "Hyde's here," and the Colonel said, "Oh shit," and I said, "What?" and he said,

"Where's Alaska?" and I said, "No," and he said, "Pudge, is she here or not?" and then we both stood up and scanned the faces in the gym.

The Eagle walked up to the podium and said, "Is everyone here?"

"No," I said to him. "Alaska isn't here."

The Eagle looked down. "Is everyone else here?"

"Alaska isn't here!"

"Okay, Miles. Thank you."

"We can't start without Alaska."

The Eagle looked at me. He was crying, noiselessly. Tears just rolled from his eyes to his chin and then fell onto his corduroy pants. He stared at me, but it was not the Look of Doom. His eyes blinking the tears down his face, the Eagle looked, for all the world, sorry.

"Please, sir," I said. "Can we please wait for Alaska?" I felt all of them staring at us, trying to understand what I now knew, but didn't quite believe.

The Eagle looked down and bit his lower lip. "Last night, Alaska Young was in a terrible accident." His tears came faster, then. "And she was killed. Alaska has passed away."

For a moment, everyone in the gym was silent, and the place had never been so quiet, not even in the moments before the Colonel ridiculed opponents at the free-throw stripe. I stared down at the back of the Colonel's head. I just stared, looking at his thick and bushy hair. For a moment, it was so quiet that you could hear the sound of not-breathing, the vacuum created by 190 students shocked out of air.

I thought: *It's all my fault.*

I thought: *I don't feel very good.*

I thought: *I'm going to throw up.*

I stood up and ran outside. I made it to a trash can outside the gym, five feet from the double doors, and heaved toward Gatorade bottles and half-eaten McDonald's. But nothing much came out. I just heaved, my stomach muscles tightening and my throat opening and a gasping, guttural *blech,* going through the motions of vomiting over and over again. In between gags and coughs, I sucked air in hard. Her mouth. Her dead, cold mouth. To not be continued. I knew she was drunk. Upset. Obviously you don't let someone drive drunk and pissed off. *Obviously.* And Christ, Miles, what the hell is wrong with you? And then comes the puke, finally, splashing onto the trash. And here is whatever of her I had left in my mouth, here in this trash can. And then it comes again, more—and then okay, calm down, okay, seriously, she's not dead.

She's not dead. She's alive. She's alive somewhere. She's in the woods. Alaska is hiding in the woods and she's not dead, she's just hiding. She's just playing a trick on us. This is just an Alaska Young Prank Extraordinaire. It's Alaska being Alaska, funny and playful and not knowing when or how to put on the brakes.

And then I felt much better, because she had not died at all.

I walked back into the gym, and everyone seemed to be in various stages of disintegration. It was like something you see on TV, like a *National Geographic* special on funeral rituals. I saw Takumi standing over Lara, his hands on her shoulders. I saw Kevin with his crew cut, his head buried between his knees. A girl named Molly Tan, who'd studied with us for precalc, wailed, beating balled fists against her thighs. All these people I sort of knew and sort of didn't, and all of them disintegrating, and then I saw the Colonel, his knees tucked into his chest, lying on his side on the bleachers, Madame O'Malley sitting next to him, reaching toward his shoulder but not actually touching it. The Colonel was screaming. He would inhale, and then scream. Inhale. Scream. Inhale. Scream.

I thought, at first, that it was only yelling. But after a few breaths,

I noticed a rhythm. And after a few more, I realized that the Colonel was saying words. He was screaming, "I'm so sorry."

Madame O'Malley grabbed his hand. "You've got nothing to be sorry for, Chip. There was nothing you could have done." But if only she knew.

And I just stood there, looking at the scene, thinking about her not dead, and I felt a hand on my shoulder and turned around to see the Eagle, and I said, "I think she's playing a dumb prank," and he said, "No, Miles, no, I'm sorry," and I felt the heat in my cheeks and said, "She's really good. She could pull this off," and he said, "I saw her. I'm sorry."

"What happened?"

"Somebody was setting off firecrackers in the woods," he said, and I closed my eyes tight, the ineluctable fact of the matter at hand: I had killed her. "I went out after them, and I guess she drove off campus. It was late. She was on I-65 just south of downtown. A truck had jackknifed, blocking both lanes. A police car had just gotten to the scene. She hit the cruiser without ever swerving. I believe she must have been very intoxicated. The police said they smelled alcohol."

"How do you know?" I asked.

"I saw her, Miles. I talked to the police. It was instant. The steering wheel hit her chest. I'm so sorry."

And I said, you saw her and he said yes and I said how did she look and he said, just a bit of blood coming out of her nose, and I sat down on the floor of the gym. I could hear the Colonel still screaming, and I could feel hands on my back as I hunched forward, but I could only see her lying naked on a metal table, a small trickle of blood falling out of her half-teardrop nose, her green eyes open, staring off into the distance, her mouth turned up just enough to suggest the idea of a smile, and she had felt so warm against me, her mouth soft and warm on mine.

———————————

The Colonel and I are walking back to our dorm room in silence. I am staring at the ground beneath me. I cannot stop thinking that she is dead, and I cannot stop thinking that she cannot possibly be dead. People do not just die. I can't catch my breath. I feel afraid, like someone has told me they're going to kick my ass after school and now it's sixth period and I know full well what's coming. It is so cold today—literally freezing—and I imagine running to the creek and diving in headfirst, the creek so shallow that my hands scrape against the rocks, and my body slides into the cold water, the shock of the cold giving way to numbness, and I would stay there, float down with that water first to the Cahaba River, then to the Alabama River, then to Mobile Bay and the Gulf of Mexico.

I want to melt into the brown, crunchy grass that the Colonel and I step on as we silently make our way back to our room. His feet are so large, too large for his short body, and the new generic tennis shoes he wears since his old ones were pissed in look almost like clown shoes. I think of Alaska's flip-flops clinging to her blue toes as we swung on the swing down by the lake. Will the casket be open? Can a mortician re-create her smile? I could still hear her saying it: "This is so fun, but I'm so sleepy. To be continued?"

Nineteenth-century preacher Henry Ward Beecher's last words were "Now comes the mystery." The poet Dylan Thomas, who liked a good drink at least as much as Alaska, said, "I've had eighteen straight whiskeys. I do believe that's a record," before dying. Alaska's favorite was playwright Eugene O'Neill: "Born in a hotel room, and—God damn it—died in a hotel room." Even car-accident victims sometimes have time for last words. Princess Diana said, "Oh God. What's happened?" Movie star James Dean said, "They've got to see us," just before slamming his Porsche into another car. I know so many last words. But I will never know hers.

I am several steps in front of him before I realize that the Colonel has fallen down. I turn around, and he is lying on his face. "We have to get up, Chip. We have to get up. We just have to get to the room."

The Colonel turns his face from the ground to me and looks me dead in the eye and says, "I. Can't. Breathe."

But he *can* breathe, and I know this because he is hyperventilating, breathing as if trying to blow air back into the dead. I pick him up, and he grabs onto me and starts sobbing, again saying, "I'm so sorry," over and over again. We have never hugged before, me and the Colonel, and there is nothing much to say, because he ought to be sorry, and I just put my hand on the back of his head and say the only true thing. "I'm sorry, too."

t w o d a y s a f t e r

I DIDN'T SLEEP THAT NIGHT. Dawn was slow in coming, and even when it did, the sun shining bright through the blinds, the rickety radiator couldn't keep us warm, so the Colonel and I sat wordlessly on the couch. He read the almanac.

The night before, I'd braved the cold to call my parents, and this time when I said, "Hey, it's Miles," and my mom answered with, "What's wrong? Is everything okay?" I could safely tell her no, everything was not okay. My dad picked up the line then.

"What's wrong?" he asked.

"Don't yell," my mother said.

"I'm not yelling; it's just the phone."

"Well, talk quieter," she said, and so it took some time before I could say anything, and then once I could, it took some time to say the words in order—my friend Alaska died in a car crash. I stared at the numbers and messages scrawled on the wall by the phone.

"Oh, Miles," Mom said. "I'm so sorry, Miles. Do you want to come home?"

"No," I said. "I want to be here . . . I can't believe it," which was still partly true.

"That's just awful," my dad said. "Her poor parents." *Poor parent,* I thought, and wondered about her dad. I couldn't even imagine what my parents would do if I died. Driving drunk. God, if her father ever found out, he would disembowel the Colonel and me.

"What can we do for you right now?" my mom asked.

"I just needed you to pick up. I just needed you to answer the phone, and you did." I heard a sniffle behind me—from cold or grief, I didn't know—and told my parents, "Someone's waiting for the phone. I gotta go."

All night, I felt paralyzed into silence, terrorized. What was I so afraid of, anyway? The thing had happened. She was dead. She was warm and soft against my skin, my tongue in her mouth, and she was laughing, trying to teach me, make me better, promising to be continued. And now.

And now she was colder by the hour, more dead with every breath I took. I thought: *That is the fear: I have lost something important, and I cannot find it, and I need it. It is fear like if someone lost his glasses and went to the glasses store and they told him that the world had run out of glasses and he would just have to do without.*

Just before eight in the morning, the Colonel announced to no one in particular, "I think there are bufriedos at lunch today."

"Yeah," I said. "Are you hungry?"

"God no. But she named them, you know. They were called fried burritos when we got here, and Alaska started calling them bufriedos, and then everyone did, and then finally Maureen officially changed the name." He paused. "I don't know what to do, Miles."

"Yeah. I know."

"I finished memorizing the capitals," he said.

"Of the states?"

"No. That was fifth grade. Of the countries. Name a country."

"Canada," I said.

"Something hard."

"Um. Uzbekistan?"

"Tashkent." He didn't even take a moment to think. It was just there, at the tip of his tongue, as if he'd been waiting for me to say "Uzbekistan" all along. "Let's smoke."

We walked to the bathroom and turned on the shower, and the Colonel pulled a pack of matches from his jeans and struck a match against the matchbook. It didn't light. Again, he tried and failed, and again, smacking at the matchbook with a crescendoing fury until he finally threw the matches to the ground and screamed, "GODDAMN IT!"

"It's okay," I said, reaching into my pocket for a lighter.

"No, Pudge, it's not," he said, throwing down his cigarette and standing up, suddenly pissed. "Goddamn it! God, how did this happen? How could she be so stupid! She just never thought anything through. So goddamned impulsive. Christ. It is not okay. I can't believe she was so *stupid!*"

"We should have stopped her," I said.

He reached into the stall to turn off the dribbling shower and then pounded an open palm against the tile wall. "Yeah, I know we should have stopped her, damn it. I am shit sure keenly aware that we should have stopped her. But we shouldn't have *had* to. You had to watch her like a *three-year-old*. You do one thing wrong, and then she just dies. Christ! I'm losing it. I'm going on a walk."

"Okay," I answered, trying to keep my voice calm.

"I'm sorry," he said. "I feel so screwed up. I feel like I might die."

"You might," I said.

"Yeah. Yeah. I might. You never know. It's just. It's like. *POOF.* And you're gone."

I followed him into the room. He grabbed the almanac from his bunk, zipped his jacket, closed the door, and *POOF.* He was gone.

With morning came visitors. An hour after the Colonel left, resident stoner Hank Walsten dropped by to offer me some weed, which I graciously turned down. Hank hugged me and said, "At least it was instant. At least there wasn't any pain."

I knew he was only trying to help, but he didn't get it. There was pain. A dull endless pain in my gut that wouldn't go away even when I knelt on the stingingly frozen tile of the bathroom, dry-heaving.

And what is an "instant" death anyway? How long is an instant? Is it one second? Ten? The pain of those seconds must have been awful as her heart burst and her lungs collapsed and there was no air and no blood to her brain and only raw panic. What the hell is *instant?* Nothing is instant. Instant rice takes five minutes, instant pudding an hour. I doubt that an instant of blinding pain *feels* particularly instantaneous.

Was there time for her life to flash before her eyes? Was I there? Was Jake? And she promised, I remembered, she promised to be continued, but I knew, too, that she was driving north when she died, north toward Nashville, toward Jake. Maybe it hadn't meant anything to her, had been nothing more than another grand impulsivity. And as Hank stood in the doorway, I just looked past him, looking across the too-quiet dorm circle, wondering if it had mattered to her, and I can only tell myself that of course, yes, she had promised. To be continued.

Lara came next, her eyes heavy with swelling. "What happeened?" she asked me as I held her, standing on my tiptoes so I could place my chin on top of her head.

"I don't know," I said.

"Deed you see her that night?" she asked, speaking into my collarbone.

"She got drunk," I told her. "The Colonel and I went to sleep, and I guess she drove off campus." And that became the standard lie.

I felt Lara's fingers, wet with her tears, press against my palm, and before I could think better of it, I pulled my hand away. "I'm sorry," I said.

"Eet's okay," she said. "I'll be een my room eef you want to come by." I did not drop by. I didn't know what to say to her—I was caught in a love triangle with one dead side.

That afternoon, we all filed into the gym again for a town meeting. The Eagle announced that the school would charter a bus on Sunday to the funeral in Vine Station. As we got up to leave, I noticed Takumi and Lara walking toward me. Lara caught my eye and smiled wanly. I smiled back, but quickly turned and hid myself amid the mass of mourners filing out of the gym.

I am sleeping, and Alaska flies into the room. She is naked, and intact. Her breasts, which I felt only very briefly and in the dark, are luminously full as they hang down from her body. She hovers inches above me, her breath warm and sweet against my face like a breeze passing through tall grass.

"Hi," I say. "I've missed you."

"You look good, Pudge."

"So do you."

"I'm so naked," she says, and laughs. "How did I get so *naked?*"

"I just want you to stay," I say.

"No," she says, and her weight falls dead on me, crushing my chest, stealing away my breath, and she is cold and wet, like melting ice. Her head is split in half and a pink-gray sludge oozes from the fracture in her skull and drips down onto my face, and she stinks of formaldehyde and rotting meat. I gag and push her off me, terrified.

I woke up falling, and landed with a thud on the floor. Thank God I'm a bottom-bunk man. I had slept for fourteen hours. It was morning. Wednesday, I thought. Her funeral Sunday. I wondered if the Colonel would get back by then, where he was. He *had* to come back for the funeral, because I could not go alone, and going with anyone other than the Colonel would amount to alone.

The cold wind buffeted against the door, and the trees outside the back window shook with such force that I could hear it from our room, and I sat in my bed and thought of the Colonel out there somewhere, his head down, his teeth clenched, walking into the wind.

four days after

IT WAS FIVE IN THE MORNING and I was reading a biography of the explorer Meriwether Lewis (of & Clark fame) and trying to stay awake when the door opened and the Colonel walked in.

His pale hands shook, and the almanac he held looked like a puppet dancing without strings.

"Are you cold?" I asked.

He nodded, slipped off his sneakers, and climbed into my bed on the bottom bunk, pulling up the covers. His teeth chattered like Morse code.

"Jesus. Are you all right?"

"Better now. Warmer," he said. A small, ghost white hand appeared from beneath the comforter. "Hold my hand, will ya?"

"All right, but that's it. No kissing." The quilt shook with his laughter.

"Where have you been?"

"I walked to Montevallo."

"Forty miles?!"

"Forty-two," he corrected me. "Well. Forty-two there. Forty-two back. Eighty-two miles. No. Eighty-four. Yes. Eighty-four miles in forty-five hours."

"What the hell's in Montevallo?" I asked.

"Not much. I just walked till I got too cold, and then I turned around."

"You didn't sleep?"

"No! The dreams are terrible. In my dreams, she doesn't even look like herself anymore. I don't even remember what she looked like."

I let go of his hand, grabbed last year's yearbook, and found her picture. In the black-and-white photograph, she's wearing her orange tank top and cutoff jeans that stretch halfway down her skinny thighs, her mouth open wide in a frozen laugh as her left arm holds Takumi in a headlock. Her hair falls over her face just enough to obscure her cheeks.

"Right," the Colonel said. "Yeah. I was so tired of her getting upset for no reason. The way she would get sulky and make refer-ences to the freaking oppressive weight of tragedy or whatever but then never said what was wrong, never have any goddamned *reason* to be sad. And I just think you ought to have a *reason*. My girlfriend dumped me, so I'm sad. I got caught smoking, so I'm pissed off. My head hurts, so I'm cranky. She never had a *reason*, Pudge. I was just so tired of putting up with her drama. And I just let her go. Christ."

Her moodiness had annoyed me, too, sometimes, but not that night. That night I let her go because she told me to. It was that simple for me, and that stupid.

The Colonel's hand was so little, and I grabbed it tight, his cold seeping into me and my warmth into him. "I memorized the popu-lations," he said.

"Uzbekistan."

"Twenty-four million seven hundred fifty-five thousand five hundred and nineteen."

"Cameroon," I said, but it was too late. He was asleep, his hand limp in mine. I placed it back under the quilt and climbed up into his bed, a top-bunk man for this night at least. I fell asleep listening to his slow, even breaths, his stubbornness finally melting away in the face of insurmountable fatigue.

six days after

THAT SUNDAY, I got up after three hours of sleep and showered for the first time in a long while. I put on my only suit. I almost hadn't brought it, but my mom insisted that you never know when you're going to need a suit, and sure enough.

The Colonel did not own a suit, and by virtue of his stature could not borrow one from anyone at the Creek, so he wore black slacks and a gray button-down.

"I don't suppose I can wear the flamingo tie," he said as he pulled on black socks.

"It's a bit festive, given the occasion," I responded.

"Can't wear it to the opera," said the Colonel, almost smiling. "Can't wear it to a funeral. Can't use it to hang myself. It's a bit useless, as ties go." I gave him a tie.

The school had chartered buses to ferry students north to Alaska's hometown of Vine Station, but Lara, the Colonel, Takumi, and I drove in Takumi's SUV, taking the back roads so we didn't have to drive past the spot on the highway. I stared out the window, watching as the suburban sprawl surrounding Birmingham faded into the slow-sloping hills and fields of northern Alabama.

Up front, Takumi told Lara about the time Alaska got her boob honked over the summer, and Lara laughed. That was the first time I had seen her, and now we were coming to the last. More than anything, I felt the unfairness of it, the inarguable injustice of loving someone who might have loved you back but can't due to deadness, and then I leaned forward, my forehead against the back of Takumi's headrest, and I cried, whimpering, and I didn't even feel sadness so much as pain. It hurt, and that is not a euphemism. It hurt like a beating.

Meriwether Lewis's last words were, "I am not a coward, but I am so strong. So hard to die." I don't doubt that it is, but it cannot be much harder than being left behind. I thought of Lewis as I followed Lara into the A-frame chapel attached to the single-story funeral home in Vine Station, Alabama, a town every bit as depressed and depressing as Alaska had always made it out to be. The place smelled of mildew and disinfectant, and the yellow wallpaper in the foyer was peeling at the corners.

"Are y'all here for Ms. Young?" a guy asked the Colonel, and the Colonel nodded. We were led to a large room with rows of folding chairs populated by only one man. He knelt before a coffin at the front of the chapel. The coffin was closed. Closed. Never going to see her again. Can't kiss her forehead. Can't see her one last time. But I needed to, I needed to *see* her, and much too loud, I asked, "Why is it closed?" and the man, whose potbelly pushed out from his too-tight suit, turned around and walked toward me.

"Her mother," he said. "Her mother had an open casket, and Alaska told me, 'Don't ever let them see me dead, Daddy,' and so that's that. Anyway, son, she's not in there. She's with the Lord."

And he put his hands on my shoulders, this man who had grown fat since he'd last had to wear a suit, and I couldn't believe what I had done to him, his eyes glittering green like Alaska's but sunk deep into dark sockets, like a green-eyed, still-breathing ghost, and don't no don't don't die, Alaska. Don't die. And I walked out of his embrace and past Lara and Takumi to her casket and knelt before it and placed my hands on the finished wood, the dark mahogany, the color of her hair. I felt the Colonel's small hands on my shoulders, and a tear dripped onto my head, and for a few moments, it was just the three of us—the buses of students hadn't arrived, and Takumi and Lara had faded away, and it was just the three of us— three bodies and two people—the three who knew what had happened and too many layers between all of us, too much keeping us from one another. The Colonel said, "I just want to save her so bad," and I said, "Chip, she's gone," and he said, "I thought I'd feel her looking down on us, but you're right. She's just gone," and I said, "Oh God, Alaska, I love you. I love you," and the Colonel whispered, "I'm so sorry, Pudge. I know you did," and I said, "No. Not past tense." She wasn't even a person anymore, just flesh rotting, but I loved her present tense. The Colonel knelt down beside me and put his lips to the coffin and whispered, "I am sorry, Alaska. You deserved a better friend."

Is it so hard to die, Mr. Lewis? Is that labyrinth really worse than this one?

seven days after

I SPENT THE NEXT DAY in our room, playing football on mute, at once unable to do nothing and unable to do anything much. It was Martin Luther King Day, our last day before classes started again, and I could think of nothing but having killed her. The Colonel spent the morning with me, but then he decided to go to the cafeteria for meat loaf.

"Let's go," he said.

"Not hungry."

"You have to eat."

"Wanna bet?" I asked without looking up from the game.

"Christ. Fine." He sighed and left, slamming the door behind him. *He's still very angry,* I found myself thinking with a bit of pity. No reason to be angry. Anger just distracts from the all-encompassing sadness, the frank knowledge that you killed her and robbed her of a future and a life. Getting pissed wouldn't fix it. Damn it.

"How's the meat loaf?" I asked the Colonel when he returned.

"About as you remember it. Neither meaty nor loafy." The Colonel sat down next to me. "The Eagle ate with me. He wanted to know if we set off the fireworks." I paused the game and turned to him. With one hand, he picked at one of the last remaining pieces of blue vinyl on our foam couch.

"And you said?" I asked.

"I didn't rat. Anyway, he said her aunt or something is coming tomorrow to clean out her room. So if there's anything that's ours, or anything her aunt wouldn't want to find . . . "

I turned back to the game and said, "I'm not up for it today."

"Then I'll do it alone," he answered. He turned and walked outside, leaving the door open, and the bitter remnants of the cold snap quickly overwhelmed the radiator, so I paused the game and stood up to close the door, and when I peeked around the corner to see if the Colonel had entered her room, he was standing there, just outside our door, and he grabbed onto my sweatshirt, smiled, and said, "I *knew* you wouldn't make me do that alone. I *knew* it." I shook my head and rolled my eyes but followed him down the sidewalk, past the pay phone, and into her room.

I hadn't thought of her smell since she died. But when the Colonel opened the door, I caught the edge of her scent: wet dirt and grass and cigarette smoke, and beneath that the vestiges of vanilla-scented skin lotion. She flooded into my present, and only tact kept me from burying my face in the dirty laundry overfilling the hamper by her dresser. It looked as I remembered it: hundreds of books stacked against the walls, her lavender comforter crumpled at the foot of her bed, a precarious stack of books on her bedside table, her volcanic candle just peeking out from beneath the bed. It looked as I knew it would, but the smell, unmistakably her, shocked me. I stood in the center of the room, my eyes shut, inhaling slowly through my nose, the vanilla and the uncut autumn grass, but with each slow breath, the smell faded as I became accustomed to it, and soon she was gone again.

"This is unbearable," I said matter-of-factly, because it was. "God. These books she'll never read. Her Life's Library."

"Bought at garage sales and now probably destined for another one."

"Ashes to ashes. Garage sale to garage sale," I said.

"Right. Okay, down to business. Get anything her aunt wouldn't want to find," the Colonel said, and I saw him kneeling at her desk, the drawer beneath her computer pulled open, his small fingers pulling out groups of stapled papers. "Christ, she kept every paper she ever wrote. *Moby-Dick. Ethan Frome.*"

I reached between her mattress and box spring for the condoms I knew she hid for Jake's visits. I pocketed them, and then went over to her dresser, searching through her underwear for hidden bottles of liquor or sex toys or God knows what. I found nothing. And then I settled on the books, staring at them stacked on their sides, spines out, the haphazard collection of literature that was Alaska. There was one book I wanted to take with me, but I couldn't find it.

The Colonel was sitting on the floor next to her bed, his head bent toward the floor, looking under her bed frame. "She sure didn't leave any booze, did she?" he asked.

And I almost said, *She buried it in the woods out by the soccer field,* but I realized that the Colonel didn't know, that she never took him to the edge of the woods and told him to dig for buried treasure, that she and I had shared that alone, and I kept it for myself like a keepsake, as if sharing the memory might lead to its dissipation.

"Do you see *The General in His Labyrinth* anywhere?" I asked while scanning the titles on the book spines. "It has a lot of green on the cover, I think. It's a paperback, and it got flooded, so the pages are probably bloated, but I don't think she—" and then he cut me off with, "Yeah, it's right here," and I turned around and he was holding it, the pages fanned out like an accordion from Longwell, Jeff, and Kevin's prank, and I walked over to him and took it and sat down on her bed. The places she'd underlined and the little notes she'd written had all been blurred out by the soaking, but the book was still mostly readable, and I was thinking I would take it back to my room and try to read it even though it wasn't a biography when I flipped to that page, toward the back:

He was shaken by the overwhelming revelation that the head-long race between his misfortunes and his dreams was at that moment reaching the finish line. The rest was darkness. "Damn it," he sighed. "How will I ever get out of this labyrinth!"

The whole passage was underlined in bleeding, water-soaked black ink. But there was another ink, this one a crisp blue, post-flood, and an arrow led from "How will I ever get out of this labyrinth!" to a margin note written in her loop-heavy cursive: *Straight & Fast*.

"Hey, she wrote something in here after the flood," I said. "But it's weird. Look. Page one ninety-two."

I tossed the book to the Colonel, and he flipped to the page and then looked up at me. "Straight and fast," he said.

"Yeah. Weird, huh? The way out of the labyrinth, I guess."

"Wait, how did it happen? What happened?"

And because there was only one *it*, I knew to what he was referring. "I told you what the Eagle told me. A truck jackknifed on the road. A cop car showed up to stop traffic, and she ran into the cop car. She was so drunk she didn't even swerve."

"So *drunk?* So *drunk?* The cop car would have had its lights on. Pudge, she ran into a cop car that had its lights on," he said hurriedly. "Straight and fast. Straight and fast. Out of the labyrinth."

"No," I said, but even as I said it, I could see it. I could see her drunk enough and pissed off enough. (About what—about cheating on Jake? About hurting me? About wanting me and not him? Still pissed about ratting out Marya?) I could see her staring down the cop car and aiming for it and not giving a shit about anyone else, not thinking of her promise to me, not thinking of her father or anyone, and that bitch, that bitch, she killed herself. But no. No. That was not her. No. She said *To be continued.* Of course. "No."

"Yeah, you're probably right," the Colonel said. He dropped the book, sat down on the bed next to me, and put his forehead in his hands. "Who drives six miles off campus to kill herself? Doesn't make any sense. But 'straight and fast.' Bit of an odd premonition, isn't it? And we still don't really know what happened, if you think about it. Where she was going, why. Who called. Someone *called,* right, or did I make—"

And the Colonel kept talking, puzzling it out, while I picked up the book and found my way to that page where the general's headlong race came to its end, and we were both stuck in our heads, the distance between us unbridgeable, and I could not listen to the Colonel, because I was busy trying to get the last hints of her smell,

busy telling myself that of course she had not done it. It was me—
I had done it, and so had the Colonel. He could try to puzzle his
way out of it, but I knew better, knew that we could never be anything but wholly, unforgivably guilty.

eight days after

TUESDAY—WE HAD SCHOOL for the first time. Madame O'Malley had a moment of silence at the beginning of French class, a
class that was always punctuated with long moments of silence,
and then asked us how we were feeling.

"Awful," a girl said.

"En français," Madame O'Malley replied. *"En français."*

Everything looked the same, but more still: the Weekday Warriors
still sat on the benches outside the library, but their gossip was
quiet, understated. The cafeteria clamored with the sounds of plastic trays against wooden tables and forks scraping plates, but any
conversations were muted. But more than the noiselessness of
everyone else was the silence where she should have been, the bub-
bling bursting storytelling Alaska, but instead it felt like those times
when she had withdrawn into herself, like she was refusing to
answer *how* or *why* questions, only this time for good.

The Colonel sat down next to me in religion class, sighed, and
said, "You reek of smoke, Pudge."

"Ask me if I give a shit."

Dr. Hyde shuffled into class then, our final exams stacked underneath one arm. He sat down, took a series of labored breaths, and
began to talk. "It is a law that parents should not have to bury their
children," he said. "And someone should enforce it. This semester,
we're going to continue studying the religious traditions to which

you were introduced this fall. But there's no doubting that the questions we'll be asking have more immediacy now than they did just a few days ago. What happens to us after we die, for instance, is no longer a question of idle philosophical interest. It is a question we must ask about our classmate. And how to live in the shadow of grief is not something nameless Buddhists, Christians, and Muslims have to explore. The questions of religious thought have become, I suspect, personal."

He shuffled through our exams, pulling one out from the pile before him. "I have here Alaska's final. You'll recall that you were asked what the most important question facing people is, and how the three traditions we're studying this year address that question. This was Alaska's question."

With a sigh, he grabbed hold of his chair and lifted himself out of it, then wrote on the blackboard: *How will we ever get out of this labyrinth of suffering? —A. Y.*

"I'm going to leave that up for the rest of the semester," he said. "Because everybody who has ever lost their way in life has felt the nagging insistence of that question. At some point we all look up and realize we are lost in a maze, and I don't want us to forget Alaska, and I don't want to forget that even when the material we study seems boring, we're trying to understand how people have answered that question and the questions each of you posed in your papers—how different traditions have come to terms with what Chip, in his final, called 'people's rotten lots in life.'"

Hyde sat down. "So, how are you guys doing?"

The Colonel and I said nothing, while a bunch of people who didn't know Alaska extolled her virtues and professed to be devastated, and at first, it bothered me. I didn't want the people she didn't know—and the people she didn't like—to be sad. They'd never cared about her, and now they were carrying on as if she were a sister. But I guess I didn't know her completely, either. If I had,

I'd have known what she'd meant by "To be continued?" And if I had cared about her as I should have, as I thought I did, how could I have let her go?

So they didn't bother me, really. But next to me, the Colonel breathed slowly and deeply through his nose like a bull about to charge.

He actually rolled his eyes when Weekday Warrior Brooke Blakely, whose parents had received a progress report courtesy of Alaska, said, "I'm just sad I never told her I loved her. I just don't understand *why*."

"That's such bullshit," the Colonel said as we walked to lunch. "As if Brooke Blakely gives two shits about Alaska."

"If Brooke Blakely died, wouldn't you be sad?" I asked.

"I guess, but I wouldn't bemoan the fact I never told her I *loved* her. I *don't* love her. She's an idiot."

I thought everyone else had a better excuse to grieve than we did—after all, they hadn't killed her—but I knew better than to try to talk to the Colonel when he was mad.

nine days after

"I'VE GOT A THEORY," the Colonel said as I walked in the door after a miserable day of classes. The cold had begun to let up, but word had not spread to whoever ran the furnaces, so the classrooms were all stuffy and overheated, and I just wanted to crawl into bed and sleep until the time came to do it all over again.

"Missed you in class today," I noted as I sat down on my bed. The Colonel sat at his desk, hunched over a notebook. I lay down on my back and pulled the covers up over my head, but the Colonel was undiscouraged.

"Right, well, I was busy coming up with the theory, which isn't terribly likely, admittedly, but it's plausible. So, listen. She kisses you. That night, someone calls. Jake, I imagine. They have a fight—about cheating or about something else—who knows. So she's upset, and she wants to go see him. She comes back to the room crying, and she tells us to help her get off campus. And she's freaked out, because, I don't know, let's say because if she can't go visit him, Jake will break up with her. That's just a hypothetical reason. So she gets off campus, drunk and all pissed off, and she's furious at herself over whatever it is, and she's driving along and sees the cop car and then in a flash everything comes together and the end to her labyrinthine mystery is staring her right in the face and she just does it, straight and fast, just aims at the cop car and never swerves, not because she's drunk but because she killed herself."

"That's ridiculous. She wasn't thinking about Jake or fighting with Jake. *She was making out with me.* I tried to bring up the whole Jake thing, but she just shushed me."

"So who called her?"

I kicked off my comforter and, my fist balled, smashed my hand against the wall with each syllable as I said, "I! DON'T! KNOW! And you know what, it doesn't matter. She's dead. Is the brilliant Colonel going to figure out something that's gonna make her less freaking dead?" But it did matter, of course, which is why I kept pounding at our cinder-block walls and why the questions had floated beneath the surface for a week. Who'd called? What was wrong? Why did she leave? Jake had not gone to her funeral. Nor had he called us to say he was sorry, or to ask us what happened. He had just disappeared, and of course, I had wondered. I had wondered if she had any intention of keeping her promise that we would be continued. I had wondered who called, and why, and what made her so upset. But I'd rather wonder than get answers I couldn't live with.

"Maybe she was driving there to break up with Jake, then," the

Colonel said, his voice suddenly edgeless. He sat down on the corner of my bed.

"I don't know. I don't really want to know."

"Yeah, well," he said. "I want to know. Because if she knew what she was doing, Pudge, she made us accomplices. And I hate her for that. I mean, God, look at us. We can't even talk to anyone anymore. So listen, I wrote out a game plan: *One.* Talk to eyewitnesses. *Two.* Figure out how drunk she was. *Three.* Figure out where she was going, and why."

"I don't want to talk to Jake," I said halfheartedly, already resigned to the Colonel's incessant planning. "If he knows, I definitely don't want to talk to him. And if he doesn't, I don't want to pretend like it didn't happen."

The Colonel stood up and sighed. "You know what, Pudge? I feel bad for you. I do. I know you kissed her, and I know you're broken up about it. But honestly, shut up. If Jake knows, you're not gonna make it any worse. And if he doesn't, he won't find out. So just stop worrying about your goddamned self for one minute and think about your dead friend. Sorry. Long day."

"It's fine," I said, pulling the covers back over my head. "It's fine," I repeated. And, whatever. It *was* fine. It had to be. I couldn't afford to lose the Colonel.

thirteen days after

BECAUSE OUR MAIN SOURCE of vehicular transportation was interred in Vine Station, Alabama, the Colonel and I were forced to walk to the Pelham Police Department to search for eyewitnesses. We left after eating dinner in the cafeteria, the night falling fast and early, and trudged up Highway 119 for a mile and a half before coming to a single-story stucco building situated between a Waffle House and a gas station.

Inside, a long desk that rose to the Colonel's solar plexus separated us from the police station proper, which seemed to consist of
three uniformed officers sitting at three desks, all of them talking
on the phone.

"I'm Alaska Young's brother," the Colonel announced brazenly.
"And I want to talk to the cop who saw her die."

A pale, thin man with a reddish blond beard spoke quickly into
the phone and then hung up."I seen 'er," he said. "She hit mah
cruiser."

"Can we talk to you outside?" the Colonel asked.

"Yup."

The cop grabbed a coat and walked toward us, and as he
approached, I could see the blue veins through the translucent skin
of his face. For a cop, he didn't seem to get out much. Once outside, the Colonel lit a cigarette.

"You nineteen?" the cop asked. In Alabama, you can get married
at eighteen (fourteen with Mom and Dad's permission), but you
have to be nineteen to smoke.

"So fine me. I just need to know what you saw."

"Ah most always work from six t' midnight, but I was coverin' the
graveyard shift. We got a call 'bout a jackknifed truck, and I's only
about a mile away, so I headed over, and I'd just pulled up. I's still
in mah cruiser, and I seen out the corner a' my eye the headlights,
and my lights was on and I turned the siren on, but the lights
just kept comin' straight at me, son, and I got out quick and run off
and she just barreled inta me. I seen plenty, but I ain't never seen
that. She didn't tarn. She didn't brake. She jest hit it. I wa'n't more
than ten feet from the cruiser when she hit it. I thought I'd die, but
here ah am."

For the first time, the Colonel's theory seemed plausible. She
didn't hear *the siren?* She didn't see *the lights?* She was sober enough
to kiss well, I thought. Surely she was sober enough to swerve.

"Did you see her face before she hit the car? Was she asleep?" the Colonel asked.

"That I cain't tell ya. I didn't see 'er. There wa'n't much time."

"I understand. She was dead when you got to the car?" he asked.

"I—I did everything I could. Ah run right up to her, but the steerin' wheel—well, ah reached in there, thought if ah could git that steerin' wheel loose, but there weren't no gettin' her outta that car alive. It fairly well crushed her chest, see."

I winced at the image. "Did she say anything?" I asked.

"She was passed on, son," he said, shaking his head, and my last hope of last words faded.

"Do you think it was an accident?" the Colonel asked as I stood beside him, my shoulders slouching, wanting a cigarette but nervous to be as audacious as him.

"Ah been an officer here twenty-six years, and ah've seen more drunks than you'n count, and ah ain't never seen someone so drunk they cain't swerve. But ah don't know. The coroner said it was an accident, and maybe it was. That ain't my field, y'know. I s'pose that's 'tween her and the Lord now."

"How drunk was she?" I asked. "Like, did they test her?"

"Yeah. Her BAL was point twenty-four. That's drunk, certainly. That's a powerful drunk."

"Was there anything in the car?" the Colonel asked. "Anything, like, unusual that you remember?"

"I remember them brochures from colleges—places in Maine and Ohia and Texas—I thought t' myself that girl must be from Culver Crick and that was mighty sad, see a girl like that lookin' t' go t' college. That's a goddamned shame. And they's flowers. They was flowers in her backseat. Like, from a florist. Tulips."

Tulips? I thought immediately of the tulips Jake had sent her. "Were they white?" I asked.

"They sure was," the cop answered. Why would she have taken

his tulips with her? But the cop wouldn't have an answer for that one.

"Ah hope y'all find out whatever y'all's lookin' for. I have thought it over some, 'cause I never seen nothing like that before. Ah've thought hard on it, wondered if I'da started up the cruiser real quick and drove it off, if she'da been all right. There mightn't've been time. No knowing now. But it don't matter, t' my mind, whether it were an accident or it weren't. It's a goddamned shame either way."

"There was nothing you could have done," the Colonel said softly. "You did your job, and we appreciate it."

"Well. Thanks. Y'all go 'long now, and take care, and let me know if ya have any other questions. This is mah card if you need anything."

The Colonel put the card in his fake leather wallet, and we walked toward home.

"White tulips," I said. "Jake's tulips. Why?"

"One time last year, she and Takumi and I were at the Smoking Hole, and there was this little white daisy on the bank of the creek, and all of a sudden she just jumped waist-deep into the water and waded across and grabbed it. She put it behind her ear, and when I asked her about it, she told me that her parents always put white flowers in her hair when she was little. Maybe she wanted to die with white flowers."

"Maybe she was going to return them to Jake," I said.

"Maybe. But that cop just shit sure convinced me that it might have been a suicide."

"Maybe we should just let her be dead," I said, frustrated. It seemed to me that nothing we might find out would make anything any better, and I could not get the image of the steering wheel careening into her chest out of my mind, her chest "fairly well crushed" while she sucked for a last breath that would never come, and no, this was not making anything better. "What if she *did* do it?" I asked the Colonel. "We're not any less guilty. All it does is make her into this awful, selfish bitch."

"Christ, Pudge. Do you even remember the person she actually *was?* Do you remember how she *could* be a selfish bitch? That was part of her, and you used to know it. It's like now you only care about the Alaska you made up."

I sped up, walking ahead of the Colonel, silent. And he couldn't know, because he wasn't the last person she kissed, because he hadn't been left with an unkeepable promise, because he wasn't me. *Screw this,* I thought, and for the first time, I imagined just going back home, ditching the Great Perhaps for the old comforts of school friends. Whatever their faults, I'd never known my school friends in Florida to die on me.

After a considerable distance, the Colonel jogged up to me and said, "I just want it to be normal again," he said. "You and me. Normal. Fun. Just, normal. And I feel like if we knew—"

"Okay, fine," I cut him off. "Fine. We'll keep looking."

The Colonel shook his head, but then he smiled. "I have always appreciated your enthusiasm, Pudge. And I'm just going to go ahead and pretend you still have it until it comes back. Now let's go home and find out why people off themselves."

fourteen days after

WARNING SIGNS OF SUICIDE the Colonel and I found on the Web:

Previous suicide attempts
Verbally threatening suicide
Giving away prized possessions

Collecting and discussing methods of suicide

Expressions of hopelessness and anger at oneself and/or the world

Writing, talking, reading, and drawing about death and/or depression

Suggesting that the person would not be missed if s/he were gone

Self-injury

Recent loss of a friend or family member through death or suicide

Sudden and dramatic decline in academic performance

Eating disorders, sleeplessness, excessive sleeping, chronic headaches

Use (or increased use) of mind-altering substances

Loss of interest in sex, hobbies, and other activities previously enjoyed

Alaska displayed two of those warning signs. She had lost, although not recently, her mother. And her drinking, always pretty steady, had definitely increased in the last month of her life. She did talk about dying, but she always seemed to be at least half kidding.

"I make jokes about death all the time," the Colonel said. "I made a joke last week about hanging myself with my tie. And I'm not gonna off myself. So that doesn't count. And she didn't give anything away, and she sure as hell didn't lose interest in sex. One would have to like sex an awful lot to make out with your scrawny ass."

"Funny," I said.

"I know. God, I'm a genius. And her grades were good. And I don't recall her talking about killing herself."

"Once, with the cigarettes, remember? 'You smoke to enjoy it. I smoke to die.'"

"That was a *joke*."

But when prodded by the Colonel, maybe to prove to him that I could remember Alaska as she really was and not just as I wanted her to be, I kept returning the conversation to those times when she would be mean and moody, when she didn't feel like answering *how, when, why, who,* or *what* questions. "She could seem so *angry*," I thought aloud.

"What, and I can't?" the Colonel retorted. "I'm plenty angry, Pudge. And you haven't been the picture of placidity of late, either, and you aren't going to off yourself. Wait, are you?"

"No," I said. And maybe it was only because Alaska couldn't hit the brakes and I couldn't hit the accelerator. Maybe she just had an odd kind of courage that I lacked, but no.

"Good to know. So yeah, she was up and down—from fire and brimstone to smoke and ashes. But partly, this year at least, it was the whole Marya thing. Look, Pudge, she obviously wasn't thinking about killing herself when she was making out with you. After that, she was asleep until the phone rang. So she decided to kill herself at some point between that ringing phone and crashing, or it was an accident."

"But why wait until you're six miles off campus to die?" I asked.

He sighed and shook his head. "She did like being mysterious. Maybe she wanted it like this." I laughed then, and the Colonel said, "What?"

"I was just thinking—*Why do you run head-on into a cop car with its lights on?* and then I thought, *Well, she hated authority figures.*"

The Colonel laughed. "Hey, look at that. Pudge made a funny!"

It felt almost normal, and then my distance from the event itself seemed to evaporate and I found myself back in the gym, hearing the news for the first time, the Eagle's tears dripping onto his pants, and I looked over at the Colonel and thought of all the hours we'd spent on this foam couch in the past two weeks—everything she'd ruined. Too pissed off to cry, I said, "This is only making me hate her. I don't want to hate her. And what's the point, if that's all it's making me do?" Still refusing to answer *how* and *why* questions. Still insisting on an aura of mystery.

I leaned forward, head between my knees, and the Colonel placed a hand on my upper back. "The point is that there are always answers, Pudge." And then he pushed air out between his pursed lips and I could hear the angry quiver in his voice as he repeated, "There are *always* answers. We just have to be smart enough. The Web says that suicides usually involve carefully thought-out plans. So clearly she did not commit suicide." I felt embarrassed to be still falling apart two weeks later when the Colonel could take his medicine so stoically, and I sat up.

"Okay, fine" I answered. "It wasn't suicide."

"Although it sure doesn't make sense as an accident," the Colonel said.

I laughed. "We sure are making progress."

We were interrupted by Holly Moser, the senior I knew primarily from viewing her nude self-portraits over Thanksgiving with Alaska. Holly hung with the Weekday Warriors, which explains why I'd previously said about two words to her in my life, but she just came in without knocking and said that she'd had a mystical indicator of Alaska's presence.

"I was in the Waffle House, and suddenly all the lights went off, except for, like, the light over my booth, which started flashing. It would be like on for a second and then off for a while and then on for a couple of seconds and then off. And I realized, you know, it was Alaska. I think she was trying to talk to me in Morse code. But, like, I don't know Morse code. She probably didn't know that. Anyway, I thought you guys should know."

"Thanks," I said curtly, and she stood for a while, looking at us, her mouth opening as if to speak, but the Colonel was staring at her through half-closed eyes, his jaw jutting out and his distaste uncontained. I understood how he felt: I didn't believe in ghosts who used Morse code to communicate with people they'd never liked. And I disliked the possibility that Alaska would give someone else peace but not me.

"God, people like that shouldn't be allowed to live," he said after she left.

"It was pretty stupid."

"It's not just stupid, Pudge. I mean, as if Alaska would talk to Holly Moser. God! I can't stand these fake grievers. Stupid bitch."

I almost told him that Alaska wouldn't want him to call *any* woman a bitch, but there was no use fighting with the Colonel.

twenty days after

IT WAS SUNDAY, and the Colonel and I decided against the cafeteria for dinner, instead walking off campus and across Highway 119 to the Sunny Konvenience Kiosk, where we indulged in a well-balanced meal of two oatmeal cream pies apiece. Seven hundred calories. Enough energy to sustain a man for half a day. We sat on the curb in front of the store, and I finished dinner in four bites.

"I'm going to call Jake tomorrow, just so you know. I got his phone number from Takumi."

"Fine," I said.

I heard a bell jangle behind me and turned toward the opening door.

"Y'all's loitering," said the woman who'd just sold us dinner.

"We're eating," the Colonel answered.

The woman shook her head and ordered, as if to a dog, "Git."

So we walked behind the store and sat by the stinking, fetid Dumpster.

"Enough with the *fine*'s already, Pudge. That's ridiculous. I'm going to call Jake, and I'm going to write down everything he says, and then we're going to sit down together and try and figure out what happened."

"No. You're on your own with that. I don't want to know what happened between her and Jake."

The Colonel sighed and pulled a pack of Pudge Fund cigarettes of his jeans pocket. "Why not?"

"Because I don't want to! Do I have provide you with an in-depth analysis of every decision I make?"

The Colonel lit the cigarette with a lighter I'd paid for and took a drag. "Whatever. It needs to be figured out, and I need your help to do it, because between the two of us we knew her pretty well. So that's that."

I stood up and stared down at him sitting smugly, and he blew a thin stream of smoke at my face, and I'd had enough. "I'm tired of following orders, asshole! I'm not going to sit with you and discuss the finer points of her relationship with Jake, goddamn it. I can't say it any clearer: *I don't want to know* about them. I *already know* what she told me, and that's all I need to know, and you can be a condescending prick as long as you'd like, but I'm not going to sit around and chat with you about how goddamned much she loved Jake! Now give me my cigarettes." The Colonel threw the pack on the ground and was up in a flash, a fistful of my sweater in his hand, trying but failing to pull me down to his height.

"You don't even care about her!" he shouted. "All that matters is you and your precious fucking fantasy that you and Alaska had this goddamned secret love affair and she was going to leave Jake for you and you'd live happily ever after. But she kissed a lot of guys, Pudge. And if she were here, we both know that she would still be Jake's girlfriend and that there'd be nothing but drama between the two of you—not love, not sex, just you pining after her and her like, 'You're cute, Pudge, but I love Jake.' If she loved you so much, why did she leave you that night? And if you loved her so much, why'd you help her go? I was drunk. What's your excuse?"

The Colonel let go of my sweater, and I reached down and picked up the cigarettes. Not screaming, not through clenched teeth, not with the veins pulsing in my forehead, but calmly. Calmly. I looked down at the Colonel and said, "Fuck you."

The vein-pulsing screaming came later, after I had jogged across Highway 119 and through the dorm circle and across the soccer field and down the dirt road to the bridge, when I found myself at the Smoking Hole. I picked up a blue chair and threw it against the concrete wall, and the clang of plastic on concrete echoed beneath the bridge as the chair fell limply on its side, and then I lay on my back with my knees hanging over the precipice and screamed. I screamed because the Colonel was a self-satisfied, condescending bastard, and I screamed because he was right, for I did want to believe that I'd had a secret love affair with Alaska. Did she love me? Would she have left Jake for me? Or was it just another impulsive Alaska moment? It was not enough to be the last guy she kissed. I wanted to be the last one she loved. And I knew I wasn't. I knew it, and I hated her for it. I hated her for not caring about me. I hated her for leaving that night, and I hated myself, too, not only because I let her go but because if I had been enough for her, she wouldn't have even wanted to leave. She would have just lain with me and talked and cried, and I would have listened and kissed at her tears as they pooled in her eyes.

I turned my head and looked at one of the little blue plastic chairs on its side. I wondered if there would ever be a day when I didn't think about Alaska, wondered whether I should hope for a time when she would be a distant memory—recalled only on the anniversary of her death, or maybe a couple of weeks after, remembering only after having forgotten.

I knew that I would know more dead people. The bodies pile up. Could there be a space in my memory for each of them, or would I forget a little of Alaska every day for the rest of my life?

Once, early on in the year, she and I had walked down to the Smoking Hole, and she jumped into Culver Creek with her flip-flops still on. She stepped across the creek, picking her steps carefully over the mossy rocks, and grabbed a waterlogged stick from the creek bank. As I sat on the concrete, my feet dangling toward the water, she overturned rocks with the stick and pointed out the skittering crawfish.

"You boil 'em and then suck the heads out," she said excitedly. "That's where all the good stuff is—the heads."

She taught me everything I knew about crawfish and kissing and pink wine and poetry. She made me different.

I lit a cigarette and spit into the creek. "You can't just make me different and then leave," I said out loud to her. "Because I was fine before, Alaska. I was fine with just me and last words and school friends, and you can't just make me different and then die." For she had embodied the Great Perhaps—she had proved to me that it was worth it to leave behind my minor life for grander maybes, and now she was gone and with her my faith in perhaps. I could call everything the Colonel said and did "fine." I could try to pretend that I didn't care anymore, but it could never be true again. You can't just make yourself matter and then die, Alaska, because now I am irretrievably different, and I'm sorry I let you go, yes, but you made the choice. You left me Perhapsless, stuck in your goddamned labyrinth. And now I don't even know if you chose the straight and fast way out, if you left me like this on purpose. And so I never knew you, did I? I can't remember, because I never knew.

And as I stood up to walk home and make my peace with the Colonel, I tried to imagine her in that chair, but I could not remember whether she crossed her legs. I could still see her smiling at me with half of *Mona Lisa*'s smirk, but I couldn't picture her hands well enough to see her holding a cigarette. I needed, I decided, to really know her, because I needed more to remember. Before I could begin the shameful process of forgetting the how and the why of her living and dying, I needed to learn it: *How. Why. When. Where. What.*

At Room 43, after quickly offered and accepted apologies, the Colonel said, "We've made a tactical decision to push back calling Jake. We're going to pursue some other avenues first."

twenty-one days after

AS DR. HYDE shuffled into class the next morning, Takumi sat down next to me and wrote a note on the edge of his notebook. *Lunch at McInedible*, it read.

I scribbled *Okay* on my own notebook and then turned to a blank page as Dr. Hyde started talking about Sufism, the mystical sect of Islam. I'd only scanned through the reading—I'd been studying only enough not to fail—but in my scanning, I'd come across great last words. This poor Sufi dressed in rags walked into a jewelry store owned by a rich merchant and asked him, "Do you know how you're going to die?" The merchant answered, "No. No one knows how they're going to die." And the Sufi said, "I do."

"How?" asked the merchant.

And the Sufi lay down, crossed his arms, said, "Like this," and died, whereupon the merchant promptly gave up his store to live a life of poverty in pursuit of the kind of spiritual wealth the dead Sufi had acquired.

But Dr. Hyde was telling a different story, one that I'd skipped. "Karl Marx famously called religion 'the opiate of the masses.' Buddhism, particularly as it is popularly practiced, promises improvement through karma. Islam and Christianity promise eternal paradise to the faithful. And that is a powerful opiate, certainly, the hope of a better life to come. But there's a Sufi story that challenges the notion that people believe only because they need an opiate. Rabe'a al-Adiwiyah, a great woman saint of Sufism, was seen running through the streets of her hometown, Basra, carrying a torch in one hand and a bucket of water in the other. When someone asked her what she was doing, she answered, 'I am going to take this bucket of water and pour it on the flames of hell, and then I am going to use this torch to burn down the gates of paradise so that people will not love God for want of heaven or fear of hell, but because He is God.'"

A woman so strong she burns heaven and drenches hell. *Alaska would have liked this Rabe'a woman,* I wrote in my notebook. But even so, the afterlife mattered to me. Heaven and hell and reincarnation. As much as I wanted to know how Alaska had died, I wanted to know where she was now, if anywhere. I liked to imagine her looking down on us, still aware of us, but it seemed like a fantasy, and I never really *felt* it—just as the Colonel had said at the funeral that she wasn't there, wasn't anywhere. I couldn't honestly imagine her as anything but dead, her body rotting in Vine Station, the rest of her just a ghost alive only in our remembering. Like Rabe'a, I didn't think people should believe in God because of heaven and hell. But I didn't feel a need to run around with a torch. You can't burn down a made-up place.

After class, as Takumi picked through his fries at McInedible, eating only the crunchiest, I felt the total loss of her, still reeling from the idea that she was not only gone from this world but from all of them.

"How have you been?" I asked.

"Uh," he said, a mouth full of fries, "nah good. You?"

"Not good." I took a bite of cheeseburger. I'd gotten a plastic stock car with my Happy Meal, and it sat overturned on the table. I spun the wheels.

"I miss her," Takumi said, pushing away his tray, uninterested in the remaining soggy fries.

"Yeah. I do, too. I'm sorry, Takumi," and I meant it in the largest possible way. I was sorry we ended up like this, spinning wheels at a McDonald's. Sorry the person who had brought us together now lay dead between us. I was sorry I let her die. *Sorry I haven't talked to you because you couldn't know the truth about the Colonel and me, and I hated being around you and having to pretend that my grief is this uncomplicated thing—pretending that she died and I miss her instead of that she died because of me.*

"Me too. You're not dating Lara anymore, are you?"

"I don't think so."

"Okay. She was kind of wondering."

I had been ignoring her, but by then she had begun to ignore me back, so I figured it was over, but maybe not. "Well," I told Takumi, "I just can't—I don't know, man. That's pretty complicated."

"Sure. She'll understand. Sure. All good."

"Okay."

"Listen, Pudge. I—ah, I don't know. It sucks, huh?"

"Yeah."

twenty-seven days after

SIX DAYS LATER, four Sundays after the last Sunday, the Colonel and I were trying to shoot each other with paintball guns while turning 900s in a half pipe. "We need booze. And we need to borrow the Eagle's Breathalyzer."

"*Borrow* it? Do you know where it is?"

"Yeah. He's never made you take one?"

"Um. No. He thinks I'm a nerd."

"You *are* a nerd, Pudge. But you're not gonna let a detail like that keep you from drinking." Actually, I hadn't drunk since that night, and didn't feel particularly inclined to ever take it up ever again.

Then I nearly elbowed the Colonel in the face, swinging my arms wildly as if contorting my body in the right ways mattered as much as pressing the right buttons at the right moments—the same video-game-playing delusion that had always gripped Alaska. But the Colonel was so focused on the game he didn't even notice. "Do you have a plan for how, exactly, we're going to steal the Breathalyzer from *inside the Eagle's house?*"

The Colonel looked over at me and said, "Do you suck at this game?" and then, without turning back to the screen, shot my skater in the balls with a blue paint blast. "But first, we gotta get some liquor, because the ambrosia's sour and my booze connection is—"

"*POOF*. Gone," I finished.

When I opened his door, Takumi was sitting at his desk, boxy headphones surrounding his entire head, bouncing his head to the beat. He seemed oblivious to us. "Hey," I said. Nothing. "Takumi!" Nothing. "TAKUMI!" He turned around and pulled off his headphones. I closed the door behind me and said, "You got any alcohol?"

"Why?" he asked.

"Uh, because we want to get drunk?" the Colonel answered.

"Great. I'll join you."

"Takumi," the Colonel said. "This is—we need to do this alone."

"No. I've had enough of that shit." Takumi stood up, walked into his bathroom, and came out with a Gatorade bottle filled with clear liquid. "I keep it in the medicine cabinet," Takumi said. "On account of how it's medicine." He pocketed the bottle and then walked out of the room, leaving the door open behind him. A moment later, he peeked his head back in and, brilliantly mimicking the Colonel's bossy bass voice, said, "Christ, you comin' or what?"

"Takumi," the Colonel said. "Okay. Look, what we're doing is a little dangerous, and I don't want you caught up in it. Honestly. But, listen, we'll tell you everything starting tomorrow."

"I'm tired of all this secret shit. She was my friend, too."

"Tomorrow. Honestly."

He pulled the bottle out of his pocket and tossed it to me. "Tomorrow," he said.

"I don't really want him to know," I said as we walked back to the room, the Gatorade bottle stuffed in the pocket of my sweatshirt. "He'll hate us."

"Yeah, well, he'll hate us more if we keep pretending he doesn't exist," the Colonel answered.

Fifteen minutes later, I stood at the Eagle's doorstep.

He opened the door with a spatula in hand, smiled, and said, "Miles, come in. I was just making an egg sandwich. Want one?"

"No thanks," I said, following the Eagle into his kitchen.

My job was to keep him out of his living room for thirty seconds so the Colonel could get the Breathalyzer undetected. I coughed loudly to let the Colonel know the coast was clear. The Eagle picked up his egg sandwich and took a bite. "To what do I owe the pleasure of your visit?" he asked.

"I just wanted to tell you that the Colonel—I mean, Chip Martin—he's my roommate, you know, he's having a tough time in Latin."

"Well, he's not attending the class, from what I understand, which can make it very difficult to learn the language." He walked toward me. I coughed again, and backpedaled, the Eagle and I tangoing our way toward his living room.

"Right, well, he's up all night every night thinking about Alaska," I said, standing up straight and tall, trying to block the Eagle's view of the living room with my none-too-wide shoulders. "They were very close, you know."

"I know that—" he said, and in the living room, the Colonel's sneakers squeaked against the hardwood floor. The Eagle looked at me quizzically and sidestepped me. I quickly said, "Is that burner on?" and pointed toward the frying pan.

The Eagle wheeled around, looked at the clearly not-on burner, then dashed into the living room.

Empty. He turned back to me. "Are you up to something, Miles?"

"No, sir. Honestly. I just wanted to talk about Chip."

He arched his eyebrows, skeptical. "Well, I understand that this is a devastating loss for Alaska's close friends. It's just awful. There's no comfort to this grief, is there?"

"No sir."

"I'm sympathetic to Chip's troubles. But school is important. Alaska would have wanted, I'm sure, for Chip's studies to continue unimpeded."

I'm sure, I thought. I thanked the Eagle, and he promised me an egg sandwich at some point in the future, which made me nervous that he would just show up at our room one afternoon with an egg sandwich in hand to find us A. illegally smoking while the Colonel B. illegally drank milk and vodka out of a gallon jug.

Halfway across the dorm circle, the Colonel ran up to me. "That was smooth, with the 'Is that burner on?' If you hadn't pulled that, I was toast. Although I guess I'll have to start going to Latin. Stupid Latin."

"Did you get it?" I asked.

"Yeah," he said. "Yeah. God, I hope he doesn't go looking for it tonight. Although, really, he could never suspect anything. Why would someone *steal a Breathalyzer?*"

———————

At two o'clock in the morning, the Colonel took his sixth shot of vodka, grimaced, then frantically motioned with his hand toward the bottle of Mountain Dew I was drinking. I handed it to him, and he took a long pull on it.

"I don't think I'll be able to go to Latin tomorrow," he said. His words were slightly slurred, as if his tongue were swollen.

"One more," I pleaded.

"Okay. This is it, though." He poured a sip of vodka into a Dixie cup, swallowed, pursed his lips, and squeezed his hands into tight little fists. "*Oh God,* this is bad. It's so much better with milk. This better be point two-four."

"We have to wait for fifteen minutes after your last drink before we test it," I said, having downloaded instructions for the Breathalyzer off the Internet. "Do you feel drunk?"

"If drunk were cookies, I'd be Famous Amos."

We laughed. "Chips Ahoy! would have been funnier," I said.

"Forgive me. Not at my best."

I held the Breathalyzer in my hand, a sleek, silver gadget about the size of a small remote control. Beneath an LCD screen was a small hole. I blew into it to test it: 0.00, it read. I figured it was working.

After fifteen minutes, I handed it to the Colonel. "Blow really hard onto it for at least two seconds," I said.

He looked up at me. "Is that what you told Lara in the TV room? Because, see, Pudge, they only *call* it a blow job."

"Shut up and blow," I said.

His cheeks puffed out, the Colonel blew into the hole hard and long, his face turning red.

.16. "Oh no," the Colonel said. "Oh God."

"You're two-thirds of the way there," I said encouragingly.

"Yeah, but I'm like three-fourths of the way to puking."

"Well, obviously it's possible. *She* did it. C'mon! You can outdrink a girl, can't you?"

"Give me the Mountain Dew," he said stoically.

And then I heard footsteps outside. Footsteps. We'd waited till 1:00 to turn on the lights, figuring everyone would be long asleep— it was a school night after all—but footsteps, shit, and as the Colonel looked at me confused, I grabbed the Breathalyzer from him and stuffed it between the foam cushions of the couch and grabbed the Dixie cup and the Gatorade bottle of vodka and stashed them behind the COFFEE TABLE, and in one motion I grabbed a cigarette from a pack and lit it, hoping the smell of smoke would cover up the smell of booze. I puffed the cigarette without inhaling, trying to smoke up the room, and I was almost back to the couch when the three quick knocks came against the door and the Colonel looked at me, his eyes wide, his suddenly unpromising future flashing before his eyes, and I whispered, "Cry," as the Eagle turned the knob.

The Colonel hunched forward, his head between his knees and his shoulders shaking, and I put my arm around him as the Eagle came in.

"I'm sorry," I said before the Eagle could say anything. "He's having a tough night."

"Are you *smoking?*" the Eagle asked. *"In your room? Four hours after lights-out?"*

I dropped the cigarette into a half-empty Coke can. "I'm sorry, sir. I'm just trying to stay awake with him."

The Eagle walked up toward the couch, and I felt the Colonel start to rise, but I held his shoulders down firmly, because if the Eagle smelled the Colonel's breath we were done for sure. "Miles," the Eagle said. "I understand that this is a difficult time for you. But you will respect the rules of this school, or you will matriculate someplace else. I'll see you in Jury tomorrow. Is there anything I can do for you, Chip?"

Without looking up, the Colonel answered in a quivering, tear-soaked voice, "No, sir. I'm just glad I have Miles."

"Well, I am, too," the Eagle said. "Perhaps you should encourage him to live within the confines of our rules, lest he risk his place on this campus."

"Yessir," the Colonel said.

"Y'all can leave your lights on until you're ready to go to bed. I'll see you tomorrow, Miles."

"Good night, sir," I said, imagining the Colonel sneaking the Breathalyzer back into the Eagle's house while I got harangued at Jury. As the Eagle closed the door behind him, the Colonel shot up, smiling at me, and still nervous that the Eagle might be outside, whispered, "That was a thing of beauty."

"I learned from the best," I said. "Now drink."

An hour later, the Gatorade bottle mostly empty, the Colonel hit .24.

"Thank you, Jesus!" he exclaimed, and then added, "This is awful. This is not fun drunk."

I got up and cleared the COFFEE TABLE out of the way so the Colonel could walk the length of the room without hitting any obstacles, and said, "Okay, can you stand?"

The Colonel pushed his arms into the foam of the couch and began to rise, but then fell backward onto the couch, lying on his back. "Spinning room," he observed. "Gonna puke."

"Don't puke. That will ruin everything."

I decided to give him a field sobriety test, like the cops do. "Okay. Get over here and try to walk a straight line." He rolled off the couch and fell to the floor, and I caught him beneath his armpits and held him up. I positioned him in between two tiles of the linoleum floor. "Follow that line of tiles. Walk straight, toe to heel." He raised one leg and immediately leaned to the left, his arms windmilling. He took a single unsteady step, sort of a waddle, as his feet were seemingly unable to land directly in front of each other. He regained his balance briefly, then took a step backward and landed on the couch. "I fail," he said matter-of-factly.

"Okay, how's your depth perception?"

"My what perwhatshun?"

"Look at me. Is there one of me? Are there two of me? Could you accidentally drive into me if I were a cop car?"

"Everything's very spinny, but I don't think so. This is bad. Was she really like this?"

"Apparently. Could you drive like this?"

"Oh God no. No. No. She was really drunk, huh."

"Yeah."

"We were really stupid."

"Yeah."

"I'm spinning. But no. No cop car. I can *see*."

"So there's your evidence."

"Maybe she fell asleep. I feel awfully sleepy."

"We'll find out," I said, trying to play the role that the Colonel had always played for me.

"Not tonight," he answered. "Tonight, we're gonna throw up a little, and then we are going to sleep through our hangover."

"Don't forget about Latin."

"Right. Fucking Latin."

twenty-eight days after

THE COLONEL MADE IT to Latin the next morning—"I feel awesome right now, because I'm still drunk. But God help me in a couple of hours"—and I took a French test for which I had studied *un petit peu*. I did all right on the multiple choice (which-verb-tense-makes-sense-here type questions), but the essay question, *In*

Le Petit Prince, *what is the significance of the rose?* threw me a bit.

Had I read *The Little Prince* in English or French, I suspect this question might have been quite easy. Unfortunately, I'd spent the evening getting the Colonel drunk. So I answered, *Elle symbolise l'amour* ("It symbolizes love"). Madame O'Malley had left us with an entire page to answer the question, but I figured I'd covered it nicely in three words.

I'd kept up in my classes well enough to get B-minuses and not worry my parents, but I didn't really care much anymore. *The significance of the rose?* I thought. *Who gives a shit? What's the significance of the white tulips?* There was a question worth answering.

After I'd gotten a lecture and ten work hours at Jury, I came back to Room 43 to find the Colonel telling Takumi everything—well, everything except the kiss. I walked in to the Colonel saying, "So we helped her go."

"You set off the fireworks," he said.

"How'd you know about the fireworks?"

"I've been doing a bit of investigating," Takumi answered. "Well, anyway, that was dumb. You shouldn't have done it. But we all let her go, really," he said, and I wondered what the hell he meant by that, but I didn't have time to ask before he said to me, "So you think it was suicide?"

"Maybe," I said. "I don't see how she could have hit the cop by accident unless she was asleep."

"Maybe she was going to visit her father," Takumi said. "Vine Station is on the way."

"Maybe," I said. "Everything's a maybe, isn't it?"

The Colonel reached in his pocket for a pack of cigarettes. "Well, here's another one: *Maybe* Jake has the answers," he said. "We've exhausted other strategies, so I'm calling him tomorrow, okay?"

I wanted answers now, too, but not to some questions. "Yeah, okay," I said. "But listen—don't tell me anything that's not relevant. I don't want to know anything unless it's going to help me know where she was going and why."

"Me neither, actually," Takumi said. "I feel like maybe some of that shit should stay private."

The Colonel stuffed a towel under the door, lit a cigarette, and said, "Fair enough, kids. We'll work on a need-to-know basis."

twenty-nine days after

AS I WALKED HOME from classes the next day, I saw the Colonel sitting on the bench outside the pay phone, scribbling into a note-book balanced on his knees as he cradled the phone between his ear and shoulder.

I hurried into Room 43, where I found Takumi playing the racing game on mute. "How long has he been on the phone?" I asked.

"Dunno. He was on when I got here twenty minutes ago. He must have skipped Smart Boy Math. Why, are you scared Jake's gonna drive down here and kick your ass for letting her go?"

"Whatever," I said, thinking, *This is precisely why we shouldn't have told him.* I walked into the bathroom, turned on the shower, and lit a cigarette. Takumi came in not long after.

"What's up?" he said.

"Nothing. I just want to know what happened to her."

"Like you really want to know the truth? Or like you want to find out that she fought with him and was on her way to break up with him and was going to come back here and fall into your arms and you were going to make hot, sweet love and have genius babies who memorized last words *and* poetry?"

"If you're pissed at me, just say so."

"I'm not pissed at you for letting her go. But I'm tired of you acting like you were the only guy who ever wanted her. Like you had some monopoly on liking her," Takumi answered. I stood up, lifted the toilet seat, and flushed my unfinished cigarette.

I stared at him for a moment, and then said, "I kissed her that night, and I've got a monopoly on that."

"What?" he stammered.

"I kissed her."

His mouth opened as if to speak, but he said nothing. We stared at each other for a while, and I felt ashamed of myself for what amounted to bragging, and finally I said, "I—look, you know how she was. She wanted to do something, and she did it. I was probably just the guy who happened to be there."

"Yeah. Well, I was never that guy," he said. "I—well, Pudge, God knows I can't blame you."

"Don't tell Lara."

He was nodding as we heard the three quick knocks on the front door that meant the Eagle, and I thought, *Shit, caught twice in a week,* and Takumi pointed into the shower, and so we jumped in together and pulled the curtain shut, the too-low showerhead spitting water onto us from rib cage down. Forced to stand closer together than seemed entirely necessary, we stayed there, silent, the sputtering shower slowly soaking our T-shirts and jeans for a few long minutes, while we waited for the steam to lift the smoke into the vents. But the Eagle never knocked on the bathroom door, and eventually Takumi turned off the shower. I opened the bathroom door a crack and peeked out to see the Colonel sitting on the foam couch, his feet propped up on the COFFEE TABLE, finishing Takumi's NASCAR race. I opened the door and Takumi and I walked out, fully clothed and dripping wet.

"Well, there's something you don't see every day," the Colonel said nonchalantly.

"What the hell?" I asked.

"I knocked like the Eagle to scare you." He smiled. "But shit, if y'all need privacy, just leave a note on the door next time."

Takumi and I laughed, and then Takumi said, "Yeah, Pudge and I were getting a little testy, but man, ever since we showered together, Pudge, I feel really close to you."

"So how'd it go?" I asked. I sat down on the COFFEE TABLE, and Takumi plopped down on the couch next to the Colonel, both of us wet and vaguely cold but more concerned with the Colonel's talk with Jake than with getting dry.

"It was interesting. Here's what you need to know: He gave her those flowers, like we thought. They didn't fight. He just called because he had promised to call at the exact moment of their eight-month anniversary, which happened to be three-oh-two in the A.M., which—let's agree—is a little ridiculous, and I guess somehow she heard the phone ringing. So they talked about nothing for like five minutes, and then completely out of nowhere, she freaked out."

"Completely out of nowhere?" Takumi asked.

"Allow me to consult my notes." The Colonel flipped through his notebook. "Okay. Jake says, 'Did you have a nice anniversary?' and then Alaska says, 'I had a *splendid* anniversary,'" and I could hear in the Colonel's reading the excitement of her voice, the way she leaped onto certain words like *splendid* and *fantastic* and *absolutely*. "Then it's quiet, then Jake says, 'What are you doing?' and Alaska says, 'Nothing, just doodling,' and then she says, 'Oh God.' And then she says, 'Shit shit shit' and starts sobbing, and told him she had to go but she'd talk to him later, but she didn't say she was driving to see him, and Jake doesn't think she was. He doesn't know where she was going, but he says she always asked if she could come up and see him, and she didn't ask, so she must not have been coming. Hold on, lemme find the quote." He flipped a page in the notebook. "Okay, here: 'She said she'd talk to me later, not that she'd *see* me.'"

"She tells me 'To be continued' and tells him she'll talk to him later," I observed.

"Yes. Noted. Planning for a future. Admittedly inconsistent with suicide. So then she comes back into her room screaming about forgetting something. And then her headlong race comes to its end. So no answers, really."

"Well, we know where she wasn't going."

"Unless she was feeling particularly impulsive," Takumi said. He looked at me. "And from the sound of things, she was feeling rather impulsive that night."

The Colonel looked over at me curiously, and I nodded.

"Yeah," Takumi said. "I know."

"Okay, then. And you were pissed, but then you took a shower with Pudge and it's all good. Excellent. So, so that night . . ." the Colonel continued.

And we tried to resurrect the conversation that last night as best we could for Takumi, but neither of us remembered it terribly well, partly because the Colonel was drunk and I wasn't paying attention until she brought up Truth or Dare. And, anyway, we didn't know how much it might mean. Last words are always harder to remember when no one knows that someone's about to die.

"I mean," the Colonel said, "I think she and I were talking about how much I adored skateboarding on the computer but how it would never even occur to me to try and step on a skateboard in real life, and then she said, 'Let's play Truth or Dare' and then you fucked her."

"Wait, you *fucked* her? *In front of the Colonel?*" Takumi cried.

"I didn't fuck her."

"Calm down, guys," the Colonel said, throwing up his hands. "It's a euphemism."

"For what?" Takumi asked.

"Kissing."

"Brilliant euphemism." Takumi rolled his eyes. "Am I the only one who thinks that might be significant?"

"Yeah, that never occurred to me before," I deadpanned. "But now I don't know. She didn't tell Jake. It couldn't have been that important."

"Maybe she was racked with guilt," he said.

"Jake said she seemed normal on the phone before she freaked out," the Colonel said. "But it must have been that phone call. Something happened that we aren't seeing." The Colonel ran his hands through his thick hair, frustrated. "Christ, something. Something inside of her. And now we just have to figure out what that was."

"So we just have to read the mind of a dead person," Takumi said. "Easy enough."

"Precisely. Want to get shitfaced?" the Colonel asked.

"I don't feel like drinking," I said.

The Colonel reached into the foam recesses of the couch and pulled out Takumi's Gatorade bottle. Takumi didn't want any either, but the Colonel just smirked and said, "More for me," and chugged.

thirty-seven days after

THE NEXT WEDNESDAY, I ran into Lara after religion class—literally. I'd seen her, of course. I'd seen her almost every day—in English or sitting in the library whispering to her roommate, Katie. I saw her at lunch and dinner at the cafeteria, and I probably would have seen her at breakfast, if I'd ever gotten up for it. And surely, she saw me as well, but we hadn't, until that morning, looked at each other simultaneously.

By now, I assumed she'd forgotten me. After all, we only dated for about a day, albeit an eventful one. But when I plowed right into her left shoulder as I hustled toward precalc, she spun around and looked up at me. Angry, and not because of the bump. "I'm sorry," I blurted out, and she just squinted at me like someone about to either fight or cry, and disappeared silently into a classroom. First two words I'd said to her in a month.

I wanted to want to talk to her. I knew I'd been awful—*Imagine,* I kept telling myself, *if you were Lara, with a dead friend and a silent ex-boyfriend*—but I only had room for one true want, and she was dead, and I wanted to know the how and why of it, and Lara couldn't tell me, and that was all that mattered.

forty-five days after

FOR WEEKS, the Colonel and I had relied on charity to support our cigarette habit—we'd gotten free or cheap packs from everyone from Molly Tan to the once-crew-cutted Longwell Chase. It was as if people wanted to help and couldn't think of a better way. But by the end of February, we ran out of charity. Just as well, really. I never felt right taking people's gifts, because they did not know that we'd loaded the bullets and put the gun in her hand.

So after our classes, Takumi drove us to Coosa "We Cater to Your Spiritual Needs" Liquors. That afternoon, Takumi and I had learned the disheartening results of our first major precalc test of the semester. Possibly because Alaska was no longer available to teach us precalc over a pile of McInedible french fries and possibly because neither of us had really studied, we were both in danger of getting progress reports sent home.

"The thing is that I just don't find precalc very interesting," Takumi said matter-of-factly.

"It might be hard to explain that to the director of admissions at Harvard," the Colonel responded.

"I don't know," I said. "I find it pretty compelling."

And we laughed, but the laughs drifted into a thick, pervasive silence, and I knew we were all thinking of her, dead and laughless, cold, no longer Alaska. The idea that Alaska didn't exist still stunned me every time I thought about it. *She's rotting underground in Vine Station, Alabama,* I thought, but even that wasn't quite it. Her body was there, but she was nowhere, nothing, *POOF.*

The times that were the most fun seemed always to be followed by sadness now, because it was when life started to feel like it did when she was with us that we realized how utterly, totally gone she was.

I bought the cigarettes. I'd never entered Coosa Liquors, but it was every bit as desolate as Alaska described. The dusty wooden floor creaked as I made my way to the counter, and I saw a large barrel filled with brackish water that purported to contain LIVE BAIT, but in fact contained a veritable school of dead, floating minnows. The woman behind the counter smiled at me with all four of her teeth when I asked her for a carton of Marlboro Lights.

"You go t' Culver Creek?" she asked me, and I did not know whether to answer truthfully, since no high-school student was likely to be nineteen, but she grabbed the carton of cigarettes from beneath her and put it on the counter without asking for an ID, so I said, "Yes, ma'am."

"How's school?" she asked.

"Pretty good," I answered.

"Heard y'all had a death up there."

"Yes'm," I say.

"I's awful sorry t' hear it."

"Yes'm."

The woman, whose name I did not know because this was not the sort of commercial establishment to waste money on name tags, had one long, white hair growing from a mole on her left cheek. It wasn't disgusting, exactly, but I couldn't stop glancing at it and then looking away.

Back in the car, I handed a pack of cigarettes to the Colonel.

We rolled down the windows, although the February cold bit at my face and the loud wind made conversation impossible. I sat in my quarter of the car and smoked, wondering why the old woman at Coosa Liquors didn't just pull that one hair out of her mole. The wind blew through Takumi's rolled-down window in front of me and against my face. I scooted to the middle of the backseat and looked up at the Colonel sitting shotgun, smiling, his face turned to the wind blowing in through his window.

forty-six days after

I DIDN'T WANT TO TALK TO LARA, but the next day at lunch, Takumi pulled the ultimate guilt trip. "How do you think Alaska would feel about this shit?" he asked as he stared across the cafeteria at Lara. She was sitting three tables away from us with her roommate, Katie, who was telling some story, and Lara smiled whenever Katie laughed at one of her own jokes. Lara scooped up a forkful of canned corn and held it above her plate, moving her mouth to it and bowing her head toward her lap as she took the bite from the fork—a quiet eater.

"She could talk to *me*," I told Takumi.

Takumi shook his head. His open mouth gooey with mashed potatoes, he said, "Yuh ha' to." He swallowed. "Let me ask you a question, Pudge. When you're old and gray and your grandchildren are sitting on your knee and look up at you and say, 'Grandpappy, who gave you your first blow job?' do you want to have to tell them it was some girl you spent the rest of high school ignoring? No!" He smiled. "You want to say, 'My dear friend Lara Buterskaya. Lovely girl. Prettier than your grandma by a wide margin.'" I laughed. So yeah, okay. I had to talk to Lara.

After classes, I walked over to Lara's room and knocked, and then she stood in the doorway, looking like, *What? What now? You've done the damage you could, Pudge,* and I looked past her, into the room I'd only entered once, where I learned that kissing or no, I couldn't talk to her—and before the silence could get too uncomfortable, I talked. "I'm sorry," I said.

"For what?" she asked, still looking toward me but not quite at me.

"For ignoring you. For everything," I said.

"You deedn't have to be my boyfriend." She looked so pretty, her big eyes blinking fast, her cheeks soft and round, and still the roundness could only remind me of Alaska's thin face and her high cheekbones. But I could live with it—and, anyway, I had to. "You could have just been my friend," she said.

"I know. I screwed up. I'm sorry."

"Don't forgive that asshole," Katie cried from inside the room.

"I forgeeve you." Lara smiled and hugged me, her hands tight around the small of my back. I wrapped my arms around her shoulders and smelled violets in her hair.

"*I* don't forgive you," Katie said, appearing in the doorway. And although Katie and I were not well acquainted, she felt comfortable enough to knee me in the balls. She smiled then, and as I crumpled into a bow, Katie said, "*Now* I forgive you."

Lara and I took a walk to the lake—sans Katie—and we talked. We talked—about Alaska and about the past month, about how she had to miss me *and* miss Alaska, while I only had to miss Alaska (which was true enough). I told her as much of the truth as I could, from the firecrackers to the Pelham Police Department and the white tulips.

"I loved her," I said, and Lara said she loved her, too, and I said, "I know, but that's why. I loved her, and after she died I couldn't think about anything else. It felt, like, dishonest. Like cheating."

"That's not a good reason," she said.

"I know," I answered.

She laughed softly. "Well, good then. As long as you know." I knew I wasn't going to erase that anger, but we were talking.

As darkness spread that evening, the frogs croaked and a few newly resurrected insects buzzed about campus, and the four of us—Takumi, Lara, the Colonel, and I—walked through the cold gray light of a full moon to the Smoking Hole.

"Hey, Colonel, why do you call eet the Smoking Hole?" Lara asked. "Eet's, like, a tunnel."

"It's like fishing hole," the Colonel said. "Like, if we fished, we'd fish here. But we smoke. I don't know. I think Alaska named it." The Colonel pulled a cigarette out of his pack and threw it into the water.

"What the hell?" I asked.

"For her," he said.

I half smiled and followed his lead, throwing in a cigarette of my own. I handed Takumi and Lara cigarettes, and they followed suit. The smokes bounced and danced in the stream for a few moments, and then they floated out of sight.

I was not religious, but I liked rituals. I liked the idea of connecting an action with remembering. In China, the Old Man had told us, there are days reserved for grave cleaning, where you make gifts to the dead. And I imagined that Alaska would want a smoke, and so it seemed to me that the Colonel had begun an excellent ritual.

The Colonel spit into the stream and broke the silence. "Funny thing, talking to ghosts," he said. "You can't tell if you're making up their answers or if they are really talking to you."

"I say we make a list," Takumi said, steering clear of introspective talk. "What kind of proof do we have of suicide?" The Colonel pulled out his omnipresent notebook.

"She never hit the brakes," I said, and the Colonel started scribbling.

And she was awfully upset about something, although she'd been awfully upset without committing suicide many times before. We considered that maybe the flowers were some kind of memorial to herself—like a funeral arrangement or something. But that didn't seem very Alaskan to us. She was cryptic, sure, but if you're going to plan your suicide down to the flowers, you probably have a plan as to how you're actually going to die, and Alaska had no way of knowing a police car was going to present itself on I-65 for the occasion.

And the evidence suggesting an accident?

"She was really drunk, so she could have thought she wasn't going to hit the cop, although I don't know how," Takumi said.

"She could have fallen asleep," Lara offered.

"Yeah, we've thought about that," I said. "But I don't think you keep driving straight if you fall asleep."

"I can't think of a way to find out that does not put our lives in considerable danger," the Colonel deadpanned. "Anyway, she didn't show warning signs of suicide. I mean, she didn't talk about wanting to die or give away her stuff or anything."

"That's two. Drunk and no plans to die," Takumi said. This wasn't going anywhere. Just a different dance with the same question. What we needed wasn't more thinking. We needed more evidence.

"We have to find out where she was going," the Colonel said.

"The last people she talked to were me, you, and Jake," I said to him. "And we don't know. So how the hell are we going to find out?"

Takumi looked over at the Colonel and sighed. "I don't think it would help, to know where she was going. I think that would make it worse for us. Just a gut feeling."

"Well, *my* gut wants to know," Lara said, and only then did I realize what Takumi meant the day we'd showered together—I may have kissed her, but I really *didn't* have a monopoly on Alaska; the Colonel and I weren't the only ones who cared about her, and weren't alone in trying to figure out how she died and why.

"Well, regardless," said the Colonel, "we're at a dead end. So one of you think of something to do. Because I'm out of investigative tools."

He flicked his cigarette butt into the creek, stood up, and left. We followed him. Even in defeat, he was still the Colonel.

fifty-one days after

THE INVESTIGATION STALLED, I took to reading for religion class again, which seemed to please the Old Man, whose pop quizzes I'd been failing consistently for a solid six weeks. We had one that Wednesday morning: *Share an example of a Buddhist koan.* A koan is like a riddle that's supposed to help you toward enlightenment in Zen Buddhism. For my answer, I wrote about this guy Banzan. He was walking through the market one day when he overheard someone ask a butcher for his best piece of meat. The butcher answered, "Everything in my shop is the best. You cannot find a piece of meat that is not the best." Upon hearing this, Banzan realized that there is no best and no worst, that those judgments have no real meaning because there is only what is, and *poof*, he reached enlightenment. Reading it the night before, I'd wondered if it would be like that for me—if in one moment, I would finally understand her, know her, and understand the role I'd played in her dying. But I wasn't convinced enlightenment struck like lightning.

After we'd passed our quizzes, the Old Man, sitting, grabbed his cane and motioned toward Alaska's fading question on the blackboard. "Let's look at one sentence on page ninety-four of this very entertaining introduction to Zen that I had you read this week. 'Everything that comes together falls apart,'" the Old Man said. "Everything. The chair I'm sitting on. It was built, and so it will fall apart. I'm gonna fall apart, probably before this chair. And you're gonna fall apart. The cells and organs and systems that make you you—they came together, grew together, and so must fall apart. The Buddha knew one thing science didn't prove for millennia after his death: Entropy increases. Things fall apart."

We are all going, I thought, and it applies to turtles and turtlenecks, Alaska the girl and Alaska the place, because nothing can last, not even the earth itself. The Buddha said that suffering was caused by desire, we'd learned, and that the cessation of desire meant the cessation of suffering. When you stopped wishing things wouldn't fall apart, you'd stop suffering when they did.

Someday no one will remember that she ever existed, I wrote in my notebook, and then, *or that I did.* Because memories fall apart, too. And then you're left with nothing, left not even with a ghost but with its shadow. In the beginning, she had haunted me, haunted my dreams, but even now, just weeks later, she was slipping away, falling apart in my memory and everyone else's, dying again.

The Colonel, who had driven the Investigation from the start, who had cared about what happened to her when I only cared if she loved me, had given up on it, answerless. And I didn't like what answers I had: She hadn't even cared enough about what happened between us to tell Jake; instead, she had just talked cute with him, giving him no reason to think that minutes before, I'd tasted her boozy breath. And then something invisible snapped inside her, and that which had come together commenced to fall apart.

And maybe that was the only answer we'd ever have. She fell

apart because that's what happens. The Colonel seemed resigned to that, but if the Investigation had once been his idea, it was now the thing that held me together, and I still hoped for enlightenment.

sixty-two days after

THE NEXT SUNDAY, I slept in until the late-morning sunlight slivered through the blinds and found its way to my face. I pulled the comforter over my head, but the air got hot and stale, so I got up to call my parents.

"Miles!" my mom said before I even said hello. "We just got caller identification."

"Does it magically know it's me calling from the pay phone?"

She laughed. "No, it just says 'pay phone' and the area code. So I deduced. How are you?" she asked, a warm concern in her voice.

"I'm doing okay. I kinda screwed up some of my classes for a while, but I'm back to studying now, so it should be fine," I said, and that was mostly true.

"I know it's been hard on you, buddy," she said. "Oh! Guess who your dad and I saw at a party last night? Mrs. Forrester. Your fourth-grade teacher! Remember? She remembered you *perfectly*, and spoke very highly of you, and we just talked"—and while I was pleased to know that Mrs. Forrester held my fourth-grade self in high regard, I only half listened as I read the scribbled notes on the white-painted pine wall on either side of the phone, looking for any new ones I might be able to decode (*Lacy's—Friday, 10* were the when and where of a Weekday Warrior party, I figured)—"and we had dinner with the Johnstons last night and I'm afraid that Dad had too much wine. We played charades and he was just *awful*." She laughed, and I felt so tired, but someone had dragged the bench away from the pay phone, so I sat my bony butt down on the hard concrete, pulling the silver cord of the phone taut and preparing for a serious soliloquy from my mom, and then down below all the other notes and scribbles, I saw a drawing of a flower. Twelve oblong petals around a filled-in circle against the daisy-white paint, and daisies, white daisies, and I could hear her saying, *What do you see, Pudge? Look,* and I could see her sitting drunk on the phone with Jake talking about nothing and *What are you doing?* and she says, *Nothing, just doodling, just doodling.* And then, *Oh God.*

"Miles?"

"Yeah, sorry, Mom. Sorry. Chip's here. We gotta go study. I gotta go."

"Will you call us later, then? I'm sure Dad wants to talk to you."

"Yeah, Mom; yeah, of course. I love you, okay? Okay, I gotta go."

"I think I found something!" I shouted at the Colonel, invisible beneath his blanket, but the urgency in my voice and the promise of something, anything, found, woke the Colonel up instantly, and he jumped from his bunk to the linoleum. Before I could say anything, he grabbed yesterday's jeans and sweatshirt from the floor, pulled them on, and followed me outside.

"Look." I pointed, and he squatted down beside the phone and said, "Yeah. She drew that. She was always doodling those flowers."

"And 'just doodling,' remember? Jake asked her what she was doing and she said 'just doodling,' and *then* she said 'Oh God' and freaked out. She looked at the doodle and remembered something."

"Good memory, Pudge," he acknowledged, and I wondered why the Colonel wouldn't just get excited about it.

"And then she freaked out," I repeated, "and went and got the tulips while we were getting the fireworks. She saw the doodle, remembered whatever she'd forgotten, and then freaked out."

"Maybe," he said, still staring at the flower, trying perhaps to see it as she had. He stood up finally and said, "It's a solid theory,

Pudge," and reached up and patted my shoulder, like a coach complimenting a player. "But we still don't know what she forgot."

A WEEK AFTER THE DISCOVERY of the doodled flower, I'd resigned myself to its insignificance—I wasn't Banzan in the meat market after all—and as the maples around campus began to hint of resurrection and the maintenance crew began mowing the grass in the dorm circle again, it seemed to me we had finally lost her.

The Colonel and I walked into the woods down by the lake that afternoon and smoked a cigarette in the precise spot where the Eagle had caught us so many months before. We'd just come from a town meeting, where the Eagle announced the school was going to build a playground by the lake in memory of Alaska. She did like swings, I guess, but a *playground?* Lara stood up at the meeting—surely a first for her—and said they should do something funnier, something Alaska herself would have done.

Now, by the lake, sitting on a mossy, half-rotten log, the Colonel said to me, "Lara was right. We should do something for her. A prank. Something she would have loved."

"Like, a memorial prank?"

"Exactly. The Alaska Young Memorial Prank. We can make it an annual event. Anyway, she came up with this idea last year. But she wanted to save it to be our senior prank. But it's good. It's really good. It's historic."

"Are you going to tell me?" I asked, thinking back to the time when he and Alaska had left me out of prank planning for Barn Night.

"Sure," he said. "The prank is entitled 'Subverting the Patriarchal Paradigm.'" And he told me, and I have to say, Alaska left us with the crown jewel of pranks, the *Mona Lisa* of high-school hilarity, the culmination of generations of Culver Creek pranking. And if the Colonel could pull it off, it would be etched in the memory of everyone at the Creek, and Alaska deserved nothing less. Best of all, it did not, technically, involve any expellable offenses.

The Colonel got up and dusted the dirt and moss off his pants. "I think we owe her that."

And I agreed, but still, she owed us an explanation. If she was up there, down there, out there, somewhere, maybe she would laugh. And maybe—just maybe—she would give us the clue we needed.

eighty-three days after

TWO WEEKS LATER, the Colonel returned from spring break with two notebooks filled with the minutiae of prank planning, sketches of various locations, and a forty-page, two-column list of problems that might crop up and their solutions. He calculated all times to a tenth of a second, and all distances to the inch, and then he recalculated, as if he could not bear the thought of failing her again. And then on that Sunday, the Colonel woke up late and rolled over. I was reading *The Sound and the Fury*, which I was supposed to have read in mid-February, and I looked up as I heard the rustling in the bed, and the Colonel said, "Let's get the band back together." And so I ventured out into the overcast spring and woke up Lara and Takumi, then brought them back to Room 43. The Barn Night crew was intact—or as close as it ever would be—for the Alaska Young Memorial Prank.

The three of us sat on the couch while the Colonel stood in front of us, outlining the plan and our parts in it with an excitement I hadn't seen in him since Before. When he finished, he asked, "Any questions?"

"Yeah," Takumi said. "Is that seriously going to work?"

"Well, first we gotta find a stripper. And second Pudge has to work some magic with his dad."

"All right, then," Takumi said. "Let's get to work."

eighty-four days after

EVERY SPRING, Culver Creek took one Friday afternoon off from classes, and all the students, faculty, and staff were required to go to the gym for Speaker Day. Speaker Day featured two speakers—usually small-time celebrities or small-time politicians or small-time academics, the kind of people who would come and speak at a school for the measly three hundred bucks the school budgeted. The junior class picked the first speaker and the seniors the second, and anyone who had ever attended a Speaker Day agreed that they were torturously boring. We planned to shake Speaker Day up a bit.

All we needed to do was convince the Eagle to let "Dr. William Morse," a "friend of my dad's" and a "preeminent scholar of deviant sexuality in adolescents," be the junior class's speaker.

So I called my dad at work, and his secretary, Paul, asked me if everything was all right, and I wondered why everyone, *everyone,* asked me if everything was all right when I called at any time other than Sunday morning.

"Yeah, I'm fine."

My dad picked up. "Hey, Miles. Is everything all right?"

I laughed and spoke quietly into the phone, since people were milling about. "Yeah, Dad. Everything is fine. Hey, remember when you stole the school bell and buried it in the cemetery?"

"Greatest Culver Creek prank ever," he responded proudly.

"It was, Dad. It *was.* So listen, I wonder if you'd help out with the new greatest Culver Creek prank ever."

"Oh, I don't know about that, Miles. I don't want you getting in any trouble."

"Well, I won't. The whole junior class is planning it. And it's not like anyone is going to get hurt or anything. Because, well, remember Speaker Day?"

"*God* that was boring. That was almost worse than class."

"Yeah, well, I need you to pretend to be our speaker. Dr. William Morse, a professor of psychology at the University of Central Florida and an expert in adolescent understandings of sexuality."

He was quiet for a long time, and I looked down at Alaska's last daisy and waited for him to ask what the prank was, and I would have told him, but I just heard him breathe slowly into the phone, and then he said, "I won't even ask. *Hmm.*" He sighed. "Swear to God you'll never tell your mother."

"I swear to God." I paused. It took me a second to remember the Eagle's real name. "Mr. Starnes is going to call you in about ten minutes."

"Okay, my name is Dr. William Morse, and I'm a psychology professor, and—adolescent sexuality?"

"Yup. You're the best, Dad."

"I just want to see if you can top me," he said, laughing.

Although it killed the Colonel to do it, the prank could not work without the assistance of the Weekday Warriors—specifically junior-class president Longwell Chase, who by now had grown his silly surfer mop back. But the Warriors loved the idea, so I met Longwell in his room and said, "Let's go."

Longwell Chase and I had nothing to talk about and no desire to pretend otherwise, so we walked silently to the Eagle's house. The Eagle came to the door before we even knocked. He cocked his head a little when he saw us, looking confused—and, indeed, we made an odd couple, with Longwell's pressed and pleated khaki pants and my I-keep-meaning-to-do-laundry blue jeans.

"The speaker we picked is a friend of Miles's dad," Longwell said. "Dr. William Morse. He's a professor at a university down in Florida, and he studies adolescent sexuality."

"Aiming for controversy, are we?"

"Oh no," I said. "I've met Dr. Morse. He's interesting, but he's not controversial. He just studies the, uh, the way that adolescents' understanding of sex is still changing and growing. I mean, he's opposed to premarital sex."

"Well. What's his phone number?" I gave the Eagle a piece of paper, and he walked to a phone on the wall and dialed. "Yes, hello. I'm calling to speak with Dr. Morse? . . . Okay, thanks . . . Hello, Dr. Morse. I have Miles Halter here in my home, and he tells me . . . great, wonderful . . . Well, I was wondering"—the Eagle paused, twisting the cord around his finger—"wondering, I guess, whether you—just so long as you understand that these are impressionable young people. We wouldn't want *explicit* discussions. . . . Excellent. Excellent. I'm glad you understand. . . . You, too, sir. See you soon!" The Eagle hung up the phone, smiling, and said, "Good choice! He seems like a very interesting man."

"Oh yeah," Longwell said very seriously. "I think he will be extraordinarily interesting."

o n e   h u n d r e d   t w o   d a y s   a f t e r

MY FATHER PLAYED Dr. William Morse on the phone, but the man playing him in real life went by the name of Maxx with two *x*'s, except that his name was actually Stan, except on Speaker Day his name was, obviously, Dr. William Morse. He was a veritable existential identity crisis, a male stripper with more aliases than a covert CIA agent.

The first four "agencies" the Colonel called turned us down. It wasn't until we got to the *B*'s in the "Entertainment" section of the Yellow Pages that we found Bachelorette Parties R Us. The owner of the aforementioned establishment liked the idea a great deal, but, he said, "Maxx is gonna love that. But no nudity. Not in front of the kids." We agreed—with some reluctance.

To ensure that none of us would get expelled, Takumi and I collected five dollars from every junior at Culver Creek to cover "Dr. William Morse's" appearance fee, since we doubted the Eagle would be keen on paying him after witnessing the, uh, speech. I paid the Colonel's five bucks. "I feel that I have earned your charity," he said, gesturing to the spiral notebooks he'd filled with plans.

As I sat through my classes that morning, I could think of nothing else. Every junior in the school had known for two weeks, and so far not even the faintest rumor had leaked out. But the Creek was rife with gossips—particularly the Weekday Warriors, and if just one person told one friend who told one friend who told one friend who told the Eagle, everything would fall apart.

The Creek's don't-rat ethos withstood the test nicely, but when Maxx/Stan/Dr. Morse didn't shown up by 11:50 that morning, I thought the Colonel would lose his shit. He sat on the bumper of a car in the student parking lot, his head bowed, his hands running through his thick mop of dark hair over and over again, as if he were trying to find something in there. Maxx had promised to arrive by 11:40, twenty minutes before the official start of Speaker Day, giving him time to learn the speech and everything. I stood next to the Colonel, worried but quiet, waiting. We'd sent Takumi to call "the agency" and learn the whereabouts of "the performer."

"Of all the things I thought could go wrong, this was not one of them. We have no solution for this."

Takumi ran up, careful not to speak to us until he was near. Kids were starting to file into the gym. Late late late late. We asked so little of our performer, really. We had written his speech. We had planned everything for him. All Maxx had to do was show up with his outfit on. And yet . . .

"The agency," said Takumi, "says the performer is on his way."

"On his way?" the Colonel said, clawing at his hair with a new vigor. "On his way? He's *already* late."

"They said he should be—" and then suddenly our worries disappeared as a blue minivan rounded the corner toward the parking lot, and I saw a man inside wearing a suit.

"That'd better be Maxx," the Colonel said as the car parked. He jogged up to the front door.

"I'm Maxx," the guy said upon opening the door.

"I am a nameless and faceless representative of the junior class," the Colonel answered, shaking Maxx's hand. He was thirtyish, tan and wide-shouldered, with a strong jaw and a dark, close-cropped goatee.

We gave Maxx a copy of his speech, and he read through it quickly.

"Any questions?" I asked.

"Uh, yeah. Given the nature of this event, I think y'all should pay me in advance."

He struck me as very articulate, even professorial, and I felt a supreme confidence, as if Alaska had found the best male stripper in central Alabama and led us right to him.

Takumi popped the trunk of his SUV and grabbed a paper grocery bag with $320 in it. "Here you go, Maxx," he said. "Okay, Pudge here is going to sit down there with you, because you are friends with Pudge's dad. That's in the speech. But, uh, we're hoping that if you get interrogated when this is all over, you can find it in your heart to say that the whole junior class called on a conference call to hire you, because we wouldn't want Pudge here to get in any trouble."

He laughed. "Sounds good to me. I took this gig because I thought it was hilarious. Wish *I'd* thought of this in high school."

As I walked into the gym, Maxx/Dr. William Morse at my side, Takumi and the Colonel trailing a good bit behind me, I knew I was more likely to get busted than anyone else. But I'd been reading the Culver Creek Handbook pretty closely the last couple weeks, and I reminded myself of my two-pronged defense, in the event I got in trouble: *1.* There is not, technically, a rule against paying a stripper to dance in front of the school. *2.* It cannot be proven that I was responsible for the incident. It can only be proven that I brought a person onto campus who I presumed to be an expert on sexual deviancy in adolescence and who turned out to be an actual sexual deviant.

I sat down with Dr. William Morse in the middle of the front row of bleachers. Some ninth graders sat behind me, but when the Colonel walked up with Lara a moment later, he politely told them, "Thanks for holding our seats," and ushered them away. As per the plan, Takumi was in the supply room on the second floor, connecting his stereo equipment to the gym's loudspeakers. I turned to Dr. Morse and said, "We should look at each other with great interest and talk like you're friends with my parents."

He smiled and nodded his head. "He is a great man, your father. And your mother—so beautiful." I rolled my eyes, a bit disgusted. Still, I liked this stripper fellow. The Eagle came in at noon on the nose, greeted the senior-class speaker—a former Alabama state attorney general—and then came over to Dr. Morse, who stood with great aplomb and half bowed as he shook the Eagle's hand—maybe *too* formal—and the Eagle said, "We're certainly very glad to have you here," and Maxx replied, "Thank you. I hope I don't disappoint."

I wasn't worried about getting expelled. I wasn't even worried about getting the Colonel expelled, although maybe I should have been. I was worried that it wouldn't work because Alaska hadn't planned it. Maybe no prank worthy of her could be pulled off without her.

The Eagle stood behind the podium.

"This is a day of historic significance at Culver Creek. It was the vision of our founder Phillip Garden that you, as students and we, as faculty, might take one afternoon a year to benefit from the wisdom of voices outside the school, and so we meet here annually to learn from them, to see the world as others see it. Today, our junior-class speaker is Dr. William Morse, a professor of psychology at the University of Central Florida and a widely respected scholar. He is here today to talk about teenagers and sexuality, a topic I'm sure you'll find considerably interesting. So please help me welcome Dr. Morse to the podium."

We applauded. My heart beat in my chest like it wanted to applaud, too. As Maxx walked up to the podium, Lara leaned down to me and whispered, "He *ees* really hot."

"Thank you, Mr. Starnes." Maxx smiled and nodded to the Eagle, then straightened his papers and placed them on the podium. Even *I* almost believed he was a professor of psychology. I wondered if maybe he was an actor supplementing his income.

He read directly from the speech without looking up, but he read with the confident, airy tone of a slightly snooty academic. "I'm here today to talk with you about the fascinating subject of teenage sexuality. My research is in the field of sexual linguistics, specifically the way that young people discuss sex and related questions. So, for instance, I'm interested in why my saying the word *arm* might not make you laugh, but my saying the word *vagina* might." And, indeed, there were some nervous twitters from the audience. "The way young people speak about one another's bodies says a great deal about our society. In today's world, boys are much more likely to objectify girls' bodies than the other way around. Boys will say amongst themselves that so-and-so has a nice rack, while girls will more likely say that a boy is cute, a term that describes both physical and emotional characteristics. This has the effect of turning girls into mere objects, while boys are seen by girls as whole people—"

And then Lara stood up, and in her delicate, innocent accent, cut Dr. William Morse off. "You're so hot! I weesh you'd shut up and take off your clothes."

The students laughed, but all of the teachers turned around and looked at her, stunned silent. She sat down.

"What's your name, dear?"

"Lara," she said.

"Now, Lara," Maxx said, looking down at his paper to remember the line, "what we have here is a very interesting case study—a female objectifying me, a male. It's so unusual that I can only assume you're making an attempt at humor."

Lara stood up again and shouted, "I'm not keeding! Take off your clothes."

He nervously looked down at the paper, and then looked up at all of us, smiling. "Well, it is certainly important to subvert the patriarchal paradigm, and I suppose this is a way. All right, then," he said, stepping to the left of the podium. And then he shouted, loud enough that Takumi could hear him upstairs, "This one's for Alaska Young."

As the fast, pumping bass of Prince's "Get Off" started from the loudspeakers, Dr. William Morse grabbed the leg of his pants with one hand and the lapel of his coat with the other, and the Velcro parted and his stage costume came apart, revealing Maxx with two x's, a stunningly muscular man with an eight-pack in his stomach and bulging pec muscles, and Maxx stood before us, smiling, wearing only briefs that were surely tighty, but not whitey—black leather.

His feet in place, Maxx swayed his arms to the music, and the crowd erupted with laughter and deafening, sustained applause—the largest ovation by a good measure in Speaker Day history. The Eagle was up in a flash, and as soon as he stood, Maxx stopped dancing, but he flexed his pec muscles so that they jumped up and down quickly in time to the music before the Eagle, not smiling but sucking his lips in as if not smiling required effort, indicated with a thumb that Maxx should go on home, and Maxx did.

My eyes followed Maxx out the door, and I saw Takumi standing in the doorway, fists raised in the air in triumph, before he ran back upstairs to cut the music. I was glad he'd gotten to see at least a bit of the show.

Takumi had plenty of time to get his equipment out, because the laughing and talking went on for several minutes while the Eagle kept repeating, "Okay. Okay. Let's settle down now. Settle down, y'all. Let's settle down."

The senior-class speaker spoke next. He blew. And as we left the gym, nonjuniors crowded around us, asking, "Was it you?" and I just smiled and said no, for it had not been me, or the Colonel or Takumi or Lara or Longwell Chase or anyone else in that gym. It had been Alaska's prank through and through. The hardest part about pranking, Alaska told me once, is not being able to confess. But I could confess on her behalf now. And as I slowly made my way out of the gym, I told anyone who would listen, "No. It wasn't us. It was Alaska."

The four of us returned to Room 43, aglow in the success of it, convinced that the Creek would never again see such a prank, and it didn't even occur to me that I might get in trouble until the Eagle opened the door to our room and stood above us, and shook his head disdainfully.

"I know it was y'all," said the Eagle.

We looked at him silently. He often bluffed. Maybe he was bluffing.

"Don't ever do anything like that again," he said. "But, Lord, 'subverting the patriarchal paradigm'—it's like she wrote the speech." He smiled and closed the door.

one hundred fourteen days after

A WEEK AND A HALF LATER, I walked back from my afternoon classes, the sun bearing down on my skin in a constant reminder that spring in Alabama had come and gone in a matter of hours, and now, early May, summer had returned for a six-month visit, and I felt the sweat dribble down my back and longed for the bitter winds of January. When I got to my room, I found Takumi sitting on the couch, reading my biography of Tolstoy.

"Uh, hi," I said.

He closed the book and placed it beside him and said, "January 10."

"What?" I asked.

"January 10. That date ring a bell?"

"Yeah, it's the day Alaska died." Technically, she died three hours into January 11, but it was still, to us anyway, Monday night, January 10.

"Yeah, but something else, Pudge. January 9. Alaska's mom took her to the zoo."

"Wait. No. How do you know that?"

"She told us at Barn Night. Remember?"

Of course I didn't remember. If I could remember numbers, I wouldn't be struggling toward a C-plus in precalc.

"Holy shit," I said as the Colonel walked in.

"What?" the Colonel asked.

"January 9, 1997," I told him. "Alaska liked the bears. Her mom liked the monkeys." The Colonel looked at me blankly for a moment and then took his backpack off and slung it across the room in a single motion.

"Holy shit," he said. "WHY THE HELL DIDN'T *I* THINK OF THAT!"

Within a minute, the Colonel had the best solution either of us would ever come up with. "Okay. She's sleeping. Jake calls, and she talks to him, and she's doodling, and she looks at her white flower, and 'Oh God my mom liked white flowers and put them in my hair when I was little,' and then she flips out. She comes back into her room and starts screaming at us that she forgot—forgot about her mom, of course—so she takes the flowers, drives off campus, on her way to—what?" He looked at me. "What? Her mom's grave?"

And I said, "Yeah, probably. Yeah. So she gets into the car, and she just wants to get to her mom's grave, but there's this jackknifed truck and the cops there, and she's drunk and pissed off and she's in a hurry, so she thinks she can squeeze past the cop car, and she's not even thinking straight, but she has to get to her mom, and she thinks she can get past it somehow and *POOF.*"

Takumi nods slowly, thinking, and then says, "Or, she gets into the car with the flowers. But she's already missed the anniversary. She's probably thinking that she screwed things up with her mom again—first she doesn't call 911, and now she can't even remember the freaking anniversary. And she's furious and she hates herself, and she decides, 'That's it, I'm doing it,' and she sees the cop car and there's her chance and she just floors it."

The Colonel reached into his pocket and pulled out a pack of cigarettes, tapping it upside down against the COFFEE TABLE. "Well," he said. "That clears things up nicely."

SO WE GAVE UP. I'd finally had enough of chasing after a ghost who did not want to be discovered. We'd failed, maybe, but some mysteries aren't meant to be solved. I still did not know her as I wanted to, but I never could. She made it impossible for me. And the accicide, the suident, would never be anything else, and I was left to ask, *Did I help you toward a fate you didn't want, Alaska, or did I just assist in your willful self-destruction?* Because they are different crimes, and I didn't know whether to feel angry at her for making me part of her suicide or just to feel angry at myself for letting her go.

But we knew what could be found out, and in finding it out, she had made us closer—the Colonel and Takumi and me, anyway. And that was it. She didn't leave me enough to discover her, but she left me enough to rediscover the Great Perhaps.

"There's one more thing we should do," the Colonel said as we played a video game together with the sound on—just the two of us, like in the first days of the Investigation.

"There's nothing more we can do."

"I want to drive through it," he said. "Like she did."

We couldn't risk leaving campus in the middle of the night like she had, so we left about twelve hours earlier, at 3:00 in the afternoon, with the Colonel behind the wheel of Takumi's SUV. We asked Lara and Takumi to come along, but they were tired of chasing ghosts, and besides, finals were coming.

It was a bright afternoon, and the sun bore down on the asphalt so that the ribbon of road before us quivered with heat. We drove a mile down Highway 119 and then merged onto I-65 northbound, heading toward the accident scene and Vine Station.

The Colonel drove fast, and we were quiet, staring straight ahead. I tried to imagine what she might have been thinking, trying again to see through time and space, to get inside her head just for a moment. An ambulance, lights and sirens blaring, sped past us, going in the opposite direction, toward school, and for an instant, I felt a nervous excitement and thought, *It could be someone I know.* I almost wished it *was* someone I knew, to give new form and depth to the sadness I still felt.

The silence broke: "Sometimes I liked it," I said. "Sometimes I liked it that she was dead."

"You mean it felt good?"

"No. I don't know. It felt . . . pure."

"Yeah," he said, dropping his usual eloquence. "Yeah. I know. Me, too. It's natural. I mean, it must be natural."

It always shocked me when I realized that I wasn't the only person in the world who thought and felt such strange and awful things.

Five miles north of school, the Colonel moved into the left lane of the interstate and began to accelerate. I gritted my teeth, and then before us, broken glass glittered in the blare of the sun like the road was wearing jewelry, and that spot must be the spot. He was still accelerating.

I thought: *This would not be a bad way to go.*

I thought: *Straight and fast. Maybe she just decided at the last second.*

And *POOF* we are through the moment of her death. We are driving through the place that she could not drive through, passing onto asphalt she never saw, and we are not dead. We are not dead! We are breathing and we are crying and now slowing down and moving back into the right lane.

We got off at the next exit, quietly, and, switching drivers, we walked in front of the car. We met and I held him, my hands balled into tight fists around his shoulders, and he wrapped his short arms around me and squeezed tight, so that I felt the heaves of his chest as we realized over and over again that we were still alive. I realized it in waves and we held on to each other crying and I thought, *God we must look so lame,* but it doesn't much matter when you have just now realized, all the time later, that you are still alive.

one hundred nineteen days after

THE COLONEL AND I threw ourselves into school once we gave up, knowing that we'd both need to ace our finals to achieve our GPA goals (I wanted a 3.0 and the Colonel wouldn't settle for even a 3.98). Our room became Study Central for the four of us, with Takumi and Lara over till all hours of the night talking about *The Sound and the Fury* and meiosis and the Battle of the Bulge. The Colonel taught us a semester's worth of precalc, although he was too good at math to teach it very well—"Of course it makes sense. Just trust me. Christ, it's not that hard"—and I missed Alaska.

And when I could not catch up, I cheated. Takumi and I shared copies of Cliffs Notes for *Things Fall Apart* and *A Farewell to Arms* ("These things are just too damned *long!*" he exclaimed at one point).

We didn't talk much. But we didn't need to.

one hundred twenty-two days after

A COOL BREEZE had beaten back the onslaught of summer, and on the morning the Old Man gave us our final exams, he suggested we have class outside. I wondered why we could have *an entire class* outside when I'd been kicked out of class last semester for merely *glancing* outside, but the Old Man wanted to have class outside, so we did. The Old Man sat in a chair that Kevin Richman carried out for him, and we sat on the grass, my notebook at first perched awkwardly in my lap and then against the thick green grass, and the bumpy ground did not lend itself to writing, and the gnats hovered. We were too close to the lake for comfortable sitting, really, but the Old Man seemed happy.

"I have here your final exam. Last semester, I gave you nearly two months to complete your final paper. This time, you get two weeks." He paused. "Well, nothing to be done about that, I guess." He laughed. "To be honest, I just decided once and for all to use this paper topic last night. It rather goes against my nature. Anyway, pass these around." When the pile came to me, I read the question:

> How will you—you personally—ever get out of this labyrinth of suffering? Now that you've wrestled with three major religious traditions, apply your newly enlightened mind to Alaska's question.

After the exams had been passed out, the Old Man said, "You need not specifically discuss the perspectives of different religions in your essay, so no research is necessary. Your knowledge, or lack thereof, has been established in the quizzes you've taken this semester. I am interested in how you are able to fit the uncontestable fact of suffering into your understanding of the world, and how you hope to navigate through life in spite of it.

"Next year, assuming my lungs hold out, we'll study Taoism, Hinduism, and Judaism together—" The Old Man coughed and then started to laugh, which caused him to cough again. "Lord, maybe I *won't* last. But about the three traditions we've studied this year, I'd like to say one thing. Islam, Christianity, and Buddhism each have founder figures—Muhammad, Jesus, and the Buddha, respectively. And in thinking about these founder figures, I believe we must finally conclude that each brought a message of radical hope. To seventh-century Arabia, Muhammad brought the promise that anyone could find fulfillment and everlasting life through allegiance to the one true God. The Buddha held out hope that suffering could be transcended. Jesus brought the message that the last shall be first, that even the tax collectors and lepers—the outcasts—had cause for hope. And so that is the question I leave you with in this final: What is your cause for hope?"

Back at Room 43, the Colonel was smoking in the room. Even though I still had one evening left of washing dishes in the cafeteria to work off my smoking conviction, we didn't much fear the Eagle. We had fifteen days left, and if we got caught, we'd just have to start senior year with some work hours. "So how will we ever get out of this labyrinth, Colonel?" I asked.

"If only I knew," he said.

"That's probably not gonna get you an A."

"Also it doesn't do much to put my soul to rest."

"Or hers," I said.

"Right. I'd forgotten about her." He shook his head. "That keeps happening."

"Well, you have to write *something*," I argued.

"After all this time, it still seems to me like straight and fast is the only way out—but I choose the labyrinth. The labyrinth blows, but I choose it."

one hundred thirty-six days after

TWO WEEKS LATER, I still hadn't finished my final for the Old Man, and the semester was just twenty-four hours from ending. I was walking home from my final test, a difficult but ultimately (I hoped) successful battle with precalculus that would win me the B-minus I so richly desired. It was genuinely hot out again, warm like she was. And I felt okay. Tomorrow, my parents would come and

load up my stuff, and we'd watch graduation and then go back to
Florida. The Colonel was going home to his mother to spend the
summer watching the soybeans grow, but I could call him long-
distance, so we'd be in touch plenty. Takumi was going to Japan for
the summer, and Lara was again to be driven home via green limo.
I was just thinking that it was all right not to know quite where
Alaska was and quite where she was going that night, when I
opened the door to my room and noticed a folded slip of paper on
the linoleum floor. It was a single piece of lime green stationery.
At the top, it read in calligraphy:

From the Desk of . . . Takumi Hikohito
Pudge/Colonel:
I am sorry that I have not talked to you before. I am not
staying for graduation. I leave for Japan tomorrow morning.
For a long time, I was mad at you. The way you cut me out of
everything hurt me, and so I kept what I knew to myself. But
then even after I wasn't mad anymore, I still didn't say anything, and I don't even really know why. Pudge had that kiss,
I guess. And I had this secret.
    You've mostly figured this out, but the truth is that I saw
her that night. I'd stayed up late with Lara and some people,
and then I was falling asleep and I heard her crying outside my back window. It was like 3:15 that morning, maybe,
and I walked out there and saw her walking through the
soccer field. I tried to talk to her, but she was in a hurry. She
told me that her mother was dead eight years that day, and
that she always put flowers on her mother's grave on the
anniversary, but she forgot that year. She was out there looking for flowers, but it was too early—too wintry. That's how
I knew about January 10. I still have no idea whether it was
suicide.

She was so sad, and I didn't know what to say or do. I think she counted on me to be the one person who would always say and do the right things to help her, but I couldn't. I just thought she was looking for flowers. I didn't know she was going to go. She was drunk, just trashed drunk, and I really didn't think she would drive or anything. I thought she would just cry herself to sleep and then drive to visit her mom the next day or something. She walked away, and then I heard a car start. I don't know what I was thinking.

So I let her go, too. And I'm sorry. I know you loved her. It was hard not to.

Takumi

I ran out of the room, like I'd never smoked a cigarette, like I ran with Takumi on Barn Night, across the dorm circle to his room, but Takumi was gone. His bunk was bare vinyl; his desk empty; an outline of dust where his stereo had been. He was gone, and I did not have time to tell him what I had just now realized: that I forgave him, and that she forgave us, and that we had to forgive to survive in the labyrinth. There were so many of us who would have to live with things done and things left undone that day. Things that did not go right, things that seemed okay at the time because we could not see the future. If only we could see the endless string of consequences that result from our smallest actions. But we can't know better until knowing better is useless.

And as I walked back to give Takumi's note to the Colonel, I saw that I would never know. I would never know her well enough to know her thoughts in those last minutes, would never know if she left us on purpose. But the not-knowing would not keep me from caring, and I would always love Alaska Young, my crooked neighbor, with all my crooked heart.

I got back to Room 43, but the Colonel wasn't home yet, so I left the note on the top bunk and sat down at the computer, and I wrote my way out of the labyrinth:

Before I got here, I thought for a long time that the way out of the labyrinth was to pretend that it did not exist, to build a small, self-sufficient world in a back corner of the endless maze and to pretend that I was not lost, but home. But that only led to a lonely life accompanied only by the last words of the already-dead, so I came here looking for a Great Perhaps, for real friends and a more-than-minor life. And then I screwed up and the Colonel screwed up and Takumi screwed up and she slipped through our fingers. And there's no sugar-coating it: She deserved better friends.

When she fucked up, all those years ago, just a little girl terrified into paralysis, she collapsed into the enigma of her-self. And I could have done that, but I saw where it led for her. So I still believe in the Great Perhaps, and I can believe in it in spite of having lost her.

Because I will forget her, yes. That which came together will fall apart imperceptibly slowly, and I will forget, but she will forgive my forgetting, just as I forgive her for forgetting me and the Colonel and everyone but herself and her mom in those last moments she spent as a person. I know now that she forgives me for being dumb and scared and doing the dumb and scared thing. I know she forgives me, just as her mother forgives her. And here's how I know:

I thought at first that she was just dead. Just darkness. Just a body being eaten by bugs. I thought about her a lot like that, as something's meal. What was her—green eyes, half a smirk, the soft curves of her legs—would soon be nothing, just the bones I never saw. I thought about the slow process of becom-ing bone and then fossil and then coal that will, in millions of years, be mined by humans of the future, and how they would heat their homes with her, and then she would be smoke billowing out of a smokestack, coating the atmosphere. I still think that, sometimes, think that maybe "the afterlife" is just something we made up to ease the pain of loss, to make our time in the labyrinth bearable. Maybe she was just matter, and matter gets recycled.

But ultimately I do not believe that she was only matter. The rest of her must be recycled, too. I believe now that we are greater than the sum of our parts. If you take Alaska's genetic code and you add her life experiences and the relationships she had with people, and then you take the size and shape of her body, you do not get her. There is something else entirely. There is a part of her greater than the sum of her knowable parts. And that part has to go somewhere, because it cannot be destroyed.

Although no one will ever accuse me of being much of a science student, one thing I learned from science classes is that energy is never created and never destroyed. And if Alaska took her own life, that is the hope I wish I could have given her. Forgetting her mother, failing her mother and her friends and herself—those are awful things, but she did not need to fold into herself and self-destruct. Those awful things are survivable, because we *are* as indestructible as we believe ourselves to be. When adults say, "Teenagers think they are invincible" with that sly, stupid smile on their faces, they don't know how right they are. We need never be hopeless, because we can never be irreparably broken. We think that we are invincible because we *are*. We cannot be born, and we cannot die. Like all energy, we can only change shapes and sizes and manifestations. They forget that when they get old. They get scared of losing and failing. But that part of us greater than the sum of our parts cannot begin and cannot end, and so it cannot fail.

So I know she forgives me, just as I forgive her. Thomas Edison's last words were: "It's very beautiful over there." I don't know where there is, but I believe it's somewhere, and I hope it's beautiful.

some last words on last words

LIKE PUDGE HALTER, I am fascinated by last words. For me, it began when I was twelve years old. Reading a history textbook, I came across the dying words of President John Adams: "Thomas Jefferson still survives." (Incidentally, he didn't. Jefferson had died earlier that same day, July 4, 1826; Jefferson's last words were "This is the Fourth?")

I can't say for sure why I remain interested in last words or why I've never stopped looking for them. It is true that I really loved John Adams's last words when I was twelve. But I also really loved this girl named Whitney. Most loves don't last. (Whitney sure didn't. I can't even remember her last name.) But some do.

Another thing that I can't say for sure is that all of the last words quoted in this book are definitive. Almost by definition, last words are difficult to verify. Witnesses are emotional, time gets conflated, and the speaker isn't around to clear up any controversy. I have tried to be accurate, but it is not surprising that there is debate over the two central quotes in *Looking for Alaska*.

SIMÓN BOLÍVAR

"How will I ever get out of this labyrinth!"

In reality, "How will I ever get out of this labyrinth!" were probably not Simón Bolívar's last words (although he did, historically, say them). His last words may have been "José! Bring the luggage. They do not want us here." The significant source for "How will I ever get out of this labyrinth!" is also Alaska's source, Gabriel García Márquez's *The General in His Labyrinth*.

FRANÇOIS RABELAIS

"I go to seek a Great Perhaps."

François Rabelais is credited with four alternate sets of last words. *The Oxford Book of Death* cites his last words as: (a) "I go to seek a Great Perhaps"; (b) (after receiving extreme unction) "I am greasing my boots for the last journey"; (c) "Ring down the curtain; the farce is played out"; (d) (wrapping himself in his domino, or hooded cloak) *"Beati qui in Domino moriuntur."* The last one, incidentally, is a pun,* but because the pun is in Latin, it is now rarely quoted. Anyway, I dismiss (d) because it's hard to imagine a dying François Rabelais having the energy to make a physically demanding pun, *in Latin*. (c) is the most common citation, because it's funny, and everyone's a sucker for funny last words.

I still maintain that Rabelais' last words were "I go to seek a Great Perhaps," partly because Laura Ward's nearly authoritative

---

*It means both "Blessed are they who die in the Lord" and "Blessed are they who die wearing a cloak."

book *Famous Last Words* agrees with me, and partly because I believe in them. I was born into Bolívar's labyrinth, and so I must believe in the hope of Rabelais' Great Perhaps.

For more information and source notes on the other quotes in the book, please visit my Web site: *www.sparksflyup.com.*

Turn the page for a
new and updated reader's guide to

looking for alaska

Hi. I'm John Green, the author of the book you just read. Well, perhaps you *haven't* read it, and you're just skipping ahead to uncover spoilers, in which case I insist that you return to your page immediately.

Now that it's just those of us who've finished reading the book: Thanks for reading *Looking for Alaska*. Books are a weird collaboration between author and reader: You trust me to tell a good story, and I trust you to bring it to good life in your mind. I can only hope I held up my end of the bargain.

In the spirit of that collaboration, I thought I might answer some questions from readers and then offer up some questions for you about the novel and your response to it. So first, here are some real questions submitted by readers via Twitter and Tumblr:

Is LOOKING FOR ALASKA AUTOBIOGRAPHICAL?

Yes. No. Kinda. Certainly, the physical campus of Culver Creek is very similar to the boarding school I attended, Indian Springs School. And many of the characters are amalgams of people I knew in high school. Indian Springs is a great school—a place unlike any other I've ever come across—and I could never have written this story if I hadn't spent three years there. That said, *Alaska* is a novel. It is well and truly made up. (And the basketball coach there would like me to note that their basketball program is really quite good.)

I'M READING LOOKING FOR ALASKA FOR SCHOOL AND I WAS WONDERING WHAT WERE TWO MAJOR SYMBOLS IN THE BOOK AND WHO WAS THE ENEMY.

I'm very grateful that *Looking for Alaska* is now taught in so many English classes, but it seems to me that books do not require either symbols or enemies to be worth reading. That said, in my opinion, there are symbols and enemies in *Alaska*. But my opinion doesn't really matter much. Books belong to their readers, and any symbols (or enemies) you find in the story can be just as interesting and important as any I could tell you about.

In short, I'm not gonna do your homework, dude.

DID YOU KNOW WHETHER OR NOT [SPOILER REDACTED BECAUSE I KNOW PEOPLE WILL READ THIS DISCUSSION GUIDE BEFORE THEY'VE READ THE BOOK, EVEN THOUGH I JUST FORBADE YOU TO DO SO LIKE SIX PARAGRAPHS AGO] WAS INTENTIONAL WHILE YOU WERE WRITING IT?

I still don't know whether [spoiler redacted] was intentional. When I started writing the book, I knew that neither I as a writer nor you as a reader would ever get inside Blue Citrus that night. I wrote the book that way because at the time I had a lot of questions—big questions about suffering and loss and faith and despair—that could not be answered. And I wanted to know whether it is possible to live a hopeful life in a world riddled with ambiguity, whether we can find a way to go on even when we don't get answers to questions that haunt us.

DID YOU LISTEN TO ANY MUSIC WHILE WRITING *LOOKING FOR ALASKA*?

I listened to a lot of old country and bluegrass music: Hank Williams, Bill Monroe, and Doc Watson. I also listened to Neutral Milk Hotel and The Mountain Goats. (These days, I often listen to songs ABOUT *Looking for Alaska* while writing. This book, astonishingly, has inspired a lot of beautiful music.)

WHY DID YOU CHOOSE THE NAME ALASKA?

For the first couple years I was working on *Looking for Alaska*, it had no title and I used a placeholder name instead of Alaska. One day, my friend Levin and I watched the movie *The Royal*

Tenenbaums, which includes in its soundtrack a cover of the great Velvet Underground song "Stephanie Says," which refers to a girl called Alaska. I loved that song in high school, and I loved the name, but it wasn't until I went home and looked up the original meaning of Alyeska, "that which the sea breaks against," that I realized it would be Alaska's name.

HAVE YOU BEEN AT ALL SURPRISED ABOUT THE SUCCESS OF *LOOKING FOR ALASKA?*

I have been entirely surprised. *Alaska* has been published all over the world, from Japan to Mexico to Lithuania, and it has enjoyed an uncommonly generous reception from readers. It has won awards that I never dared to hope for, and most importantly, people still read it and like it enough to share it with their friends. Honestly, I never thought this book would even still be in print seven years after its publication, let alone that I would be answering questions about it in a New and Expanded Discussion Guide.

ARE THERE ANY LAST WORDS YOU LIKED THAT DIDN'T MAKE THE BOOK?

Tons! I love Emily Dickinson's last words: "I must go in. The fog is rising." Winston Churchill said, "I'm bored with it all." British MP Lady Astor awoke from a stupor to find her family surrounding her and asked, "Am I dying or is it my birthday?" (It wasn't her birthday.) The Irish playwright Brendan Behan turned to a nun who was drawing his blood and said, "Bless you, Sister. May all your sons be bishops." And the great short story writer O. Henry, who knew a thing or two about endings, said, "Turn up the lights. I don't want to go home in the dark."

SOME INTENTIONALLY VAGUE AND BROAD
DISCUSSION QUESTIONS

1. Is forgiveness universal? I mean, is forgiveness really available to all people, no matter the circumstances? Is it, for instance, possible for the dead to forgive the living, and for the living to forgive the dead?

2. I would argue that both in fiction and in real life, teenage smoking is a symbolic action. What do you think it's intended to symbolize, and what does it actually end up symbolizing? To phrase this question differently: Why would anyone ever pay money in exchange for the opportunity to acquire lung cancer and/or emphysema?

3. Do you like Alaska? Do you think it's important to like people you read about?

4. By the end of this novel, Pudge has a lot to say about immortality and what the point of being alive is (if there is a point). To what extent do your thoughts on mortality shape your understanding of life's meaning?

5. How would you answer the old man's final question for his students? What would your version of Pudge's essay look like?

p.s. The great and terrible beauty of the Internet now makes it possible for us to continue the strange conversation between reader and writer indefinitely. Here are some of the places you can catch me online:

My Web site: **http://www.johngreenbooks.com**
The video channel I built with my brother:
http://www.youtube.com/vlogbrothers
My tumblr: **http://fishingboatproceeds.tumblr.com**
(that url is a very long story)
My twitter: **http://www.twitter.com/realjohngreen**

Turn the page to read an excerpt from
John Green's #1 *New York Times*
bestselling novel

The Fault in Our Stars

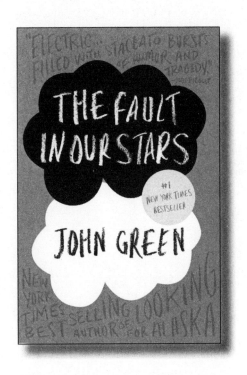

CHAPTER ONE

Late in the winter of my seventeenth year, my mother decided I was depressed, presumably because I rarely left the house, spent quite a lot of time in bed, read the same book over and over, ate infrequently, and devoted quite a bit of my abundant free time to thinking about death.

Whenever you read a cancer booklet or website or whatever, they always list depression among the side effects of cancer. But, in fact, depression is not a side effect of cancer. Depression is a side effect of dying. (Cancer is also a side effect of dying. Almost everything is, really.) But my mom believed I required treatment, so she took me to see my Regular Doctor Jim, who agreed that I was veritably swimming in a paralyzing and totally clinical depression, and that therefore my meds should be adjusted and also I should attend a weekly Support Group.

This Support Group featured a rotating cast of characters in various states of tumor-driven unwellness. Why did the cast rotate? A side effect of dying.

The Support Group, of course, was depressing as hell. It met every Wednesday in the basement of a stone-walled Episcopal church shaped like a cross. We all sat in a circle right in the middle of the cross, where the two boards would have met, where the heart of Jesus would have been.

I noticed this because Patrick, the Support Group Leader and only person over eighteen in the room, talked about the heart of Jesus every freaking meeting, all about how we, as young cancer survivors, were sitting right in Christ's very sacred heart and whatever.

So here's how it went in God's heart: The six or seven or ten of us walked/wheeled in, grazed at a decrepit selection of cookies and lemonade, sat down in the Circle of Trust, and listened to Patrick recount for the thousandth time his depressingly miserable life story—how he had cancer in his balls and they thought he was going to die but he didn't die and now here he is, a full-grown adult in a church basement in the 137th nicest city in America, divorced, addicted to video games, mostly friendless, eking out a meager living by exploiting his cancertastic past, slowly working his way toward a master's degree that will not improve his career prospects, waiting, as we all do, for the sword of Damocles to give him the relief that he escaped lo those many years ago when cancer took both of his nuts but spared what only the most generous soul would call his life.

AND YOU TOO MIGHT BE SO LUCKY!

Then we introduced ourselves: Name. Age. Diagnosis. And how we're doing today. I'm Hazel, I'd say when they'd get to me. Sixteen. Thyroid originally but with an impressive and long-settled satellite colony in my lungs. And I'm doing okay.

Once we got around the circle, Patrick always asked if anyone wanted to share. And then began the circle jerk of support: everyone talking about fighting and battling and winning and shrinking and scanning. To be fair to Patrick, he let us talk about dying, too. But most of them weren't dying. Most would live into adulthood, as Patrick had.

(Which meant there was quite a lot of competitiveness about it, with everybody wanting to beat not only cancer itself, but also the other people in the room. Like, I realize that this is irrational, but when they tell you that you have, say, a 20 percent chance of living five years, the math kicks in and you figure that's one in five . . . so you look around and think, as any healthy person would: I gotta outlast four of these bastards.)

The only redeeming facet of Support Group was this kid named Isaac, a long-faced, skinny guy with straight blond hair swept over one eye.

And his eyes were the problem. He had some fantastically improbable eye cancer. One eye had been cut out when he was a kid, and now he wore the kind of thick glasses that made his eyes (both the real one and the glass one) preternaturally huge, like his whole head was basically just this fake eye and this real eye staring at you. From what I could gather on the rare occasions when Isaac shared with the group, a recurrence had placed his remaining eye in mortal peril.

Isaac and I communicated almost exclusively through sighs. Each time someone discussed anticancer diets or snorting ground-up shark fin or whatever, he'd glance over at me and sigh ever so slightly. I'd shake my head microscopically and exhale in response.

So Support Group blew, and after a few weeks, I grew to be rather kicking-and-screaming about the whole affair. In fact, on the Wednesday I made the acquaintance of Augustus Waters, I tried my level best to get out of Support Group while sitting on the couch with my mom in the third leg of a twelve-hour marathon of the previous season's *America's Next Top Model*, which admittedly I had already seen, but still.

Me: "I refuse to attend Support Group."

Mom: "One of the symptoms of depression is disinterest in activities."

Me: "Please just let me watch *America's Next Top Model*. It's an activity."

Mom: "Television is a passivity."

Me: "Ugh, Mom, please."

Mom: "Hazel, you're a teenager. You're not a little kid anymore. You need to make friends, get out of the house, and live your life."

Me: "If you want me to be a teenager, don't send me to Support Group. Buy me a fake ID so I can go to clubs, drink vodka, and take pot."

Mom: "You don't *take* pot, for starters."

Me: "See, that's the kind of thing I'd know if you got me a fake ID."

Mom: "You're going to Support Group."

Me: "UGGGGGGGGGGGGGG."

Mom: "Hazel, you deserve a life."

That shut me up, although I failed to see how attendance at Support Group met the definition of *life*. Still, I agreed to go—after negotiating the right to record the 1.5 episodes of *ANTM* I'd be missing.

I went to Support Group for the same reason that I'd once allowed nurses with a mere eighteen months of graduate education to poison me with exotically named chemicals: I wanted to make my parents happy. There is only one thing in this world shittier than biting it from cancer when you're sixteen, and that's having a kid who bites it from cancer.

Mom pulled into the circular driveway behind the church at 4:56. I pretended to fiddle with my oxygen tank for a second just to kill time.

"Do you want me to carry it in for you?"

"No, it's fine," I said. The cylindrical green tank only weighed a few pounds, and I had this little steel cart to wheel it around behind me. It delivered two liters of oxygen to me each minute through a cannula, a transparent tube that split just beneath my neck, wrapped behind my ears, and then reunited in my nostrils. The contraption was necessary because my lungs sucked at being lungs.

"I love you," she said as I got out.

"You too, Mom. See you at six."

"Make friends!" she said through the rolled-down window as I walked away.

I didn't want to take the elevator because taking the elevator is a Last Days kind of activity at Support Group, so I took the stairs. I grabbed a cookie and poured some lemonade into a Dixie cup and then turned around.

A boy was staring at me.

I was quite sure I'd never seen him before. Long and

leanly muscular, he dwarfed the molded plastic elementary school chair he was sitting in. Mahogany hair, straight and short. He looked my age, maybe a year older, and he sat with his tailbone against the edge of the chair, his posture aggressively poor, one hand half in a pocket of dark jeans.

I looked away, suddenly conscious of my myriad insufficiencies. I was wearing old jeans, which had once been tight but now sagged in weird places, and a yellow T-shirt advertising a band I didn't even like anymore. Also my hair: I had this pageboy haircut, and I hadn't even bothered to, like, brush it. Furthermore, I had ridiculously fat chipmunked cheeks, a side effect of treatment. I looked like a normally proportioned person with a balloon for a head. This was not even to mention the cankle situation. And yet—I cut a glance to him, and his eyes were still on me.

It occurred to me why they call it eye *contact*.

I walked into the circle and sat down next to Isaac, two seats away from the boy. I glanced again. He was still watching me.

Look, let me just say it: He was hot. A nonhot boy stares at you relentlessly and it is, at best, awkward and, at worst, a form of assault. But a hot boy . . . well.

I pulled out my phone and clicked it so it would display the time: 4:59. The circle filled in with the unlucky twelve-to-eighteens, and then Patrick started us out with the serenity prayer: *God, grant me the serenity to accept the things*

I cannot change, the courage to change the things I can, and the wisdom to know the difference. The guy was still staring at me. I felt rather blushy.

Finally, I decided that the proper strategy was to stare back. Boys do not have a monopoly on the Staring Business, after all. So I looked him over as Patrick acknowledged for the thousandth time his ball-lessness etc., and soon it was a staring contest. After a while the boy smiled, and then finally his blue eyes glanced away. When he looked back at me, I flicked my eyebrows up to say, *I win.*

He shrugged. Patrick continued and then finally it was time for the introductions. "Isaac, perhaps you'd like to go first today. I know you're facing a challenging time."

"Yeah," Isaac said. "I'm Isaac. I'm seventeen. And it's looking like I have to get surgery in a couple weeks, after which I'll be blind. Not to complain or anything because I know a lot of us have it worse, but yeah, I mean, being blind does sort of suck. My girlfriend helps, though. And friends like Augustus." He nodded toward the boy, who now had a name. "So, yeah," Isaac continued. He was looking at his hands, which he'd folded into each other like the top of a tepee. "There's nothing you can do about it."

"We're here for you, Isaac," Patrick said. "Let Isaac hear it, guys." And then we all, in a monotone, said, "We're here for you, Isaac."

Michael was next. He was twelve. He had leukemia.

He'd always had leukemia. He was okay. (Or so he said. He'd taken the elevator.)

Lida was sixteen, and pretty enough to be the object of the hot boy's eye. She was a regular—in a long remission from appendiceal cancer, which I had not previously known existed. She said—as she had every other time I'd attended Support Group—that she felt *strong*, which felt like bragging to me as the oxygen-drizzling nubs tickled my nostrils.

There were five others before they got to him. He smiled a little when his turn came. His voice was low, smoky, and dead sexy. "My name is Augustus Waters," he said. "I'm seventeen. I had a little touch of osteosarcoma a year and a half ago, but I'm just here today at Isaac's request."

"And how are you feeling?" asked Patrick.

"Oh, I'm grand." Augustus Waters smiled with a corner of his mouth. "I'm on a roller coaster that only goes up, my friend."

When it was my turn, I said, "My name is Hazel. I'm sixteen. Thyroid with mets in my lungs. I'm okay."

The hour proceeded apace: Fights were recounted, battles won amid wars sure to be lost; hope was clung to; families were both celebrated and denounced; it was agreed that friends just didn't get it; tears were shed; comfort proffered. Neither Augustus Waters nor I spoke again until Patrick said, "Augustus, perhaps you'd like to share your fears with the group."

"My fears?"

"Yes."

"I fear oblivion," he said without a moment's pause. "I fear it like the proverbial blind man who's afraid of the dark."

"Too soon," Isaac said, cracking a smile.

"Was that insensitive?" Augustus asked. "I can be pretty blind to other people's feelings."

Isaac was laughing, but Patrick raised a chastening finger and said, "Augustus, please. Let's return to *you* and *your* struggles. You said you fear oblivion?"

"I did," Augustus answered.

Patrick seemed lost. "Would, uh, would anyone like to speak to that?"

I hadn't been in proper school in three years. My parents were my two best friends. My third best friend was an author who did not know I existed. I was a fairly shy person—not the hand-raising type.

And yet, just this once, I decided to speak. I half raised my hand and Patrick, his delight evident, immediately said, "Hazel!" I was, I'm sure he assumed, opening up. Becoming Part Of The Group.

I looked over at Augustus Waters, who looked back at me. You could almost see through his eyes they were so blue. "There will come a time," I said, "when all of us are dead. All of us. There will come a time when there are no human beings remaining to remember that anyone ever existed or that our species ever did anything. There will be no one left to remember Aristotle or Cleopatra, let alone you. Everything that we did and built and wrote and thought and discovered will be forgotten and all of this"—I gestured encompassingly—"will have been for naught. Maybe that time is coming soon and maybe it is millions of years away, but even if we survive the collapse of our sun, we will not survive forever. There was time before organisms experienced consciousness, and there will be time after. And if the inevitability of human oblivion worries you, I encourage you to ignore it. God knows that's what everyone else does."

I'd learned this from my aforementioned third best friend, Peter Van Houten, the reclusive author of *An Imperial Affliction*, the book that was as close a thing as I had to a Bible. Peter Van Houten was the only person I'd ever come across who seemed to (a) understand what it's like to be dying, and (b) not have died.

After I finished, there was quite a long period of silence as I watched a smile spread all the way across Augustus's face—not the little crooked smile of the boy trying to be sexy while he stared at me, but his real smile, too big for his face. "Goddamn," Augustus said quietly. "Aren't you something else."